Immigrant Ancestors
of
Marylanders

*As Found in
Local Histories*

Compiled by
Martha & Bill Reamy

HERITAGE BOOKS
2007

HERITAGE BOOKS

AN IMPRINT OF HERITAGE BOOKS, INC.

Books, CDs, and more—Worldwide

For our listing of thousands of titles see our website
at
www.HeritageBooks.com

Published 2007 by
HERITAGE BOOKS, INC.
Publishing Division
65 East Main Street
Westminster, Maryland 21157-5026

International Standard Book Number: 978-1-58549-527-6

PREFACE

This project was undertaken for two reasons. The first being to help researchers specifically pinpoint immigrant ancestors. Finding an ancestor who is pointedly named as the immigrant to America leads the researcher to change the focus of his or her research to another geographic arena. It is an important turning point in research, and if it goes unrecognized, can result in wasted time and effort.

The second reason that this project was undertaken was to provide a partial index to many worthy, out-of-print, unindexed Maryland source records. The entries here are brief and researchers should follow up by obtaining a print of the original article. Most contain extensive additional data on the family.

The books used in this study are available in most Middle-Atlantic states' libraries. Most are also available through the Latter Day Saints local Family History Libraries.

It should be noted that none of the sources used in this compilation is documented. Each is to be used as a clue to lead you to source documents and to tell you specifically in which county and/or state records you might find your immigrant ancestor or his immediate descendants, as well as family origins in the old country.

Martha & William Reamy
Waipahu, Hawaii
March 1993

REFERENCES USED

6TH = *Portrait and Biographical Record of the Sixth Congressional District, Maryland: Containing Portraits and Biographies of many well known Citizens of the Past and Present* (New York, Chicago: Chapman Pub. Co., 1898)

AAH = *The Founders of Anne Arundel and Howard Counties, Maryland. A Genealogical & Biographical Review from wills, deeds and church records*, J. D. Warfield, A.M. (Baltimore, 1905; reprinted by Regional Publishing Co., 1980)

C = *History of Cecil County, Maryland: Early Settlements Around the Head of Chesapeake Bay and on the Delaware River, Sketches of Some of the Old Families of Cecil County*, George Johnston (Elkton, MD, 1881)

FR1 & FR2 = *History of Frederick County, Maryland, With a Biographical Record of Representative Families*, T. J. C. Williams and Folger McKinsey (1910: reprinted Baltimore, Regional Publishing Co., 1979, with added index by Jacob Mehrling Holdcraft)

GME = *Genealogical and Memorial Encyclopedia of the State of Maryland: A Record of the Achievements of Her People in the Making of a Commonwealth & the Founding of a Nation* under editorial supervision of Richard Henry Spencer, Etc. (New York: The American Historical Society, Inc., 1919)

H/C = *History of Harford & Cecil Counties*

MDC = *The Biographical Clycopedia of Representative Men of Maryland and District of Columbia* (Baltimore: National Biographical Publishing Co., 1879)

TR3 & TR4 = *Tercentenary History of Maryland Embodying Biographical Records of Colonists, Pioneers, Judges, Governors, Military Officers, etc.*, Henry Fletcher Powell (Chicago-Baltimore: The S. J. Clarke Publishing Co., 1925) Only volumes 3 & 4 were used in this compilation, with a few brief entries from volume 2, which was not available.

BBOTT, JOHN H., b. Liverpool, England, manufacturer of weaving implements. 1815 with wife & 6 children to US via. Ireland. After a bad voyage their ship was towed into Newport, RI & he took his family to Philadelphia, PA & finally settled in Frederick, MD. His son, John H. Abbott, machinist, b. Frederick City, MD 30 June 1835. *FR2:869-70*

ABELL, ROBERT, settled in MA Bay Colony. Preserved Abell, with 3 brothers, all sons of Robert of England, to MA early days of the colony. Preserved settled in town of Sukonk (then known as Rehoboth). His grandson Robert served in Revolutionary War. Caleb, s/o Robert (Rev. veteran), served in War of 1812. Robert s/o Caleb had son A. S. Abell, founder & prop. of the *Baltimore Sun*, b. East Providence, RI, 10 Aug. 1806; d. Baltimore 1888. He is 6th in desc. from Robert, the immigrant, above. *MDC:18; GME:11*

ABERCROMBIE, DAVID, of Scotch birth & ancestry, to Baltimore c. 1847; connected with news agency of William Taylor & Co., later succeeded by the Baltimore News Co. His son John was b. at Stirling, Scotland 2 Jan. 1842 & was age 12 on immigration. John, who d. 7 Jan. 1911, m. Elizabeth Sarah Daniel, a d/o Thomas Daniel of Dumfries, Scotland who was b. there in 1807 & studied at the Univ. of Edinburgh. Thomas Daniel was a physician who settled first in Canada in Port Stanley & in St. Thomas, Ontario. He d. at the Protestant Hospital 4 May 1866. John & Elizabeth Sarah Abercrombie had sons b. in Baltimore: 4 April 1871, Harry Netherclift Abercrombie & Ronald Taylor Abercrombie b. 19 Jan. 1879. *TR3:711-12, 1000-1003*

ABRAHAMS, JOSEPH, from England to America c. 1660. His son William, b. Chestertown, MA in 1694, m. 19 Nov. 1719 Martha Boylston. William d. 1763. Their son Woodward b. 1727, m. 1751 Tabitha Smithurst; she d. 1793, aged 64. In 1757 Woodward removed to Marblehead, MA, where he d. 1813. His son Woodward, b. Marblehead, 14 July 1762, m. Miss Gallison --- on 4 June 1790 & had one son, William, b. 10 June 1792. William removed to Baltimore & 4 Dec. 1803 m. Hannah Wooley of Harford Co. He resided in Baltimore until 1818; resided in Cecil Co. until 1827, when he removed to Port Deposit, where he d. 16 Dec. 1827. Methodist Episcopal. *MDC:449*

ABRAMS, LEVY, & wife Sarah Karlins, m. in Poland & came to the US soon afterward when Levy was aged 25. Sarah was b. in Suwalki,

Russia & Levy was b. Poland. They had 6 children, son, Michael A. b. in Baltimore, MD 27 Feb. 1885; physician. Levy was an interpreter for the supreme court & adherrent of the Jewish faith. He d. 1915, aged 56 & Sarah d. 1918, aged 54. *TR3:679-80*

ABRAMSON, JENNIE, d/o Solomon, a rabbi of a Jewish temple at Shavly, Russia. Jennie m. Abraham Levinson & their son Frank was b. in Rochester, NY 25 April 1890. Frank physician of Baltimore. Abraham, father of Abraham Levinson, b. Kovno, Russia & migrated to US in the 1880's. He res. for a time in Rochester, NY & in early 1890's to Baltimore. Rabbi of the B'nai Israel synagogue on Lloyd St. until his death in 1912. *TR3:591*

ACTON, NATHANIEL, & wife Jane McDevit, to America from Ireland c. 1828 & settled in Augusta, ME. Removed to Philadelphia in 1844, where Nathaniel d. in 1859. Their eldest son Samuel Graham Acton, b. in Augusta, ME 3 Aug. 1829, removed to Anne Arundel Co., MD 1857, where he established the summer resort at Brooklyn known as Acton Park House. Samuel served in the side of the Confederacy during the Civil War. He m. in 1852 Ann Elizabeth, d/o Sumner Prentiss of MA; she d. Jan. 1877. Episcopal. *MDC:566*

ADAMS, GEORGE (REV.), clergyman of England, to America in 18th century & settled in Prince George's Co., MD, where he had a parish & where he died. He had a son, Benjamin, who participated in the War of 1812; b. Prince George's Co. *MDC:93*

ADAMS, HENRY, b. Duisberg, Prussia, 11 Feb. 1858, s/o Henry & Elizabeth (Ludwig) Adams, the former a native of Friemersheim, Germany, the latter a d/o John Ludwig, member of old Duisburg family. Henry Adams Sr. was a s/o Peter Adams & immigrated to America, settled in Peoria, IL. Henry Sr. was a builder & d. in Peoria at age of 78; Elizabeth d. there in 1871, aged 37. Henry Adams Jr. immigrated to the US at age of 22 in 1880 & settled in Baltimore. He m. in Florida, OH, 9 Sept. 1884, Mary Elizabeth, b. Baltimore & d/o Ernest & Mary (Altvater) Klingelhofer, both of German lineage. *TR3:699-700*

ADAMS, JOHN, from Ireland in 1820, m. Ann Kuhn, b. Adams Co. PA. Ann was d/o Henry Kuhn, a miller of PA & later of Richmond, VA. John F. Adams, s/o John & Ann, b. Ellicott's Mills, MD 30 Jan. 1829. *MDC:673-74*

ADDISON, ROBERT, from Edinburgh, Scotland in 1743, settled in Calvert Co., MD; m. Isabella Cook, d/o Rev. Cook, Protestant Episcopal clergyman who sailed on the same ship with him to America. Robert d. 1785 & is bur. in graveyard of Lower Chapel, his wife d. 28 Nov. 1809 in Baltimore at home of son George Mitchell Addison. They also had: Isabella, John, Montgomery, James, Elizabeth & Nancy. *TR4:289*

ADLER, CHARLES, b. 8 Dec. 1839, in mountain town near Cassel, Germany, s/o Simon & Malchen (Stern) Adler. He arrived in MD in Sept. 1854 & settled in Montgomery Co.; merchant. In Feb. 1865 to Baltimore & enetered wholesale shoe house of H. Frank & Co. & changed name of the firm to Frank & Adler. 19 Feb. 1865 he m. Caroline Frank, d/o Henry Frank. *TR3:946-59*

ADLER, PHILIP, & wife Nytta, both b. Germany & after marriage to the US, settled in Baltimore. Their dau. m. M. E. Reinhard of Baltimore. *TR3:684-5*

AHALT, ---, with wife from Germany to America at early date & settled near Burkittsville, MD. Their children: John, hunter in the mountains of MD, later to IN; Jacob, m. Miss Slifer & d. near Palmyra, MO; Matthias, m. Miss Routzhan, d. at Middletown Valley; Samuel; Joshua, m. Miss Maught, d. in Middletown Valley; & several daus., names unknown. *FR2:1573*

ALBAUGH, JOHAN WILHELM, with four sons: Zachariah, Johan Wilhelm, Johan Gearhardt & Johan Peter, emigrated in 1734 from Germany on the ship *Hope,* landing in Philadelphia. Settled first in NJ & later removed to near Frederick, MD. Name has been spelled Alibach, Albach, Aulabaugh, Allbaugh & Albaugh. Johan Wilhelm, the emigrant, wife's name was --- Gearhardt. *FR2:1261-2*

ALBERT, LAWRENCE, from Wurtzbeg, Bavaria to America 1752, settled in York Co., PA. Descendant Jacob Albert to Baltimore 1805, hardware business. Jacob's son, Hon. William Julian Albert, Congressman, b. Baltimore 4 Aug. 1816, m. 15 May 1838 Emily J., d/o Talbot Jones of Baltimore. *MDC:47*

ALLAN, WILLIAM, b. Scotland, settled in Charleston, SC in 1790. He m. Sarah Haig & dau. Mary Kerr Allan m. Joseph Waties Allston, a veteran of the War of 1812. Their son, Joseph Blyth Allston, b. Georgetown, SC, 8 Feb. 1833, served in the Confederate Army from Georgetown County. In 1867 he removed to Baltimore, attorney, m. 1857, Mary C. North, d/o John North & Jane Petigru. *MDC:302-03*

ALLEN, EDWARD, b. Scotland & served as soldier under Oliver Cromwell, to American upon the restoration of the Stuarts under Charles II. An original settler of Suffield, CT, m. Mary Kimball; he d. 22 Nov. 1696, she d. 12 June 1969. Their 7th child, Benjamin Allen, m. Mercy Bardwell (or Cooley) Townsley & their son Joseph, b. Suffield 1701, served in militia, m. Hannah Clesson, d/o Capt. Joseph & Hannah (Arms) Clesson. Their eldest son Zebulon, b. 21 Nov. 1731 in Deerfield, MA, was military officer in French & Indian War (1755-8). Three of Zebulon's sons, Asaph, Simeon & Joseph, served in the Rev. Jonathan Allen, his 6th child, b. 20 April 1766. Desc. George Hanford Allen, b. Columbus, Muscogee Co., GA, was a sign painter & gilder. He m. Lillian May Price, d/o Lewis C. & Mary Elmore (Longbothum) Price, who res. in Selden, Long Island, NY; Port Jefferson, Long Island; New Haven, CT; Brooklyn, NY & Patchogue, Long Island. They had Rev. Louis St. Clair Allen, b. Brooklyn, Kings Co., NY 11 July 1883. Rev. Allen served as divine of the Methodist Episcopal Church in Baltimore. He m. at the brides' home in Irvington, MD, Bertha Webb Steinacker, d/o Joseph Toomey & Mary Emma (Webb) Steinacker. *TR4:275-6*

ALLEN, PATRICK, b. Ireland, to America at age 18 & settled first in DE, manufacturer of woolen cloth; afterward removed to PA. His son, Thomas C. Allen, b. in Delaware Co., PA, blacksmith & machinist in Burmond. Thomas C. d. in Philadelphia in 1876, aged 59; m. Elizabeth Rudolph of Delaware Co., d/o William Rudolph. Their son, John R. Allen, b. 2 Oct. 1843 in Delaware Co., PA. 1861 enlisted in Co. F., 91st PA Inf. After the war he res. Delaware Co., PA, Armstrong Co., PA & in 1881 to Cecil Co., MD & settled on the William Kirk place. *H/C:382*

ALLEN, THOMAS, came into MD 1634, in the *Ark & the Dove*. He was murdered by Indians in 1648 at "Piney Point," St. Mary's Co. His son Charles had dau. Elizabeth who m. Richard Roberts. *TR4:343*

4

AMELUNG, JOHN FREDERICK, from Bremen, brought a colony of 300-400 persons for a settlement in Frederick Co., MD; 1789 opened glass factory. *FRI:268*

AMMIDON, ROGER, assumed that he came from Holland & settled in Salem, MA before 1637. Desc. John Perry Ammidon m. Sarah E. Crombie, of Scotch descent. Their son, Daniel C. Ammidon, b. Wakefield, MA 28 Jan. 1857, res. in Baltimore. Daniel m. in Nov. 1885, Julia A. Bevan, who d. the following year, leaving a dau. Julia who m. William G. Pierson. Daniel m. (2) Estelle Josephine Hoyt, Oct. 1902. She a desc. of Simon Hoyt who settled in Stamford, CT in 1641. *TR4:542-3*

AMOS, WILLIAM (REV.), b. England, emigrated to America in early manhood & settled on a farm near Fallston, MD; Quaker. In 1806 he called a meeting of his descs. in America & over 140 gathered in Baltimore. *H/C:506-7*

AMTHOR, JOHANN MICHAEL ROBERT (M.D.), b. Gotha, Germany, 4 March 1821, s/o Andrew & Caroline (Poller) Amthor. To America in 1852 & settled in Baltimore. Lutheran. He m. 1852 Fredericke Oschman, also b. Gotha. *MDC:640*

ANDERSON, JAMES (DR.), b. Scotland, to Chestertown, Kent Co., MD, where he practiced in the middle of the 18th century. *MDC:385*

ANDERSON, PATRICK, b. Ireland, 1 Jan. 1838, s/o William & Ellen (McKelvey) Anderson. To America at age 14 & employed in cotton factory in Philadelpha, after which he removed to Chatham, Chester Co., PA to apprentice under James A. Kendall. 1859 to Cecilton, MD. His brother John served in the Civil War in Co. E, 10th OH Inf., killed in action. Patrick m. in 1862 Henrietta Register, b. Cecil Co. Methodist-Episcopal Church Members. *H/C:334-5*

ANGUS, FELIX (GEN.), b. Lyons, France, 4 July 1839. He grew up in Paris and left home to travel world-wide in 1852. In 1860 he came to the US, served in the Civil War in the 65th NY (2d Duryen Zouaves); after the war settled in Baltimore, MD. 13 Dec. 1864 he m. Annie E., dau. of Charles C. Fulton, proprietor of the *Baltimore American,* where Felix was later Treasurer & General Manager. *MDC:122-23.*

ANNAN, ROBERT (M.D.), b. town of Cupar Fife, Scotland in 1742 & emigrated to America, arriving in NY in 1761; ordained & installed at Neelytown, NY in 1766, where he remained 14 years. Removed from Neeleytown to Boston in 1783; 1786 to Old Scots Church, Philadelphia until 1801/2 when he removed to Baltimore, MD. He retired to a farm in York Co., PA, where he d. 1819. He was m. 2 times: 1. Margaret Cochran, d/o William of Carrollsburg, York Co., PA. By her had Robert Landsale & William, both physicians. Robert L. settled at Emmitsburg, MD & d. 1827. William located in Philadelphia & d. 1797. Margaret d. 1793 & 1794 Robert m. 2d Elizabeth Hawthorne, d/o Samuel & Elizabeth of Strasburg, Lancaster Co., PA. Son Samuel, also a physician, res. at Emmitsburg, Baltimore, Lexington KY & St. Louis, MO. Another son, Andrew Annan, M.D., b. in Emmitsburg, MD in 1805 is mentioned in the first reference here. *FR2:1502-3, 1503-4*

APPLEBY, ---, ran away from his home in England & d. in Montgomery Co., MD. His children: Nicholas, went to NE; Rufus (b. c. 1830); Walter; Wesley; Somerset, d. aged 21; Mary Jane, m. Benjamin Hilton; Sarah, m. Joshua Brown; Harriet, m. Thomas Phillips; Fanny, m. Mr. Carlisle; & Martha, m. Alexander Hempston & to NE. *FR2:1138-9*

APPLEMAN, PHILIP, b. Heidelberg, Germany 20 Oct. 1755. To America in early manhood & settled in Pleasant Valley, Washington Co., MD. He was one of the first to build on the present site of town of Middletown. He m. Maria Brunch, of Heidelberg, Germany. Children: John; Catherine of Middletown, d. unm.; Sarah of Middletown, unm.; Jacob & Susan, dec'd. Members United Brethren Church in Middletown. *FR2:871-2*

ARBUCKLE, DANIEL, one of 4 brothers to America from Ireland & settled in Philadelphia Co., PA. His son, Daniel Jr. b. Montgomery Co., PA; manufacturer of cotton & woolen goods. He retired to Cecil Co., MD in 1869, where he d. in 1891, aged 78. He m. Mary S. Magargle of Philadelphia Co., PA & they had 9 children: sons Daniel T. & Paul T. res. of Cecil Co., MD. *H/C:130, 426-7*

ARCHER, JOHN, s/o Robert of Northern Ireland, m. Esther Irwin & to America in early part of last century from Londonderry with his family of wife and 3 sons & 1 dau. Settled in Cecil Co., later Harford Co., MD. *MDC:40*

ARMSTRONG, JOHN, from England to Cumberland Valley, PA; had son John, a gun & white smith & master mechanic, settled near Emmitsburg, MD & m. a Miss --- James, an only child, who lived near Emmitsburg of Welch desc. Their children: William, Robert, Samuel & James, all gunsmiths & daus. Anna, Jane & Elizabeth. *FR2:805*

ARNOLD, ABRAHAM B. (M.D.), b. Jebenhausen, Kingdom of Wurtemburg, Germany 4 Feb. 1820, of Jewish parentage. To US with uncle at age 14 & 5 years later joined by his parents. Abraham m. 1847, Ellen, d/o Adam Dennis, Esq. of Easton, PA; settled in Baltimore. *MDC:80*

ARNOLD, DAVID, b. Germany, settled in Middletown Valley, Frederick Co., MD, where he d. in 1841, aged 84; farmer. His children: John H., b. 1795; Peter, m. Polly (Mary) Harshman, d. in Burkittsvile, MD; Lydia m. John Ausherman & d. at Arnoldstown, Frederick Co., MD. Son John H. m. 5 March 1818, Sarah Karn. *FR2:1061-2, 1188-9*

ARTER, HENRY, b. Germany, m. Magdalen Cook of Philadelphia, PA. Henry to America as a young man. *6TH:424-27*

ASH(E), DANIEL HEINRICH (ESCH), of Hachenburg, Germany, emigrated to Philadelphia 1741; lost at sea in 1747 while returning to his native land. His granddau. Rachel Ashe m. Jonathan Webb & resided in Pine Grove, Lancaster Co., PA. Her dau., Rebecca E. Webb m. John Creswell & their son John A. J. Creswell b. 18 Nov. 1828 at Port Deposit, Cecil Co., MD. *MDC:624*

ASHFORDBY, WILLIAM, b. England 1638, one of the earliest settlers of NY, where he d. 1697. He res. in Esopus & was Ulster Co. sheriff 1680-1685. Miss Elizabeth Grant McIlvain of Baltimore, MD is a desc. *TR4:103*

ATKINSON, ALEXANDER, b. & reared in Ireland, in young manhood emigrated to US & settled in Cecil Co., MD. School teacher at Rising Sun. He d. c. 1825. Methodist. His son Stephen b. 17 July 1820 in Cecil Co. & m. 23 June 1842 Hannah Maria, d/o William Ramsey, of Bay View, Cecil Co. *H/C:435-6*

ATKINSON, THOMPSON (CAPT.), German sea captain who met his wife in Ireland; to Portland, ME, where dau. Mary was born. Dau. Mary

m. Lt. William M. Atkinson of Baltimore, where they resided. Their dau. Ruth C. m. Dr. J. Charles Norton 3 Dec. 1912 at St. Martin's Roman Catholic Church in Baltimore, MD. *TR3:228*

AUCHER, ELIZABETH, d/o Edward of Bishopsbourne & Mabel Wrothe, d/o Sir Robert Wrothe & sister of Sir Anthony Aucher, member of council of the VA Company. She was also the first cousin of Joan Aucher, who m. Sir Humphrey Gilbert, the half-brother of Sir Walter Raleigh. Desc. was Mrs. Fillmore Beall of MD. *TR4:432*

AUMEN, BARNABAS, & wife Margaret, from Baden, Germany to PA. Their son Francis John b. on the voyage. The family settled near Littlestown, PA. Francis John served in the Civil War in the Union Army; farmer & later guard on the battlefield of Gettysburg, which job he held until his death. Francis' wife, Martha Henrietta, was of English desc. & the d/o William & Harriet Rider of Round Top, PA, near Gettysburg. Francis & Martha had a son, William Sylvester Aumen, b. Littlestown, PA, 12 July 1870, 2d of 10 children. William to Waynesboro, PA & later to Baltimore, MD & after the fire of 1904 founded Aumen Machinery & Supply Co. William Sylvester m. (1) Elizabeth Brown, d/o Harry & Mary of Baltimore. She d. leaving a dau., Mary M. He m. (2) Annie Agnes McGee, d/o Thomas & Annie McGee of Baltimore & had 2 children. Roman Catholic. *TR3:729-30*

AUSHERMAN, ---, b. Germany, came from Hesse Cassel to Frederick Co., MD c. 1790. Son John, farmer, m. Lydia Arnold; members of the River Brethren. Their son David b. 7 July 1838 in Middletown Valley; d. 24 April 1907. He was a minister of the German Baptist Church & res. near Burkittsville, Middletown District & m. Amanda L. Rensburg, d/o Samuel & Maria (Bowlus). *FR2:872-3*

AYRES, JOHN, (EYRES), mariner who took the oath of fealty to Lord Baltimore in 1647. His name appears in the Accomac Co. Order Book of 1697 as "Surveyor of ye King's High Waies". In 1703 he m. Mary Hill, d/o Capt. Richard & Mary of Hunting Creek. Desc. Richard Johnson Ayres, b. Aryesley, Craddockville, Accomac Co., VA 10 July 1842, m. Elizabeth Hack Dawson, d/o Capt. Samuel & Sarah Ann (Bayne) Dawson, of Leesburg, Loudoun Co., VA. Mrs. Dawson d. in Baltimore 15 March 1893, aged 54. Their dau., Henrietta Dawson Ayres, b. 19 Feb. 1871 at Shepherd's Plain, near Pungotague, Accomac Co., VA & was educated in Baltimore. 22 Dec. 1896 she m. Harper Donelson

8

Sheppard, b. Pitt Co., NC, 9 Oct. 1868, s/o William Henry Haywood Sheppard, b. 1813 in Snow Hill, Greene Co., NC & Anne Elizabeth Neal, b. Murfeesboro, NC 1842. *TR4:467-70*

AYRES, THOMAS, b. Scotland, took up residence in Harford Co., MD, a large land owner. His son, Thomas J., m. Elizabeth Albany, both b. Harford Co. Their son, Thomas J. also b. there 9 March 1833. *H/C:535-6*

ADAGLIACCA, FRANCIS L. (M.D.), b. Palermo, Sicily, 26 April 1895, s/o Vincent J. & Josephine (Zaffarano), Josephine d. Paterson, NJ. Vincent m. Catherine Baldanza & 1897, with family, settled Paterson, retail shoe merchant. Francis m. 25 Oct. 1922, Elizabeth, b. Baltimore, d/o James T. & Margaret (Gourley) O'Connor; res. Baltimore. *TR3:186*

BADER, DOMINICK (CAPT.), of the German Yagers, who with others was captured at Bladensburg in War of 1812-15. His dau. Margaret m. 3 May 1833 Lewis Turner, b. Baltimore 15 June 1810. *MDC:303*

BAER, PHILIP, b. Germany 1 May 1747, settled in Lancaster Co., PA 1765, where he m. Elizabeth ---. Some time later removed to Middletown Valley, Frederick Co., MD near Bealsville. He d. there 28 April 1828. His dau., Elizabeth, b. Lancaster, PA 9 April 1782, m. Adam Miller of Frederick Co. *FR2:897-8*

BAKER, ---, b. Germany, early located in Frederick Co., MD. His son Frederick, b. Frederick City in 1775, d. 1862. Frederick was a farmer & had 10 children: Ezra, William, Aaron, Augustus, Daniel, Edward, Sophia, Matilda & 2 others d. young. Member of the Reformed Church. *FR2:1493*

BALDWIN, ---, b. Bucks Co., England, in 1639 to America on the ship *Marvin*. He landed in Milford, CT. One branch of the family migrated to PA & descs. later settled in OH. Desc. Jacob H. Baldwin, b. CT, m. Lucy Hicks, also member of old family of CT & their son, Hiram was b. in Kinsman, OH; atty. Hiram m. Lucy Clarke, d/o Reuben Clarke & member of old family of Brookfield, MA. Reuben Clarke, the American progenitor, was of Dorset, England & came to America in 1641. Hiram Baldwin d. 1874 aged 55 & his wife d. 1884, aged 65. They had 7 children, 4 sons & 3 daus.; 4 lived to maturity. Their youngest son was

9

Reuben S. Baldwin, b. 7 Dec. 1865 in Columbus, OH. He is now gen. manager of the MD Steel Rolling Co., in Baltimore, MD. He m., in Anne Arundel Co., MD, in 1886, Amy Hollingsworth, b. Youngstown, OH & d/o Sheldon & Charlotte (Sutcliffe) Hollingsworth of Huddersfield, England. *TR3:1033-4*

BALTZELL, JOHN JACOB, from Alsace, Germany in middle of last century, during the Seven Years' war there. He settled at Philadelphia & c. 1750 located in Frederick, MD. He came with his brother Charles, who served in the Revolutionary War, a major in the German regiment of MD line. *6TH:317-18*

BAMFORD, HENRY, b. Co. Tyrone, Ireland, to America aged 17 in company of John Binn, owner of the Antietam iron works near Sharpsburg, where he was employed. Member of the Lutheran Church, d. aged 78 in 1868. He m. Sarah Wilcox, b. Frederick Co., MD; she d. at the home of her son Robert C., aged 84. She a d/o John Wilcox, who came from England to America in young manhood & served as a private in War of 1812. *6TH:559-61*

BANNON, MICHAEL, b. in County Tyrone, Ireland, 1 Aug. 1827, s/o Philip & Alice (Gallagher) Bannon. At age 18 to America & landed in Baltimore in 1847; teacher. [2d ref. says he arrived in NY July 1846.] He later removed to Anne Arundel Co., studied law & opened an office in Baltimore. He m. Eveline Clark of Anne Arundel Co. They had 8 children, one was James, political leader of Anne Arundel Co., MD. AAH:324-5, *MDC:118*

BARBER, LUKE (DR.), to St. Mary's Co., MD 1658. His dau. Mary m. William Nichols & had dau. Susannah. Susannah m. Richard Blake. *TR4:344*

BARCLAY, HUGH, son of an English esquire, residing in Ireland, m. Elizabeth ---, b. Ireland. Hugh to America & settled in Baltimore "over 60 years ago." Son Rev. Joseph H. D.D., Pastor of 1st Lutheran Church in Baltimore was b. there 1 April 1834. *MDC:555-56*

BARKER, LEWELLYS FRANKLIN, b. Norwich, Ontario, Canada, 16 Sept. 1867, s/o James Frederick & Sarah Jane (Taylor) Barker. James was a Quaker minister & the s/o William P. & Sarah (Stover) Barker. The Barker family originally from England & settled in Dutchess Co.,

NY. Lewellys is a physician associated with the Johns Hopkins Hospital in Baltimore. He served in WWI. *TR3:511-12*

BARNARD, RICHARD, b. Bandon, Co. Cork, Ireland, 1840, m. Frances Duncan. Their son Alfred D. Bernard, physician, atty. & political economist, b. Baltimore, 25 March 1868. *GME:271*

BARNARD, ROBERT, b. Boston, England, in early life settled at Normanstone, DC & was connected with the Chesapeake & Ohio Canal Co. His dau. Sophia D. m. John Higgins, and is still living at age 74. Their son Frank, attorney of Rockville, b. 22 May 1861; m. 21 Oct. 1885 Roberta Baker, d/o Reuben. She is a descendant of Samuel Ogle, ex-governor of MD. *6TH:674-75*

BARROLL, WILLIAM, b. Hereford, England, 1734, s/o Sir Knight Barroll, settled in Kent Co., MD in 1774. Minister, rector of St. Stephen's Protestant Episcopal Church, Sassafrass Neck, he succeeded his uncle, Rev. Hugh Jones. Had one son, William, who settled in Chestertown, MD, an attorney. William (d. 1875, aged 87) m. Ann Williamson in 1761; she was b. 1734. Their son, James E., b. Easton, Talbot Co., MD, attorney who in 1854 removed to Baltimore. James E. m. Henrietta J. Bedford Hackett, b. 1788, d/o Major Hackett of Queen Anne's Co., MD. *H/C:258, TR3:722-3, TR4:75, H/C:257-8*

BARTGIS, MATHIAS, with 2 of his brothers, natives of France, to America with William Penn. Landed at Philadelphia, PA & Mathias settled in Fredericktown, MD, the first printer to settle there. He m. & had 2 sons: Franklin & Mathias, Jr. Franklin was b. near Fredericktown; farmer & m. Elizabeth Hoffman & they had 6 children, one of whom was Titus Bartgis, b. Nov. 1818. Franklin d. near his home & is bur. in the Old Cronis' graveyard near Fredericktown. *FR2:858-9*

BARTLETT, THOMAS, b. Yorkshire, England 1635, to America 1692 with his family & settled in Talbot Co., MD, near Easton. "In mature life" became Quaker, "which may account for his migration to a new country at age of fifty-seven." Named his 1200 acre estate in MD Ratcliffe Manor. He m. Mary Goodchild, also of York & their 5 children all b. in England: Thomas, John, James, Mary & Esther. Thomas d. in MD 1711. His second son, John (1675-1748) m. Mary Townsend, d/o Robert, who came to PA with William Penn on ship *Welcome* in 1682. *TR4:635-7*

BARTON, THOMAS (REV.), minister of Church of England who emigrated to America from Ireland between 1750-1765. Served as chaplain in the army of Gen. Braddock & was rector of churches in York & Lancaster, PA. He m. a sister of David Rittenhouse, representative of the PA-Cassel-Rittenhouse family. Great grandson Randolph Barton m. Agnes P. Kirkland of Winchester, VA. Their son David Walker Barton b. in Baltimore Co., MD 8 April 1890. *TR4:141*

BASKIN, WILLIAM, of French lineage, family migrated to England during the reign of Cromwell. William to America c. 1700, settled on land at the junction of the Susquehanna & Juniata Rivers, place afterward known as the Baskin Ferry. His son Andrew capt. in the Continental Army & 1st state senator from Lancaster Co., PA. Desc. Thomas Edmund Baskin m. Sarah B. Peebles. Their son, William Peebles Baskin was b. Richland, SC, farmer. William m. Sallie Stuckey, also of SC, & had son Eldridge Baskin, b. Bishopville, SC, 11 Aug. 1877. William d. aged 37; Sallie, b. 1839, d. 1921. Eldridge grad. Univ. of MD Medical College in 1903 & opened an office in Baltimore. Methodist. *TR4:789-90*

BAUER, JOHN, and wife Catherine (Kreitler), resided at Gruenrethersbach, Germany, John a Capt. in the German Army. Dau. Catherine m. John Conrad and son Dr. John Joseph Heck b. in Baltimore 26 May 1879. *TR3:246*

BAUER (BOWER), JOHN (SIR), Burgermaster of Strasburg, Germany, left that city on the occupation by the French, to America & settled in Baltimore County, where he patented land in 1774. *MDC:68-9*

BAUMGARDNER, JOHN, b. Germany, 30 April 1840, s/o Thomas & Margaret Baumgardner. He emigrated with his parents & settled in Frederick Co., MD 1843. John was in partnership with John W. Stonebraker of Hagerstown in the manufacture of fertilizers. He was a founder of the Frederick Brick Works. 1863 he m. Fannie Sinn & had 7 children. *FR2:853-4*

BAUMGARDNER, THOMAS, b. Prussia, Germany 1805. His siblings: Henry, of WI; John of Prussia; Margaret & Catharine, both also of Prussia. Thomas to America in 1843 & settled in Frederick City, MD, where he d. 1873. Shoemaker, Lutheran. He m. Margaret Sheffler, also b. Prussia & had: Henry; John F.O. of Frederick; Barbara A. m. Nicholas

Lochner of Frederick; Charles of Frederick & Lizzie, m. August Ebert of Frederick City. *FR2:1276-7*

BAYNE, WALTER (BEANE), transported himself & one able man-servant in 1640/41, for which he received 100 acres of land from Cecil Calvert. He was a burgess for St. George's Hundred 1641-50. Desc. Rev. Colmore Bayne of MD & Accomac Co., VA, was b. Prince George's Co., MD 22 April 1774 & m. Elizabeth Smith Hack, d/o Peter. He was a s/o Lt. William Bayne & Mary Fenley who were m. 4 Nov. 1753 in the Broad Creek Church, in St. John's or Piscataway Parish, Prince George's Co., MD. *TR4:467-9*

BEACHLEY, HENRY, ancestor of the Beachley family in this country, purchased the old homestead in Middletown Valley, Frederick Co., MD prior to the Revolution. He settled among the early Swiss settlers; member of the Reformed Church. His wife was Barbara Flook. Children: Peter, Jacob, John, Conrad, Henry, Daniel (b. 1802), Barbara, m. John Flook; Mollie, m. Henry Ahalt; Catharine, m. Mr. Leinbach & 2 other daus. *FR2:857-8*

BEALL, NINIAN, (1625-1717), b. Largo, Fifeshire, Scotland. In 1650 he fought against Cromwell at Dunbar, was captured & transported to Calvert Co., MD in 1655. Capt. of militia in Calvert Co. 1778. Became owner of several large tracts of land in Southern MD. He was lt. of Lord Baltimore's vessel, the *Royal Charles*, was commander in chief of the MD Militia & served in many political capacities. His will is dated 15 Jan. 1717. Under his supervision in 1690 a party of 200 Presbyterian immigrants from Scotland entered MD & he located them along the Potomac & named the settlement New Scotland. The pastor of this flock was Rev. Nathaniel Taylor. Col. Beall d. 1717 & was bur. on his plantation, "the Rock of Dunbarton," now Gay St. in Georgetown. He m. c. 1670 Ruth Moore, d/o Richard & Jane Moore, barrister, of St. Mary's Co., MD; they had 12 children. *TR4:345, 429, 825-7, MDC:373, AA:101*

BEARD, JOHN, to America from Germany & settled at Rock Hill, Woodsboro District, Frederick Co., MD. Grandson John Beard m. Sarah Locke & had son John D. Beard 30 Dec. 1851 in Frederick Co. *FR2:1251-2*

13

BEARD, JOHN (REV), believed to have been a native of Ireland. In 1762 was pastor of church in Cecil Co., MD. His will, proved in 1802, mentions sons James, Hugh & George. *C:280*

BEATTY, ARTHUR, b. Co. Tyrone, Ireland, his son, William, b. DE, removed to Cecil Co., MD; millwright & railroad worker. In 1848 druggist in North East, MD; Methodist Episcopal, d. 1882 aged 82. *H/C:576*

BEATTY, JOHN, emigrated from Ireland to America & settled in NY. Was sheriff of Ulster Co. 1691 & he d. 1721. His son, Thomas Beatty, b. in NY 4 March 1703 & to MD 1732. Miss Elizabeth Grant McIlvain of Baltimore is a desc. *TR4:102*

BEDINGER, ADAM, b. Alsace, after his marriage came to America in 1736, setled in York Co., PA. Oldest son Henry m. Mary VonSchlegel & in 1762, with his family, Henry removed to Mecklenburg (now Shepherdstown), Frederick Co., VA, where he died. He had 3 sons who served in the Revolutionary Army: Henry, George M. & Daniel. Henrietta Bedinger, b. Bedford, 7 Feb. 1810, is the d/o Daniel & she m. Charles W. Goldsborough, M.D., of Walkersville, MD, b. 1841 in Frederick Co. *6TH:416-21*

BEIERFELD, ABRAHAM, b. Germany, 1890 to US, settled in Baltimore; optometrist. He m. in Baltimore Mollie Honigsberg, b. Russia, to America 1891 with her parents, who also settled Baltimore. *TR3:263*

BEITLER, SAMUEL, b. Germany 1 Sept. 1790, hatter. Emigrated to PA in early life. He m. & removed to farm in Adams Co., PA & later settled near Loy's Station, Creagerstown District, Frederick Co., MD, where he d. 21 March 1867. He & wife bur. in old graveyard at Creagerstown. Both were members of the Reformed church. His wife was Susanna Kramer, b. Germany 22 Aug. 1802, to America in youth, settling in PA. Their children: Sophia, b. 13 Oct. 1918, d. unm.; Jessie, b. 31 July 1824, dec'd.; Samuel J.; Sarah E., widow of the late George Beird, b. 20 Feb. 1839; John H., miller & farmer of Loy's Station, b. 23 Oct. 1843. *FR2:1435-6*

BELL, ADAM, to America from Scotland c. 1820. Adam m. Eleanor Tyffe & their son Silas Adam Bell m. Emma Rebecca Cashell. Silas &

14

Emma had a son, Alton Cashell Bell, b. 4 Oct. 1875 in Laytonsville, MD. *TR3:641-2*

BELL, ALEXANDER, b. at Blackadder-Mains, Parish of Edwin, County of Berwick, Scotland, s/o William Bell, b. Maincliffe, on the south bank of the Tweed. To US on visit to a brother at age 27 & returned to Scotland. In 1848 he settled in Baltimore in the malt business. In 1857 m. Margaret, d/o John Boyd, a native of Ayrshire, Scotland, carried on maltster business in Baltimore. *MDC:453*

BELL, HUGH, b. Ireland of Scotch parentage. He fought in Baltimore in War of 1812 in Chase's Six Gun Battery. His wife was Ann Chambers & they had 7 sons, two of whom, Edward & Robert, were killed while serving in the Confederate Army in the Civil War. Ann was d/o William & Mary (Brown) Chambers of Harford Co., MD. She was desc. from one of four brothers who came to America from Antrim, Ireland early in 1700 & who settled Chambersburg, PA. *TR4:748-9*

BELLESON, WILLIAM, b. England. To America, when he met on the ship a German girl, whom he married. They landed at Baltimore where they settled; he was a gunsmith. His son, William, b. in Baltimore, was a ship carpenter. William (2) removed to Franklin DIstrict, Carroll Co., MD, where he died. His wife was Lucretia Fowler & they had: Mary, d. unm.; Richard; Henrietta, m. Frederick Koons; Annie, m. John Malohan; George W.; William & Corella m. Perry Green. *FR2:1500-01*

BELT, HUMPHRY (SIR), sailor from Gravesend, England in ship *Arden*, landed Anne Arundel Co., MD 30 June 1663. His son John Belt m. Elizabeth Tidings. *FR2:920*

BELT, MIDDLETON, m. Mary Ann Dyer at St. John's Church, Surrey, England, 25 March 1763. Their dau., Anna Maria, b. in Bristol, England 24 Nov. 1771; another dau. Middletown, b. in VA 24 April 1777. Others of the family included William Dyer, b. in Montgomery Co., MD 26 Feb. 1788 & James Harrick, b. 31 Jan. 1792 in the same place. *H/C:571-3*

BENGSTON, ANDREAS, b. Stockholm, Sweden 1640 & res. in province of New Sweden 1656-1706. Miss Elizabeth Grant McIlvain of Baltimore is a desc. *TR4:103*

BENJAMIN, JOSEPH, from London, England to America in 1766 & settled in VA, where he joined "Light Horse Harry Lee's Legion" of VA Cavalry at Amelia Court House in 1775. After the Rev. War settled in Cecil Co., MD & m. Elizabeth Grace Winchester. He converted to Christianity after his marriage & was eventually one of the founders of the Methodist Episcopal church of Charlestown, where he is buried. His son George, b. Cecil Co. April 1780. *TR4:331-2, H/C:315-17*

BENJAMIN, SOLOMON, to America with his parents c. 1819, at age of 4; settled in Richmond, VA. His son Solomon served in the Confederate army & was the father of Levi, b. in Richmond. Levi to Baltimore in the late 1870's and d. here 1896, aged 38; m. Mollie G. Beckwith. *TR3:306*

BENNETT, RICHARD, b. England in the early 17th century. Emigrated to VA, was agent of his uncle, Edward Bennett, wealthy London merchant. Took refuge in MD in 1642, settled near present site of Annapolis, at "Towne Neck" on the severn in 1649. After his death his widow [not named here] m. Philemon Lloyd, by whom she had many children & from whom the MD Lloyds of Wye House are descended. His wife's kinsman is named as Col. Nathaniel Utie, secretary to the governor. Richard's will was probated 1675. *TR4:899-900, AA :41*

BENSON, STEPHEN, of the kingdom of France, settled in MD 1641. His dau. Elizabeth m. (2d) Richard Bond of Calvert Co. "24th day of ye 7th month, called September, 1702 . . . at Herring Creek Meeting House in Anne Arundel County, Maryland." Their son, Benson Bond, member of assembly 1751, m. Mary Holdsworth. *TR4:314, 344*

BERRY, BENJAMIN, of England, with brother-in-law Charles Bell, son of the man who beheaded Charles I, to America & settled in Prince George's Co., MD. Benjamin m. Miss Clagett. *MDC:55*

BERRY, JAMES, settled in James City County, VA c. 1630-32. Removed to MD 1652 with wife Elizabeth & son William & received grants for tracts in Calvert Co. (now Prince George's Co.) on the Patuxent River. James d. c. 1685. Quaker family. *TR4:322*

BESER, LOUIS, and wife Sophia, both b. in Russia, to America & settled in Cincinnati, OH. Son Nicholas b. in Cincinnati 1 May 1889, practices law in Baltimore. *TR3:301*

BESLER, CHARLES S. M., b. Germany 27 Nov. 1817, s/o Christian H. & Rachel J. (Snell) Besler, both b. Germany. Charles was the eldest of their 2 children, the other being his sister Johanna S. E. W., who d. unmarried 16 Sept. 1890, at the home of her brother. At age 15 Charles accompanied his father to America, landing in Baltimore 30 Aug. 1832 & on the 17th of the following month settled on farm in Harford Co. He m. at the age of 27, Christiana Seaman, also b. in Germany, with her parents to America at age of 15 in 1840. No issue. Members Bethel Presbyterian Church. *H/C:528-9*

BEST, ---, b. Germany, settled in PA in 18th century, bur. near Littlestown, Adams Co., PA. His son David, farmer near Lewistown, Frederick Co., MD, d. aged 77 & bur. at Mount Olivet Cemetery in Frederick. David m. Mary Lantz of near Uniontown, Carroll Co., MD. She d. aged 68. *FR2:899-900*

BESTER, WILLIAM JOHN, s/o French Huguenots who fled into the Protestant German state of Hesse-Cassel. William was b. in Hesse-Cassel. His father was head gardener for King Frederick William of Prussia. William John emigrated to America & eventually settled in Hagerstown, MD, where in 1847 he established a horticultural business that he carried on until his death in Sept. 1859, aged 57, & continued by his sons. His wife was Elizabeth Wort, b. Wurtemberg, Germany, who came to America in 1835. She d. in 1903, aged 84. *TR3:656-7, 6TH:191-2*

BEVARD, CHARLES, to America in colonial days, served in Rev. Both he & his wife lived to age 95. Their son James was a merchant at Bush, Harford Co., MD. James' son George b. at Bush, m. Mary Wallace, d/o Randall of Harford Co. George was a cooper & served in the War of 1812. Presbyterian. *H/C:257*

BIDDLE, JOHN, & Mary his wife, emigrated from England before 1692 & settled in Cecil Co., MD. Vestryman & warden of St. Stephen's Episcopal Church. Their son, John, b. 1 Oct. 1695, m. Mary Mouned, b. 2 Feb. 1715. *H/C:343-4*

BIELFELD, HERMAN (REV.), b. Germany, 4 Sept. 1815, d. in America 26 Nov. 1895. Minister of the German Reformed Church, m. Friederecke Piele, b. Germany. Son J. J. Bielfeld was reared in Frederick City, MD; res. for a time in Harrisburg PA, Baltimore MD & became a

17

student of fresco painting. After traveling he eventually located in Frederick City in 1879. Engaged in printing & publishing business with V. M. Marken. Member Reformed Church. *FR2:855*

BIRELY, ---, two brothers from Germany to America before 1776, both settled in Frederick Co., MD. One settled in Frederick City (tanner) & the other settled at Double Pipe Creek, (now Detour), over the county line in Carroll Co. *FR2:1252-3*

BIRELY, WILLIAM, b. Germany, to America before Rev., paper manufacturer of Frederick Co., MD; m. Charlotte --- in Germany, resided near Myersville. Their children: Margaret, Rebecca, Charlotte, Mary Elizabeth & John William, b. Frederick Co. 1816. *FR2:702*

BIRNIE, CLOTWORTHY (II), from Co. Antrim, Ireland & settled at Glenburn farm, near Taneytown, MD in 1810. He is of Scotch-Irish desc. Desc. Rogers Birnie m. Amelia Knode Harry, whose Dutch ancestors came from Holland in 1760 & settled in Hagerstown, MD. *TR4:774-6*

BISER, CHARLES C., to America from Hesase Darmstadt. His son John had a son, Henry Biser, b. in Middletown area of Frederick Co., MD 30 April 1821, m. Sophia ---, b. there in Feb. 1826. Sophia also of German desc. Their son, Charles Calvin Biser, b. near Middletown 28 Oct. 1862. *TR3:574-5*

BISER, FREDERICK, b. Germany, to America with 3 brothers. Settled in Frederick Co., MD, early inhabitant. Member Reformed Church & m. Margaret Coblentz. Children: Daniel; John; Peter; Jacob; Henry; Polly, m. Henry Brandenburg; Elizabeth, d. unm.; & Catherine m. Daniel Routzahn. *FR2:951-52, 1059-60*

BITTINGER, HENRY, b. Germany, settled in OH, later to PA & still later to Allegany Co., MD to the present site of town of Bittinger, named for him, where he d. aged 70. Lutheran. *6TH:180-81*

BITTLE, ---, family of German ancestry, first settled in PA. George Bittle, removed from Adams Co., PA to Middletown Valley, Frederick Co., MD. He was among the earliest of settlers to that region. Son Jonathan m. Rachel Bogner & had son Thomas F. b. on homestead 1 mile north of Bellsville (now called Harmony), Jackson District, Frederick Co.,

23 Sept. 1838. Member St. John's Lutheran Church, at Church Hill, where he & his wife are buried. *FR2:876-7*

BLACK, ANDREW L., b. 23 Aug. 1840, town of Jedburgh, County of Roxburgh, Scotland, s/o George. George was the s/o John A., & John A. s/o George of the parish of Minto. To NY in 1865, settling in Rochester; later resided in Richmond, VA, Philadephia, and still later to Baltimore (1871) & established the Belvedere Nursery. In June 1866 he m. Annie, d/o John Turnbull, formerly of Henderside, Scotland. *MDC:201*

BLACK, GEORGE (MAJOR), b. Londonderry, Ireland, to Kent Co., MD c. 1740, with his father, James, & settled at Fairfields. He m. 1770 Margaret Wallace, d/o Andrew & Eleanor. Was a patriot & contributed food & clothing to the Continental army. *MDC:613*

BLADEN, WILLIAM of Hemsworth, Yorkshire, England, to America 1690, d. Annapolis 1718. His son, Thomas Bladen, b. Annapolis, MD in 1698 & was proprietary gov. of MD, 1742-1749. His wife was Barbara, d/o Sir Thomas Janssen, Baronet. Thomas d. in England in 1780. *TR4:31*

BLAKE, CHARLES, s/o & heir of Charles Blake of the parish of St. George, Hanover Square, London, settled in Queen Annes Co., MD prior to 1700. He m. Henrietta Lloyd, d/o Col. Philemon Lloyd & wife Henrietta Marie Neale. Their dau., Dorothy Blake, became the wife of Dr. Charles Carroll of Annapolis & mother of Charles Carroll, barrister. *TR4:453-4*

BLAKE, GEORGE A., b. in Co. Mayo, Ireland, 23 Aug. 1834. With his parents to America in 1846, landed in Boston, MA and went on to Baltimore, where they settled. He m. 1856, Harriet Grigg, d/o William of St. Mary's Co., MD. His brother, Charles D., also b. in Co. Mayo, Ireland 10 Jan. 1836, removed to Baltimore with parents in 1846. He m. in 1876 Marrion Wolcott of Baltimore. Another brother, Henry C., b. 10 March 1840, to America with parents. All three were builders. *MDC:157*

BLAKE, JOSEPH, settled early in Calvert Co. Thomas Blake (no definite relationship given to Joseph) in 1692 was a military officer in Calvert Co. Another early Blake of Calvert Co. named here is Richard of My Lordship's Favor. He m. Susanna Nichols, d/o William Nichols, who was sentfrom England to MD in 1695. *TR4:454*

BLAKE, THOMAS (CAPT.), to MD via Barbadoes & VA & first settled in Somerset Co., MD before 1671. He signed himself of the town of Galloway in the Kingdom of Ireland & was desc. from Richard Blake, the founder of the family in Ireland. Thomas removed to the western shore & settled in Calvert Co. after 1671. He m. (1) Jane, widow of Robert Webb of Calvert Co., before 1694; m. (2) Jane Sutton, widow of Edward Isaac. By his 2d m. he had a son Richard, d. 1746. Richard m. Susannah Nichols, d/o William of St. Mary's Co., MD & Mary Barber. *TR4:311-17*

BLAND, THEODRICK, to America from England 1654, settled in Tidewater VA & m. the dau. of the gov. of the colony. He is bur. at Westover churchyard in Charles City Co., VA. His son Richard had son Richard who was very active in politics. The second Richard had a son Peter, had son Peter Jr., who left VA & res. MO. A son Richard Edward Bland, physician & surgeon of St. Louis, MO, m. Henrietta Williams. Their son, John Randolph Bland, settled in Baltimore. *TR3:1017-18, TR4:112*

BLICKENSTAFF, YOST, from Germany, one of the earliest settlers in the Middletown Valley, Frederick Co., MD. To America in early manhood & took up tract of timberland known as "Yost's Claim," where he married, raised a family & died. He was buried on the home place. His son John m. Mary, d/o --- Fair. His son Jacob, res. Catoctin District, Frederick Co., b. March 1832. *FR2:862*

BLOOMER, JAMES, & wife Catherine, b. England, to Baltimore in early life. Their dau., Catherine Elizabeth Bloomer, m. Thomas William Biddle Sr., of NY City. Their son, Thomas William Jr., b. Brooklyn, NY 31 March 1885, in 1916 to Cumberland, MD, architect. Thomas Jr.'s wife is Augusta Tate, d/o Henry of New York city & they m. 6 June 1908. Res. Cumberland. *TR3:633-4*

BLUMBERG, LEOPOLD (GEN.), b. in Province of Brandenberg, Prussia 28 Sept. 1827, the 21st child in a family of 17 sons & 5 daughters, whose parents, Abraham & Sophia, were of the Hebrew faith. He grew up at Frankfort-on-the Oder & served in the Prussian army. In 1854 he resigned his commission & came with his wife to Baltimore;

served in the Union Army during the Civil War as Major of the 5th MD Regiment. He d. as a result of wounds of the war 12 Aug. 1876. *MDC:478*

BOLLMAN, THOMAS, b. in Bremen, Germany 28 May 1775, to Baltimore, MD c. 1778; a baker. Thomas d. 17 April 1819. His wife was Ann Barbara Raab, b. Weissenbach, Germany 20 Sept. 1786; came to Baltimore 1 Jan. 1800; were m. 16 April 1805. She d. 30 Jan. 1866, aged 79. She was the d/o Adam Gottlieb Rabb, who kept the German Lutheran day school connected with Zion Church in Baltimore. Her mother was Magdalena Schaefer of Weissenbach. *MDC:599-600*

BOND, PETER, to MD from England before the Rev. War. His son (or perhaps his nephew), Thomas Bond, res. Pleasant Hills, a large landowner in what is now the Baltimore City area. *TR4:792-3*

BOND, PETER, progenitor to America from England, set. VA, to MD 1660. *GME:48*

BOND, THOMAS (DR.), English emigrant, his son Richard m. Elizabeth Chew in 1702 at the Quaker meeting house on West River, Anne Arundel Co., MD. Drs. Thomas & Phineas Bond, s/o Richard & Elizabeth, moved to Philadelphia in 1734 & 1738, respectively & became famous physicians. *TR4:298*

BONNER, CHARLES (COL.), from England to Bath, NC, served in Rev. Descendant Anne Bonner Marsh m. John Long, their grandson John Stevenson Long Yost b. 18 May 1892, Baltimore, MD. *TR3:104*

BONSAL, RICHARD, to America from village of Bonsal, in Derbyshire, England, landed in Philadelphia in 1682. Desc. Stephen Bonsal m. Frances Land Leigh. She of colonial families who settled in PA & VA. Their son, Leigh Bonsal, b. in Norfolk, VA 4 July 1862, spent most of his life in Baltimore, MD; attorney. Leigh m. Mary C. Pleasant, 16 Oct. 1890 & had 6 children. *TR3:967-8*

BOOTH, ---, left England in 1829 accompanied by 11 children, 2 remaining in England. Of the 11, William was a farmer in Harford Co., MD; Adam was a commission merchant in Baltimore & was killed during the riots at the breaking out of the Civil War. The father of this family was a weaver in England, where he invented the first power mill for weaving cloth. He died aged 87 & his wife, Elizabeth (Carter) Booth, died aged 85. Their son Joseph Booth, b. Lancashire, England, 9 April 1811, came with his parents to America in 1829. Farmer, dealer in ice & large manufacturer of ice cream. He d. 20 Dec. 1891. Joseph's wife was Barbara Ann Schuh, b. in PA in 1820, d. 1884. *H/C:436*

BOOTH, BARTHOLOMEW (REV.), and sons William and Robert & Miss Mary Valens and sister Mrs. Bardsley to America before beginning of the Revolutionary War. Settled at 'Needwood Forest' near Petersville, Frederick Co., MD. Rev. Booth d. Washington Co., MD c. 1786. *FRI:328*

BORDLEY, THOMAS, b. Yorkshire, England, to America 1694 with an elder brother, a clergyman, settled in Kent Co., MD. Thomas m. Ariana Vanderheyden of Cecil Co., MD. She m. 2d Edmund Jennings of Annapolis and in 1737 to England with him where she died. *MDC:49*

BOTELER, HENRY, CHARLES & RUPERT, received a large grant from Lord Baltimore in what is now Upper Marlboro, Prince George Co., MD. Edward m. Priscilla Lingon (Lincoln). This branch of the family the Frederick Co., MD Botelers. *6TH:239-41*

BOUIC, PIERRE AMABLE TRANQUILLE, of village of d'Ocqueville in province of Lower Seine, Normandy, France, c. 1785, settled near Poolesville, Montgomery Co., MD. His 2d wife was Mrs. Doracas Fletchall, widow & a d/o William Veirs of Montgomery Co. They had son William Viers Bouic, b. 12 May 1816, near Poolsville. Pierre d. c. 1821. William res. for a time in Jefferson Co., MO, atty., returned to Montgomery Co. 1843 & m. Mary Ann Matilda Viers, eldest d/o Samuel Clark Viers & settled in Rockville, MD. *TR4:482 & 6TH:158-61*

BOWDLE, ---, family established in MD early in the 17th century & the immigrant ancestor [not named here] was a vestryman of the First Protestant Episcopal, founded in Talbot Co., MD in 1649. *TR4:450*

BOWEN, ---, to America from England before 1750 & settled in DE. Desc. Levi Bowen, b. Baltimore, MD, ship chandler. *TR3:589-91*

BOWEN, WILLIAM, b. Wales in 1816, s/o James, b. Wales, a miner. In 1840 William m. in England Eliza Vaughn, b. Gloucestershire. After marriage ran an inn in Gloucester & to America 1846 with wife & 3 children. Settled at Mt. Savage, Allegany Co., MD. One year later to Frostburg & worked in coal mines. He d. 10 April 1896, aged 80; Eliza d. Oct. 1896. Members of the Methodist Episcopal Church. *6TH:380-81*

BOWIE, JOHN, b. Scotland 1688, d. 1759; To America c. 1705/06, at the invitation of his maternal uncle, John Smith, who had settled on the Patuxent river, a few miles north of the village of Nottingham. John m. Dec. 1707, Mary d/o James Mulliken. Their son, Capt. William Bowie, m. Margaret Sprigg & had a son Robert, b. on family estate of Mattaponi, near Nottingham, Prince George's Co., MD in 1750. Robert was the 12th & 15th gov. of the state of MD. *TR4:55, GME:386*

BOWIE, JOHN, b. Scotland, to America in 1707 & settled in Prince George's Co., MD. Desc. Col. Allan Bowie, Jr., served in the MD militia in the Rev. War. *TR4:443*

BOWLY, DANIEL, b. c. 1695, s/o Samuel, to America & settled at West River, below Annapolis, MD & m. Elizabeth, d/o Capt. Darby Lux. Their only son, also Daniel, b. 1744, m. his cousin Nancy, member of the Scottish royal clan of Stewart, in St. Paul's Church of Baltimore, 25 July 1775. *TR4:808-9*

BOWMAN, HENRY, b. Germany, to America as young man, settled at what is how Hopewell Cross Roads in MD. He was a Methodist Protestant church member in 1769, then called the Bush Forest Church, later known as the Log Meeting House and now known as Bush Chapel. Henry d. aged 96; chairmaker. *H/C:242*

BOYD, JAMES ALEXANDER, b. Kilwinning, Ayrshire, Scotland 22 Dec. 1823. Served as apprentice to a stonecutter. He took out a contract to work in Kingston, Jamaica & after 3 years, at age 25 he landed in Philadelphia. He later resided in WV, OH, Baltimore MD, Memphis TN & Brazil. 1865 he settled in Montgomery Co., MD & called his estate Boyds. Presbyterian. 22 June 1854 he m. Sarah, d/o Jonathan & Zilpah (Allen) Rinehart. Jonathan was of Allegany Co., MD & d. at age 45. James Alexander Boyd d. 21 Dec. 1896. *6TH:169-71*

BOYER (BYERS), GABRIEL, to America from Germany in early manhood & settled near Westminster (now Carroll Co.), MD. Gabriel's children: Michael, John Henry, Elizabeth, m. John Power; Catherine, m. Peter Slagle; Sarah, m. Solomon M. Myesli; Polly, m. James Orndorf.

Son Michael, cooper & farmer, spent his whole life near Westminster; was veteran of War of 1812; m. Elizabeth Dutrow of Emmitsburg District. Lutheran; both bur. at Krider's Church, near Westminster. *FR2:860*

BOYLE, EDWARD, b. Co. Fermangh, Ireland; m. Ellen Smith b. same place. Son Rev. Francis Edward Boyle b. Baltimore 6 Sept. 1827. *MDC:14*

BOYLE, PATRICK, b. Ireland, to America c. 1730, settled in Cecil Co., MD. His son Patrick m. Hannah Harland. *H/C:338*

BRACE, WILLIAM, b. London, England, in boyhood shipped on a merchant vessel & later settled in Cumberland, MD. He m. Susan C. Stafford in Keyser, WV. *6TH:574-75*

BRACKENRIDGE, W. D., b. near Ayr, Scotland, 1810. To Philadephia in 1837, Superintendent of Public Grounds in Washington, D.C. till 1854, when he removed to Baltimore Co., MD. He m. 1843, Isabella A. Bell, of Jedborough, Scotland. *MDC:199*

BRADFORD, WILLIAM, from England to America with his wife Elizabeth Lightbody before the Rev. War. Their son, William Jr., m. Sarah McComas. Descs. res. in Harford & Baltimore Counties, MD. *TR4:656-9*

BRADY, JAMES, b. Dublin, Ireland, with wife Margaret (McCrone), emigrated from Ireland & settled in Wilmington, New Castle Co., DE, 1828. James was a linen manufacturer & he d. c. 1850; wife d. 1866. Their son Henry H. was b. there 24 Jan. 1831. Other sons named were George F., William & Samuel. Henry H. removed to Chesapeake City, MD. He m. 27 March 1861 Rebecca S., d/o Joseph & Rebecca Cooper. Presbyterian. *MDC:155 & H/C:253*

BRAND, JOSEPH, b. Scotland, to America at an early day & located in Hanover Co., VA; engaged in merchandising during the Rev. War. His son William was b. there & went to LA previous to 1800, architect & builder. He d. 1850; Episcopal. William m. Hettie Reed of PA & had 5 children surviving to adulthood. His son, Rev. William Francis Brand, rector of the Episcopal Church at Emmorton, Harford Co,. MD, b. New Orleans, LA, 17 June 1814. Served in NY & then sent to Anne Arundel

Co., MD & later Emmorton, where his wife's family had built for him a church, consecrated in 1851. 25 May 1842 he m. Sophia Hall, d/o Haney of Carpenters Point, Cecil Co., MD. *H/C:581-2*

BRANDENBURG, JACOB, b. Brandenburg, Germany, a member of a wealthy family connected with nobility, to America with his brothers, Mathias & William. Mathias settled in KY; William in Middletown Valley, Frederick Co., MD & Jacob in the wilderness of Frederick Co. on farm in New Market district called "Chance," now property of J. L. Baker, a desc. Jacob Brandenburg m. Elizabeth Rine; he d. 1829, "at a ripe old age," his wife d. in 1833. Lutherans. Their children: William, m. Rachel Purdum, d. in Carroll Co., MD; John, dec'd.; Jacob, d. Montgomery Co., MD; Jesse, m. in Flushing OH to Miss Turner, both dec'd.; Lemuel; Mary Polly, m. --- Walker, d. near Fountain Mill Frederick Co.; Mahala, m. Denton Watkins, both d. in OH; Priscella, m. Thomas Baker. *FR2:878-9*

BRASHEARS, BENJAMIN, from France to VA, and thence to MD in 1658, & naturalized an English subject, 4 Dec. 1662. Benjamin m. Mary ---; was a Judge of Calvert Co., May 1661. *GME:408*

BRAUN, JOHN R., b. Bremen, Prussia 1 June 1817. To NY & later to Baltimore, MD, in 'segar' business with A. Bohn & Co. *MDC:323*

BREADY, GEORGE, b. Switzerland, c. 1775 to America, settled in Frederick Co., MD, farmer. *6TH:801-02*

BREESE, JOHN, and wife Aseneth, both of French Huguenot descent. Their son Oscar F., b. 26 March 1825, Dist. of Montreal, Canada, at age 18 on the death of his father, went to Hartford, CT & later resided as life insurance company agent in PA & VA. To Baltimore where he m. Louisa Kleckner of New Berlin, PA, d/o Joseph. Member Brown Memorial Church in Baltimore. *MDC:29*

BRENAN, J. F., from Bordeaux, France to San Domingo, Central America. Fled the island on an uprising of Negroes and made his way to Baltimore, where he resided until his death. Lumberman. *TR2:48-9*

BRENT, MARGARET, b. in England 1601, a d/o Richard & Elizabeth (Reed) Brent. Margaret arrived at St. Marys, MD in Nov. 1638. With her sister Mary she patented in 1639 land near St. Mary's City. Margaret was a sister-in-law of Gov. Leonard Calvert who d. leaving 2 children in England in 1647. Mistress Brent was appointed his sole executrix. Between 1654 & 1657 Margaret took up several hundred acres of land in Westmoreland Co., VA & there spent her declining years. She d. c. 1671 unmarried. *TR4:857-8*

BREUNINGER, J. HENRY, b. Germany 1818; his grandfather Henry was a jeweler, his father Jacob F. to America only on a visit. Jacob F. d. in Germany in 1856, aged 74 & his wife Dora (Krout) & J. Henry removed to America. Settled in Baltimore Co. for 3 years; 1850 to Harford Co. Dora d. 1860. J. Henry worked for George P. Cook in tannery at Cooksville on Deer Creek & later at Peach Bottom, PA for James D. Wiley & Son and later still at Bel Air, MD for John Moor. J. Henry set up a tannery in 1864 at what is now called Lafayette Valley. In 1846 he m. Lizzie Sommer, b. Germany. *H/C:226*

BREVITT, JOHN, b. England, to America aged 20, at the time of the Revolutionary War & served in that war on the American side, a son of a wealthy manufacturer of Wolverhampton. After the war settled in Baltimore & d. there 1818, aged 64. His brother served as surgeon in the British Army through the war & afterwards joined his brother John in Baltimore. *MDC:355*

BREWER, JOHN, b. in the South of Wales at beginning of 17th century. Emigrated in early life to MA (Puritan) & in 1645 to VA; 1649 to MD & settled in Puritan City of Annapolis on South River. Established "Brewerton," patented 1659. He m. Sarah d/o Henry Ridgely. John d. 5 April 1690. *MDC:65*

BRICE, JOHN (CAPT.), early from Hamershire, England to MD, gentleman, merchant, planter, political servant & was Captain of the Severn Hundred (Anne Arundel Co., MD); m. Sarah, widow of Capt. John Worthington. Children: Ann, m. Vachel Denton; Rachel, m. Philip Hammond, Annapolis merchant; John Jr., m. Sarah Frisby, d/o James & Ariana (Vanderheyder) Frisby. *AAH:156-7*

BRIDGES, ROBERT FERGUSON, of County of Fife, Scotland, Presbyterian family, was the younger of 7 sons. In 1816 he immigrated to America & settled in Hancock, MD. Three years later he m. Rebecca Leopold, who had moved with her parents from PA to MD. Her grandparents were res. of Reading, PA. Robert & Rebecca's son, Robert,

b. in Hancock 21 May 1830 & d. 1908. He m. Priscilla William Breathed, b. Berkeley Springs, WV. *TR3:559-60*

BRILLHART, ---, b. Germany, to America in early life & settled in York Co., PA; extensive land owner. The emigrant's son, Isaac, was b. York Co., veteran of the Rev. War, farmer. His son, Joseph Brillhart, m. Elizabeth Strayer & had son Jacob, b. in York Co. 25 Jan. 1831. He m. at age 28 Elizabeth Venus, b. York Co., the d/o Ann Sykes Venus, b. England & her father of French extraction. Member of the Evangelical Church, she d. Jan. 1888, aged 64. *H/C:558-9*

BRISCOE, JOHN (DR.), b. 1590, Cumberland County, England, one of 20 gentlemen "of very good fashion" who accompanied Leonard Calvert on the *Ark & Dove* expedition & settled in Saint Mary's City, MD in 1634. Family is of Crofton Hall, Cumberland County, England & is the Briscoe family, originally "deBrikskeugh," from the name of the estate near New Biggin, Cumberland Co., England. He brought his wife & 3 sons, George, Dr. John & a third, said to have been father of Philip of St. Mary's Co. This Col. Philip was a justice of Charles Co., MD 1694-1701 & d. 1724, leaving 4 sons & 4 daus. John, the immigrant, m. in England Elizabeth DuBose & his 3rd son was the father of Philip Briscoe, who m. Susanna Swann, d/o Col. Samuel. Elizabeth DuBose (DuBois) was a desc. of the Huguenot, Marquis de Roussey. *TR4:168, 199-200, 368, 770-1, 859*

BROADWATER, CHARLES, English immigrant, had son Col. Charles Broadwater who served in the French & Indian & Rev. Wars. *TR4:302*

BROME (DE BROME), JOHN, one of three brothers from Herefordshire, England to America before 1650 & settled at Calvert Co., MD. He d. at Plymouth while on a visit to England. He m. Margaret --- & his son John (II), commissioned by the king in 1692 to lay out parishes in MD m. Margaret Winifred Jones. Thomas Brome, brother of John the immigrant, settled in NY. Henry, the third brother, settled in the Carolinas. *TR4:654-6*

BROOKE, JOHN, 4th s/o Hon. Thomas Brooke, member of British Parliament 1604-1611. John arrived in MD 30 June 1650 & settled Della Brooke on the Patuxent river, m. a great-granddau. of Thomas Beaumont of Whiteley, & their dau. m. John Hanson of Woodhouse. *TR4:208*

BROOKE, ROBERT, b. London 3 June 1603, served as commissioner of Charles Co. 1650, acting gov. of MD in 1652 & president of the provincial council of MD in 1652. Robert brought his wife (Mary Baker of Battle [another reference gives Mary Mainwaring, his 2d wife, as emigrating with him]) & ten children from England in 1650 [1649?] & settled at Delabrook (now in Calvert Co., MD), on the Patuxent River [Battle Creek, named in honor of Robert's first wife.]. "Her [Mary Baker of Battle] 2 sons, Baker & Maj. Thomas Brooke of Brookfield accompanied the immigrants." Robert d. 1855. Entry gives Baker Brooke, s/o Col. Baker Brooke, b. at Battle, Sussex, England, 16 Nov. 1628, d. St. Marys Co., MD 1679. Baker m. Anne Calvert, d/o Gov. Leonard Calvert, 1st gov. of MD. *TR4:344, 779-81, MDC:128, 6TH:838-40, AAH:321*

BROOKE, ROGER, s/o Robert & Mary (Mainwarring), b. 20 Sept. 1637, at Brecknock College, Wales, the Episcopal residence of his maternal grandfather, the Bishop of St. Davids, and came to America with his parents at age 13. Resided Battle Creek, Calvert Co., MD.; m. 1st Dorothy Neale, d/o Capt. James & Ann (Gill); m. 2d Mary Wolseley, d/o Walter, and grandau. of Sir Thomas Wolseley, of Staffordshire. *GME:232*

BROOKE, THOMAS (HON. COL.), Gentleman, eldest s/o Major Thomas Brooke, Sr. & Eleanor Hatton who was b. England 1642, the d/o Hon. Richard Hatton of London. Major Thomas & wife Eleanor immigrated to MD & had son Thomas b. Prince George's Co., MD c. 1660. Thomas m. as his 2d wife Barbara Dent & had dau. Priscilla who m. 1707 Thomas Gantt. *TR4:575-8*

BROOKS, JACOB, b. England, to America before the Revolution, m. Mary Conway, eldest d/o William Conway of the Conways, North Wales. Son Nathan Covington Brooks b. in West Nottingham, Cecil Co., MD, 12 Aug. 1809. *MDC:689-90*

BROWN, ---, early German settler of VA, res. Loudoun Co., stone mason. His son Joseph L. Brown had a son William b. Loudoun Co. & settled Lovettsville, Loudoun Co. & later res. at Point of Rocks, MD. William m. Mary Jane, d/o Samuel & Christianna (Stoneburner) Fry of Loudoun Co. Their son William T. Brown b. 19 April 1848, later farmer near Doubs, Buckeystown, MD & removed to Point of Rocks, MD in

1898. William T. Brown m. Hannah A., d/o Samuel & Hannah (Williams) Compher of Loudoun Co., VA & had 4 children. *FR2:969-70*

BROWN, ALEXANDER, Ireland to America 1797, settled Baltimore, MD; d. 1834 (three score years & ten [age 70]), banking firm. *TR2:54-6*

BROWN, GEORGE, 2d of 4 sons of Alexander and Grace (Davison) Brown, b. 17 April 1787 in Ballymena, County Antrim, Ireland. To US at age 15 [1800?]. Was assoc. with his father in he management of the Baltimore banking house of Alexander Brown & Sons, Baltimore. He m. Isabella McLanahan, b. Newcastle, PA. Mr. Brown d. 26 Aug. 1859 at his home in Baltimore, a very wealthy man. Son George Stewart Brown b. May 1834, Baltimore. *GME:371 & MDC:74*

BROWN, GEORGE (DR.), from Ireland to Baltimore in 1783; d. 1822. His son George John Brown b. Baltimore m. Esther Allison, d/o Rev. Patrick Allison of Baltimore. *MDC:391*

BROWN, HENRY, b. Waterford, Ireland; mariner. He m. Michol Magdalene Boyer, b. Chester Co., PA 1 Feb. 1772. She was a descendant of a German refugee family that settled early in PA. They m. 3 Feb. 1791 & settled in Cumberland Co., PA at what is now Kingston, east of Carlisle. Their son James H. joined the Methodist Episcopal Church & received license to preach in 1828. He served the Baltimore Conference in MD, PA, VA & DC. James H. m. 26 March 1837 Ann Maria Hines of New Oxford, Adams Co., PA. *MDC:559*

BROWN, HUGH, from Ireland to Cecil Co., MD in early manhood. His dau. Emeline m. Amor Cameron, s/o Robert, of Cecil Co., MD; she d. 1850. *H/C:318-21*

BROWN, JESSE, b. Scotland, d. c. 1837/8; mariner, m. Eleanor d/o John Sweeting of Baltimore. Son George W. b. 4 Jan. 1835 in Baltimore. *H/C:276*

BROWN, JOHN SMITH, b. 7 Nov. 1809, near Plymouth, England. To America with parents at age 10, settled in Washington, D.C. Father was William Brown, contractor, went west & left family in DC. John Smith Brown at age 16 to Baltimore to learn shipbuilding with James Beacham on Fells Point. Methodist Episcopal. John Smith Brown married 3 times: 1) Sarah Harrison Ald of Baltimore 5 Nov. 1832; 2) at Richmond,

VA to Elizabeth A. Coleman, 6 Dec. 1842; 3) Cassie F. Whiteford of Harford Co., MD 28 Dec. 1871. *MDC:28*

BROWN, ROBERT, b. Ireland, wife Mary F. Sardin, b. on the ocean while her parents coming to America. Son Robert Jr. also b. Ireland, to America with parents as a boy. [sic] Robert Jr. before the Civil War owned 1800 acres of land from the 7th St. Pike to Rock Creek, & included Kensington, Forest Glen & Chevy Chase, MD. *6TH:726-27*

BROWN, ROBERT, of Dumfries, Scotland, settled in America. Descendant William Brown had a dau. Mary A., who m. George W. Mobley & their son William B. b. 28 Feb. 1843 in Clarksburg, MD. *6TH:720-21*

BROWN, SAMUEL, Englishman, from Scotland to America before the Revolution, which he served in. Descendants settled in Howard Co., MD. *MDC:623*

BROWNE, ABELL, from Dumfries, Scotland, was sheriff of Anne Arundel Co., MD & in 1692 was an Associate Justice of the county. He m. (1) a d/o Samuel Phillips of Calvert Co., a sister of Mary, wife of Michael Taney. His son Samuel removed to Baltimore Co. on Bush River c. 1689. *AAH:168*

BROWNE, HUGH, b. near Belfast, County Down, Ireland in 1784. At age 7 to America with his family. He m. Eliza Manley & son Nicholas Manly Browne b. at North-East, Cecil Co., 16 Sept. 1837. [Could be the same as Hugh Brown above, but no concrete evidence.] *MDC:307-08*

BROWNING, JOSHUA, b. England, to America with Braddock's army at the time of the Rev., spent the rest of his life in Frederick Co., MD. His son Meshack was a famed hunter b. in Frederick (now Montgomery) Co. *6TH:131-33.*

BROWNING, WILLIAM, and wife Sarah, first known settlers in America of this family, res. in Portsmouth, RI; surmise that they came from England. Desc. Ralph Browning, M.D., b. at Griswold, New London Co., CT 26 April 1869, removed to Myersville, Frederick Co., MD. *FR2:867*

BRUCE, ANDREW, from Scotland to America before the Revolution & settled in Frederick Co., MD & later in Alleghany Co., MD, west of Fort Cumberland in 1805. He d. 1813 & left a large family. *MDC:569*

BRUNE, FREDERICK W. (SR.), b. Bremen, to Baltimore 1799, where he d. 1860; m. Ann Clark, b. Dublin, Ireland, to Baltimore as infant in 1787 by her parents. Frederick was a merchant. *MDC:10*

BRUNNER, JOSEPH, b. City of Manheim, Upper Germany, to the colonies in ship *Oliver*, landed in Philadelphia, PA 11 Sept. 1726, & settled on Carroll's Creek, near present City of Frederick, MD in 1726. He had: Jacob, John, Elias & Henry; also 2 daus. not named here. *FR2:747, 916-17*

BUCKEY (BOQUET), HENRY (COL.), b. Rolle, Switzerland in 1719, d. in Pensacola, FL Feb. 1766. A second source says he is a Frenchman. Soldier in service of the Dutch & later that of Sardinia & in 1748 was in service of Holland as lt.-col. of Swiss guards. Entered the English army in 1756, was a friend of Washington. He served in the Rev. & settled in Frederick Co., MD east of Mt. Pleasant, farmer. He had son George Peter, b. 28 Feb. 1771 & dau. Susan. Members of Reformed Church & George m. Susan Creager. His descs., spelling the name Buckey, res. Frederick Co., MD. *FR2:1129-30, 1596-7*

BUDEKER, CARL A., & wife Anna Elizabeth Schone, d/o Ludwig Schone, both b. Germany. To America & their son, William Budeker, M.D., b. Baltimore 21 Sept. 1870. Lutheran. *TR3:661-2*

BUHRMAN, JOHN, from Germany to America before the Rev. War. His son Henry b. in Germany. Early settlers of Frederick Co., MD in the Hauvers Dist. *FR2:983-4*

BULL, JOHN, one of 5 brothers to emigrate from England to America, John the only one who settled in MD (Harford Co.). His son William who m. Elizabeth d/o Henry Ruff. William was a farmer & tanner & d. 1853, aged 80. Edmund L., another son of the immigrant John, b. Harford Co. in what was then called Bulltown. Edmund served in the War of 1812 & m. Margaret Gay, b. Harford Co. Their son Jacob b. 1848. *H/C:151, 173*

BUNTING, WILLIAM, of England, enlisted in the Continental Army Flying Camp in 1774. Desc. Rev. James Bunting m. Eleanor Shemwell. James b. Baltimore 14 NOv. 1814, was minister at the Methodist Episcopal church, taught at Dickinson College & was superintendent of public schools. He d. 24 June 1880. His widow was b. Chaptico, St. Mary's Co., MD 22 July 1831 & she d. 28 Jan. 1901. *TR4:770-1*

BUPPERT, JOHN, left Germany as a boy & settled in Baltimore Co., MD, where son Henry was b. at Hebbville. The family later settled in Baltimore City. Henry m. Annie Elizabeth Wolf and had William Irwin Buppert in April 1878. *TR3:238*

BURALL, WILLIAM, one of 3 brothers to America from Germany. One brother settled in VA, one in NY or NJ & William in Frederick Co., MD. Son Adam Burral, b. 1796 in Frederick Co. He m. (1) Miss --- Runkles, had 8 children; m. (2) Charlotte, d/o Edward & Mary (Brandenburg) Walker. *FR2:862-3*

BURGER, WILLIAM H., b. Germany in 1827 & to Frederick Co., MD c. 1842. Some years later his father located in Frederick, having also immigrated. William in retail grocery business & m. Annie M. Drehr who d. in 1905. They had 9 children, 5 of whom reached maturity: Henry C. of Frederick: William Alexander; Charles Edward of Frederick; Annie Margaret, who is unmarried; and Annie Rosetta, also never married. *FR2:1105*

BURKHART, GEORGE, early German settler of Frederick Co., later removed to east TN, where he d. He had children: Peter, George, Charles H. & Margaret. Son Charles, b. 1797, d. on the Yellow Springs farm now owned by his son in 1879, farmer. Charles m. c. 1821, Elizabeth R. Neighbors. Both bur. at Mt. Olivet cemetery at Frederick City, MD. *FR2:1397-8*

BURNS, FRANCIS, of Scotch-Irish ancestry, brought by his parents to America at age 6. In 1818 to Baltimore. Son Samuel b. Baltimore 2 March 1822 & m. 17 Nov. 1846, a d/o James Wilks. *MDC:674*

BURRIDGE, JOHN, into Province of MD 1658 & settled in Anne Arundel Co., MD. *TR4:343*

BURTT, THOMAS W., b. London, England, to America in early life & settled in Baltimore where he m. Esther Spear, d/o Henry of Kent Co., MD. They located in Montgomery Co., PA, where son Alfred Patterson Burt was b. 10 Feb. 1823. Alfred to Baltimore to settle in 1848, book business, where he m. 1848 Christiana Shaw, d/o Thomas of Philadelphia. Episcopal. *MDC:573*

BUSSARD, PETER, b. Germany, to America & settled in PA & later to Hauver's District, Frederick Co., MD. He d. 1802; m. a Miss --- Householder. Children: Daniel; Ulstey; Peter; John Wesley (b. 1794); Samuel; Susan, m. a Mr. Kinney & removed to OH where she d. at an advanced age; & Sophia, m. George Fox of Hauvers District. John Wesley Bussard was b. 1794 & res. at Cavetown, Washington Co, MD & later in Frederick Co. He m. 1815, Susan Ann Delaugter. *FR2:860-1, 1381-2, 1541-2*

BUTLER, MARY, "a Welsh lady," d/o Absalom Butler, m. Nicholas Morgan, and their son Gerard Morgan, b. 8 June 1784, in Baltimore County, MD. Methodist Episcopal. *MDC:649*

BUTLER, THOMAS, to this country at the same time with the Carroll family & owned c. 9,000 acres of land in the Montgomery Co. area. *6TH:763-64*

BUXTON, JOHN, emigrated from the North of Ireland with an unnamed brother & settled in MD. Desc. John Buxton, blacksmith, res. near Frederick, MD. This John m. Massey Soper & had: Brook; Susan, m. --- Mullinix; John; Lizzie, d. young; Samuel; Basil; James; Upton. *FR2:1034*

ABELL, WILLIAM, b. 9 March 1699, Warminster, England; in British navy as surgeon. To VA c. 1723, res. Henrico Co. His youngest son Nicholas b. 1750. Desc. Elizabeth Caskie Cabell, b. 1851 in Richmond m. Albert Ritchie, governor of MD. in 1875. *GME:94*

CADDEN, R. (REV.), of Scotch-Irish ancestry, to America where son Charles William was b. 11 March 1830 in Jefferson Co., VA. Rev. Cadden m. in SC Margaret McCord, also of Irish descent. *MDC:82*

CADWALLADER, ROBERT, to America from Wales c. 1698, with wife & 3 sons & 1 dau. Two of their sons had previously emigrated.

Family settled in Gwynedd, Montgomery Co., PA c. 1700 & joined Friends Society. According to custom of Wales, the children adopted the surname Robert, which was later changed to Roberts. Eldest son Cadwallader Roberts, b. in Wales 1673, res. Gwynedd. 9 April 1714 m. Eleanor Ellis, b. 17 Aug. 1693. Caldwallader d. of smallpox 7 March 1731. He & Eleanor had Rebecca & Robert (b. 1719-d. 1760). Son Robert m. Sarah Ambler (1721-1769) & had 7 children. The eldest, Cadwallader Roberts, b. 18 Oct. 1743, farmer of Montgomery Co., PA d. 7 Feb. 1816. He m. Mary Shoemaker of Montgomery Co. 24 May 1768 & had 7 children. Their youngest child, Mary, b. 1786, d. 1830, in 1808 m. Edward Spencer, s/o Job & Hannah Spencer of Horsham Twp., PA. They had two children: Cadwallader R., b. 1810 & Agnes S. (b. 30 July 1816), m. Josiah Engle Willis. Josiah (b. 1807), res. Gwyneed, PA & removed to Harford Co., MD before the Civil War. About 1881 family res. in Poplar Ridge, NY where Agnes d. 8 March 1896 & Josiah d. 26 Nov. 1889. *TR4:568-9*

CAIRNES, GEORGE, b. Ireland, with parents to America at age of 4, settled in Harford Co., MD. Farmer, Presbyterian. He d. at age 90 & buried in Bethel cemetery. His son William m. Elizabeth Vance, both b. Harford Co. & their son George A. Cairnes b. there 5 July 1846. *H/C:507*

CALLAGHAN, TIMOTHY, cattle dealer of Ireland who came to America in 1845 with his family. He took up res. at Harford Furnace, where he d. 1885. His wife was Mary Lynch, b. Ireland; she d. aged 92. His son, Patrick, b. Ireland 18 March 1831, settled first in PA & later at Ashland Furnace, Baltimore Co., MD; purchased land near Creswell in Harford Co. In canning business. Patrick m. Ann Ready of Baltimore who d. 1896. They had a son, also Patrick, who had a son, Daniel, b. near Gunpowder Neck, Harford Co., 7 Nov. 1862. Catholic. *H/C:255, 533-4*

CAMERON, ROBERT, from Scotland to Cecil Co., MD; his son Amor b. Cecil Co. (d. 1885), m. Emeline Brown, d/o Hugh who came to Cecil Co. from Ireland in early manhood. Emeline d. 1850. *H/C:318-21*

CAMPBELL, CHARLES, of Scotch-Irish descent, came from the North of Ireland to America in 1849 & settled in Baltimore. He m. Mary J. Harrison of Baltimore. Charles was a florist & horticultural gardner. *MDC:156*

CARLIN, JOHN, from England to Montgomery Co., MD, farmer; m. Miss Knott of MD. Son John T., b. Montgomery Co., MD m. Frances R. Hammel of Frederick. Their son, John J., sole owner of Carlin's of Baltimore, "a nationally known world's model amusement resort," b. Frederick, MD 20 Oct. 1880. *TR3:243*

CARPENTER, WILLIAM, & family, sailed from Southampton to the American colonies in 1638 on the ship *Bevis.* He is listed on the passenger list as "one William Carpenter of Wherwell, aged 62 years, who returned to England on the same ship; William his son, aged 33 years; son's wife Abigail, aged 32 years; and four grandchildren of ten years or less and a servant, Thomas Bansholt, aged 14 years." William, the son, was b. 1605 & d. in Rehoboth, MA 7 Feb. 1659; admitted a freeman of Weymouth 13 May 1640. He served in local politics & in the militia. His eldest son, John Carpenter, b. England c. 1628, m. Hannah Hope & d. 23 May 1695. At age 17 became res. of CT Colony & in 1660 bought land in Hampstead, Long Island. Samuel, s/o this John & wife Hannah, b. Jamaica, NY c. 1666, was landowner there in 1685. His eldest son, Joseph, b. Jamaica c. 1692, settled in Goshen before 1775. His wife was Susanna & their 3rd son, John b. 1735 in Chester, NY to MD & bought land near St. Clements Bay. He m. Susanna Turner, d/o Edward, s/o Edward, the 2d s/o William Turner, early MD settler. *TR4:211*

CARROLL, CHARLES, to MD 1 Oct. 1688 & m. (1) in America, Martha Underwood, d/o Anthony of St. Mary's Co., MD (she d. 1690) & (2) Mary Darnall, d/o Henry of "Portland Manor" & wife Elinor Hatton, widow of Major Thomas Brooke of "Brookefield." An extensive landowner & was atty. of the widow Lady Baltimore. His will was probated in MD in 1720. Charles' children: Henry, d. at sea; Charles Jr., b. 1702; Daniel, b. 1707, m. Ann Rozier of "Notley Hall." *AAH:501-2*

CARROLL, THOMAS, b. Ireland, near city of Dublin, to US & settled in Baltimore. He m. Sarah King, b. Baltimore Co., of English ancestry. Thomas d. 1832, aged 64, his wife d. at age of 38, both in Baltimore. Their son John King Carroll, b. in Baltimore 21 May 1806. *MDC:692-93*

CARSWELL, JOHN S., b. Paisley, Renfrewshire, Scotland 8 Jan. 1807, s/o George, a magistrate of Palsley. John to America in 1827 & settled in Canada for 20 years. In 1840 he m. Harriet Von Ripper, b. Bellville,

NJ, who d. in Baltimore in 1856. John S. resides in Baltimore. Presbyterian. *MDC:226*

CASHELL, JAMES, b. Ireland, settled in Montgomery Co., MD, where his descendants have lived ever since. Son George b. 3 Sept. 1776, m. Elizabeth, d/o Hazel Butt 17 June 1804. He d. 1861, a farmer near Layhill. *6TH:629-30*

CASHMYER, HENRY, b. in Palatine, one of the Rhemish Provinces, 6 Sept. 1835, s/o Peter & Madeline (Schuinacher). Peter was a farmer & came to America & settled in Baltimore 1839. Henry was a cooper; he m. 1846 Mary Elizabeth Zinland of Baltimore. Roman Catholic. *MDC:108*

CASSARD, MICHEL, with wife Margueritte Marcorelle, m. in Nantes, France 28 Dec. 1766. During the French Revolution they fled to San Domingo. At the uprising of slaves in that place, they, with other French families of the island, fled & settled in Baltimore, where a French community was formed. The boats were separated and some landed in New Orleans. Their children Gilbert & a brother finally reached MD destitute. Gilbert, b. Nantes 1782, d. in Baltimore in 1857. He m. Sarah Inloes of Baltimore in 1811, d/o Catherine Weller & Thomas Inloes, & they had 12 children. *TR4:761-2*

CASTLE, JOSEPH, b. Germany, emigrated to Middletown Valley, Frederick Co., MD, an early settler; shoemaker. His son Otho b. c. 1792 & d. 1822. Otho m. Elizabeth Baker & had 6 children: Mahlon; Malinda, m. Hezekiah Young; Henry; Daniel & Elizabeth, m. Benjamin Pettingill. *FR2:1140*

CASTLEBERG, JACOB, b. London, England, as a youth apprenticed to Edholm Ericsson, a Swede, considered at that time the best chronometer maker in the world. In 1848, at age of 18, Jacob to America, first to NY & later to Baltimore, where he res. until his death in 1910, aged 80; jeweler. President of the Eden St. synagogue & member of the Benevolent Society. He m. 1856, Emma Isaacs, b. NY City of German parents. They had 12 children. *TR3:723-4*

CATHCART, JOSEPH, b. Ireland, to America at an early day, farmer of Harford Co. His son, William Cathcart, b. Harford Co., farmer, veteran of War of 1812. *H/C:544-5*

CHAISTY, EDWARD, b. Ireland, settled in Baltimore in 1811. He m. in Baltimore the same year. Son Edward J., a physician, was b. near Baltimore 22 Dec. 1813. *MDC:672-73*

CHALLONER, THOMAS, b. England, m. Mary Emma Meredith; their son William b. Baltimore. Grandau. Mary Edith m. Miller Reid Scott, b. 15 June 1900, Baltimore. Ancestral estate Cravens Arms, in Shropshire, London still owned by family in 1925. Methodist. *TR3:77*

CHANDLEE, BENJAMIN, s/o William Chandlee of Kilmore, of the County of Kildare, Ireland, probably b. c. 1658 [one ref. says b. in France] with his father's family fled to Ireland to escape religious persecution during the reign of Louis XIV. Came alone to America in 1699/1700, first locating at Philadelphia, where he apprenticed himself to Abel Cottey, a watch & compass maker of Philadelphia. He m. 25th day 3d month 1710, at Philadelphia, in the Friends' Meeting House, Sarah, d/o Able & Mary Cottey. They settled in Nottingham, Cecil Co., MD; iron worker. Had at least three children, Cottey, John & Benjamin. In 1741 he removed with his younger children to Wilmington, DE. Benjamin (2d), s/o Benjamin, b. at Nottingham, Cecil Co., MD, c. 1728, was founder of the firm of Chandlee & Sons of Nottingham, manufacturers of clocks, surveyors' compasses & mathematical instruments. He d. 9th month, 18th, 1794 aged 69. His wife was Mary Fallwell, d/o of Goldsmith Edward Fallwell of Wilmington. Cottey, son of the immigrant, b. at Nottingham c. 1713, d. there in 1807, Quaker, unmarried. *H/C:158, 424-6*

CHANNELL, ---, from Scotland to America "at a very early day" & settled in PA. His son, Isaac Channell, m. Mary Anderson, like himself, b. in PA. Their son William was b. in PA 9 Nov. 1824, at age 28 m. Mary J. Herbert, b. PA, & moved to Harford Co., MD. Presbyterian. *H/C:489*

CHAPLINE, ISAAC, of the Royal Navy of England, to America with Lord Delaware as King's Council to the Colony of VA in 1610. Settled on tract called "Hundred Chapline's Choice." Had son John who lived in VA who had son William who d. in MD in 1682. "This William Chapline was the father of another William Chapline, who was one of the passengers on the *Mayflower*." Another source says: "William's son, Moses Chapline, was one of the passengers on the *Mayflower* & in 1620 he removed from Boston, MA to the Eastern Shore of MD & there m.

Jeanette Caton, a cousin of Richard Caton. Moses d. 1762 & is buried in the family cemetery." William Chapline 2d became member of King's Council in MD & had 3 sons: William, b. 1700 who removed to Frederick Co., farmer; Moses, b. 1703, d. 1762, removed to the Eastern Shore of MD, m. Jeannette Caton; & Joseph, b. 1707, ancestor of the Sharpsburg Chaplines. *FR2:913-14 & 6TH:346-8*

CHASE, THOMAS (REV.), English clergyman of the Protestant Episcopal church, first rector of St. Paul's church of Baltimore. His wife was Mathilda Walker. Their son, Judge Samuel Chase, b. 17 April in Somerset Co. MD, became member of Sons of Liberty in Jan. 1763; was a signer of the Declaration of Independence. His dau., Eliza Chase Dugan Coale, was wife of Dr. Skipwith Holland. *TR4:115 & MDC:184*

CHEW, JOHN, of "Chewtown," Somersetshire, England, to VA in the *Sea Flower* in 1622 & joined family members who had preceded him in 1618. He settled at James City, VA; his wife's name was Sarah. He removed to MD with neighbors, wife & sons, Samuel & Joseph, in 1649. His will is dated 1676. *AAH:109*

CHILD, HENRY, of Hertfordshire, who res. in Coldshill, parish of Rindersham; Quaker. 20 Jan. 1687 Henry purchased 500 acres of land in Plumstead, Bucks Co., PA. He brought his son Cephas to America in 1693, and returned to England. In 1715 he gave the 500 acres to this son. Cephas was a carpenter, res. in Philadelphia and m. Feb. 1716, Mary Atkinson. Grandau. Grace Child, b. 26 Dec. 26 1765, dau. of John and Sarah (Shoemaker) Child, m. Joseph Kirk. (See Kirk entry.) Their 3d son, Samuel Kirk b. 15 Feb. 1793, moved to Baltimore where he d. 5 July 1872. Silversmith. *GME:279*

CHILD, SAMUEL, s/o Samuel, b. near St. Paul's, London, England & to America when young; carriage builder of Baltimore. He m. Margaret Worrall, of English descent, her ancestors were among the early settlers of MD. *MDC:640*

CHISELIN, CESAR, with wife Catherine Reverdy, both French Huguenots, to MD; settled Annapolis early 18th century. *TR3:92*

CHRISTIE, JAMES, b. Ireland, located in NY & later Cecil Co., MD. Served in War of 1812. Son John m. Sophia Logan & their son George M. b. Cecil Co., MD 1844. *H/C:283*

CHURCHMAN, JOHN, of Saffron Waldron, Essex Co., England, to America at age 17 & settled in Darby, PA in 1682. At the time he was under the care of Thomas Cerie. They settled at Chester, PA, but in 1704 removed to the woods of Nottingham (Cecil Co., MD). John became a famous Quaker preacher, self-taught surveyor; he d. 1745, & left only son George, b. 1730. George m. Hannah, d/o Mordecai & Gainor James, in 1752 & d. 1814, leaving a large family. *C:525-6*

CIOTTI, ANDREW, b. in province of Como, Italy 12 Dec. 1863, s/o Joseph & Marie. To America in 1893 & settled in Baltimore. Now president of Baltimore & Jamaica Trading Co., fruit importers. He m. in Barosso, Italy in 1893, Agnes Vincenti, d/o Paul. *TR3:625-6*

CLAGETT, THOMAS (CAPT.), (1635/40-1703), was s/o Col. EDWARD CLAGETT of London and his wife Margaret, d/o Sir Thomas Adams, lord mayor of London. Capt. Thomas was an officer in the British Army & emigrated to MD by 1659 [c. 1670?]. He received a patent for 1,000 acres in Kent Co. Capt. of provincial militia of Calvert Co. He was a resident of St. Leonard's Town in that county. His will of 1703 names his sons, Thomas & Richard and his wife Sarah Patterson. Sarah was of London, England, where they had married before coming to America. Son Thomas Jr. b. 1675, m. Mary ---; Richard Clagett b. 1681, m. 1704 Deborah (Dorsey) Ridgeley, d/o John Dorsey & widow of Charles Ridgely of Hampton. TR4-28-9 gives another son, Rev. Samuel Clagett, m. Elizabeth Gantt & had Thomas John Clagett, b. Prince George's Co., MD 2 Oct. 1742, first Protestant Episcopal prelate consecrated on the soil of the English settlements in America. Sided with the Americans in the Revolutionary War. *TR4:28-9, 642-4, 806-8, FR2:1344-5*

CLAIBORNE, WILLIAM, b. Kitterby, York Co., England, s/o Edmund, Esq. of Claeborne Hall, Co. of Westmoreland, England, and Grace, d/o Sir Alan Billingham of the same County. William's elder brother Thomas inherited the Manor. In 1621 William was appointed surveyor of VA Company of London & arrived at Jamestown, VA 1622. He purchased Kent Island & settled there. He left 3 children. Desc. F. G. Claiborne m. Ella Palmer of Richmond, VA. F. G. served in the Civil War in the Confederate infantry. Their son, Thomas D., businessman of Baltimore m. 15 April 1918, Elizabeth McComis, d/o Fred W. of Hagerstown, MD. *TR4:296-7 MDC:50*

CLARK, ---, 3 brothers, John, James & David, from the North of Ireland & settled in Anne Arundel Co. subsequent to the Revolution. Founded a carding wool business on their manor which were later changed to grain mills. James Sr. m. Jemima Ward of London, then living with her father on "Carroll's Manor." *AAH:533-4*

CLARK, MATTHEW (CAPT.), b. County Cavan, Ireland 4 Nov. 1841. With parents at age 2 to America & settled at Philadelphia. Matthew settled in Baltimore. He served the Confederacy during the Civil War. He m. Kate McWilliams, d/o John of Baltimore & resides in Baltimore. *MDC:537-38*

CLAYTON, WILLIAM, s/o Thomas of London & grandson of William Clayton of Oakenshaw, Co. Yorkshire, England. He had a patent granted by the British govt. for 400 acres at Chichester, PA, where he settled in 1671. Generations that followed him were: William Jr., Richard, Richard Jr. and Powell, also b. PA, farmer. Powell Clayton's grandson, Wesley Clayton, b. in Delaware Co., PA 27 Feb. 1835, to MD in 1866 & settled in Cecil Co., farmer. Powell m. Mary P. Goodley, in 1862. Another desc. Susan Smith Clayton, (2d d/o John Clayton Jr., b. 1795, d. 25 Nov. 1848, s/o John, Sr. b. 1763, d. 1797; a Rev. War soldier) m. John Philips of Frederick Co., MD. She was b. in DE. *H/C:411, TR4:268-9*

CLEMSON, ---, Quakers who settled with William Penn's people in Lancaster Co., PA c. 1656, reported to have first settled in DE with the Swedes in 1656, then to Philadelphia & later to Lancaster PA. Before the Rev. War they moved to Frederick Co., MD. John Clemson (1757-1846), s/o James (III), represented Lancaster Co., PA in Provincial convention at Philadelphia. James' (III) will probated in Lancaster, PA 25 July 1792 & his sons James & John were bequethed the residue of his estate, with payment of shares to his widow Margaret & to the other 7 children, who were daus. who m. into the families of Skiles of Salisbury PA, the Whitehill family of Frederick Co. MD, the Brady family of Lancaster Co. PA, the McCausley family of Kinkers PA, the Watson family of Donegal PA, the Atlee family of Frederick Co. MD, & the McCausland family of Leacock, PA. The first Marylander of this family was John Clemson (1757-1846), who m. Mary Haines after he had removed to Frederick Co., where he purchased land before the Rev. War near Clemsonville. *TR4:353*

CLINE, ALEXANDER, b. Waterford, Ireland of Scotch-Irish ancestry, to America at an early day, settled in Chester Co., PA. Later to York Co., PA & d. there. Methodist Episcopal Church member. Son Capt. Casper Cline, b. Abbottstown, York Co., PA 1775, at age 21 spent several years in Baltimore. He m. Catherine, d/o Col. Robert Evans, In 1822 removed to Frederick. His 2d wife was Corilla Evans, sister to his 1st wife. Son George T. b. near Frederick, MD 4 March 1835. Casper d. at his home near Frederick City, MD 18 April 1871. Carriage manufacturer. *6TH:791-93, FR2:1087-8*

CLINE, PHILIP, cooper, from Germany to America in early manhood. Was among the early settlers in Middletown Valley, Frederick Co., MD, near what is now known as Ellerton. He m. Elizabeth Ambrose & they had a son Thomas. Members of St. John's Lutheran Church at Church Hill. Philip d. at age of 88 & is bur. in St. John's Church graveyard. *FR2:1468-9*

COALE, WILLIAM, (c. 1592-1669) from Bristol, England to America, first settling in VA & later to St. Jerome, Calvert Co., MD. His wife was Sarah --- & they had: Sarah, m. Elias Beck; Richard; William; John; Nicholas & Mary who m. a Mr. Guyther. The 2d William, son of the immigrant, was b. c. 1623 & d. 30 Aug. 1678. His 1st wife was Hester --- & they had a son William, b. 21 Sept. 1655, who m. c. 1684 Elizabeth (Thurston) Skipworth, widow of George Skipwith. His 2d wife was Hannah --- & they also had a son named William, b. 20 Oct. 1667, who m. Elizabeth Sparrow, d/o Thomas & Eliza, 30 July 1689. William (2d) m. for his 3d wife Elizabeth, d/o Philip & Sarah (Harrison) Thomas. William to MD in 1671; Elizabeth in 1651 with her father, Lt. Philip Thomas, who settled in Anne Arundel Co. & d. 1675. Their dau. Elizabeth, b. 30 Aug. 1671, m. Nathan Smith; Philip; & Samuel, b. 9 April 1676. *TR4:798-9, 825-7*

COALE, WILLIAM, b. England, was one of the first settlers on Deer Creek, Harford Co., MD. William had a son Isaac, who had a son Skipworth H. Coale, physician & farmer who d. 1832, aged 42. *H/C:128*

COBLIENTZ, HERMAN [HARMON], b. at Fort Coblentz-on-the-Rhine, Prussia & emigrated to US & settled at Littlestown, Adams Co., PA. In 1766 removed to Frederick Co., MD. Member of the Reformed Church & is bur. in the old Reformed graveyard at Middletown. His son John Philip Coblentz had a son Philip b. in Frederick Co. in 1812 & d. there 1899. Herman had a brother Peter who also came to Frederick Co. *FR2:1288-9, TR4:590*

COCKEY, THOMAS & JOHN, brothers, s/o William & Mary of Cuckold Point, Devonshire, England. Both settled in Anne Arundel Co., MD 1679. John m. Elizabeth Slade & had a son John who served in the Rev. War. *TR4:291*

COCKRILL, THOMAS, b. Scotland, to America 1794. Served as 1st Lt. in War of 1812 in 3d Brigade of MD Militia. Thomas m. Rebecca Veazey, of English descent. *MDC:532*

CODD, JOHN FRANCIS, & wife Amelia Dittman, both b. Liverpool, England. Their dau. Regina m. Terence Aloysius Donohue of Baltimore on 24 June 1908, at St. Pius Memorial Roman Catholic Church in Baltimore. [Does not state if family immigrated to US or just Regina.] *TR3:743-4*

COLE FAMILY, left Tewksbury, in the northern part of Gloucestershire, England in 1785; settled Baltimore. Presbyterian. *TR3:29-30*

COLGAN, CHARLES, b. Co. Derry, Ireland, to America 1830; landed in NY, settled in Baltimore, later Harford County, MD, d. 1886; m. Elizabeth Clarke, b. Baltimore 1822, d. 13 Aug. 1892. Catholic. *TR3:50*

COLLENBERG, THEODORE, b. Reithburg, Germany, to US at age of 9 & in 1836 took up res. in Baltimore; merchant. He was the s/o John Henry Collenberg. Theodore m. Louise, d/o Daniel Koch of Baltimore. Their son, John Henry, b. Baltimore 7 March 1852; physician. John Henry m. 26 Aug. 1881, Mary Josephine Hodges, d/o Joseph & Annie (Hunt) Hodges. *TR3:635-6*

COLSTON, JAMES, of England, purchased land in Talbot Co., MD Nov. 1664. His son James who d. 1729, was twice married. His 2d wife was Elizabeth, d/o Henry & Elizabeth (Clements) Bayley. They m. 14

Sept. 1714. They had 5 children; son James only one named here.
TR4:85-6

COLTON, JOHN, b. Portsmouth, England, m. Elizabeth Moore, b. Little Hampton. John was a soldier in the British Army & emigrated to US in 1819, settled in Leonardtown, St. Mary's Co., where he d. at age of 52. Elizabeth d. aged 43. Son George, b. Portsmouth 31 Oct. 1817 to America with his family. George was a newspaperman & in 1865 purchased the *Maryland Republican*, published at Annapolis. George m. 27 Sept. 1842, Lydia Jane Hamilton. *MDC:295-96*

COMBS, WILLIAM, possibly the immigrant, of Combs family of Old Stratford, Co. of Warwick, England, b. 1672. His will probated 1740 in Leonardstown, MD. He m. Mary Hatton & had 8 children: Mary Waughap, Ellen Woodley, Enoch (b. 1756), Thomas Hatton, William Jr., James, Phillip & Susannah. *TR4:566-8*

CONLEY, THOMAS Y., b. in the north of Ireland, to America in 1801 or '02. He m. Helen Mary Fuller, d/o Aaron Fuller, who at one time owned the old Kirkwood Hotel in Washington, DC. Thomas & Helen had son, Charles William Conley. *FR2:848-9*

CONRAD, ALEXANDER, and wife Jeannette, both b. France, res. in province of Alsace until 1868, when they migrated to Louisville, KY. Alexander served as a drummer boy under Napoleon I, and later under Louis XVIII and Charles X. Dau. Fannie, b. 27 Aug. 1837, d. in Louisville, KY, Nov. 28, 1897, m. Isaac Lionel Lehman. Their son Clarence Morton Lehman b. 3 Aug. 1875, removed to Baltimore, MD; merchant. *TR3:121*

CONTEE, JOHN, of England, to America with his uncle, John Contee, & settled in Prince George Co., MD. He m. Jane Brook. Their youngest dau., Barbara, m. John Reid Magruder. Barbara & John were parents of Alexander Contee Magruder who m. his cousin Rebecca B. Thomas. Alexander's will was dated 1730. *6TH:721-24*

COOK, CONRAD P., b. 9 Sept. 1826, Nedar, Hesse-Darmstadt, Germany. At age 23 to America & settled in Baltimore, baker. Removed to Havre de Grace after 18 months. He m. Catherine A. Schreitz, d/o John & Margaret, 7 April 1852. Catherine b. 25 Aug. 1829 near Frickburg, Germany & to America with her parents at age of 3. *H/C:518*

COOKE, MORDECAI, from England in 1650, was sheriff of Glouces-ter, VA in 1698. Desc. John K. Cooke, lumber merchant of Portsmouth, VA & postmaster. Served in the Mexican War as 1st lt. Co. F, VA Regt. & in the Civil War as postmaster of Gen. Lee's Army of Northern VA. He d. at Portsmouth 6 Feb. 1887; m. Fannie Bracken of Gloucster Co., VA who d. 1867, leaving a son & 3 daus. Their son, Giles Buckner Cooke, b. Portsmouth 13 May 1838; grad from VA Military Institute in 1859; served in Confederate army. Since 1891 rector of North Elk parish, MD. Giles m. 19 Oct. 1870, Mrs. Martha F. (Mallory) Southall, she d. 2 Jan. 1894. *H/C:576-7*

COOPER, BENJAMIN, b. 1623, s/o William, attended Merton College (now Univ. of Oxford) in 1641, became professor in 1652. Benjamin's son, George, b. 1667, succeeded his father as registrar at Merton in 1682 & d. 1737. Two of the 3 sons of George, Benjamin & John, also students at the university, emigrated to Dorchester Co., MD, where they patented land from King George; Benjamin d. a batchelor. John m. Miss --- Smith of Tuckahoo, Dorchester (now Caroline) Co. *H/C:493-4*

COOPER, FREDERICK T., b. England, to America 1851, settled in San Francisco, CA; m. Pauline Touillon, b. San Francisco, d/o Bouchard Touillon, who came to America from France & crossed the plains with the '49ers, a pioneer settler of CA. Pauline d. in San Francisco, aged 61, 26 Nov. 1922. Their 3d child, Robert H. Cooper, b. San Francisco 6 May 1889, is vice-president of the Oriole Steamship Line & resides in Baltimore. *TR3:279*

CORBIN, HENRY, b. Shropshire, England, was a member of the VA house of burgess. His dau. Letitia m. Col. Richard Lee. Desc. Henry Lee Smith, physician of Baltimore, b. 23 March 1868 in Ashland, Hanover Co., VA, s/o John Thomas & Margaret Lewis (Marshall) Smith. *TR4:194-5*

CORIELL, DAVID, Huguenot, from Corsica in 1659 to GA & later settled in NJ. Desc. Isaac Coriell m. Hannah Maria VanVliet & had son Alvin, b. Plainfield, NJ 4 Dec. 1844. At age 9 Alvin came with his parents to Baltimore, where he d. in Sept. 1904, aged 60; lumber dealer. Episcopalian. In 1868 he m. Mary A. Lawrence, b. 7 Feb. 1847, a d/o Dr. Thomas J. & Emerald (Sutton) Lawrence of Anne Arundel Co., MD. Mary d. 14 June 1921, aged 74. *TR3:765-6*

CORRELL, GEORGE, ABRAHAM, LEWIS & CHRISTOPHER, brothers, to America just after the Revolution. One settled in Jersey City, NJ; one in Lancaster, PA & 2 in DE. Lewis settled in Jersey City, where he owned Correll's Ferry. Descendant Abraham Correll m. Ann Lyder & son J. William b. Winchester, VA 26 Aug. 1826 studied medicine in VA & NC, later to Baltimore. Dentist. J. William m. 1850 Lulu Latham, of Chester, VA. *MDC:416*

COSENS, HENRY JOHN (D.V.S.), b. 23 March 1837, Sussex, England, served as veterinary surgeon in the Confederate service. He came to the US just before the Civil War & located in Stanton, VA. Since 1864 has made his home in Hagerstown, MD. He was s/o Henry John & Frances (Rudwick) Cosens. The father Henry John d. in 1860, aged 58; his wife d. 1855, aged 57. *6TH:558-59*

COTTMAN, BENJAMIN, from Great Yarmouth to America. 25 June 1671 purchased land in Somerset Co, MD. He d. 1703 & left a son, John Cottman, who had a son John. The 2d John's son, Joseph Cottman, b. 1713, d. 1793; m. Margaret Bozman & had a son, Lazarus, b. 14 Jan. 1764. *TR4:183*

COWDEN, JOHN, b. Scotland 1806, as young man to St. Johns, New Brunswick & later to the US, where he settled in Cumberland, MD. His children: Peter G., John & William F. Peter b. St. Johns in 1838 & d. in Cumberland in 1913. Peter served in the Union Navy during the Civil War. He m. Sarah M. Pitzer & had 4 children: Alexander H., Catherine Ann, Nellie Palmer & Peter Gibson. *TR3:611-12*

COWDERY, NATHANIEL, b. England 1600, settled in MA. His grandson, Jabez Cowdery, surgeon in the Continental Army, had son Jonathan who served as surgeon in the US Navy. Desc. in the 4th generation is Robert Tunstall Taylor, b. Norfolk, VA 16 Jan. 1867, only child of Robertson & Baynham (Tunstall) Taylor. Robert grad. of Johns Hopkins Univ., practiced at Kernan Hospital for Crippled Children in Baltimore. *TR4:621-2*

COX, NEWMAN H. D., b. Kingsport, Nova Scotia, Canada 28 Jan. 1868, & traces his ancestry to Sir Richard Cox, English loyalist. This paternal grandfather was Thomas Cox who m. a Miss Bigelow & their son Ebenezer became the father of Dr. Newman H. D. Ebenezer m. Emma Dewis, b. in Advocate Harbor, Nova Scotia, d/o Joshua & Naomi

(Spicer) Dewis. Representatives of the Dewis family migrated to Canada from England in the 18th century & were among the earliest settlers of Cumberland Co., Nova Scotia. Ebenezer & Emma had 8 children & Newman H. D. was their only son. He studied medicine at Univ. of NY & completed his studies in the Univ. of MD, 1895. After gradu. he served as a missionary in Africa for 4 years. On his return to the US he began practice in Arlington, MD. He m. 2 June 1896, Louise Heyn, b. Baltimore & d/o Martin Heyn, deceased, who was a merchant tailor of German extraction. *TR3:934-5*

COX, WILLIAM, & wife Mary Goldhawk, both b. near London, members of Society of Friends, to America & settled in Harford Co., MD in 1744 in area known as Cox's Mills. *MDC:644*

CRAIN, JOHN, from Wales to Charles Co., MD c. 1700 & m. Miss --- Maston. His mother was the d/o Peter Wood & Elizabeth Thomas. *MDC:104*

CRAMER, JOHN GEORGE, one of 3 brothers b. Germany, to America & landed at Philadelphia, PA 1705. Two located near Atlantic City, NJ, but not for long because of mosquitos, one settling in PA. Around Camden, NJ are still many of the Cramer name. John George Cramer removed to Frederick Co., MD. Member Reformed Church. His son, also John, was a large landowner, his land part of the old Dulaney Manor in hands of desc. William A. Cramer. In John's will, made in 1820, he mentions his son Lewis and his own brother Henry. John's son Ezra is named in the 2d entry. Ezra was b. on the homestead 2 March 1797. *FR2:1111-12, 1267-70*

CRAMER, LUDWIG, b. Germany, d. c. 1869; his dau. Margaret m. William Creswell, b. Clayton, MD; their son Charles E. b. 14 May 1849. *H/C:264*

CRANWELL, JOHN, s/o Patrick of Co. Wexford, Ireland, settled in Baltimore 1796. His son George W. (1830-1884), m. Clara B. Holton, d/o George C. Their son James Harford Cranwell, b. Baltimore. *TR4:273-4*

CRAPSTER FAMILY, can be traced to 2 brothers & a sister, of Swedish desc., whose parents immigrated to what was then Frederick Co., MD & settled near Pipe Creek & Taneytown, now Carroll Co. Hannah, the sister & the dau. of the immigrants, m. Deacon John Jones of the Piney Creek Church & moved to Liberty, Frederick Co., MD. They had one son, Daniel Jones. *TR4:834-6*

CRAWFORD, JOHN (M.D.), b. 3 May 1746 in the North of Ireland; served as surgeon at Barbadoes and at the Dutch Colony of Demarara. 1796 settled in Baltimore and d. there 9 May 1813; bur. Westminster Churchyard. *TR4:16-7*

CREAMER, HENRY, from Germany & settled in Westminster MD. His son, Valentine, removed in 1803 from Baltimore to OH where he d. 1831. *MDC:309*

CRESAP, THOMAS (COL.), b. at Skipton-in-Craven, Yorkshire, England c. 1702; to MD at age 13. 1726 m. Hannah Johnson & settled near Havre de Grace; to VA and later to Western MD. D. Old Town, MD 1788. *FRI:21*

CRIST, JACOB ADAM, & elder brother, John George Crist, sailed from Rotterdam in ship *Robert & Alice*, landed in Philadelphia, PA 24 Sept. 1742. Jacob Adam was then age 17. With his brother to the Tulpehocken, in Berks Co., PA, where he married [wife's name unknown.] With wife's relatives to York Co., PA c. 1755, where his son Philip Crist was m. 1781 to Elizabeth Long of York Co. All of the children of Philip & Elizabeth settled in Perry Co., PA c. 1800. Philip's son Daniel, b. 15 April 1787, d. 18 Feb. 1870, m. 1814 to Mary Bicetine; Lutherans. Daniel's son David, shoemaker & farmer, b. 1 March 1815, m. Margaret E., d/o William & Anna (Olinger) Campbell. David & Margaret had Rev. George W. Crist, pastor of the Monocacy Valley Lutheran Charge, Walkersville, Frederick Co., MD. He was b. at Markelsville, Perry Co., PA 17 April 1849. He has served at Harper's Ferry, WV & Duncannon, PA (1879), Philipsburg, PA, Millersville, PA (1896), Dauphin Co., PA (1902) & Monocacy Valley Charge, Frederick Co., MD (1906). Rev. George m. 27 Dec. 1877, Anna B., d/o Robert & Jane (Alexander) Orr of New Bloomfield, PA. *FR2:883-4*

CROMWELL, JOHN HAMMOND, of England, a lineal descendant of Oliver Cromwell through his son Sir Henry Cromwell & Lady Mary Russell. John Hammond Cromwell m. Mary Hammond Dorsey. *MDC:556*

CROSS, JOHN, immigrant ancestor, b. in Co. Antrim, Ireland, 1730, d. Baltimore, MD 29 Sept. 1807; settled in Cecil Co., 1771/2. He m. Jane Young, an immmigrant, b. in Co. Monahgan, Ireland, 1743, d. in Baltimore 6 March 1826. Their son Andrew b. Cecil Co. 4 Oct. 1772 & d. Baltimore 23 Sept. 1815. He m. Rachel, d/o Thomas & Esther (Patterson) Wallace, b. 15 Dec. 1780, d. 12 March 1843. *GME:54, TR4:173*

CROTHERS, JAMES & WILLIAM, b. Ireland, settled early in America. William, sea captain, lost at sea & his descs. live in Baltimore. James had a son, John Lawrence, b. Cecil Co., farmer, d. at an early age. One of John's sons, Richard H. res. Cecil Co.; another son, Alpheus, b. in Cecil Co., 17 May 1820, d. aged 77 of heart disease 26 March 1897. Alpheus m. Margaret Orelia, d/o John Hart Porter, of Cecil Co. *H/C:555-6*

CROTHERS, JOHN, b. Ireland, to America & settled near village of Calvert, Cecil Co., MD. His son, another John, died at age 74, 7 July 1873. He had m. Rachael, d/o James Cameron of Cecil Co. who d. in 1847. *H/C:394-5*

CROW, JOHN, with family to America from England, settled in neighborhood of Snicker's Ferry, on the Shenandoah River, Frederick (now Clarke Co.) VA. Son John m. Ann Mildred Newton and had John Taylor Crow, managing editor of the Baltimore Sun, b. at Adelphi Mills, 29 Dec. 1822. *MDC:21*

CROXALL, RICHARD, from England to MD in 1715, later res. on his estate in Baltimore Co. known as "Garrison Forest." Richard m. in Ireland Joanna Carroll, a lineal desc. of the O'Carrolls--Princes & Lords of Ely. Charles Moale Croxall, a grandson of Richard & Joanna, served in the Rev. War. *TR4:681-2*

CRUM, CASPER, b. Germany, to Frederick City 'nearly a hundred years ago.' He was the father of Casper, b. Frederick City, MD; stone mason & Catholic. Casper (2) m. Mary Wirtz, b. in Bo-byer Overhauser, Germany, who came to America at age of 18. Their children: Charles of Frederick; George C.; Mollie, m. William Kline; Catharine, m. Guy Albaugh of Frederick; Harry, res. NC; Alice, unm. res. Frederick; & Frank of Frederick. *FR2:1574-5*

CRUSE, THOMAS, Irish patriot who emigrated to America to escape the vengence of the British. His dau. Mary m. Thomas Wilson & their son Franklin b. Baltimore 8 Dec. 1822. Mary d. 1824. *MDC:387*

CULLER, MICHAEL, one of 3 brothers from Germany to America; Michael settled in Western MD, between Creagerstown & Lewistown. His property confiscated by the British & he crossed the mountain & settled 1 1/2 miles northeast of Jefferson. He m. Miss --- Rhinehart & had: Jacob, Philip, John, Michael, Henry, Elizabeth who m. Philip Coblentz, Susan who m. George Willard & a son [unnamed here] who m. Miss --- Remburg. *FR2:1085-6*

CULVER, EDWARD (COLVER), 1610-1685, grandson of Rev. Edward Culver, whom Queen Elizabeth, in 1575, presented to the Rectory of Harmondsworth, County Middlesex, England. Edward Culver, Puritan, left England c. 1635 for Boston; settled in Dedham, MA & m. Anne Ellis 19 Sept. 1638. Moved to Roxbury & later to New London, CT (1653), where he d. 1685. Through their 7th child, Lt. Edward Culver, the present Baltimore family is descended. He was b. 1654 in New London & d. in Litchfield, CT 7 April 1732; living in Norwich, CT in 1680, when he m. Sarah Backus d/o William of Norwich, on 15 Jan. 1681/2. 1698 to Leganon, CT. They had 12 children. Samuel, their 6th child, b. 11 Feb. 1691 in Norwich, CT, d. c. 1770 in Litchfield; m. 13 May 1714, Hannah Hibbard, d/o Robert of Windham. Samuel Culver was a founder of Litchfield, 1722. Samuel & Hannah had 9 children. Their son Jonathan Culver m. in Litchfield 16 Nov. 1749, Sarah Hinman, d/o Capt. Samuel Hinman of Goshen, CT. He moved to Spencertown, Albany (now Columbia) Co., NY, had 6 children & d. in Canaan in 1808. Son Solomon moved to Upper Plymouth, Luzerne Co., PA in 1792/93; 1809 west to Knox Co., OH & in 1813 took up res. in Richland Co., OH, where he d. 2 April 1835. He had 13 children. Son William Edward Culver, b. Luzerne Co., PA 3 July 1803, d. Washington, DC 12 March 1876, was twice married: (1) Martha Hawkins Craig (1805-66) whom he m. in KY 15 June 1826 & (2) Jane McClintock, b. Philadelphia, 23 Dec. 1833 & later moved to Baltimore with her parents. She was d/o Matthew McClintock, of old Scotch-Irish stock, b. 3 March 1806 & d. 13 Dec. 1885. Matthew McClintock m. Susan Appleby, b. 8 Jan. 1815, d. 13 Oct. 1877. Jane d. 19 May 1920, aged 87. William Edward Culver & Jane had a son, William Edward Culver Jr., b. in Baltimore 12 Nov. 1868. *TR4:470-6*

49

CUMMINGS, ---, from Ireland to Philadelphia, son James b. Philadelphia 1814. James res. Pleasant Grove, PA & later Oakwood, Cecil Co., MD. In 1859 settled on farm near Pilot Town, where he died (1891). James m. Jane McColgan of Lancaster Co., PA. *H/C:287*

CUMMINGS, JAMES W., b. Dublin, Ireland 1814, to US when a boy & settled in Chevy Chase, MD, 1832. Farmer; m. Mary Ellen Wall who d. Chevy Chase, aged 75. Their son, Andrew J. Cummings, b. Chevy Chase 8 Sept. 1878. *TR3:109-10*

CUNNINGHAM, JOHN, from Scotland to NY 1790, where he m. Elizabeth Gibson, d/o Lewis, an Englishman. His posthumous son, James Bell Cunningham b. in NY City 5 Sept. 1815, d. 23 Jan. 1877. He m. 1 July 1856 in Wilmington, DE Mary Rosalie Thompson, eldest child of Dr. James William & Sarah Peters (Robinson) Thompson. They had 7 children & Sarah d. 26 June 1898. Their youngest child, Elizabeth, b. at Chatterton Hill, White Plains, Westchester Co., NY 14 March 1870, m. 20 April 1895, at St. Peter's Episcopal Church of Baltimore, Richard James Leupold, s/o Heinrich & Elizabeth Charlotte (Dobree) of London, England. He was a desc. of Lord James de Sausmarez, British admiral. *TR4:187*

CUPPETT, JOHN, b. Germany, to US c. 1750 & settled in Bedford Co., PA. In 1814 located in Preston Co., WV & d. there aged 87. He m. Eva, d/o George Fear. Son Jacob, b. Bedford Co., PA 1798 later removed from Preston Co. WV to Allegany Co. MD. He died at the home of his son Thomas H., Garrett Co., MD, 1892, aged 98. *6TH:128*

CURLEY, MICHAEL JOSEPH (MOST REV.), archbishop of the Roman Catholic church in the Baltimore diocese, b. in Golden Island, Athlone, Ireland, 12 Oct. 1879, a s/o Michael & Maria (Ward) Curley. He was first assigned to parish at St. Augustine, FL, 1904-14; appointed to Baltimore in 1921. *TR3:521*

CURTIS, DANIEL, b. London, England in 1723, emigrated to America aged 18, settling in Baltimore 1741/42. Colonial Justice & High Sheriff under King George III. He lived to the age of 100. *MDC:545*

CUSHWA, JOHN, with wife Catherine to America 1670-80 from Alsace-Lorraine. They settled near Womelsdorf & Stouchsburg, Berks Co., PA. Their son John moved from PA with his wife to western MD, settled in the valley of the Conococheague, near where is today Clear Spring. Their son David served as an officer in the War of 1812. Members of the German Reformed Church; later generations were Catholic. *6TH:535-56*

CUSTER, EMANUEL, "probably" came from Germany. He was a brother of the famous Gen. Custer, the Indian fighter. He settled in Western MD, near Grantsville. His son David b. there in 1811 & m. Margaret Stark, b. of Irish parentage & d. age 80. *6TH:572-73*

AILEY, PATRICK, & wife Anna Case, both b. Ireland. Patrick to America in 1858, settled at Baltimore until his death 1 Feb. 1907, aged 63. Anna to Baltimore as a girl in 1864 & was m. Nov. 1880. Members of St. Mary's Star of the Sea, Roman Catholic parish in Baltimore. They had 9 children, 7 sons & 2 daus., only two now living: Gilbert A., b. 30 Nov. 1881, & Mary A. Dailey. *TR3:552*

DALLAM, RICHARD, b. England, nephew of the first Duchess of Marlborough (nee Sarah Jennings) who m. John Churchill, Duke of Marlborough. Richard setled at Joppa, barraster. He m. Elizabeth (Betty) Martin. *H/C:129*

DALTON, WILLIAM, Englishman who immigrated with brothers Tristran & Charles. Tristran settled in MA & was 1st US senator from MA; Charles settled at Dalton, GA, which city was named for him. William settled first in VA & removed to Rockingham Co., NC. Desc. William F. Dalton m. Elizabeth Hand. They res. near Madison, NC & their son --- m. Ida Frances Bennett, d/o William W. & Sara (Robertson) Bennett of Rockingham Co. Son William Bennett Dalton, M.D. is their eldest of three children. He grad. Univ. of MD medical dept. in 1918 & in 1916 m. in Baltimore May Schley Egerton, d/o Bayard Calvert Egerton. *TR4:746-7*

DANNOCK, DENNIS, of English/Irish desc., settled in Somerset Co., MD in 1665; atty. His son John, also an atty., judge of Provincial Count 1710. Descs. removed to Frederick Co., MD. *FR2:808*

DARE, WILLIAM, b. England 1720, to America in early manhood & settled in NJ. Another William Dare, b. England, to NY in 1695 [see below]. William's (who settled in NJ) son, John, b. in NJ 25, Oct. 1796, to Baltimore & later to Jefferson, Frederick Co., MD. He m. Susan Hersberger, d/o Henry who was b. 1760, d. 1812. Henry was s/o Bernard, who settled in the area in 1798. *6TH:259-61*

DARE, WILLIAM, b. England, settled in NY as early as 1695. William Dare, 4th in desc. from the immigrant, b. Sept. 1736, m. Elizabeh Rose. Of their 7 children William H. Dare d. in Baltimore. Another MD connection was William (5th), s/o William (4th) & Elizabeth, b. 1770, d. 1830. He m. Rebecca Belange & they res. in Bridgeton. Their second son, John Dare, removed to Baltimore, MD at a young age & learned tailoring with his uncle Ephraim Dare. John m. Susan Hershberger, d/o Henry, of Jefferson, MD. John d. 6 Oct. 1878 & Susan in 1886. *FR2:1594-5*

DASHIELL, JAMES, Huguenot desc., from England located on English land grant on the Eastern Shore of MD (Somerset Co.) in 1666. He res. in Somerset Co. & m., in England, Anne Fairfax who d. 27 Feb. 1696 in Somerset Co. James d. there in 1697. His son James patented lands in the same county in 1672, 1673 & 1696. *TR4:686-8, MDC:606-7*

DAVIDGE, HENRY, ex-capt. in the British Army, settled in MD, m. Honora, d/o Sir Henry & Sarah (Dorsey) Howard, of Anne Arundel Co., MD. Henry Davidge d. young. *TR4:15*

DAVIDSON, JAMES (DR.), of Aberdeen, Scotland, his son George had son Philip Thomas Davidson who m. Marcella Blunt & had son Charles Fitzsimmons Davidson in Queenstown, MD 29 Sept. 1865. *TR4:116*

DAVIS, JOHN, 1705 from Wales to Long Island, where he died at an advanced age; Quaker. His eldest son, Isaac, moved to Salem Co., NJ in 1725. Isaac's second son, David, res. near Pittsgrove, NJ where he died. He m. Dorothy Cousins (b. in England 1693). Their son David, b. 1730, m. Martha Cole. Their eldest son, Isaac Davis, b. 1762, mariner, veteran of War of 1812, m. Susanna Newman, d/o John, of Red Bank, NJ & with his family to Cecil Co., MD in 1820. *H/C:466-7*

DAVIS, JONATHAN C., b. England & when a boy emigrated to America. He learned trade of tailor in DE & later bought a farm in that part of Frederick Co., MD which is now Carroll Co. His wife was Mary Winters & they had: John W.,; A. Maria; Edward Aaron; Joseph, res. in Carroll Co.; Jonathan C. & William. Lutheran. *FR2:1170-1*

DAWKINS, JOSEPH, b. England, from Oxfordshire to Calvert Co., MD 1668 or earlier. He m. Mary Hale & his will was probated 1685 May 9. *GME:417*

DAWSON, JAMES, with two brothers from England to MD. One brother settled in New England & the other in the south. James settled in Prince George's Co., MD, planter. *6TH:607-08*

DAWSON, JOHN, CHARLES & THOMAS, from England to America. On shipboard John m. Mary Doyne, an Irish girl. Their children settled in VA. Thomas settled where is now Dawsonville. George settled in Washington Co., MD. *6TH:825-26*

DE BOUCHELLE, LEGE, to America, settled Bohemia Manor, Cecil Co., MD 1640. Family of French origin. *H/C:247*

DE COURCY, HENRY, Englishman, to MD with Lord Baltimore & settled on estate near the mouth of the Chester River, "My Lord's Gift," *MDC:695-96*

DE COURSEY, JOHN & WILLIAM, emigrated from Ireland to MD, of an illustrious Anglo-Norman family. They were granted the estate of Cheston in 1642. *MDC:578-79*

DEBAUGH, PHILIP, m. Mary Clatonia, both b. on the Rhine in Germany where they married. To America c. 1830 & settled in York Co., PA. He was a shoemaker & huckster. They later settled in Baltimore Co., MD. Philip d. 1863, aged 63. Catholic. *H/C:175*

DEFORD, THOMAS, with brother, landed at Kent Island c. 1730. His son, Benjamin Deford m. Anne Hutton in 1798, d/o Thomas Hutton of Anne Arundel Co. & the d/o Thomas Graham, who was of Calvert Co. (the Huttons m. 1703). Benjamin Deford Sr. moved from Kent Island to West River, Anne Arundel Co. in 1791, where he d. Feb. 1810. Wife Anne, d. four days later. Joseph Hutton emigrated from Scotland & settled in Anne Arundel Co. He was the first tobacco inspector, appointed by the British gov't. in 1720. *TR4:761*

DENISON, JOHN MORGAN, of Londonderry, Ireland, to Baltimore and established grocery business; he d. 1810. *MDC:171*

DENNIS, ADAM, b. Scotland, m. Susan Whitesal of an old PA family. Their dau., Mary Dennis, b. Schuylkill Co., PA, m. Franklin S. Moyer. Their son, Dr. Frank A. G. Moyer, b. Easton, Northampton Co., PA 25 Nov. 1858, grad. 1881 with M.D. from College of Physicians & Surgeons in Baltimore. The Moyer family founded in America by Frank, b. France & came to America in early part of 19th century. His son, Franklin S. Moyer, reared & educated in Schuykill Co., PA had as his vocation fresco painting. Franklin was a soldier of the Civil War, Co. K, 51st Regt., known as the Iron Brigade. He d. at the battle of the Wilderness at age of 32. *TR3:848*

DENNIS, DANNOCH, to MD from England in 1632 & settled in Somerset Co., MD 1665; lawyer. Desc. George R. Dennis served as US senator 1876-1882. His son, John Upshur Dennis, b. MD had son J. Murdoch Dennis, b. Baltimore 13 April 1882. Littleton Dennis, 3rd in desc. from Donnach, served in the Continental Army. He m. Susannah, d/o Col. John Upshur of Northampton Co., VA. Their son, John Dennis (1771-1807), atty. of Somerset Co., MD & US congressman. *TR3:862-3, TR4:866, MDC:662-3*

DENT, THOMAS, 1st lord proprietor of Giesborough Manor, estate granted him by the crown. He was b. in Yorkshire, England in 1630 & immigrated to MD. He m. Rebecca Wilkinson, d/o Rev. William, the 1st Episcopal clergyman in MD. Served as sheriff of St. Mary's Co. (1664) & justice of the co. court & other offices. Desc. res. Oakley, St. Mary's Co. *TR4:549-50*

DERR, SEBASTIAN, desc. from an old family of Bavaria, Germany, came from the Palatinate to America on the ship *James Goodwill*, landing in Philadelphia in 1728. He res. for a time in Alexandria & later removed to Frederick Co., MD. He was a Protestant refugee & one of the founders of the Reformed Church in Frederick. Two of his sons [not named here] settled in Rock Bridge Co., VA & later removed to KY. Sebastian d. 1802 & was bur. in old graveyard back of the old Reformed Church on Church St. in Frederick City. His son John m. Catharine Steiner, d/o Capt. John. *FR2:1246-7*

DEVRIES, SAIB, from Holland to America 1803 at age of 3 with his parents. He m. Sarah Elder, of English desc., and resided in Sykesville, Carroll Co., MD. His son, Henry O. Devries, b. near Sykesville, MD 1826. *AAH:488-9, MDC:178*

DEWHURST, PATRICK, & wife Mary, b. England. Their son Edward b. in England 1878, brought to US. Edward m. Mary Ann Welch & had James Patrick Dewhurst, b. Fall River, MA 26 May 1890. James Patrick is a dentist of Cumberland, MD. He served in the 1st World War & m. Grace Ann Getzendanner, d/o P. D. & Sarah Ann of Cumberland, MD. *TR3:635*

DIAMOND, JOHN, from England to Philadephia, PA in early life. His son William C., b. Philadelphia & became resident of Montgomery Co., MD as a young man. He d. there in 1873. His wife was Josephine Jenkins, d/o John, and b. in Baltimore. Son John B., the only survivor of his father's family, b. 25 March 1857 & grew up in neighborhood of Gaithersburg, MD. 7 Nov. 1877 he m. Grace Ranney, d/o Judge Israel, of Delaware, Delaware Co., OH. *6TH:683*

DIEHL, JOHN, from Germany to Baltimore in 1857, merchant. He m. Mary Louise Fremin, b. near Paris, France & d. 1915. They had a family of 9 children who are yet living. Roman Catholic family. Their son, Julius F., b. Baltimore 4 July 1878. In 1905 Julius m. Nellie Dyer, b. Owings Mills, MD, a d/o James Dyer. *TR3:761-2*

DIFFENBALL, JOHN, to America from Germany & settled on a farm near Westminster (now Carroll Co.), MD. Granddau. Ellen Gilbert, d/o Adam & Catherine (Diffenball) Gilbert, b. 7 June 1828 near Westminster, m. Joseph Byers at Bridgeport, MD. *FR2:860*

DILLER (DE LLER), CASPER, b. Holland. To England, where he m. & emigrated to America c. 1729 & settled at New Holland, PA, farmers. Desc. Martin Diller, settled in area of Johnsville, Frederick Co., MD c. 1829 & m. a Miss Wolf. Their son John was a boy when his parents removed from PA to MD; farmer, d. near New Market, Frederick Co., MD in 1890, aged 69 years; Lutheran & m. Margaret Ellen Cramer, d/o Jacob & Susan (Umstead) Cramer. She now res. in Mt. Pleasant District, aged 79. *FR2:118-19*

DINTERMAN, GEORGE, b. England, settled in Frederick Co., MD about "150 years ago." *FR2:1512-13*

DISTLER, JOHN CYRUS, b. Bavaria, Germany, to America in the late 1840's. His son, John Cyrus Distler, Jr. was b. in Pittsburgh, PA in 1859. John Jr. has been a res. of Baltimore most of his life. He m.

Elizabeth Felber & their son, also John Cyrus Distler, was b. Baltimore 19 Oct. 1884. Elizabeth's grandparents were b. in Saxony, Germany & came to the US in the late 1840's; she was b. Baltimore. *TR3:911-12*

DODSON, THOMAS, with brother John & sister Mary to Burlington, NJ in 1677 with small colony of Quakers. He b. Knaresborough, Yorkshire, England 19 Oct. 1669, s/o Daniel & Susannah. He m. in Burlington & soon removed to Talbot Co., MD. His son Robert, b. Talbot Co., 1700. *TR4:537-40*

DOHME, CHARLES, b. Oberkirchen, Germany in 1807, in 1852 to US with wife & 7 children & settled in Baltimore. Charles was of Hessia, Germany, owner of White Sand Stone Quarry of Hessia. Imported to US brownstone for building from Germany. He d. in Baltimore in 1880. He was m. in Germany to Sophie Graebe, b. Germany, she d. in 1855 at age of 48. They had 7 children & their eldest was Louis, b. Germany 6 July 1837. He learned the drug business under Alpheus P. Sharp in Baltimore & founded the business of Sharp & Dohme, manufacturing chemists in 1845 in Baltimore. Another son of the emigrants was Charles Emil Dohme, a clerk of their business. Charles was b. Obernkirchen, Germany 12 March 1843, aged 9 when he accompanied his parents to America. In 1866 he m. Ida Schulz, d/o Wilhelm & Louisa (Jacobi) Schultz. Wilhelm was b. Ulm, Germany & fought under Napoleon in the battle of Leipzig. Another son of the immigrant was Gustavus Christian Dohme, b. Hessia, 17 March 1837, became a pharmacist of Baltimore & m. in Oct. 1867, Laura Doscher of Bremen, Germany. She d. 6 Jan. 1873 & on 18 Jan. 1876 he m. Mrs. Martha Cooper of Baltimore. *TR3:636-40, MDC:186*

DOLLMAN, JOHN G., b. Germany 1847, s/o John & Christina (Helm) who emigrated to America c. 1854 & settled Pottsville, PA where he carried on tin shop. John G. to America with parents at age of 7. *H/C:254*

DONNELLY, JAMES W., b. Ireland, to America in boyhood with his parents & settled in Cumberland, MD; carpenter. He m. Harriet R. Ways, b. Frederick Co., d/o Samuel D., who settled in Cumberland. *6TH:539*

DONOHUE, JOHN, b. Ireland 1814, to US as a young man of c. 20 years & settled in Baltimore, where he died aged 24. Livery business. John was s/o Charles Donohue & Anna Patrick. John m. Rose Kelly &

had son Terence Aloysius Donohue, b. Baltimore Co. 7 Feb. 1874. Roman Catholic family. *TR3:743-4*

DONOVAN, RICHARD (LT.), b. Co. Waterford, Ireland 17 Nov. 1731, m. in Dublin, Sarah Ann Delafield on 19 March 1763 & sailed for America 1764, settled in Baltimore Co., where is now Clifton Park. His grandmother was Catherine DeBurgo, d/o William Gall DeBurgo of Irish ancestry & wife of Edmond O'Donovan, desc. of the ancient Milesian kings. Richard served in the MD Line & was killed 16 Aug. 1780 at Camden, SC. *TR4:433*

DONSIFE, CATHARINE MARY, b. Germany, 14 Aug. 1816, to America with her parents at age of 4. Settled first in PA & later in Frederick Co., MD. She m. Henry Saylor, b. 10 March 1807 in Frederick Co., near Woodsboro, where he d. 30 June 1854. She d. 3 Nov. 1900. Her parents are not named here. *FR2:1139-40*

DORSEY, EDWARD, Englishman, immigrant ancestor of the Dorsey MD line. Desc. is traced as follows: Edward (I) to Edward (II), John Dorsey to William Hammond Dorsey, Richard Brooke Dorsey, Vernon John Dorsey & Vernon M. Dorsey, b. Washington, DC, 1 Dec. 1869. Richard Brooke Dorsey & wife Anne were res. of Olney, Montgomery Co., MD. Vernon in 1849 joined rush of gold seekers to CA & on his return studed law in Baltimore. *TR3:879-80*

DORSEY, JOHN, with brothers Edward & Joshua, emigrated from "Hockley in the Hole," England to Anne Arundel Co. 1660 & took up land on Bush River, now the Severn, where Annapolis now stands. They named their land "Hockley in the Hole" to commerate the place in England from which they had come. John d. 1714. *TR4:322, FR2:1448-9*

DORSEY, PATRICK, b. south of Ireland 1818, youngest of 9 children of Daniel & Mary (Kelley) Dorsey. His sister is Mrs. Bridget Blake of OH. Daniel d. 1825, aged 65 years. After Daniel's death his widow to America & settled in NY, later to OH, where she d. aged 40. Patrick accompanied his mother to America & grew up in Muskingum Co., OH. About 1840 to Frostburg, MD & then Somerset Co., PA. He later removed to Johnstown, PA & in 1872 to Garrett Co., MD. In 1851 he m. Sarah J. McKusker, d/o John of Allegany Co., MD. *6TH:23-24*

DORTON, HENRY FREDERICK, b. Germany, left as a youth; m. Anna M. Resau. Henry was a seaman & later an officer of the US Navy during the Civil War. Son Frederick Theodore Dorton b. Baltimore 19 Jan. 1872. *TR3:179-80*

DOTTERER, JOHN, b. Germany, emigrated & settled in what is now Waynesboro, PA, where he died. His wife was Mary Catharine --- & they had John & Frederick, and probably others. Son John, b. 9 Dec. 1785, Franklin Co., Pa. He m. Mary Hoffman, b. 2 May 1785, d. 15 Feb. 1855. They res. on farm near what is now Detour, Carroll Co., MD. *FR2:1262-3*

DOUGLAS, ROBERT, b. Scotland, m. Mary Robertson, d/o John & b. Ireland; they m. in Hagerstown & resided in VA. Son Henry Douglas b. in Shepherdstown, Harper's Ferry District, VA 29 Sept. 1840. Henry served in the Confederate Army, Co. B, 2d VA Infantry; a general. *6TH:205-07*

DOWNEY, WILLIAM, from Scotland to America 1742 & settled at Lancaster, PA, where he d. leaving 4 sons. His son John served in the Rev. War & after the war settled at Williampsort, MD, Washington Co., & later removed to VA near Charlestown, where he d. 1825. John m. three times: (1) 1782 Ruhana Stocksadale. Desc. William Downey b. 11 May 1789 removed to Frederick Co., MD. He m. Cordelia, d/o Basil Dorsey, Jr. *FR2:936*

DOYLE, JAMES, b. Clanegal, County Carlow, Ireland, of the clan of O'Doyle. Desc. James Doyle m. Maria J. --- & res. Westminster, MD. *TR4:324*

DOYNE, ROBERT, from Ireland, settled in Charles Co., MD & served as high sheriff. He received grants from Lord Baltimore & owned thousands of acres in Charles Co. He m. Mary Stone before 3 March 1674. She was d/o Virlinda (Cotton) Stone, widow of Gov. William Stone of Nanjemoy, Poynton Manor, Charles Co. Mrs. Stone was a sister of the Rev. William Cotton of Northampton Co., VA & her mother was Joan Cotton of Bunbary, Cheshire, England. *TR4:467-9*

DRAKE, MARY, m. John Fitzgerald, 2 June 1795, d. 22 Oct. 1850, aged 76 years; d/o Francis Drake who came from Devonshire, England and m. c. 1775 Ann Slowey. Grandson of John and Mary (Drake)

Fitzgerald, William Francis Clautice, b. in Baltimore 24 Nov. 1838 & d. there 12 July 1913. He was a son of George and Catherine (Fitzgerald) Clautice of Baltimore and grandson of Peter and Mrs. (Adelsberger) Clautice. *GME:301*

DRONENBURG, JACOB, from Germany with 2 brothers & settled in Frederick Co., MD, where he owned a smithy. He m. & had a son Jacob, b. Clarksburg & res. on a farm near Urbana. Jacob m. Mary M. Madery. *FR2:1074-5*

DRURY, CHARLES, from England to America & m. Mrs. Alice Adney, widow of Moses Adney. After her death he m. Miss Cole of Sudley, Anne Arundel Co. & had 3 sons: Charles, William & Samuel. Charles, the immigrant, and his sons forfeited lands in England because of their support of the American Revolution. *TR4:757*

DU FIEF, NICHOLAS G., b. in France, to America & settled in Washington, DC. His dau., Mary, m. William H. Fowler & son William C. b. 17 Aug. 1836. *6TH:827-28*

DUDDERAR, GEORGE PHILIP, b. Germany. His son Conrade m. Miss --- Dukensheets & settled at Oak Orchard, MD. Son William Dudderar, b. at what is now Linganore District, Frederick Co., MD, m. Margaret, d/o Jacob Shriner. *FR2:1222-3*

DUKE, RICHARD, to MD with Gov. Leonard Calvert in 1634; Catholic. In 1653 he left MD for England with wife & 2 sons, Richard & Thomas. Was descended from the House of Devon of East Devon. One son, James, settled in Calvert Co., MD before 1651. *TR4:359, 489*

DULANY, ---, records make mention of 2 Delany brothers & 3 sisters from Cork, Ireland, landing in VA in 1700. The eldest brother, William, to Culpeper, VA & later to Wye in Queen Annes Co., MD, where he d. The MD record mentions William & Daniel Delany, brothers, s/o Thomas & Sarah Delany, from Queen County, Ireland; in 1700 changed the spelling to Dulany. Daniel was age 18 on emigration & admitted to the MD bar 1710. His son Daniel (1721-1797), educated in England, m. on his return to America in 1747, Rebecca d/o Benjamin Tasker. *AAH:184, TR4:890-1*

DULANY (DELANEY), DANIEL (SR.), a cousin of Rev. Patrick Delaney, b. 1686 in Queen's Co., Ireland. He indentured himself & came to MD. He m. 1st Miss --- Plater of Calvert Co., MD who d. young. He m. 2d Rebecca Smith, d/o Col. Walter Smith of Calvert Co. *MDC:380*

DUNN, ANDREW, scion of an old family of Ulster, in the north of Ireland. His son, James F. Dunn, b. Baltimore 27 Aug. 1851. Merchant of fine china & cut glass. James m. Sarah Henderson of Baltimore & their son, James F. Jr., b. there 17 June 1881. *TR3:551-2*

DUNN, CHARLES B., b. Devonshire, England, became financier of Philadelphia, PA. His son, George G. Dunn m. Lillie Blye, who was related to the Garrett family of Baltimore. Their dau., Katherine Wright Dunn, m. William Watters Pagon, of Baltimore, 22 June 1916 in Philadelphia. *TR4:788-89*

DUNNIGAN, JOHN, b. Ireland, the eldest of 5 sons of John Dunnigan, who brought his family to America in 1863 & took up residence in Harford Co., MD, where he d. in 1865. Son John, farmer, m. Anna Clark. Catholic. *H/C:562*

DUNSTER, HENRY (REV.), b. Lancshire, England; first president of Harvard College. His sister Jane m. 17 Jan. 1706, Samuel Waters, Jr. of Prince George's Co., MD. Their son Mordecai b. 18 March 1722 & d. 1783. He m. Rachel --- & had son Benjamin who settled at Bealls Manor, then in Prince George's, now in Montgomery Co., MD. *TR4:704-7*

DURHAM, ---, from England at an early day & settled near Bel Air, Harford Co., MD. His son Samuel Durham had a son David, b. Harford Co. David's son Abel m. Sarah Devoe & 25 Feb. 1831 had William A. Durham. *H/C:525*

DUVALL, MAREEN (MAUREEN/MARIN), French Huguenot of Norman French lineage, from area of Nantes, Brittany, to MD 1659 [c. 1650] as one of 150 adventurers brought over by Col. William Burgess & settled in Anne Arundel Co. (Prince George's), MD. His original grant of land in Anne Arundel Co., given by Lord Baltimore, is dated 28 Aug. 1659. He named this land "LaVal" in memory of family estate in France. He m. 3 times : (1) ---; (2) Susanna & (3) Mary Stanton. At his death he held a vast estate & his widow m. Col. Henry Ridgely & later Rev.

Mr. Henderson, commissary of the Church of England. Mareen's will probated 1694. Mrs. Henderson's will, probated at Upper Marlborough, shows that she had a brother in Philadelphia & that her maiden name was Mary Stanton. Benjamin, youngest son of Mareen & his wife, m. 1713, Sophia Griffith and their 3d child, Benjamin m. Susanna Tyler, d/o Robert of Queen Anne Town in 1744. *AAH:104, TR4:238-9, 490, FR2:948-9, GME:132*

DUVALL, MARSH M., b. Germany, to America, settled first in PA & later in Frederick, MD. His son William T. b. & resided in Frederick. William d. 1880; his wife was Rebecca Staub, d/o Peter, a chair manufacturer in PA. She d. 1893. Both buried in Mt. Olivet Cemetery. *6TH:248-49*

DUYCKINCK, LEVI HOLDEN, b. in Holland 12 Jan. 1754, to America in the service of the Spanish government. Was proprietor of book store in NY City. His son Richard B. res. in NJ, farmer. Richard's son, Horace H., b. in Somerset Co., NJ 1819; 1852 removed to Cecil Co., MD. Member of Zion Presbyterian Church. He m. Emily Longstreet of NJ & he d. 8 April 1891, aged 72. *H/C:524-5*

ARLE, JAMES, b. in England 25 July 1631, settled in MD on the Corsica River, near Centreville with his wife Rhode 15 Nov. 1683, and d. 24 Sept. 1684. The family are believed to be of the Craglethorpe family, Lincolnshire, England. Descs. fought in the Revolutionary War & the War of 1812. Desc. Richard T. Earle m. Mary Tilghman, a d/o Judge James Tilghman. Richard & Mary's son, Samuel T. Earle, m. Mary Brundage, a d/o William & Rosetta (Usher) Brundage. The Brundage family was established near Norfolk, VA. *MDC:133, TR3:857-8*

EASTERDAY, MICHAEL, b. Germany, to America with his brother [not named here] & settled near Jefferson, MD. He served during War of the Rev. as bodyguard of Gen. George Washington. After the war he settled near Jefferson & married. His first wife is not named here, but he m. 2d Miss Dagenhart. Their children: Conrad; Christian; Jacob of Washington Co., MD; Lawrence; Samuel; Daniel; Tracy, m. G. F. Clinck, of Washington Co., MD; Sarah, m. Joshua A. Warrenfeltz; Lavinia, m. John Metz of Washington Co., MD. All are now dec'd. except Jacob. After death of his first wife, Michael removed to a farm near Boonsboro,

Washington Co., MD, where he d. He is bur. at old Shunk graveyard near Boonsboro. *FR2:1477-8*

EATON, CLARENCE JACKSON, b. St. John, New Brunswick, Canada, 14 March 1875, s/o Abijah H. & Emma Delia (Andrews) Eaton. His maternal grandfather, John D. Andrews, res. Milltown, New Brunswick, Canada. The Eaton name is of Welsh & Saxon origin. Clarence Jackson Eaton studied at Baltimore City College & in March 1878 eastablished the Eaton & Burnett Business College. He m. 24 April 1915, in Dover, DE, Blanche Ferguson Harman of Baltimore, d/o Walter & Caroline (Richardson) Harman, res. of Centerville, MD. *TR3:1019-20*

EBERHART, PAULUS, from Paltz to Philadelphia, PA 1744 & in 1752 removed to Baltimore Co., MD, near the present town of Manchester (now Carroll Co.). His son, George Eberhardt, b. 11 Aug. 1745, d. 12 July 1830; m. Elizabeth Zacharias, b. 12 Feb. 1749. Their son George Jr., b. 10 Nov. 1771, m. Elizabeth Weaver. *TR4:594-5*

EBERT, HANS MICHAEL, from Wurtemberg, Germany to PA in 1831. Desc. Martin P. Ebert, b. Frederick Co., VA 1854, m. Mary Elizabeth Rutherford, d/o John H. & Camilla (Baker) Rutherford of Winchester, VA. Rutherfords came to America from Scotland c. middle of the 18th century. Their son, Dr. John William Ebert, m. Louise Bowly 29 Sept. 1909. Louise b. in Baltimore 1890; Dr. John practices medicine in Towson, MD. *TR4:808-09*

EBY, THEODOUS, b. in canton of Zurich, Switzerland 25 April 1663, a Mennonite who fled Germany where he resided 1704-1715. He sailed for Philadelphia in 1715 & settled at Mill Creek Place, now known as Roland Mill, south of New Holland, in Lancaster Co., PA, where he d. 1737. Desc. James W. Eby m. Jennie V. Shorb, d/o Samuel J. Shorb & Catherine Parr, & their son, Dr. J. Cyril Eby, b. Littlestown, Adams Co., PA 14 Dec. 1884. Dr. Eby res. Baltimore, Catholic & member of parish of Saints Philip & James. *TR4:415-16*

ECCLESTON, CHARLES A., b. England, a descendant of a prominent landed family. To the US at the outbreak of the Civil War, he entered the Army. In 1863 he m. Martha Brown, d/o Robert of Montgomery Co., MD. *6TH:613-14*

ECCLESTON, RICHARD & JOHN, came in 1648 to MD in ship *Good Intent.* They were sons of Lord Charles Eccleston of Dorset, England. With them came William Byus, son of Lord William Byus of Wexford, Ireland. Richard was unmarried at the time of his emigration. Descs. Joseph Byus m. Ann Eccleston & lived at "Burlin Hall," near Cambridge, MD. *TR4:135*

ECKE, GEORGE, settled Baltimore 1883, where he m. Therese Hohman 21 Oct. 1883. She m. 2d George Haensler. *TR3:85*

ECKER, ---, emigrated from Germany to Frederick Co., MD, Liberty District. His son, Samuel Ecker, b. in MD, farmer. His wife was of Irish desc. & they had Levi, b. MD, farmer. Levi m. Elizabeth Giddings, of Montgomery Co., MD, d/o George W. Giddings, farmer Washington, DC. *FR2:1514-15*

ECKSTEIN, CHRISTIAN, the elder, b. 1822 in Dernichein, near Frankfort-on-the-Rhine, Germany. He & wife emigrated to America in 1845, landed in Baltimore where he worked in the dairy business until 1854, when he removed to Frederick, MD, where he d. 1874. His wife was Elizabeth Kepple & they had 7 children: Christian H, aged 9 on emigration, atty. & public office holder, m. 1875, Mary K. Feinour of Washington, D.C.; Elizabeth, m. George Brengle of Frederick; Annie m. Charles Haller of Frederick; William F. of Frederick; Mary, m. Edward Koontz; Louisa, widow of Capt. William Haller of Frederick & Ella V., m. George Shaffer. *FR2:1096-7*

EDEN, ROBERT, the last Proprietary Governor of MD, came in 1769; m. Lord Baltimore's dau. He d. & was buried in Anne Arundel Co., MD. *AAH:214-15*

EDMONDSTON, ARCHIBALD, to MD from Scotland & became military officer & magistrate of Prince George's Co., MD. *TR4:345*

EDWARDS, EDWARD, b. Wales, m. Mary Miller, b. Lehigh Co., PA. Edward president of Slatington Rolling Mill Co., of Slatington, PA. Their son, John M. [E?] b. 8 May 1869, in Catasauqua, Lehigh Co. He m. Mary Lamar Read, d/o Nelson Clark Read of Cumberland, MD. John was principal of the Allegany Co. Academy, Cumberland, MD. *6TH:137-38, 694-5*

EDWARDS, PHILIP (REV.), b. England, to US in 1880 with his wife, Mary Josephine Vincent, & their family. Mary d. 1882, leaving children: John R. of Washington, DC & Richard N. of Westminster, MD, both members of the Methodist Episcopal church; and Annie, m. Reverdy U. King of Calvert Co., MD. *TR3:814-17*

EDWARDS, ROBERT, with Hayden & another brother whose name cannot be learned to America from Wales prior to 1740. Hayden settled in VA, the other brother settled in CT. Robert settled in NY, & remained a batchelor, supposed to have been killed in the Revolution. Hayden had a son Benjamin who went to Montgomery Co., MD. *6TH:710-11*

EICHELBERGER, JOHN E., b. 1670 in Germany, to America 1728. Family came from Ittlingen, near Sinsheim, County of Heidelberg in the Grand Duchy of Baden. John's son Philip Frederick, who immigrated with him, was b. 17 April 1693, d. 19 Aug. 1776. Philip Frederick was accompained by his wife & 4 children. His 2d wife was Mary Magdalene ---. Lutheran Church members. Philip Frederick's son, John Frederick Eichelberger, b. 18 Feb. 1722, d. 1783, was a Rev. War patriot. His son, John, b. 1749 in Frederick Co. MD, d. 22 April 1822, was a Rev. soldier. He m. Mary Leonard, d/o Michael, b. Germany, who settled in Reading, PA. Another son of Philip Frederick was Martin, who had a son Leonard, who was a hero of the Revolution & was later harbormaster in Baltimore. Leonard m. Elizabeth Smyser of York, PA. Still another son of Philip Frederick was Leonard, b. PA 1750, d. 1811, had a son George M. who m. Jane Gayson & had son George b. Carroll Co., MD 1784, d. in Frederick 1854. George was register of wills for Frederick Co. for 20 years. *TR4:268, 6TH:427-8; FR2:974-5*

EISENBRADT, CHRISTIAN H., to Baltimore from City of Goettingen, Hanover, Germany. His dau. Sophia W. m. Ernest Mann & only son Harry E. Mann, b. in Baltimore 2 Aug. 1851. *MDC:254-55*

ELDER, WILLIAM, b. Lancashire, England 1707, to St. Mary's Co., MD by 1728/32. He m. Ann Wheeler in England, she d. 1739. Children: William, m. Miss Wickham; Guy, m. twice & by his 2d wife had 13 children (Joseph, Judith, James, Polly [all went to KY], Benjamin, Guy, Priscilla, Edward, Thomas & George; Charles, m. Julia Ward of Charles Co., MD. Mary, m. Richard Lilly of VA; Richard, m. Phoebe Delovier). William from St. Mary's Co. to Frederick Co., MD in 1734, where he was the first white man to settle in Emmitsburg in 1734. William m. 2d

1794, Jacoba Clementina Livers, d/o Arnold, b. England & fled from there on the colapse of the reign of James II & settled at large estate in MD called "Arnold's Delignt" on Owing's Creek. Children of William's 2d marriage: Elizabeth, Arnold, Thomas, Ignatius, Anna & Aloysius. *FR1:10-11, FR2:835*

ELLICOTT, ANDREW, of an old Collumpton, Devonshire family in England, to PA in 1730, accompanied by his son Andrew Jr. Andrew Sr. res. in Bucks Co., PA & d. there. Andrew Jr. m. in Bucks Co., PA 17 June 1731, at Friends Meeting House, Ann Bye, both d. in Bucks Co. Andrew 3d, s/o Andrew and Ann (Bye), b. 22 Jan. 1734, d. 1809. In 1772 with brothers Joseph & John removed to Baltimore Co., MD. This family settled site known as Ellicott City, Howard Co. Millers & merchants on a large scale, the town is named for them. *AAH:497-8, GME:235-6*

ELLINGER, JACOB, b. 7 Dec. 1820, Bavaria, Germany, Hebrew. From Breman to Baltimore, MD aged 19, arrived 26 July 1840; partner with brother Samuel in livestock business. He m. 12 Aug. 1845, Mary Eliza, d/o George Baker of Baltimore. Brother Samuel, b. Germany, early settler of Baltimore; m. Emma Wolf. Dau. Rosalie m. Solomon Straus and their son was b. here 24 Nov. 1873. *MDC:100, TR3:338*

ELLIS, ROWLAND, b. Wales & a priest of the Established Church. Sent to America by the society for the diffusion of Christian knowledge, located in Burlington, NJ in 1701, he became early connected with St. Mary's Church, of which, for 175 years in direct line his descs. were wardens, the line terminating with the death of Dr. Charles Ellis. Desc. Rowland Ellis m. Elizabeth Rudulph, d/o Esther Synge, a dau. of Philip Synge the "patriot silversmith of the Revolution." Philip Synge, a German, landed as a youth in 1701 at Annapolis, MD & removed to Baltimore & later to Philadelphia. He was the intimate personal friend of Benjamin Franklin. Their son, Francis Asbury Ellis m. Eliza Ann Howard, had son Dr. Charles M. Ellis, b. at Elkton, MD 13 Dec. 1838. *H/C:551-3*

ELMER, EDWARD, Puritan, (1610-1676), supposedly a res. of Braintree in Co. of Essex, England, to America & was killed by Indians during King Philip's War in 1676 at South Windsor, MA. His son Samuel b. 1649, had Jonathan b. 1686, d. 1758, leaving a son, Dr. Nathaniel Elmer (1758-1816), who m. Mary Allison, d/o Gen. William

Allison. Horace Elmer (of the 6th American generation) (1783-1850) m. Susan Stewart, d/o Luther & Keziah (Carpenter) Stewart. Lewis Elmer (1814-1892), b. Goshen, NY, m. 5 Jan. 1837, Mary Ann Wickersham. They had William Stewart Elmer, b. 2 Nov. 1840, d. 17 May 1915. He was b. Morristown, NJ & later res. at Pittsburgh, PA. To Baltimore with his maternal grandfather, Isaac Wickersham & m. Mary Elizabeth Addison 5 April 1865 & d. aged 74. *TR4:289-91*

ELY, RICHARD, from Plymouth, England in 1660 & settled at Lyme, CT. Descendant Elias S. Ely m. Hester Wright & their son Charles Wright Ely, b. Madison, CT 14 March 1839. Charles was Principal of the State Institution for the Education of the Deaf & Dumb at Frederick City, MD. He m. Mary Darling of Ohio 24 Oct. 1867. Presbyterian. *MDC:381*

EMMERICH, ---, b. Germany, to America in 1830 & wedded a Miss Harper, b. Centerville, VA, who was of family for whom Harpers Ferry was named. Their son, George Washington Emmerich, m. Mary Elizabeth Shepherd & their dau., Ellen Cora, was b. at Bristol, Anne Arundel Co., MD 3 May 1873 & brought to Baltimore as an infant. *TR4:757*

EMMONS, WILLIAM (SR.), emigrated to America from England in 1718 with his wife, Sarah Way, & settled in Taunton, MA. William was s/o Major Gen. Carolus Emmons. The family later to Litchfield, CT, where Sarah d. in 1735 & the next year William m. Sarah Barnes. WIlliam Sr. d. in Litchfield in 1793. His children: Woodruff, William Jr., Arthur & Tabitha; children by 2d wife: Hannah, Mary & Lydia. Woodruff, the eldest son, b. aboard ship on the Atlantic ocean, in 1718, m. in Cornwall, CT 10 March 1743 to Esther Prentice (2 May 1717-9 Nov. 1817) & had: Samuel, Elizabeth, Simeon, Elizabeth (II), Sarah, Salmon, Solomon, Asa & Asaph. Woodruff d. in Cornwall 1793. His 6th son & 9th child, Asaph, b. in Cornwall c. 1760 & d. 20 Feb. 1831, while on a visit to the home of his son, Lewis, in Washington Hollow, Dutchess Co., NY & was bur. in the Quaker churchyard at that place. Asaph served in the Revolutionary Army & was m. 1784 to Nancy Suley, who d. in 1830 in town of New Marlboro, MA. Children of Asaph & Nancy: Lewis, Samuel, Laura, John, Mariah, Nancy, Katherine, Mira & Franklin. John Emmons, s/o Asaaph, b. Cornwall, CT 13 Dec. 1791, d. 1864. Served in War of 1812 & m. Mehitable Trescott in 1812 & had: Burton, Charles Trescott, John S., Ann S. & Isaac T. John was a Quaker preacher & both he & his wife bur. in old Quaker Churchyard near Canaan Valley. Son Charles Trescott Emmons was b. 1 Oct. 1819 & m. Lucy Caldwell & became the father of Charles Cadwell Emmons, b. in New Marlboro, MA 21 Jan. 1846. Newspaper man, removed to LaFayette, IN & lived in Cleveland & Pittsburgh. His wife was Jennie M. Briney, d/o Mark D. & Amanda (Ebersole) Briney of Woodstock, OH. Their youngest child & only son was Charles DeMoss Emmons, b. LaFayette, Tippecanoe Co., IN 13 Feb. 1871, is president of the United Railways & Electric Co. of Baltimore. Charles DeMoss Emmons was raised in Pittsburgh, PA; Presbyterian. He m. 1 May 1894, Bertha, d/o Samuel & Mary (Brackenridge) Ewart of Pittsburgh. *TR3:935-6*

EMMORD, FRED, b. Hanover, Germany 1813; to America & his son Fred Emmord b. in Magnolia, Harford Co., MD 27 Nov. 1854. Family to Baltimore, where Fred Sr. employed on the Balto. & OH railroad. Later farmer of Harford Co. & d. there in 1883. Lutheran. *H/C:567-8*

EMORY, ARTHUR, to MD in 1666 with wife Mary & 2 children. Son Arthur was early member of Queen Annes Co. court (1708); was member of Wye Church & a warden of St. Paul's parish. *TR4:250-1*

ENGEL (ENGLE), NICHOLAS, b. Hesse Cassel, Germany 9 Nov. 1816. Orphaned young & put to the shoemaking trade. Also trained as a cabinet maker. Immigrated to America, landing at Baltimore & settled at Thurmont, Frederick Co., MD. Later removed to Mechanicstown District, near Eicholtz's Mill, Frederick Co., farmed. He d. at Graceham, MD; member of the Moravian Church at that place. Nicholas m. 18 Dec. 1845, Anna E. Gall, d/o William & Elizabeth Gall. William Gall had brought his wife & family to America in 1824 & settled in Frederick Co. Mrs. Engel d. 19 Jan. 1903, the mother of 12 children. *FR2:1425-7*

ENGLAND, JOSEPH, minister in the Friends' Society, was s/o John England & Loue his wife. Joseph b. 1680 at Burton, on the River Trent, in Staffordshire, England. In 1710 he m. Margaret, d/o Samuel & Joanna Orbel, b. at Deal in Kent in 1685. They came to America in 1752, bringing children John, Samuel & Joanna. Joseph & Lydia were b. after their arrival in America. Joseph d. 1748, Margaret in 1741. They settled in Cecil Co., MD, on North East Creek. *C:159*

ENGLAND, SAMUEL, "son of an Englishman," and founder of the family in America, settling in Cecil Co., MD. His great-grandson Joseph

T. England, b. on famly homestead in 1821, son of Isaac & grandson of John. Quakers. *H/C:335*

ENSOR, LUKE & JOHN, before 1776 emigrated from England & settled in Baltimore Co., MD near Cockeysville. *FR2:1354-5*

EPSTEIN, JACOB, b. 28 Dec. 1864, Lithuania (then part of the Russian empire) to Baltimore at age 17, wholesale dealer. 1891 m. in Baltimore Lena Weinberg. *TR3:107-09*

ERICH, AUGUSTUS (M.D.), b. 4 May 1837 at Eisleban, Prussia. In 1856 to Baltimore with his family. Graduated Univ. of MD 1861, practiced in Baltimore. 1 Nov. 1862 m. Annie, eldest d/o Henry Baetjer, Esq. of Baltimore. *MDC:193*

ERKENBRACK, PHILIP ADAM, of an ancient Holland family, settled in the Hudson River country in 1698; he had 12 sons. Desc. Frederick Philip Erkenbrack, b. Brooklyn, NY, m. Isabel Beresford & had Dr. Clarence Phillip, b. Rochester, NY 2 June 1879. He was a physician of Baltimore & veteran of WWI. 19 Oct. 1904, in Baltimore, he m. Teresa Rose, d/o Francis Edward & Catherine (Blondell) Rose of early Baltimore family. *TR3:848-51*

ESCHBACH, JOHN, b. Germany 15 [13?] Sept. 1747, to America when young, settled in Bucks Co., PA (now Lehigh Co.), farmer. He m. Catherine Bush, also b. in Germany, 1749. Their son Anthony, b. 10 May 1772 in PA, farmer & mechanic, killed c. age 40, thrown from a horse. Anthony's wife was Barbara Roemig of Allentown, PA. Their son, David b. in Paradise Twp., Northumberland Co., PA 27 Oct. 1802, [second source says David was b. in Bucks Co. & removed with his parents as a child to Northumerland Co.] d. 15 Feb. 1879, m. (1) 11 Oct. 1824, Elizabeth B. Rishel, b. 18 Nov. 1806, d. 14 Oct. 1844 [1841], the anniversary of their marriage. They had 4 children. Their son Rev. E. R. Eschbach was pastor of the Reformed Church of Frederick, MD. He was b. in Chillisquaque Twp., Northumberland Co., PA 9 Nov. 1835 & removed to Turbot Twp. as a child & d. in MD. Anthony's second wife was Sarah --- & they had 2 children. *6TH:320-22; FR2:909-10*

ESTABROOK (ESTEBROK), JOSEPH & THOMAS, Puritans of Okehampton, Co. Devon, England, to America 1660. Joseph, pastor at Concord, MA, m. Mary d/o Capt. Hugh & Esther Mason in 1668 & d.

1711. Their son, Joseph Estabrook, b. Concord, MA 6 May 1669, citizen of Lexington, m. Melicent, d/o Henry Woodis of CT & d. 1733. Their son John Estabrook, b. at Lexington 1694 m. Prudence Harrington 27 Oct., 1720. Their son, Nehemiah, b. at Lexington, MA 2 March 1735, served in the French & Indian War (1775) & in the Rev. In 1759 Nehemiah m. Elizabeth, d/o Samuel & Hannah Winship, & he d. Hopkington, NH 1812. His son, Eliakim, b. Lexington, MA, 1773, in 1793, m. Hannah Crosby Cook, d/o Ephraim & Hannah Cook of West Cambridge. Their son Endor, b. 1795 at Lexington, served in West Cambridge Light Infantry. 1817 Endor m. Lydia, d/o Deacon John & Hannah (Phelps) Adams of West Cambridge. Endor & Lydia's son, Endor, b. 5 Nov. 1825, in 1853, m. Catherine Allen, b. in Baltimore 17 March 1835, d/o Solomon & Elizabeth (Simms) Allen of Baltimore Co. & res. in MD. Their dau. Ida Estabrook, b. in Baltimore 26 Feb. 1855, in 1877 m. Rudolf Stehl. *TR4:151-2*

ETCHBERGER, WILLIAM, to America 1643 with William Penn & settled in PA. Desc. Capt. James Etchberger m. Frances Anne Despeaux, both b. Baltimore. Their dau., Frances Ann, b. Baltimore 13 Jan. 1841, m. Dr. John F. Hancock, b. Anne Arundel Co., MD 9 Sept. 1834, s/o John Hancock & Mary Leake. Dr. Hancock d. 12 Nov. 1923; res. Baltimore. *TR4:349-50*

EVANS, ---, 3 brothers from Scotland to MD. Catherine, d/o one of the brothers, m. Caspar Cline, b. Hanover, PA, resided in Frederick, MD. Their dau., Mary, m. William Yeakle of Frederick on 19 Oct. 1845. Another of the brothers, Col. John Evans, located in Ross Co., OH. *6TH:492*

EVANS, DAVID (REV.), first pastor of Pencader Presbyterian Church, Cecil Co., MD, was s/o David Evans & b. Wales. *C:165-6*

EVANS, JOB, of Wales, with his family to America & located in Baltimore Co., near Owings Mills, farmer. His children: John m. Miranda Owings, d/o Edward of Fountain Rock, Frederick Co. & removed to Chillicthe, OH in 1815 & son Robert was father of Catharine & Corilla Evans. Robert was b. in Wales & came to this country with his father Job. His dau. Catherine was the 1st wife of Casper Cline & dau. Corilla Casper's 2d wife. Son George T. Cline b. near Frederick, MD 4 March 1835. *6TH:791-93, FR2:1089*

EVANS, JOHN, probably b. in Wales in 1680; settled at Iron Hill, Newcastle Co., DE in 1725. He d. at Nottingham, MD 1738. His son John, b. in Cecil Co., d. there 1775. John Jr. m. Mary Oliver, b. Beverly, MA, 1795, reared in Boston & d. Jan. 1881. *H/C:579-80*

EVANS, JOHN, JAMES & ROBERT, brothers who settled in Cecil Co., MD 'about a century & a half ago,' believed to have been s/o John Evans, b. c. 1680, who also immigrated to America. James purchased land in Drumore Twp., Lancaser Co., PA, where he res. until 1752 when he sold it to his brother John. James & Robert m. sisters, Isabella & Margaret, d/o John Kilpatrick of West Nottingham, Cecil Co. James settled c. 1750 in Cecil Co. on 'Evans Choice,' c. 4 miles north of town of Port Deposit. Robert settled on Big Elk Creek, Cecil Co. in 1730. John Evans, the eldest brother (21 May 1709-28 Jan. 1798), served in the French & Indian War as a volunteer from Lancaster Co. He m. a Sarah Denny & had 8 children; his eldest son James b. 1749, m. (1) Susan Allison. John later to Erie Co., PA; served as a volunteer in the War of 1812. Robert, youngest of the 3 immigrant brothers, settled on the Big Elk, west of Cowantown in 1730; tanner. He & wife Margaret Kilpatrick had sons Robert & John Evans, & daus. Jean who m. Henry Hollingsworth of Elkton; Hannah who m. Rev. James Finley, pastor of the Rock church; Mary, m. Zebulon Hollingsworth of Elk Landing; Isabell, m. William Montgomery; Margaret, m. James Black; & Elanor, m. Amos Alexander of New Munster. *C:485-95, H/C:126*

EVANS, JOHN N., b. Pembrokeshire, South Wales, left there with wife and 5 children in 1862, to US & settled in Northumberland Co., PA; miner, d. Shamokin, PA 1885, aged 60. He m. Mary Evans, d/o William and Martha who resided in Sandersfoot, South Wales. Mary d. at Altoona, PA 1913. They had 3 sons & 5 daus., one son, John Absolom Evans, M.D., b. Northumberland Co., PA 27 Jan. 1866, practices medicine in Baltimore. *TR3:215*

EVANS, THOMAS, from Wales, settled in what is now Upper Darby, PA, near Philadelphia. Descendant William Warrington Evans, D.D.S., b. Baltimore 30 April 1843, third s/o Elizabeth & Rudulph H. Evans, who in 1849 founded the Baltimore Cemetery. *MDS:*

EVANS, WILLIAM, son of John who was from Wales & settled in city of London, England in 1762. William to America & settled at head of Elk River, Cecil Co. He was joined in America by his brother Henry who located in the Freedom District Baltimore (now Carroll Co.). Farmers. *MDC:172*

EVERSFIELD, JOHN (REV.), youngest s/o William who d. 1705, County of Kent, England. John b. 4 Feb. 1701, ordained deacon in 1723 & grad. Oxford in 1727. To MD 1727 where he took up parish of St. Pauls, Prince Georges Co., where he was rector for nearly 50 years. He was arrested for treason during the Rev. War. He m. 9 May 1730, Eleanor Clagett (1712-1730), 2d d/o Richard Clagett of Croome & wife Deborah Dorsey, d/o of the Hon. John the immigrant. Rev. John d. 8 Nov. 1780 & was interred under the alter in St. Thomas Church, at his own request. It is mentioned that among his pupils was Thomas J. Clagett, his wife's nephew, who later became bishop. *TR4:323, 806-8*

EWEN, RICHARD (MAJOR), in 1649 brought his wife Sophia & 5 children & 3 servants at his own charges to MD, for which he received a patent for 1,000 acres. He was s/o William Ewing. Joshua Ewen's son Patrick was b. Cecil Co., & served as squire of Octoraro Hundred. He was captain in continental army. Patrick Jr., farmer of Cecil Co., d. 1864. Joshua's oldest dau., Elizabeth, m. Richard Talbott, Quaker of West River, Anne Arundel Co., MD. *AAH:530, H/C:438-9, 473-4*

EWING, SAMUEL, b. Glasgow, Scotland, to America & settled in Cecil Co. Established grist & sawmill; he m. in the 2d Presbyterian Church of Philadelphia His son, Amos Ewing Sr. had Amos Jr., who was b. on homestead 21 July 1793; farmer & miller. He m. Mary Steel. *H/C:570*

EYLER, FREDERICK, b. Switzerland 9 April 1776; with a brother in early manhood to America & settled in north part of Frederick Co., MD & named his settlement Eyler's Valley. Farmer. Frederick m. 15 Dec. 1809, Margaret Willier, b. 11 Sept. 1783. Their children: one d. in childhood; J. Frederick, dec'd., farmer of Mechanicstown District; Caroline, dec'd., m. Robert Clugston of Waynesboro, PA; Marie, dec'd., m. John Benchoff of Hagerstown, MD; Lizzie E. [Jane E.], dec'd., m. Samuel M. Diffendall of Mechanicstown District; William, dec'd.; Charles A.; Rebecca, widow of George Favorite of Thurmont [Graceham], MD. Members United Brethren Church. *FR2:837, 1455-6*

EYLER, GEORGE, with wife Elsie Kauffman, b. Germany, settled in Eyler's Valley, Frederick Co., which was named for him. Moravians, had 12 children. Son David, farmer of Frederick Co., Mechanicstown

District, b. there 22 Feb. 1813 & d. on his farm 2 1/2 miles north of Thurmont, 26 June 1863. *FR2:836*

 ABER, PETER J. (REV.), b. at Cologne, the capital of Rhenish Prussia, 21 July 1847. At age 20 he became a member of the Franciscan Order. 8 April 1872 he arrived in NY, where he became a member of the Methodist Episcopal Church. He later converted to the philosophy of Emanuel Swedenborgh and in 1875 came to Baltimore, MD to serve as Pastor of the First German New Jerusalem Society. *MDC:127*

FACIUS, G. (REV.), b. at Mainz, on the Rhine, 22 Sept. 1830. His grandfather on his mother's side served in the Prussian army in the War of 1812. Rev. Facius was s/o Charles Facius, a merchant of Hesse Darmstadt. In 1847 Rev. G. with parents to U.S., settled in Baltimore. He served as pastor of the German Reformed Zion Congregation. 1863 he m. Leopoldina, d/o John Lorz, of Bavaria. *MDC:140-41*

FAHREY, PETER (DR.), b. Germany, of French descent, 8 May 1767, emigrated to Lancaster Co., PA as a youth. Tanner & later physician. Removed to MD & settled near Boonsboro, Washington Co. *6TH:406-08*

FAIR, CAMPBELL (REV.), b. Hollymount, County Mayo, Ireland 28 April 1842, s/o John Fair of town of Ballina who d. in 1846. His mother was Maria Wilson, d/o Thomas Wilson, lawyer of Dublin. Campbell was a minister of the Church of England & Ireland, ordained 1865 in North Wales & appointed to the curacy of Holy Trinity Church, Birkenhead. He was injured in a train collision & paralyzed for some time. A seavoyage was ordered & he arrived in NY with his mother & proceeded to New Orleans, where he apparently recovered. He m. Alice, youngest d/o William J. McLean of New Orleans. Settled in NY & Later to Baltimore. *MDC:459*

FALKENFIELD, THEODORE (REV.), b. Western Germany; 1753-55 served as pastor of the Reformed Church at Frederick, MD. *FR1:408*

FALLS, HUGH, b. Ireland, d. Cecil Co., MD 1816. He m. Emily Riddle, b. Cecil Co., d/o William & Mary. Emily d. 1886 at an advanced age. *H/C:396*

FARNANDIS, PEDRO, to America from England before 1694. Family early from Portugal to England, Pedro Farnandis appears in Domesday Book, 1066. Pedro (the immigrant) settled in Annapolis, MD, his will 24 July 1775. His wife was Eleanor --- & they had a son Peter & a son James who m. (1) Anne Elizabeth Wallace of Port Tobacco & (2) Miss --- McPherson. *TR4:107*

FARRIS, WILLIAM, to America from England; was first English settler on what is known as the "Welsh Tract," in New Castle Co., DE. His son Jacob Farris of Penceaddy Hundred, New Castle Co.; his dau. Sarah Sharp Farris m. --- Moore & res. in Elkton & Baltimore after 1826. *MDC:246*

FASSITT, RALPH, b. France, a desc. of Huguenots. Descs. res. in Worcester Co., MD, and William Fassitt to Philadelphia, PA in 1800, Presbyterian who m. Margaret Barclay of Philadelphia, d/o John Allen, Revolutionary veteran. William d. in Philadelphia 1874, aged 74. Their son, Thomas Fassitt b. in Philadelphia, m. Catherine Van Sant of Bucks Co., PA & they removed to the old Kirk Brown farm in Cecil Co.,; dairy farmer. *H/C:559*

FAULK, GEORGE (CAPT.), b. France, m. Rebecca McCarthy, b. Germany. To America 1772, settled in Philadelphia; operated line of merchant ships. Son George Jr. ran away to sea as a boy of 12 & was taken as prisoner of war during the War of 1812. He was a seafarer for 60 years, d. in Philadelphia aged 90. George Jr.'s dau. Josephine, m. Pierce Woodward, b. Philadelphia, res. in TX & served in the Confederate Army during the Civil War. To Baltimore in 1875, broker. Pierce was desc. from Samuel T. Woodward, Sr., b. England & to America c. 1770. Samuel was a capt. in the Continental Army through the Rev. War, after which he settled in Philadelphia. *TR4:838-40*

FAZENBAKER, GEORGE, b. Hesse-Cassel, to America, a Hessian soldier, in the service of King George, to fight the colonists. He became a permanent resident of Allegany Co., MD. He had children Marcus & Godfrey. *6TH:643-44*

FEARHAKE, GEORGE, (FUERHACKE), b. Westphalia, Germany, to America around the close of the Revolutionary War with Colony that came over with John Frederick Amelung as glass workers. Factory in

Urbana District of Frederick Co., MD the first glass works in this country. His son Adolphus b. Frederick Co. 1795. *FR2:827*

FEAST, JOHN, b. Yorkshire, England 3 June 1802; sailed for America 1823 & landed in Philadelphia, after 3 days to Baltimore, where he had a brother Samuel who had come to US in 1817. Both were floriculturalists. John was one of the founders of the MD Horticultural Society in 1830. He married twice: 1st 1831 to Mahala Spencer of Harford Co., 2d to Sarah A. Uppercue, of Baltimore Co. *MDC:583*

FEISER, JACOB, of German parentage, he located in York Co., PA & in 1850 removed to Frederick Co., MD. Later (c. 1869) removed to York Co., PA, where he died. He had: Jacob, Henry, Peter, Sarah, Maria, Louisa, Rebecca, Kate, Ella & Leah. Jacob, s/o Jacob, b. York Co., PA in Oct. 1825; to Frederick Co., MD as a young man & d. on his farm there 29 Jan. 1871. He m. (1) in PA, Matilda Diehl & had David, now res. in Jackson Co., MD [sic] & Mary, res. in Westminster [MD] & m. to the late Judge Shaffer. Jacob m.(2) to Mrs. Phoebe Shank, widow of Frederick. *FR2:1292*

FENWICK, CUTHBERT, one of the founders of the colony of MD, was b. in England c. 1613 & belonged to the Fenwicks of Fenwick Tower, Northumberland. He was in MD before the end of 1634 & came into the colony as a redemptioner. He was a Roman Catholic, was twice married & it is suspected that his 1st wife was of the family of Thomas Cornwallis. His 2d wife was Jane Eltonhead Moryson, widow of Robert Moryson of VA & d/o Richard Eltonhead of Eltonhead, Lancashire, England. Her brother, Hon. William Eltonhead, was a member of the MD privy council. *TR4:862-3*

FERGUSON, JOHN, b. Wallace, Nova Scotia, March 1822. He served in the US navy 1844-1870, when he retired to Woburn, MA, where he d. 1903. His wife was Annette Elizabeth Teare & she res. in MA. Their son, John Berton Ferguson, b. Woburn 8 Jan. 1877; 1909 removed to Hagerstown, MD. He m. in Williamsport, MD, Beulah L. Darby, d/o Frances H. & Rebecca T. (Haines) Darby, both b. MD. *TR3:394-5*

FETTERHOFF, JOHN (M.D.), graduated Breslau University of Germany & migrated to US c. 1834. Married Elizabeth Fahrney, b. PA, d. 1880, aged 49. Son Hiram R. b. in Fetterhoff Church, Franklin Co.,

PA, 1874 to Baltimore until 1886, when he went to CA and back to Baltimore, where he d. 1900. aged 62. *TR3:190*

FEY, HENRY, b. 5 Oct. 1825, Schwartzenbasel, Germany; m. Christina Keartz 1855. Served 6 years in German Army as Lt., discharged at city of Cassel 21 March 1856, and soon after to US, settled in city of Cumberland, MD 1857. Tailor. *TR3:178*

FISHER, GEORGE N., and wife Barbara Hachtel, both b. Bavaria; to America in 1851 & landed in Baltimore, then moved to Fulton Co., PA. George was a wheelwright & d. 15 July 1892, aged 67. Lutheran Church member. Their son George L. with them to America at age 5. He was b. 20 Nov. 1846 & reared in PA. Served in Co. A, 7th MD Infantry during the Civil War. He became a member of the Regular US Army in 1866, Co. A, 2d Regt. of Infantry & was stationed in KY, GA, AL, SC, FL, ID. He later made his home in Hagerstown, MD. On 6 Nov. 1867 he m. Margaret, d/o Michael Hanely. *16TH:842-43*

FISHER, THOMAS, b. Germany, to America as a young man & settled in Adams Co., PA, near what is now Littlestown. He m. Catharine Mitten & they had 8 children. One son, Isaac, a twin, was b. in 1799. Farmer of Frederick Co., MD, where he d. 1875 & is bur. in the Lutheran Cemetery at Emmitsburg, MD. Isaac m. Mary E. Rowe, d/o Daniel of Emmitsburg District. They had 13 children. *FR2:828 & 1617-18*

FLACK, FRANCIS, b. Wurtemberg, Germany, to US as a young man, a stonemason. Settled on farm near Garrett Park. Catholic. Francis m. Elizabeth Sherren, b. in Darmstadt, Germany, to America in girlhood. *6TH:675-76*

FLANAGAN, HUGH, b. Ireland; weaver. Emigrated to US 1822, with his wife, Catharine Oaks & one child, Margaret. He & Catharine m. in Dundalk, Ireland 14 Dec. 1817. He d. 27 Feb. 1830, was survived by his wife, who d. 25 Ja. 1882. They had settled in Emmitsburg District, Frederick Co., MD. Members of the Roman Catholic Church. Children: Margaret, m. James Hovis; James d. Lewistown District in 1896; Mary Ann, d. 1907, never mar.; & John F., b. 8 July 1829, d. 10 Aug. 1880. *FR2:1384-5*

FLECK, GEORGE, b. Germany 1748, settled in Sinking Valley, Blair Co., PA, where he d. 10 June 1836. He paid taxes in Philadelphia (1769,

1774 & 1779) & served as private in Capt. George Homey's Co., Northern District of the City Guards, Philadelphia Militia in Rev. War. In 1773 he m. Mollie Weeks & had: George b. 1774; Conrad b. 1780, m. Mary Moore; Margaret b. 1782, m. John Fleck; Jacob b. 1783, m. Nellie Mattay; Catherine b. 1785, m. Daniel Crissman; Elizabeth b. 1787, m. Abram Crissman; Henry b. 1791, Catherine Ramey; David b. 1793, m. Mary Ramey & Mary b. 1797, m. Peter Burket. The son of David Fleck & Mary Ramey was Gabriel (1820-1891) who m. Rebecca Stoner (1826-1902) & had Cyrus Lemuel Fleck who in 1887 m. Annie Catherine Leas of Granite Hill, Adams Co., PA, d/o John Bender Leas & Mary Ann Walter. Cyrus b. in Sinking Valley & res. in Riegelsville (Bucks Co.), PA where he was pastor of St. Peter's Lutheran Church 1887-1891. Their son, Rev. John Gabriel Fleck, b. in Riegelsville, Bucks Co., PA 3 Oct. 1891, pastor of St. John's Evangelical Lutheran church in Baltimore, MD. He served in WWI. *TR4:562-66*

FLOOK, ---, five brothers of French Hugenot origin, sailed from Bristol, England & landed in Philadelphia, PA c. 1760. Three of the brothers settled in MD & two in PA. One of the former, Henry, later removed to VA, where he d. 1840, nearly 100 years of age. Another brother who had first settled in Lancaster, PA, went to Oneida & located near Smith's Falls, in province of Ontario, Canada, whence his descs. removed to IA & IN. The ancestor of the MD branch was Jacob Flook. He had a son, also Jacob, who m. Esther ---, by whom he had 4 sons & 3 daus.: Percy (Perry), Daniel, Jacob, Hanson, Elizabeth, Eveline & Catharine. *FR2:1032-3*

FOARD, ---, c. 1680 to America & obtained from Lord Baltimore a grant to a tract of land adj. the property of the Roman Catholic Church on Sassafras Neck. The Foards are one of the oldest & largest famlies on Bohemia Manor. Before 1741 Richard Foad m. Mary, d/o Richard Boulding of Back Creek Neck. *H/C:502-3*

FOLEY, ---, progenitor of US family, from Ireland to US & settled in WV, where he spent the remainder of his life. He was a veteran of the Civil War on the Confederate side. His son, John J. Foley, b. Frankfort, near Piedmont, WV. Roman Catholic. John had 5 surviving children; one was a twin, Edgar M. Foley, dentist of Baltimore City. *TR3:547-8*

FOOTER, THOMAS, b. England 8 March 1847, s/o James & Mary (Sparks) Footer. James was a paper manufacturer. Thomas to America

& settled in Cumberland, MD with his family. He is owner of Footer Dye Works, a dying & cleaning establishment. His wife was Eliza Booth & they m. 17 March 1866 & had 9 children, 5 now living: Henry, Joseph W., Edmund B. (all associated with his business); a dau. m. C. H. Gloss & another dau. now Mrs. Spitzna. *TR3:607-8*

FORD, JAMES R., from Scotland to Baltimore & had son Elias Ford who had son John Thompson Ford, b. Baltimore 16 April 1829, who m. Edith Branch Andrews of Hanover Co., VA. John T. Ford was manager of the Baltimore Ford's Theatre, in 1870 purchased the Holliday Street Theatre, which he sold in 1877. In 1871 opened the present Ford's Opera House. Owner of 3 theaters in Washington, DC, including the one in which President Lincoln was shot. *TR4:668-70*

FORSYTHE, THOMAS & JAMES, from Scotland in 1779. James went west & Thomas settled near Sykesville (now Howard Co.). He m. (1) Elizabeth Hasgood of Devonshire, England by whom he had son Henry, b. 1804. He m. (2) Mary Warfield, d/o John & Mary Chaney Warfield & (3) Amelia Gaither. *AAH:486*

FORSYTHE, WILLIAM, from Scotland to America, settled Baltimore; m. Cornelia Bryden. William d. 1894, aged 47; Cornelia d. 1922, aged 68. *TR3:71*

FOSS, JOHN N., b. 16 Jan. 1838 at Wesselburen, Germany, son of John N. Foss. His father sent him to America with friends. John N. resided for a time in NY, in 1851 to Baltimore; butcher/meat packing house of Foss & Homer. In 1859 he m. Amelia, d/o George Vieweg of Baltimore; she d. 1863 & in 1864 he m. (2) Amelia, d/o Volantine Menger of Baltimore. *MDC:188*

FOX, ---, b. in Germany, to America in early manhood, an early settler of PA, His son George Fox, removed to Frederick Co., MD where he bought land in Hauvers District & named his place "Foxes Ranges," and afterward Foxville. George's son, George P., b. near Foxville, MD; m. Sophia, d/o John & Susan Bussard. Their son, Thomas C. Fox, b. on family farm near Foxville 19 July 1841. *FR2:899*

FOX, E. A. C., b. Westphalia, Germany in 1820. In 1844 to America & located near Hartsgrove, near the Washington Co. line, in Frederick Co., MD. In 1857 he established a tinware & stove store in Frederick City, now run by his son. He was member of the Lutheran Church & his first wife was Catherine Gladhill, of Frederick. Their children: Lewis, tinner of Baltimore; E. August, coppersmith of Washington, DC; Ida, dec'd., m. William Bartholow; Wilhelmina, m. Charles Myers of Washington, DC & Lizzie, d. unm. Mr. Fox m. 2d Caroline M. Babel, b. Bavaria, Germany. They had: H. K. C. & Calvin O. C. Fox. *FR2:1358*

FRANCE, JOSEPH, b. 5 Sept. 1762, s/o Joseph France, b. St. Ives, Kimbolton, England. To Baltimore at an early age. He m. there 22 Aug. 1793, to Mary Harding, who was b. Baltimore 15 April 1778 & d. 9 Sept. 1834. Joseph d. 25 Oct. 1854, aged 92, at the home of his son, Richard France, in Baltimore. Children of Joseph & Mary: George, b. 1 Dec. 1794; John, b. 14 April 1797; James, b. 20 April 1799; Lewis, b. 1 March 1802 & Richard, b. 18 Sept. 1805. Lewis France d. 26 March 1848, leaving a son, Lewis, who settled in Denver, CO; jurist & writer. James, 2d s/o Joseph, merchant of Baltimore & m. Margarita Boyle, d/o Capt. Thomas of Baltimore who had been b. in Marblehead, MA 29 June 1776 & d. at sea 13 Oct. 1825. *TR3:677-8*

FRANK, HENRY, b. Bavaria, to America from Germany c. 1830, settled in Baltimore, where he d. 1880 [1879], aged 71. Member of Baltimore Hebrew congregation. His wife Sarah Truehart to Baltimore as a young girl from Bavaria. She d. 1897, aged 84. They had 7 children, including Moses Frank, b. 20 July 1844, m. Isabella Cohen, d/o Moses & Mina (Preiss) Cohen. Other children Solomon, res. of Baltimore now aged 84; Henrietta, m. Jacob Miller of Baltimore; Louis H, m. Caroline Brafman; & Bertha, wife of the late Simon Rosenberg. Dec'd. children: Caroline, m. Charles Adler & Frances, m. Ansel Mandelbaum. *TR3:367, 713-14*

FRAZEE, ELISHA, b. France, settled in NY City during the Rev. War. He later to MD & purchased land near Selbysport, MD. *6TH:552-53*

FREELAND, JOHN, & wife Mary to US from Scotland & settled in Baltimore, where they died. Son John Jr., b. in Baltimore, spent much of his life in WV, m. Patty McCann who d. aged 78. *6TH:188*

FREEMAN, CELIA, b. London, England, d/o Joseph, m. 7 Nov. 1897, Dr. Moses M. Savage, in Baltimore. Jewish. *TR3:345*

FRICKER, JOHN, migrated from England to America while quite young & settled in Baltimore in 1812; molder. He m. a Miss Stroud, also

b. England, & their son, John A. Fricker, b. Baltimore 24 May 1878; m. Louisa B. Magers, d/o Elias (b. PA) & --- (Davis) Magers (of an old Baltimore family). *TR3:976-9*

FRIEDMANN, MENKA, b. 21 Dec. 1823 in Bavaria, Germany. To US in 1854, settled in Baltimore, wholesale clothier. Feb. 1856 he m. Caroline, d/o Benjamin Prager of Bavaria, Germany. *MDC:713-14*

FRIEND, JOHN (DR.), b. France, settled NJ c. 1725 & m. a Miss Levis & subsequently moved to MD, near Swan Pond, not far from Cumberland. They later moved to Turkey Foot (now Confluence), PA. Son Gabriel, b. PA, one of the first settlers of Garrett Co., MD. The town of Friendsville named in his honor. *6TH:548-49*

FRIEZ, JULIEN P., b. at Grandvillars, near Belfort, France 16 Aug. 1851 & d. at his home in Baltimore 9 March 1916. He was s/o Joseph Friez and Marguerite (Roy), d/o Francis Roy of household of Louis XVI of France. Julien to US at an early age, located in NY state, at age 16 to Ottawa, IL, thence to Philadelpia; manufacturer of telegraph instruments. To Baltimore; founder of Westen Electric Co. He m. Cordelia Schimff of Philadelphia. *GME:332*

FRIEZE, SIMNI, from Germany to MD & m. a Miss Reese. Descendant John Thompson Freize resided in Havre de Grace, MD. *MDC:301*

FULTON, GEORGE, from the banks of the River Tweed (Scotland) to Philadelphia; m. Ann Ware of DE, and ward of Benjamin Chew. George & Ann both d. 1826, left 5 sons, including Charles Carroll Fulton, editor *Baltimore-American* 1853-1883. *GME:2-3.*

FULTON, WILLIAM (REV.), b. Glasgow, Scotland, to US in early youth & settled on Eastern Shore of MD after the Civil War. Family resided Snow Hill, MD in 1861. Episcopal clergyman, rector of St. Peter's Church of Salisbury at his death, 6 Dec. 1877. William m. Nancy Organ who was b. in Cable, OH. Their dau. Margaret m. 13 April 1893, Marion V. Brewington of Salisbury, MD. *TR2:24, TR4:511-12*

ADDESS, ---, from Dumfries, Scotland in the 18th century & settled in Stafford Co., VA. His son Alexander m. Katie, d/o Joshua & Catharine Kendal, also of VA. He d. 1825. His grandson, Alexander Geddess, b. in Stafford Co. 29 Sept. 1799, came to Baltimore at age of 12 & became apprenticed to Capt. Towson in stonecutting business. He resided in Baltimore Co., where he d. 9 April 1873. Alexander was m. Nov. 1821 to Mary A., d/o John Westford, b. London, England, & settled in MD in latter part of last century. *MDC:704*

GAITHER, JOHN, came in the ship *Assurance* from England to VA in 1635. He was a member of the Non-Conformist Church. By 1662 he was a landowner in Anne Arundel Co., MD. His wife was Ruth Morley & she m. after his decease, Francis Hardesty. *AAH:107-8*

GALL, WILLIAM, b. Germany, to America & settled in Thurmont, Frederick Co., MD, wheere he died. His children: William of Lewisburg, KS; Edward, went to OH; Eva, m. Nicholas Engle; John; & Henry. Henry was b. Germany, to America as a child. Tanner, employed at the old John Rouzer tannery at Thurmont. Henry d. aged 72. He m. Catharine S. Martz & left a son, Charles M. Gall. Member of St. John's Lutheran Church of Thurmont. *FR2:1545*

GALVIN, WILLIAM, b. Co. Galway, Ireland, to US as young man, settled in Baltimore 1857. Veteran of Civil War; m. Mary Leleand, b. Co. Roscommon, Ireland, who came to America alone c. 1867, settling in Baltimore. Roman Catholic. *TR3:305*

GANS, WILLIAM, b. Germany, m. Rebecca DeWolff of Baltimore & of Holland ancestry. Rebecca's great-grandfather, Levi Benjamin, was among the first American settiers from Amsterdam, Holland. William & Rebecca's dau., Henrietta, b. in Baltimore 4 Dec. 1885, spent her childhood in Richmond, VA. On 24 Jan. 1906 she m., in Baltimore, Solomon Juhn Solmson, who is now dec'd. *TR3:568*

GANTT, THOMAS, of "Myrtle Range," on the Patuxent River near White Landing, Prince George's Co., MD. He was bapt. at Staffordshire, England in 1615, s/o Roger Gantt of Rowley Regis, England & Ann Cobham his wife, d/o William of Rowley, County Stafford and wife Alice Mainwaring; settled early in MD. Thomas the immigrant m. Edith [Mary?] Graham of Scotland and left one son, Edward, who m. Anne

Baker. Edward & Anne had son Thomas who m. in 1707, Priscilla Brooke, d/o Hon. Col. Thomas Brooke & 2d wife Barbara Dent. [This data disagrees with that found below.] *TR4:322, 575-8*

GANTT, THOMAS, to Province of MD 1654; was high sheriff of Calvert Co. 1673, m. Anne Greenfield, d/o Col. Thomas Greenfield of Prince George's Co., MD, who immigrated in 1666. Son Thomas m. Priscilla Brooke, d/o Col. Thomas Brooke (1660-1750) & wife Barbara Dent, d/o Thomas Dent, Gentleman who immigrated to MD in 1662 with his wife Rebecca Wilkinson, d/o Rev. William Wilkinson of St. Mary's Co. *TR4:344*

GARRETT, AMOS, English merchant, was mayor of Annapolis in 1708; d. 8 March 1727, aged 56, a bachelor. He was a s/o James & Sarah Garrett, late of St. Olive Street, Southwork, England. *AAH:121-3 & 218*

GARRETT, JOHN, b. North of Ireland. He m. Margaret MacMechen, b. in Scotland. John, taken ill during the voyage to America, d. before land was reached. His widow and their children continued and settled in Cumberland Co., PA; in 1798 she removed to Washington Co., PA. Robert, s/o John and Margaret, b. Lisburn, Co. Down, Ireland, 2 May 1783, d. 4 Feb. 1857. To American at age 7. Shortly after 1800 he moved to Baltimore, MD, to Middletown, Washington Co., PA & returned to Baltimore c. 1820. Banker & railroad financier. Robert m. 19 May 1817 Elizabeth d/o Henry Stouffer; b. 18 Sept. 1791, d. 17 July 1877. Son John Work Garrett was President of B&O Railroad. *GME:359*

GARRETT, MICHAEL, b. Ireland, to America in 1846 & settled in Baltimore. He later removed to Allegany Co., MD where he d. aged 85. He m. Bridget McGough, who d. in 1891, aged 78. *6TH:582-83*

GARROTT FAMILY,, of Scotch-Irish descent. Many years ago several brothers of that name came from one of the lower counties of MD in the neighborhood of Knoxville, Frederick Co., MD. *FR2:1576-7*

GARY, JOHN, farmer of Lancashire, England, with his brother James, emigrated to America 1712 & settled in NH; James settled MA. James Sullivan Gary, grandson of John, s/o --- Gary & Mary Witherell, m. Pamelia, d/o Ebenezer Forrest, of Foxboro, MA. James Sullivan resided in MA, CT & RI; in 1838 removed with his family to Prince George Co., MD. *MDC:502-03*

GASSAWAY, NICHOLAS, Englishman, in 1689 named by the assembly of MD one of the committee to regulate the affairs of the province. His son John was an officer in the Revolution & member of the MD regiment. *6TH:639-41*

GASSAWAY, NICHOLAS (MAJOR), to MD from England in 1649; deputy governor for Lord Baltimore. *GME:217*

GAULT, SAMUEL, b. in a town of the Frith-of-Forth, North of Scotland 1680. He removed to Wales where he m. Elsie Carlton. They returned to Scotland & later removed to Londonderry, Ireland & in 1721 to America, settled in Chester, now Hooksett, NH, on what was known as the "Londonderry Grant." His children Andrew, Samuel & Jane b. Scotland & son Patrick b. Ireland. Andrew located in Pembroke, NH & m. Mollie Ayer of Londonderry, NH, by whom he had a son Matthew, b. Pembroke in 1747. Matthew m. Elizabeth Buntin, served in the Rev. War. Matthew & Elizabeth had a son Andrew b. 1781 who m. Sallie Knox & had son Matthew b. Bow, NH 24 Aug. 1819. This son Matthew worked in Baltimore & Washington. He m. Laura Cordelia Deale, d/o the late William G. of Washington, DC. Methodist Episcopal. Matthew's brother Cyrus also resided in Baltimore. Granite workers. *MDC:404-05*

GAVER, HENRY, b. in Holland, emigrated to America in early manhood & landed at Baltimore. He settled near what is now Ellerton, MD, one of the earliest settlers of the Middletown Valley. He m. in MD & had one son, John Gaver who married & left 2 sons: Daniel & George. George m. Mary Raymor & d. aged 44 & is bur. at Church Hill. Their son John was b. near Ellerton 22 Jan. 1817. *FR2:1605-6*

GAVER, JOHN T., b. & raised in Holland; to America in early manhood. He landed at Baltimore, settled near what is now Ellerton, MD, one of the earliest settlers in the Middletown Valley (Frederick Co.). He m. in MD & had one son, John. *FR2:826*

GAYLORD, AARON, to America 1629; desc. of William Gaillaird of Lincolnshire, England. His dau. Lorena m. Lynde Phelps & their dau. Maria Phelps m. Chaucey Brooks, of a Baltimore family. *TR4:76*

GEDDES, JAMES, b. Aberdeen, Scotland, to Baltimore 1816; copper-smith. He m. --- Robinson of Baltimore, d/o Samuel. James d. 1837. Son James W., b. 10 Jan. 1824, Baltimore, m. 1850 Sarah Ann, d/o John Hulse of Baltimore, originally of England. *MDC:68*

GEORGE, A. FREDERICK, b. Staffordshire, England 27 Jan. 1856, s/o Rev. William E. & Jane E. George. Father to US in 1859 & settled in Barton, Allegany Co., MD. Rev. William served in Co. A, 3d Regt., Potomac Home Brigade during the Civil War. In 1870 to western part of Allegany (now Garrett) Co., MD, farmer. A. Frederick George was aged 3 when to America with family. In 1878 m. Mary Elizabeth Brady. *6TH:811-12*

GEORGE, ANTHONY, b. Cuba, to US in early manhood & settled in Philadelphia, PA. Sea Captain; Catholic. His son Anthony, Jr., b. Philadelphia, manufacturer of block tin metal cups & saucers, he d. in Cecil Co., MD aged 76 in 1892. *H/C:351*

GERARD, RICHARD, one of the gentlemen who accompanied Lord Calvert on his expedition to MD on the *Ark & the Dove* in 1633/4. He was the s/o Sir Thomas Gerard of St. Clement's, England, who was granted a manor of 14,000 acres in MD in 1634. Sir Thomas presented the manor & island of St. Clement's to his dau. Elizabeth, who in 1669 m. Chief Justice Nehemiah Blakistone. *TR4:292*

GESEY, ELIAS, b. Switzerland, to US & m. a Miss Stimmel who d. 1889. They had: Theodore; Sarah m. Daniel Stauffer & d. 1908; Martha m. Jacob Perry of Walkersville & Catherine, m. a Mr. Conley of Chicago. *FR2:1524-5*

GETTEMULLER, HERMAN H., from Germany to America with family in 1856, merchant. One son was Henry J. Gettemuller, a child when the family came to Baltimore, merchant of Old Town. *TR3:272*

GETTY, JOHN, emigrated from Ireland in 1790 & settled near Cresaptown, Alleghany Co., MD, one of the 1st settlers of that part of MD. *MDC:256*

GETTY, ROBERT, b. Ireland, to US at age 8 years & was educated at Philadelphia. He engaged in mercantile business with cousin Amber

Ross. He d. 1843, aged 64. Presbyterian. He m. Margaret d/o John Wilmot, of Annapolis. She d. in Georgetown, aged 86. *6TH:764-65*

GETZENDANNER (KITCHADANNER), CHRISTIAN, b. Switzerland & to America & settled at what is now Frederick Co., MD 1729. Christian took up res. in Schiefferstadt, Germany, where in 1723 he m. Ann Barbara Brunner. 1729 with the Brunner family to America, landing in Philadelphia. They settled near the present city of Frederick, MD. Christian d. 1766, bequeathing the land to his son Adam. Adam d. in 1783 & the land was divided among his sons John, Christian & Jacob. John, another son of Christian the immigrant, had a son Jonathan, a farmer. *FR2:822, 1456; 6TH:338-9*

GIESKE, GUSTAVE, b. Oldenburg, Germany 1844. Settled in Baltimore & in 1858 employed in leaf tobacco business on commission basis, in partnership with the late Edward Neimann. Lutheran. He d. 14 April 1916, aged 72. His wife was Auguste Driver, who now res. in Catonsville, where their son, Walter M., was b. 9 Jan. 1883. *TR3:655-6*

GIFFORD, JOSEPH, and his son James, both b. England, Joseph near Portsmouth, to US & settled in Philadelphia Co., PA. Later removed to Bucks Co., PA. Joseph was a stock farmer, James was a blacksmith. James m. in England, Ruth Edmonds. In 1856 they removed to Cecil Co., MD near Principio, where James d. 1882, aged 84. *H/C:146, 241*

GILBERT, ---, b. England & his son was b. in Harford Co., MD., a hero of the Revolutionary War. Micah, of the 3d generation of Gilberts in America, was b. near Avondale & his son, Michael Gilbert, was also born there. Michael's son, Robert J. Gilbert, m. 23 May 1839 , his cousin, Elizabeth Gilbert. Robert d. 17 Feb. 1879. *H/C:530*

GILBERT, HENRY, b. in Germany; he & two brothers to US & settled in MD. He m. Miss Runkles, a sister of Samuel Runkles of Frederick Co. & settled in the Woodsboro District of that county. Their children: Margaret, m. John Doty; Lizzie, m. Jacob Purdum; John, m. Rachel Hood & settled near Zanesville OH. Henry m. 2d Mary (Polly) Long, an aunt of Mrs. John H. Harn, & had only one child, George Henry Gilbert, b. 7 Feb. 17 1853. *FR2:1162*

GILES, WALTER, b. Plymouth, England 5 Feb. 1800. In 1830 to NY & then to Canada. There he m. Alice Ann Wells, d/o Levi, of Halifax,

Nova Scotia. They res. for a time in Boston, then Baltimore, where their son E. Walter Giles was b. 2 Oct. 1844. *TR4:245*

GILL, ---, s/o John of Yorkshire, England, to VA & m. in Alexandria & a few years later settled in Baltimore, where he d. at the advanced age of 91 years. His son George M. Gill b. 15 Feb. 1803 in Baltimore. *MDC:290-91*

GILL, STEPHEN, immigrated from Yorkshire Co., England with his 4 brothers & settled c. 1805 in Baltimore Co., MD, in the section now known as Garrison Forest, near old St. Thomas Episcopal Church. His wife was Elizabeth Hubbard & they had 4 children. Their eldest son, John, m. Mary Rogers, a sister of Col. Nicholas Rogers who served in the Revolutionary War. One of their sons, Nicholas, m. his cousin Elizabeth Gill. *TR3:873-4*

GILLIS, ALEXANDER F., b. at Irish Cove, Nova Scotia, was physician of NY City & d. aged 68 on 28 Feb. 1915. He was s/o Roderick Gillis & of Scotch ancesty. Alexander's wife was Anna A. Boyle, d/o Francis W. of New Milford, PA. They had 3 sons & 3 daus. Anna survives Alexander & now res in Baltimore, aged 68. Their son, Dr. Alexander James Gillis, b. Carbondale, Lackawanna Co., PA 13 Oct. 1888, is physician of Baltimore. *TR3:781-2*

GILMOR, ROBERT, English, to America late 1700's, merchant; settled MD. *TR3:67.*

GILPIN, JOSEPH, b. Dorchester, Oxfordshire, England 1664; to America & settled at Chester Co., PA [Philadelphia/Birmingham, Delaware Co., PA, 1695] 1696. Quaker. He had a son Joseph & descs. resided Parkersburg WV, Montgomery Co. MD, Frederick City MD & Lancaster Co. PA. Joseph the immigrant's eldest son Samuel, progenitor of Cecil Co., MD branch of the family, b. in England in 1694, settled at Gilpin's Rocks, on the Great North East. His eldest son Joseph removed from Gilpin's Falls before 1761 & settled on what is now known as "Gilpin Home Farm," on the Big Elk, north of Elkton, MD. Joseph m. Eliza Reed & had: John, Hannah, Elizabeth, Joseph, Mary & Rachel. Joseph d. 1790, aged 63 years. Bernard Gilpin, a desc. of the immigrant Joseph, m. Letitia (Canby) to came to MD c. 1800 from Chad's Ford, PA. *FR2:823, MDC:262, C:511-13*

GINGELL, GEORGE, b. England, settled in MD as a young man, employed in the Newport Mills. His grandson, James Madison Gingell, s/o Joseph & Mary (Johnson) Gingell, b. village of Bethesda, MD 28 Feb. 1819. *6TH:733*

GIST, CHRISTOPHER, m. Edith Cromwell, niece of Oliver Cromwell in England, to MD c. 1650. Settled in Baltimore Co. Christopher d. 1691; wife died 3 years later. Their son, Richard, surveyor for the western shore of MD & assisted in the laying out of Baltimore Town in 1736. *FRI:216, TR4:853-4*

GITTINGS, THOMAS, to MD c. 1684 & in 1720 obtained patents for a tract of land in Long Green Valley, Baltimore County, Gittings's Choice. *MDC:553-54*

GLEN, ALEXANDER LINDSEY, b. 1610 near Inverness, Scotland, to Holland & then to New Netherlands before 1643, d. Schenectady, NY. Grandson Jacob Alexander Glen, b. Schenectary, NY 1686, removed to Kent Co., MD and d. there; m. Jane Beedle, widow, 7 June 1762. *TR4:74*

GLIDDEN, CHARLES, of ancient family that went from France to England in 1066, emigrated from England to America in 1660 & settled in Boston, later moving to Portsmouth, NH. Descs. founded the town of Newcastle, ME. Desc. Joseph Glidden had a son Joseph b. 1757, who had son Joseph (III) b. 1791. Joseph's (III) son was William Pierce Harrington Glidden, b. 7 Aug. 1830 & d. c. 1910. His only son, Edward Hughes Glidden m. Pauline Boucher of Cleveland, OH & had a son Edward Jr., b. Baltimore, MD 27 March 1901. *TR4:693-4*

GLUCK, HENRY, of Heilbach, Hesse, Germany, with wife Anna Margaret Manns of the same place, m. in America. Henry sailed on the *Julius*, landed at Baltimore 27 Nov. 1855. He settled at Chambersburg, PA, bought farm near Markes, PA. His wife d. 26 June 1898. He now resides at Shippensburg, PA. Their son, Aaron Manns Gluck, Reformed Church minister at Emmitsburg, MD (1903). *FR2:825*

GNAGY, CHRISTIAN, & wife Elizabeth, from Switzerland c. 1750 to Somerset Co., PA. Later moved to Harrison Co., OH, where he d. 1812. Son Christian b. in PA, resided in Somerset Co. He m. in 1813, Barbara Blocher & he d. 1880, aged 90 years. His son Emanuel Gnagy, b. PA, removed to Grantsville (then in Allegany Co., MD), 1846. Farmer, member of Dunkard church & d. in 1890, aged 70. *6TH:634-35*

GOLDBACH, OTTO, b. Bavaria 1846, at age 22 to US, settled in Baltimore, where he d. 1918. He m. Barbara Steinmetz, b. Bamberg, Bavaria; d. 1904, aged 55. *TR3:351*

GOLDSBOROUGH, NICHOLAS, b. Malcolm [Melcorn] Regis, near Weymouth, England in 1640/41 [1636]. Immmigrated to Barbadoes 1669, then New England and finally settled Kent Island in Chesapeake Bay (Queen Anne Co.) in 1670. Later removed to Talbot Co., MD. His date of death is given in different sources as 1670 & 1672. His wife was Margaret Howes of Newberry, Berks Co., England; they m. 1659. She was only d/o Abraham Howes (s/o William of Newburg, Berks Co., England). Their children: Robert, Nicholas & Judith. Margaret m. (2) George Robbins of Talbot Co. Their son Robert, b. Dec. 1660 & m. 2 Sept. 1679, Elizabeth Greenbury, dau. of an Indian chief. He [Robert] came into MD in 1678 & d. 25 Dec. 1746. Other children of Nicholas were: Nicholas who d. 1705 & Judith. Desc. Charles Goldsborough, b. at Hunting Creek, Dorchester Co., MD 15 July 1765 [1760?], was the 18th Governor of MD. Another desc. Dr. Robert Goldsborough m. Eleanor Dall Lux, a niece of Gov. Charles Ridgely of Hampden in Towson, MD. Robert had res. many years in Centerville, MD. Another desc., Robert Goldsborough, Rev. patriot, m. Mary Emerson Trippe & had Robert Henry, US senator, b. at Myrtle Grove, near Easton, Talbot Co., MD 4 Jan. 1779. *AAH:260; 6TH:591-3; MDC:255; TR4:24, 51, 324-5, 795-8; FR2:1241-2*

GOLDSBOROUGH, ROBERT, b. Blandford, Co. of Dorchester, England in 1660 & to America in 1678, settling on tract "Goldsborough's Neck," near Easton, known as "Ashby." *MDC:476*

GOLDSBOROUGH, ROBERT, an Englishman who came to America in 1670, lawyer. *MDC:650-51*

GOLDSTROM, BERNHARDT, of German birth, m. Sarah Rosenstein. Bernhardt immigrated to the US & became a jeweler in Baltimore, MD, where his widow Sarah still resides. They had 4 children: Isidor, b. 23 Dec. 1874, m. in 1913, Dora Davis; Stella, m. Simon Schwartz of NY City; Marion, m. Max Kohn, banker of Baltimore; & Helen, m. --- Swartz of Mt. Vernon, NY. *TR3:918-19*

GORDON, CHARLES, to American colonies from Carrich Fergus, Co. Antrim, Ireland in early 18th century. He m. a Miss McKenzie from Scotland & d. 1740. His son David d. 1783 & was the father of 2 sons who served in the Rev. Peter served the state of NJ & Archibald saw active service in the artillery at the battle of Brandywine. 1779 Archibald Gordon m. Psyche Van Sicklen; he d. 1829 & is bur. in Presbyterian churchyard in Glasgow, New Castle Co., DE. His son Archibald res. in Monmouth, NJ but d. in MD on Miller's Island. Archibald m. Sarah Hart, d/o Joseph & Betsy (Porter) Hart, whose people owned Miller's & Hart's Islands in Chesapeake Bay. *TR4:152-5*

GORMAN, JOHN, to America from Ireland c. 1800 & settled in Harrisburg, PA & later removed to Baltimore. *MDC:623*

GORSUCH, CHARLES, s/o Rev. John Gorsuch, D.D. & wife, Anne Lovelace, both of kingdom of England. Desc. Edward Gorsuch b. 17 April 1795 & d. in Christiana, Lancaster Co., PA 11 Sept. 1851, while pursuing runaway slaves. *TR4:337*

GORTER, GOSSE ONNO, b. in City of Amsterdam, Holland, 8 Feb. 1818. He visited America on several occasions & in 1849 he settled in Baltimore. He d. in Baltimore 20 Feb. 1879. 12 Aug. 1847 he m. Mary Ann Polk, d/o the late Col. James Polk of Baltimore. She was b. in Princess Anne, Somerset Co. MD. Their son, James P. Gorter, b. 27 Aug. 1858 in Baltimore. *MDC:205-06, TR3:184*

GOUGH, HARRY, b. England, to America & settled at South Hampton, near Bel Air. Dau. Hannah E. m. Preston McComas 10 Oct. 1809. Son Harry D. Gough served in the MD Legislature. *MDC:252-53*

GOUGH, WILLIAM, b. England, to America 1673 & settled in Charles Co., MD. Desc. Stephen Gough m. Clare Baldwin & had son James who m. Elizabeth --- (his will probated 1700). Their children & desc. res. in Leonardtown, MD. "It is stated in *Genealogical Gleanings in England* that Elizabeth, widow of William Gough, married Lawrence Washington, great-great-great-grandfather of George Washington, in 1564, and the name Thomas Washington is found in several generations of the Gough family, which was originally established in St. Marys County, Maryland." *TR4:221-2, 533-4, 555-6*

GOULD, ALEXANDER, b. Balcorn, Parish of Logey, Co. Clackmannanshire, Edinburgh, Scotland, 1780, s/o John & Ellen (Drysdale) Gould. Ellen was d/o Alexander Drysdale. Family to America & settled in Baltimore, MD, 1784, where he purchased land from John Moale near Spring Gardens. John was a butcher & when he died Alexander took over his business. Alexander d. 16 April 1859 & left 4 sons & 3 daus. out of the 14 children born to him. *MDC:604-05*

GRABILL, JOHN, b. Germany, to US & settled on Beaver Dam, Frederick Co., MD. His son, also John, m. Hannah Myers & had a son, Abraham. *FR2:1258-9*

GRAFF, ---, from Germany to America early in life & settled in Lancaster Co., PA & later to Frederick Co., MD, where he bought a farm near Ceresville. His son William was b. in Frederick Co. in 1805. He res. in the Urbana District of the county, 2 miles east of Buckeystown. William m. Anna, d/o Matthew Brown, retired editor of Baltimore who removed to Frederick Co. Children of William & Anna: Charles B., dec'd.; Elizabeth E. of Buckeystown; Sophia T., widow of the late Rev. Thomas Scott Bacon, dec'd., of Buckeystown; and John P. Members of Episcopal Church in Urbana. William d. Feb. 1880 & is bur. in Mt. Olivet Cemetery in Frederick. Anna d. 1887, lies by his side. *FR2:1411-13*

GRAFTON, NATHAN, England to America, settled in MD. Son Martin b. Harford Co., served in War of 1812; Martin's son Basil b. near Forest Hill, Harford Co., 16 Sept. 1832. Baptists. *H/C:277*

GRANT, WILLIAM, of Scotland, to Prince George's Co., MD during the Revolutionary period. He here m. Isabella Grant, also of Scotland, who lost her parents on their passage to America. Isabella had been accompanied by her brother William & sister Rachel. Children of William & Isabella: John; Robert & Daniel, both single & James who m. Elizabeth Madden. *AAH:475*

GREASLEY, JACOB F., b. 7 March 1814, in Notingen, Baden, Germany, son of Philip H., a farmer, and Christana, dau. of George A. Daub. Jacob emigrated to America & arrived in NY, from which place he removed to Baltimore, where he apprenticed himself to butcher Louis Weiss. Jacob m. 5 Jan. 1837, Louisa Lenox, d/o Richard & Elizabeth.

Member of Otterbein Church of United Brethren in Christ, Baltimore. *MDC:147*

GREEN, JAMES E., b. Ireland, of English parentage, his father being George Green. He was a first cousin to Sir Robert Ball, royal astronomer of Ireland. James brought his wife & son to Americca, settling first at Norrisville, PA & in 1876 removed to Baltimore Co., MD. James m. Margaret Vida Stanley Lane, d/o George & Vida Lane of Clommel, Ireland who was b. 29 Aug. 1849. Their son, James E. Jr., b. Clommel, County Tipperary, Ireland 22 Nov. 1871. James Sr. d. at Baltimore Co. Nov. 1913, aged 74. Member of Trinity Church in Towson, MD. *TR3:642-3*

GREENBERRY, NICHOLAS (COL.), b. England 1627, d. MD 1697, commissioner for Anne Arundel Co. 1683 & other political appointments. Arrived with wife Anne & children Charles & Katherine & 3 servants in the ship *Constant* in 1674, settled in Anne Arundel Co., MD, a large landholder. Ann d. 1698. Both bur. at Greenberry Point Farm, on the north side of the Severn River, opposite Annapolis. Their son Charles m. a d/o Thomas Stimpson & Rachel Clark & had a dau. Ruth wno m. --- Williams. *AAH:162, TR4:355*

GREENE, THOMAS, proprietary Governor of MD 1647-48; b. England, to MD in 1634; d. in MD. *TR4:33-4*

GREENFIELD, THOMAS (SIR), early settler of southern MD from England. Desc. Rev. Nathan Greenfield, minister of the Methodist Episcopal church m. Miss --- Hatton & had Caleb Greenfield of Greenwood, Baltimore Co., who m. Anne Brooke Dilworth. Their dau., Sarah Marie, b. Baltimore Co. & d. Baltimore City 24 May 1899, m. Charles Ridgely Richardson, physician of Baltimore who served in the War of 1812. His first wife was Julianna Smith. *TR4:679-81*

GREENWOOD, DOROTHY, b. Kalgoorlie, Western Australia, m. Clarence J. Holloway & their only son, Jack, b. in Atlantic Highlands, NJ 6 Aug. 1900. The Holloway family is English & was in America before the Revolutionary War. Clarence's parents were John Quincy Adams Holloway & Susanna (McKew). Clarence was raised in Baltimore. *TR3:889-90*

GRIER, JAMES, s/o John, to US from Ireland & settled in Chester Co., PA, farmer & potter of near Oxford. He d. in Chester Co. aged 82 years. He was twice married, his first wife Elizabeth Patterson, she d. 4 March 1817. His 2d wife was Martha Hindman. Son of his first marriage, James A. Grier, b. Chester Co., PA, settled near Towson in Baltimore Co., MD & later removed to Washington, D.C., & still later retired to Harford Co., MD. His wife was Mary Jane Thomas, of Harford Co. *H/C:431-2*

GRIFFISS, EDWARD, b. Wales, to US & settled in Baltimore. His son was Thomas J. Griffiss, b. Baltimore, who m. Sophia Anna Von Hitzel. Sophia's father was a court physician & surgeon of Germany & on her father's death in 1837 she & her mother came to America & settled in Baltimore. Living children of Thomas & Sophia Griffiss: Blanche, Mrs. Alfred W. Jacobsen & Warren. Warren was b. Baltimore, 18 May 1867. *TR3:746-9*

GRIFFITH, THOMAS, ENOCH MORGAN, MARY JOHNS, MARGARET MATTHIAS & JAMES DAVID, pioneer band of Baptists who in 1701 came from counties of Pembroke & Carmarthenshire, South Wales, in Great Britian & settled in the Welch Tract of PA & Cecil Co., MD. They were later joined by Reese & Catharine Ryddarcks, Peter Chamberline & Thomas Jones, also from South Wales. Reese Ryddarcks, according to his tombstone found "on the northern slope of the Iron Hill, near the murmuring waters of the Christiana" was b. at Hanwenog, in the county of Cardigan & was bur. in 1707, aged 87. Members of the 3rd Baptist Church founded in America in 1747. *C:164-5*

GRIMES, ---, b. Ireland, to America & was early settler of Frederick Co., MD. His son Samuel res. near Catoctin Furnace. *FR2:1009*

GRINDALL, ---, founder of MD family, was a ward of Lord Baltimore, whom he accompanied on his voyage to America as his secretary. He settled in St. Mary's Co., where descs. resided until Dr. John Grindall removed to Harford Co. *MDC:339*

GRINDER, MICHAEL, from Germany with three brothers & landed in Baltimore, MD. Farmer of Frederick Co., near Woodsboro. He m. & had 6 children, the youngest was Samuel, b. 3 Sept. 1813, farmer, hotel keeper, lime butner at Buckeystown. Had a farm in Urbana District, Frederick Co. Samuel m. Harriet A. Null. *FR2:1002*

GROSS, AUGUST, b. Germany, to Baltimore where he settled before the Civil War, carriage manufacturer; m. Amelia Poehnert who d. 1880 at age of 28, she b. in Baltimore d/o Charles, who came to America in early 19th century. *TR3:262*

GROSS, JACOB, b. Germany 6 Sept. 1820, the 3rd of 8 children of Jacob Sr., also b. in Germany, and Catherine Cooper; farmer & manufacturer. In 1827 Jacob Sr. brought his family to America & settled in Harford Co. Son Jacob Jr. m. at age 26 to Keziah Bryley. Members of Bethel Presbyterian Church. *H/C:530-1*

GROSS, JONATHAN, b. Germany, to America & settled in Frederick Co., early settler of Middletown Valley near Jefferson. His son Henry, farmer of Frederick Co., m. Elizabeth Cost. *FR2:977-8*

GROSSNICKLE, JOHN, from Germany to America in company with a brother [not named here]. His son Peter b. in Middletown Valley, Frederick Co., MD, was farmer & dealer in lumber; was a large land owner. He m. Hannah Grossnickle, a distant cousin, & had 12 children, 9 lived to maturity (all now dec'd. except Rebecca): Elizabeth, m. John Harshman; Peter Jr.; Mary, m. Benjamine Limebaugh; Christianna, m. Samuel Kesselring; Lydia, m. Daniel Harshman; Jacob; Susan, m. Daniel Wolf Jr.; Daniel, farmer of Catoctin District; Rebecca, widow of Jacob Mangins of Catoctin District. *FR2:1369-70*

GRUMBINE, JACOB, b. Germany, as a young man emigrated to the US & located at Hanover, York Co., PA. Later removed to Frederick City, MD. His wife was Margaret ---. Their son Daniel M. Grumbine was b. Hanover, PA 15 May 1815. Daniel was connected with the Evangelical Lutheran Church of Frederick & m. Mary A. Schaeffer, d/o Jacob & Susan of Carroll's Manor, Frederick Co., MD. *FR2:1358-9*

GUILFOYLE, WILLIAM, & wife Eliza Henderson, both b. Ireland, in 1848 with 2 children, Henry W. & Mary E., to America & settled in Baltimore, where he d. William was a veteran of the Civil War in the Union Army. Son Henry W., business man of Whiteford, MD, b. in Ireland 16 Oct. 1846; he was age c. 16 when both his parents died. Employed by Frank Hamway, woolen manufacturer of Harford Co. Later was blacksmith. Age of 21 he m. Maggie E. Hildt, b. Harford Co. of a PA family. *H/C:568-9*

GUNNING, JAMES, b. Ireland, res. in Eckhart, near Frostburg, MD. He m. Rose Donohue, b. PA, of Irish lineage. Their dau., Helen, m. John J. Foley & had son Edgar M. Foley b. 15 March 1896 in Piedmont, WV. Edgar is dentist of Baltimore City. *TR3:547-8*

GUNTER, SOPHIA, d/o Frederick, b. Germany, m. Thomas Hanson of MD. Sophia d. 22 Feb. 1895. [See Hanson entry.] *H/C:204*

GUNTHER, GEORGE, & wife Catherine Schleinniger, both b. Bavaria, Germany, he 29 March 1845; brewer. He came to Baltimore as a young man [first source says he res. for a time in NY & to Baltimore 1875] & started his own brewing plant in Canton & in 1900 organized the George Gunther, Jr. Brewing Co.. George d. in Baltimore in Sept. 1912 aged 67. He is survived by his widow, now aged 73 years. They had 6 children, 3 sons & 3 daus. Son Frank Henry Gunther, the youngest in the family, in 1906 became associated with the family business. His brother George Jr., b. Baltimore 1876, is also a member of the company. Frank m. 9 Jan. 1907 in Baltimore to Mary R. Spiegel Robinson, d/o Mary O'Rourke & Ernest Spiegel, res. of Chestnut Hill, near Philadelphia, PA. Her family is of Irish & German ancestry. When she was 4, Mary's father Ernest died & her mother subsequently m. Wilbert Robinson of Baltmore. *TR3:499-500, 996-9*

GUNTHER, JOHN F., b. Germany, to Baltimore before the Civil War. John served in MD company during the war. His dau., Rose Elizabeth, m. Alexander Hoffmann, also of Baltimore, in 1906. *TR3:367*

GUNTHER, LUDOLPH WILHELM, b. City of Nienburg in the Kingdom of Hanover, 6 Feb. 1821, s/o George John Gunther, b. Hanover, Chief-Surgeon in King's German Legion, and Caroline Mansching. Gunther family was of Schwartzburg, Sonderhausen. 1839 from Bremen to Baltimore, later settled in KY & returned to Baltimore. Ludolph m. 1st Catharine Upshaw, d/o Col. Edwin of King & Queen Co., VA; m. 2d Jan. 1855, Martha Ann Cecil of King WIlliam Co., VA. *MDC:83*

GUTMAN, JOEL, b. 3 Sept. 1829, at Merchingen, Grand Duchy of Baden, s/o Moses & Ella. To America 1849, sailing from London, landed in NY July 1849. Went directly to Baltimore & later VA. Dry goods business in Baltimore. Hebrew. He m. 15 Aug. 1852, Bertha Kayton, d/o Louis & Caroline of Baltimore. *MDC:116*

GWYNN, HUGH, recorded to have saved Pocahontas from drowning & given Gwynn's Island in token of gratitude. He patented land at the mouth of the Pyanketauk (1642) & was one of the first burgesses for the new county of Gloucester & also for York in VA. He d. c. 1659 & in his will named Elizabeth Gwynn as executrix. He left 2 children, John & David. John had son John who m. Mildred Reade. David m. Katherine Griffin Faunteloy & had: Elizabeth, Sarah, Katherine & probably Humphrey & John, who in 1681 laid claim to the estate of Col. John Burnham. Desc. Capt. Andrew Jackson Gwynn, b. 1837 in Piscataway, Prince George's Co., MD, s/o John Hillery & Ann Eliza Dyer, & in 1877 settled in Spartanburg, SC. He was one of the first Catholics to locate in the district. He m. Marie Louise Keene. *TR4:393*

AGAN, JOHN, b. Norway 6 June 1873, of Norwegian parentage, was brought to America as a small boy by his parents, John Ernest & Mary E. (Williams) Hagen, who settled in Brooklyn, NY. On the death of his father, John removed to Ocean City, MD & was connected with the fishing industry; removed to Salisbury in 1910. Now owns & conducts the largest public garage in the city & has the agency for the Cadillac & Chevrolet motor cars. He m. in Ocean City in 1899 Louella C. Quillen, d/o Ase & Mary, both b. MD. *TR3:612-13*

HAHN, ADOLPHUS [ADOLPH], b. Germany, to America 1855 & settled in Frederick City, MD; tanner, Lutheran. He m. Caroline Jacobs & their adult children: Henry A.; Charles, d. aged 48, 28 July 1902, tinner & stove dealer of Frederick; Annie C., never m.; William A.; & Clara A., m. Henry Blackstone of Frederick City. Son Henry A., b. Hanover, Germany, 26 Oct. 1852, d. 20 March 1910. *FR2:818, 1560; 6TH:378-9*

HAINES, ---, husband & wife from Scotland to US where they had son Thomas, b. Cecil Co., MD. Thomas served in the War of 1812 & d. aged 88. Thomas had a son Samuel, b. near Port Deposit, Cecil Co., farmer, m. Mary Ann Rockwell, who d. 1885. Thomas d. 1880. Methodist Protestant. *H/C:234*

HAINES, RICHARD, & Margaret from Northampton Co., England, to America in 1682 on the *Amity* where son Joseph was born. Richard d. aboard ship before reaching America & Margaret setttled in Burlington Co., NJ. 1714 Joseph to Nottingham Twp. (today in Cecil Co., MD), then part of Chester Co., PA. Joseph had an older brother, John, who came to America c. 1679 & obtained a grant for the father in West Jersey. Name has been found spelled Eaune, Ayne, Hayne, etc. *H/C:314-15, 487-8*

HALL, HENRY (REV.), priest of the church of England, sent to MD 1698 by Henry Lord Bishop of London, with letters to Francis Nicholson, Governor. Henry was first rector of St. James Parish, Anne Arundel Co., MD. In 1701 Henry m. Mary Duvall, of Mareen, the Huguenot; he d. 1722. *AAH:99, TR4:721*

HALL, RICHARD, believed to be a s/o Bishop Joseph Hall of England, patented large tract of land called "Mount Welcome," on east side of the Susquehanna River, Cecil Co., MD in 1650. His son Elisha m. Sarah Winfell (or Wingfield), believed to be of the VA Wingfield family, 16 Sept. 1688. Their son Elisha, b. 1663, m. & had: Richard b. 1690; Elihew b. 1692; & Sarah b. 1694. *C:480-5*

HALL, WILLIAM (CAPT.), b. England, to America c. 1793, at an early age. He m. Mary Ann Drebert, b. 21 Jan. 1791. Their dau., Sophia, b. 2 Jan. 1846, m. Edward Walter Giles in Baltimore & dau. Emma b. there 5 June 1882. *TR4:245*

HALLIDAY, ROBERT, nurseryman of Baltimore, b. Dumfries, Scotland; to America 1835, settled Baltimore. Son Robert J. b. Baltimore 4 March 1840. *MDC:87*

HAMERIK, ASGER (PROF.), composer & music director of the Peabody Institute, Baltimore, MD, b. 8 April 1843 in Copenhagen, Denmark. His ancestors had come from Germany during the 30 Years War. He was the son of --- Hamerik & Julie Scheuerman, b. Copenhagen of German descent. Asger in 1864 to Paris & then to Baltimore. *MDC:84*

HAMILL, PATRICK, Protestant Irishman b. Ballymena, Co. Antrim; m. Mary Morrison, both of Co. Antrim, Ireland. Patrick a rebel under Robert Emmett, in 1798 forced to flee to America. Catholic. Mary was

Methodist. He first located in Philadelphia, school teacher & later to Chester Co. He then removed to Allegany Co., MD, where he died. His son, Patrick Jr., b. in Ingman Place, Allegany Co., 28 April 1819, at that time Garrett Co. He res. at Georges Creek Hills, Western Port, Cranberry Glade Grove & Oakland, MD. Held many public possitions & was Methodist. He d. in Oakland; his wife, Isabel Kight, d. the same place 25 Jan. 1895, aged 78. *MDC:418-19; TR3:516-17*

HAMILL, ROBERT, and wife Catharine Conant from Ireland in early 1800's, to Baltimore & he fought in the defense of Baltimore in War of 1812. *MDC:429*

HAMILTON, CHARLES, b. in Tynon, County Armagh, Ireland in 1828, s/o Cornelius Hamilton & the d/o Charles Case. To NY in 1851 & then on to Baltimore. Horticulturalist. Charles m. Margaret Barnhill, d/o William of Londonderry, Ireland & of Scotch descent. *MDC:220*

HAMILTON, WILLIAM, b. Scotland, settled in Baltimore as a teacher. His son was William C., who died in the service of the Confederate Army during the Civil War. Grandson W. Campbell Hamilton b. in Baltimore Dec. 1849. *MDC:211-12*

HAMMOND, JOHN (MAJOR-GENERAL), b. Isle of Wight [England] in 1643, was bur. 29 Nov. 1707 at St. Anne's Parish, Anne Arundel Co., MD. He emigrated to MD c. 1664, at the age of 25, settled in Annapolis 1685. His wife was Mary Greenbury & they had sons, Thomas, Charles, John B. & William D. *FR2:297-8, 1212-14*

HANCE, JOHN, to Province of MD 1659; was of Calvert Co. & his will is dated 1684. His son, Capt. John Hance, justice of Calvert Co. (1696) *TR4:343*

HANCOCK, STEPHEN, to St. Mary's Co. 1664, military officer of Anne Arundel Co. under Lord Baltimore. *TR4:349*

HANKEY, JOHN, b. in Germany 23 May 1736. His wife, also German, b. in May 1740. In early manhood, John, with 2 brothers, came to America where he settled in Frederick Co., MD. He was a wheelwright. He & wife, Barbara Gall, bur. in the old Lutheran Cemetery at Emmitsburg, MD. She also b. Germany in May 1740, to America early in life. Their son Isaac, b. 15 April 1769 & d. 19 July 1840, farmer of Frederick

Co. Isaac m. Susan M. Apple, b. 1773, d. 1851. They are bur. in graveyard at Apple's Church in Frederick Co. *FR2:810, 1166-7, 1490-1*

HANNA, JOHN, from Ireland to settle on farm in Harford Co., MD. His son Alexander farmer in Harford Co. & left is property his son William who m. Jane McGaw & had 9 children. One child was Robert F. Hanna, b. 1840. Alexander Hanna, desc. of John the immigrant, d. in Harford Co. & divided his farm among 3 sons: Robert, William & Stephen B. James W. is sole survivor of the sons at the time of pub. of this book. In 1857 he m. Anna M. Hanna, a lineal desc. of William Hanna; no issue. Presbyterian. *H/C:514-15, 527*

HANNA, WILLIAM, from Scotland to PA in 1790. He m. Lydia Davis, of Irish descent & of old MD family. Their son Joseph m. Margaret Josephine Batson. Their son, Martin Jay Hannah, physician of Baltimore, b. in Dayton, Howard Co., MD 22 May 1887, served in WWI & m. Sara Shane Rust, d/o William Demetrius & Mary Townsend (Shane) Rust. *TR4:573-5*

HANSON, ANDREW, & wife Annika, Swedes who settled on Kent Island, MD in the Chesapeake in 1653. Their son Daniel, b. Charles Co., MD in 1723, served in the Rev. War & was a member of the continental congress. *TR4:864-5*

HANSON, JOHN (COL.), of the Swedish army, removed to MD 1653 & after short res. on Kent Island, went to St. Mary's Co., MD. He settled in Charles Co. after 1656. His will, dated 12 Dec. 1713, he mentions 7 children. *TR4:770-1*

HANSON, THOMAS, b. in Holland, sailor, to America in early manhood & settled in Baltimore. He retired to Harford Co., dairy farmer, & d. 20 Nov. 1887 at Seneca Ridge farm. Lutheran. *H/C:204*

HANSON BROTHERS: Andrew, Randolph, William & John, s/o Col. John Hanson who was slain in battle of Leitzue in 1632. His sons placed under the care of the King & in 1642 Queen Christina placed them under the care of Gov. Printz of New Sweden, who brought them to DE. Andrew m. Annika --- & had son Hans Hanson, b. on Tuncum Island, New Sweden in 1646. Hans was judge of Kent Co., MD 1685-97 & delegate from Kent to MD legislature 1694-1697 from Cecil Co. In 1679 he m. Martha Kelto Ward & he d. 1703. His estate was known as

"Kimbolton," & on the north side of the Chester River. Their son, Frederick Hanson, b. 1693, d. 1738, chief justice of Kent Co. He m. Mary Lawder & had son Benjamin in 1714. Col. John Hanson, s/o Col. John, the officer of the Swedish army & brother to Andrew, to MD & settled in St. Mary's Co. 1653; 1656 in Charles Co., MD. He had been b. in the kingdom of Sweden c. 1630 & was youngest s/o Col. Hanson of the Swedish army & grandson of John Hanson of London, a desc. of that Roger de Rastrick who had his seat at Rastrick in parish of Halifax in York county (Yorkshire), England as early as 1251. *TR4:204, 659-61*

HARBAUGH, YOST, a Swiss who came to America c. 1736. His name appears in the Land Office at Harrisburg, PA as Joust Harbaugh. His 1st wife was also a native of Switzerland. Their children: George Ludwig, Jacob, John, Henry and Yost. His second wife was Mary Elizabeth ---, their children: Leonard, Mary Elizabeth, Ann Margaret & Ann Catherine. Yost was member of the German Reformed Church & supposed bur. in the graveyard at the Kreutz Creek Church. His son Jacob, b. Switzerland 5 Feb. 1730, was aged 6 years on the family's emigration to America. Jacob settled in the upper part of Harbaugh's Valley, "where the gap opens out towards Frederick." He m. April 1761 to Anna Margaretta, d/o George Smith, who was b. 3 April 1740. *FR2:1178-9*

HARCOURT, RICHARD, b. Ireland, to America c. 1800 & later m. Sallie Thompson of Stonington, CT; son William b. at Tompkinsville, Staten Island, NY in 1823. William was a mariner, served in the TX Navy, later sailed on whaler out of New Bedford. After travels m. 2 May 1850, Mary E., d/o Capt. William M. Betts of Norfolk, VA & settled in Washington, DC; worked at the Navy Yard. Now res. in Baltimore, member of the Methodist Episcopal Church. *MDC:223-4*

HARDCASTLE, ROBERT, b. England, to America in 1748 & settled in what is now Caroline Co., MD (then Queen Anne's Co.). His eldest son, Thomas, founded the family seat, known as Castle Hall in upper Caroline Co. Thomas m. & left 8 sons. Robert's 3d son, Peter, was soldier in the Rev. War. *TR4:668-70; MDC:584-5*

HARGETT, PETER, to America in 1750 on the ship *Two Brothers* from Rotterdam. He had son Abram Hargett, who had a son John. *FR2:1256-8*

HARLAN, MICHAEL & GEORGE, to America from England with William Penn in 1687, early Quakers. Michael's son David res. in Chester Co., PA. David's son Jeremiah to Harford Co., MD from London Grove Twp., PA in last quarter of 18th century, miller. Jeremiah m. Esther Stump, d/o Henry & Rachel (Perkins) Stump in 1800. Desc. Jeremiah Harlan [could be Jeremiah s/o David, but not so stated] was read out of meeting for having "exercised" with a light horse artillery. His son, Dr. David Harlan, a desc. of the first Michael Harlan, was b. Harford Co., MD. David was surgeon with the US Navy. He m. Margaret Rebecca Herbert, also b. Harford Co., d/o James & Mary Ann (Baker) Herbert, old MD settlers of English ancestry. *TR3:962-3; H/C:133*

HARLEY, JOSHUA, from England with the Giddings family & settled on the Merryland tract. He was a major in the Continental Army. After the war he settled in Frederick Co., MD, where Burkittsville now stands. Joshua m. Miss Whitenight of VA & had: William, farmer of VA; Joshua, farmer at Paw Paw, WV; Mahlon, merchant at Paris, MO, m. Miss Biser, sister of Daniel S. Biser; Thomas, physician of Hedgesville WV; Elizabeth, m. Capt. William Lamar; Eliza [sic], m. Miss Butler, settled in LA; & Sophia, m. A. Biser, res. near Broad Run, MD. *FR2:1566-7*

HARLEY, WILLIAM, b. Dumbarton, England, settled in Fauquier Co., VA, where he m. Mary Hartson. Their son, Thomas H. m. Jane Harley, who was b. Annapolis, MD. A. G. Harley, son of Thomas H. & Jane, b. Fauquier Co., VA 26 May 1834 & became principal of the public school of Comus, Montgomery Co., MD. In Worcester Co., MD 9 June 1857, he m. Josephine, d/o Levin & Margaret A. (Brettingham) Ames, of Accomac Co., VA. *16TH:844-45*

HARP, JOHN, of Meyersville, MD is either a desc. of Daniel Harp who came to America from Rotterdam in ship *Molly* in 1707 & settled in Berks Co., PA; OR he is a desc. of John Michael Harp or Michael Harp, who came to America from Rotterdam at ages of 30 and 27, in 1741 in ship *Thackleberry* [see below]; both settled in Berks Co., PA. That branch of the Harps who settled in what is now known as Carroll, Anne Arundel and Montgomery Counties & in Baltimore City and throughout the South, were of English desc. The Harps from Scotland, through the aid of Queen Anne, settled in MD, VA & the South. John, s/o George Harp, b. 1798 near Myersville, Frederick Co. John m. Elizabeth Doub, d/o Jacob Doub 4th, whose ancestors were the first settlers in Western MD c. 1712, from Germany, Huguenots of French descent who first settled in DE, & from there to Cecil Co., MD & still later to Myersville, Frederick Co. They called the settlement "Jerusalem." *FR2:903-6*

HARP, JOHN MICHAEL, of French Protestant family, came in ship *Thackleberry* from Rotterdam & settled in Berks Co., PA. John Harp & 2 brothers left Berks Co. & settled near what is now known as Wolfsville, Frederick Co., MD in 1760 & later John moved to Graceham, where he d. aged 80 & bur. at Rocky Hill, near Woodsboro, 1795. He had 7 children, 3 sons & 4 daus., of whom the oldest son was George, b. 1765, d. 5 March 1844, bur. in St. John's cemetery near Myersville, Frederick Co. He was a shoemaker & was a member of the German Reformed church & later joined the United Brethren church. George m. Catherine Toms, d/o William, a German. Their eldest son, John Harp, b. 1798, near Myersville, settled at that place in 1833. His wife was Elizabeth Doub, d/o Joseph, whose forebears came to western MD in 1712, a French Huguenot family that came from Germany & first settled in DE, thence to Cecil Co., MD. *TR4:162*

HARRIS, THOMAS, from England to America in Colonial days (c. 1660) & settled at St. Mary's Co., MD. His grandson Thomas m. Sarah Offutt & left a number of children, among them Nathan who settled in Frederick Co., MD. Nathan m. the widow of Capt. Philemon Dorsey (Rachel, d/o Levin Lawrence). *FR2:940*

HARRIS, THOMAS, b. southern part of England in 1815; age 19 to US & settled in GA, 1848 to Liberty District, Frederick Co., MD. Merchant at Libertytown, Methodist Episcopal Church member, m. Mary Blamey & had 7 children, only 2 lived to maturity: Mary Elizabeth, d. 1902, m. Thomas R. Phillips of Frederick City & James H. *FR2:815*

HARRIS, WILLIAM, of London, to MD 1662 & located at The Cliffs, Calvert Co. in 1698; Quaker. *TR4:343*

HARSHMAN, CHRISTIAN, b. Germany [second entry says he was b. in Frederick Co., MD], minister of the German Baptist Church, to America in early manhood with his father [not named]. He married & had 4 children, the eldest John b. on homestead, farmer & businessman. John m. Elizabeth Grossnickle. Their son Elias b. near Wolfsville, MD 11 April 1831. *FR2:819, 1346-8*

HARTOGENSIS, HENRY S., b. Hertogenbosch, Holland (Netherlands) 27 Oct. 1829. To US 1848 & settled in Baltimore, MD where he m. Rachel de Wolff, a native of Holland, who had come to this city 'at a tender age.' They had 6 children who reached maturity & she d. 20 May 1902, aged 77 years. Henry d. 25 Dec. 1918; manufacturer of business forms & sporting goods business. Jewish. Their son, Benjamin Henry Hartogensis, b. Baltimore 9 April 1865 & m. 10 June 1896, Grace Bendann, d/o Daniel & Hannah (Lissner) Bendann. *TR3:512-16*

HARWOOD, THOMAS, of Streatley, Berks County, England deeded to his son Richard land on Muddy Creek in Anne Arundel Co., MD. Richard lived on the land, m. Mary --- & their first son, Thomas Harwood, b. 1698. *AHH:96*

HATTON, ELEANOR, came to Province of MD with her mother, Margaret Hatton, in 1649. She m. Major Thomas Brooke (1632-1676) of Calvert Co. *TR4:344*

HAUER, NICHOLAS, b. Dildendorf, district of Nassau Farbrucken in German Lotheringen, Germany, 6 Aug. 1733 & d. in Frederick Co., MD. To America as a young man & in Frederick City in 1754. Manufacturer of hats & tavern keeper. Later removed to Lancaster Co., PA, but returned to Frederick. His wife was Catharine Zealer & they had: Henry, Daniel, Catharine m. Peter Manta, Elizabeth m. Jacob Steiner, Barbara m. John C. Fritchie (she became famous through the poem of Whittier), Margaret m. a Mr. Stover of Baltimore, and Mary who m. William Adams & removed to KY. Son Daniel, b. Lancaster Co., PA in 1768. About 1790 located in Frederick City, MD & manufactured hats until he retired in 1830. Daniel m. Margaret Mantz, b. Frederick, d/o David Mantz a saddler, & had: Catharine m. Jacob Byerly; Matilda m. William Randolph Fleming; Harriet m. Allen G. Quynn; George; Mary & Nicholas D. *FR2:1047-8; 6TH:395*

HAUGH, HEZEKIAH, from England to America with brother. The brother settled in NJ & Hezekiah located in Frederick Co., MD, taking up land along Little Pipe Creek, at what is now Haughsville. Hezekiah served as a soldier in the Rev. War. His son Paul, a blacksmith, inherited the family farm. *FR2:1052-3*

HAUGH, POWELL, b. Switzerland, was early settler of the northern part of Frederick Co., MD at Haugh's Church, now in possession of

Samuel C. Haugh. Powell gave land to the church & is bur. in the churchyard. His son William b. Frederick Co. William & wife were members of the German Reformed Church, known as Haugh's Church & they are also buried in the graveyard there. William's son William b. on homestead near Ladiesburg, 11 Nov. 1811, after retirement to Johnsville & later Frederick. *FR2:935-6*

HAUVER, PETER, b. Germany 1 March 1754; to America as young man & settled on what is now Hauver's District, Frederick Co., MD, one of the earliest settlers in the district, which was named for him. He m. Hannah --- & had at least one son, Christopher, b. 12 Nov. 1801, on homestead 1 mile south of Foxville, on road to Catoctin Furnace. Christian m. Mary, d/o William Brown of Frederick Co. *FR2:809, 1084, 1126*

HAWKINS, JOHN, sea captain who "lived & flourished in the days of Good Queen Bess." Desc. Capt. William L. Hawkins, b. LA, in 1865 removed to Harford Co., MD & in June 1866 m. Etta Harlan, d/o Dr. Reuben S. Harlan of Harford Co. *H/C:509*

HAWKINS, JOHN, received 100 acres of land in Anne Arundel Co., MD for transporting himself from England, was settled on the Magothy River in 1657. His wife was Margaret Hawkins. *AAH:43*

HAWKINS, NICHOLAS, b. England, to America at young age. Farmer, veteran of the Rev. War. His son, John Hawkins, b. Harford Co., m. Susan Thompson & their dau. Mary J., b. Harford Co. 28 Feb. 1828; m. at the age of 17 John S. Hutchins, b. Harford Co. *H/C:518-19*

HAWLEY, JEROME, b. Brentford (now possibly a part of London), England, one of the first commissioners & councillors of MD, he d. there in 1638. A Roman Catholic, he m. Eleanor --- before sailing for America. Eleanor was a widow & had a son, Sir William Courtney, by her 1st husband. There are no Hawley descendants recorded in colonial records, and it is believed that his dau. [not named here], who lived in Belgium & never came to America, was his only living child. *TR4:863-4*

HAYDEN, JOHN, b. Wales & after coming to America was known as the "Iron King." He established the Haydentown Iron Works in PA, the first located west of the Allegany Mountains. His son John Jr. b. in Fayette Co., m. Ruth, d/o John & Martha Fowler. Jacob, s/o James A.

b. in Fayette Co., PA 1842. Served as an apprentice printer & in the Union Army. In 1877 he established the *Oakland Republican* in Western MD. In 1875 he m. Letitia V. Savage, d/o Nelson. *6TH:633-34*

HAYDEN, WILLIAM, from England to CT. Desc. -- Hayden, dental surgeon, established first dental college in the US in Baltimore, MD. His son [not named here] owned land now known as Lake Rowland, which in early days contained his farm & homestead. His son, George Gillette Hayden, merchant, d. April 1898, aged 42. He had been b. in St. Louis & m. Jennie Gibson Reid, d/o a shipbuilder, real estate dealer & farmer of Baltimore City & Co. *TR3:736-9*

HAYES, JONATHAN, of England, s/o Jonathan, served in British Army at Philadelphia; m. Elizabeth Elliott. Settled in DE, farmer. They had 12 sons, one of which Jonathan, with Edward Dulany & John Drummond to Western MD. Jonathan m. Miss --- Henderson, who came from Nova Scotia. *FR2:804*

HAYES, WALTER COONEY (CAPT.), b. Ireland, Captain in English Navy; 1797 resigned commission & emigrated to America. He m. Margaretta Wonderly of Carroll Co., MD. *MDC:80*

HAYWARD, ---, from England at an early day & settled in SC, removing thence to PA. Son Thomas Hayward, b. SC, farmer, removed to PA. His son Joseph J., b. Philadelphia, physician of York Co., PA; m. Sarah Briarly, b. Franklin, PA. They had 9 children, including Thomas B. Hayward, b. York Co., PA 4 May 1838, removed to Harford Co., MD & m. Helen M. Bussey, b. in Harford Co. of French desc. *H/C:541-2*

HAYWARD, NEHANNAH, of St. John's New Brunswick, an Englishman, who settled at Wilton, NH. Nehannah m. --- Hutchinson, b. Milford. Son Jonas Hutchinson Hayward, b. 23 June 1815, at Milford, NH, to Baltimore May 1839. Congregational. He d. 15 May 1866 in Baltimore. 16 March 1842 he m. Mary A. Bromwell of Baltimore. *MDC:246-7*

HEALEY, MICHAEL, farmer & distiller of Ireland, to America 1818 & settled in Baltimore & later removed to Cumberland. He d. at age 76. *MDC:305-06*

HEAPS, ROBERT, b. England, to America before the Revolution & settled in Harford Co., farmer. His son [not named in the second source, but a son Robert L. is named in the first source] was b. Harford Co. in 1800, and his son was John Heaps who m. Martha Alexander, both b. Harford Co. Their 2d son Hugh T., b. in 1830, in Harford Co. *H/C:267, 557*

HEATHMAN, SARAH ENDICOTT, b. Devonshire, England, m. Dr. John Waller Key. Their son, Dr. J. Albert Key, an alumnus of Johns Hopkins University, MD, b. Jackson, Hinds Co., MS, 21 April 1892. John Key was b. in Raymond, MS, the s/o John Albert & Mary Elizabeth (Bradley) Key; John Albert b. in Columbia, TN, was a veteran of both the Mexican & Civil Wars, & lost his life in the latter conflict, dying in Raymond, MS. *TR3:802-3*

HEATWOLE (HUTWOHL), MATHIAS, b. Germany, to America in 1747 & first settled in PA, later removing to VA, where descs. have since resided. Desc. David A. Heatwole, s/o Abram Heatwole, m. Catherine Driver & their son Timothy O. Heatwole, b. in Dale Enterprise, Rockingham Co., VA 18 Feb. 1865. Catherine was the d/o John & Catherine (Funk) Driver, early settlers of Rockingham Co. Mennonite family. Timothy O. grad Univ. of MD dental Dept. in 1895 & rec'd. an MD from the same 2 years later. Became dean of the dental school in 1911 & served in the US Dental Corps in WWI. He m., in Baltimore 17 June 1914, Mrs. Annie (Blackwell) Lathan, widow of F. M. Latham & formerly a res. of New Bern, NC. The doctor is Presbyterian & a member of Brown Memorial Church. *TR3:883-4*

HEATZIG, WILLIAM B., b. Dresden, Saxony 1822; 1854 to America & settled on Long Island, later removed to Elkton, MD; furniture store. He m. prior to leaving Saxony, Eleanor Stein, who d. in Elkton 1891. *H/C:224*

HEBB, WILLIAM, from England to America in early 17th century & settled in St. Mary Co., MD, having received a grant of land. He was in the British navy. He spent his entire life at his home at Porto Bello & is buried in the family graveyard there, as is his son Vernon. *6TH:147-521*

HECK, CHARLES, s/o Philip Martin Heck & Elizabeth Hoffman, b. Germany 1818; to US 1850, brewer in Baltimore 2 years & removed to Sandy Hook. He m. 1842 Cassandra E. Morgan. *H/C:278*

HECK, JOHN CONRAD, b. Berlin, Germany, to US with parents at age 3 months. Settled in Baltimore where his son John Joseph was b. 26 May 1879. John Conrad Heck m. Catherine Bauer & he d. as the result of pneumonia after an illness of 3 days, 3 March 1904, aged 62. *TR3:246*

HEFFNER, DANIEL, b. Brevair, Germany, to America in early manhood, landing at Baltimore. Blacksmith & machinist, res. near Lewistown, Frederick Co., MD. He m. Susan Eyler & had a son Frederick b. 1 July 1832. *FR2:979*

HEINEKAMP, WILLIAM, b. Lippe, Detmold, Prussia 1826, s/o John, of Detmold, who recently d. at the age of 87. In 1848 to Baltimore. He m. Mary Marischen, d/o John, of Oldenburg, Prussia. Catholic. *MDC:396*

HEINEKAMP, WILLIAM T., b. Bavaria in 1826, emigrated at age 21 and settled in Baltimore; piano manufacturer, Confederate veteran. He d. 1903. Wife Mary Morrison also b. Bavaria, still living. Son Rudolph J. b. 3 March 1892, Baltimore. *TR3:340*

HEINLEIN, FREDERICK, b. in province of Batavia, Germany 21 May 1836, s/o Frederick Sr., a butcher & hotel keeper of Neustadt, Bavaria & wife Johanna. To America as a young man & settled in Frederick, MD. He m. Dorcas Dunkhorst, b. Hanover, Germany in April 1849. *6TH:462-63*

HEISSE, JOHN F., b. Darmstadt, Germany 22 Jan. 1830, m. Rebecca A. Cuddy, b. near Monkton, MD, a d/o John P. & Ruth C. Cuddy. Rebecca d. in Baltimore Co. 1881, aged 43. Their son, Rev. John Frederick Heisse, b. in Monkton, 28 Sept. 1862, 4th child in family of 5 sons & 2 daus. He was a minister of the Methodist Episcopal church & his first charge was West Harford Circuit, Harford Co., MD (1888). In 1889 appointed junior pastor of City Station Church in Baltimore. In 1891 he m. Mrs. Elizabeth Estelle Galbreath, formerly Elizabeth Estelle Rusk of Baltimore. Dr. Heisse traveled extensively & was very active in the church. *TR3:988-92*

HELLER, CASPER, & wife Anna R. Hepps, to Baltimore from their native Bavaria in "ante-bellum days." Casper b. in Lehanthal, Bavaria, located in Baltimore in 1852, where he d. 1912, aged 79; clothing cutter

& tailor. Anna was from Muelhausen, Bavaria; she d. 1908, aged 75. Their son George, b. in Baltimore, physician. *TR3:652-3*

HELLMAN, JOHN JOSEPH, b. Germany, emigrated to MD. Desc. John Joseph Hellman, b. Baltimore Co., grocer & merchant, m. Maria Regina Rex, d/o Dr. John R. & Mary Alice (DuVal) Rex of Elk Ridge, Howard Co. Charles Joseph Hellman, eldest s/o John J. & Maria R., b. 25 Aug. 1883 in Relay, Baltimore Co. *TR3:717-18*

HELLMAN, JOHN RUDOLPH (CAPT.), eldest child of Abraham & Elizabeth (Schorter) Hellman, b. Staffelbach, Switzerland 7 Oct., 1825. Abraham was a farmer & d. 1869; Elizabeth d. 1866. John R. to US in 1850 & settled in Rochester, NY as a bookkeeper. He served in the Union Army during the Civil War; afterwards settled in MD. He m. 25 April 1845, Elsie Wolf. *MDS:54*

HEMP, ---, from Holland to America & settled in Frederick Co., MD, near Lewistown in early settlement days. Son Frederick was a miller & farmer of Frederick Co. & m. Julia, d/o John Keller, another early settler of the county. *FR2:807*

HENCH, JOHN, from Germany to PA, settled in Chester Co. c. 1750. His grandson Samuel Hench, b. Perry Co., PA, farmer, Lutheran. His son George W. b. Perry Co. 1828 & still resides there. Samuel m. Frances R. Rice, b. 1824. Their son, Silas M. Hench of Perry Co., PA, minister, ordained at Walkersville, Frederick Co., MD Nov. 1879. Pastor Glade Reformed Church Frederick Co., m. Jan. 1880, Martha J. Beaver, d/o John K. Beaver of Montgomery Co., PA; no issue. *FR2:813*

HENDERSON, JOHN, Capt. b. Ireland, to America & took part in the War of 1812. He first res. in Baltimore, MD, later removed to Elkton & later still to Dist. No. 4, where he d. in 1856, aged 74. He married as his second wife Rebecca A. Groves. *H/C:383-4*

HENDERSON, ROBERT, b. England, m. Margaret Vail of NJ & son George was b. in NY City 3 July 1828. They removed to Philadelphia in 1835. In 1853 George removed to Alleghany Co., MD. Episcopal. *MDC:225-6*

HENKEL, HENRY A., b. Alsace-Lorraine, France, came to US as a child, m. Elizabeth Vuchald; their son Harry A. located in Baltimore at age of 19. Lutheran. *TR3:57*

HENRIQUES, JOSEPH (Capt.), b. Kingston, Jamaica 18 June 1825. At age 6 weeks his parents removed to NY City. His father, Moses, b. & reared in London, England, in the West Indies trade, where he met & m. Sarah Nunes, b. Kingston, West Indies. In NY Moses was agent for banking house of Rothschild. Joseph served in the Union Army during the Civil War & eventually removed to Harford Co., MD. His wife was Sarah B. Hoke, b. in Harford Co. *H/C:560-1*

HEPBRON, Thomas, Scotch, to America, one of the first settlers in Kent Co., MD. *MDC:284*

HERBERT, HENRY, & wife Louisa (Coleman), to US from England 1871. Their son, Arthur Wiliam Herbert, b. Ilion, NY 21 April 1873, to Frederick, MD 1917. Presbyterian. He m. 22 July 1892, Jessie Stuart Howden of Hartford, CT. She of Scotch parentage, her parents, James & Jessie Stuart (Cummins) Howden, to US from the north of Scotland. *TR3:403-04*

HERMANN, CHARLES M., b. in Middle Germany in 1842, s/o Rev. Gotlieb of the Lutheran Church. He settled in Frederick, MD, florist. Another son of the Rev. was Gotlieb, Jr., in the book-binding business in Atchison, KS. Other children did not emigrate to America. Charles M. to US in 1866 & settled in Quincy, IL, & after 2 years to MD & up to 1877 resided in Baltimore. In 1877 to Frederick, MD. He m. Lizzie Diehl in Frederick in 1871. She was d/o Albert, in the shoe business. *6TH:435-36*

HERSHBERGER, BERNARD, b. Germany. Brought his wife & family with him to America in 1798. Settled in Frederick Co., & town of Jefferson was laid out by him & called New Town. He had several sons & 4 daus., 3 of whom married men by the name of Kemp. His son Henry was aged 5 on their immigration to America. Henry m. Catherine Remsberg & had: John B., m. Miss Wiles, d. in Jefferson, MD before 1872; Mary, m. (1) George Herring & (2) Peter Boyer, her brother-in-law, husband of her sister Catherine, she d. in Jefferson aged 83; Henry, m. Julia Scott, has 12 children, d. at Broad Run, Frederick Co., MD; Elizabeth, m. James Wiles, dec'd.; Catherine, m. Peter Boyer, d. in

Jefferson; Thomas, moved West & m. Miss Dever; Susan, m. John Dare, d. aged 83. Reformed church members. *FR2:1595*

HERSHBERGER, JOHN, b. Germany, settled "over a hundred years ago" near Cearfoss Crossroad, Washington Co., MD--farmer & j.p. His children: Hiram; Missouri who m. James Murray of Parsons, KS; David, dec'd.; Joseph C.; Clarissa wife of James Rhodes of Broadfording, Washington Co., MD. *FR2:943-4*

HERVEY, NICHOLAS, Englishman, Lord of St. Joseph's Manor on the Patuxent River in St. Marys Co., MD before 1639. He brought with him to the Province of MD his wife Jane, dau. Frances & 4 servants. Frances m. George Beckwith, of an English family of Yorkshire. George came into MD 1648. *TR4:251*

HESS, CHARLES, b. Hesse-Cassel, Germany. Member of the Hessian Army hired by England & brought to America during the Revolution. In 1781 he became an American citizen. He erected a mill in Carroll Co., MD, near the Mason-Dixon Line. He left a son, Samuel. *FR2:1367-8*

HETRICK, NICHOLAS, b. Germany c. 1790, d. 1827, aged 30. To America c. 1790 & located in Perry Co., PA; m. in Germany Elizabeth Rator. Their 3rd son, John, b. c. 1821 in Perry Co., m. Susan Bird (d. 1823) d/o Andrew Bird, Revolutionary soldier. Adam, s/o John & Susan Hetrick, b. 1821 Perry Co., to Harford Co., MD in 1850. *H/C:306*

HETT, JOHN, b. Hesse Cassel, Darmstadt, Germany 12 Feb. 1804, d. Frederick Co. March 1886, bur. Mt. Zion Reformed Cemetery. Member German Reformed Church of Frederick; weaver. Aug. 1841 to America with his wife. Landed at Baltimore City & immediately removed to Harper's Ferry, VA (WV) & worked on the canal. Later bought land from Daniel Getzendanner one mile northwest of the Mt. Zion Church in Frederick District (MD) & later purchased land from Joseph Routzahn in the same area. He had m. in Germany Mary C. Schultz. All children b. in this country but only 2 lived to adulthood--Henry & Margaret J. (wife of William H. Brengle of Frederick City). *FR2:821*

HETZEL, CHRISTIAN F., b. Goeppingen, Wurtemberg, Germany 25 Sept. 1858, s/o Philip Joshua Hetzel b. 1 Jan. 1809 in the same district. Christian F. to America in 1844 with his father. He lived in NY until 1850 when to Cumberland, MD until his death in 1871. Member of the

German Lutheran Church. The wife of Philip Joshua Hetzel was Margaret Yauss, d/o John Jacob. Other children of Philip & Margaret were: Christina Matilda, b. 11 Jan. 1836, m. John G. Bauer, sheriff of Allegany Co., MD; Caroline Frederick, b. 12 July 1837 & m. John Appel of Cumberland; and John Joshua, b. 1 Feb. 1849 in NY City. *6TH:556-58*

HETZELL, JOHN G., b. Wurtemburg, Germany, 1 April 1821, s/o George, a farmer who d. when John was 8 years of age. In 1831 with his mother to Baltimore. He later resided in Cumberland, MD as a journeyman & later still returned to Baltimore. He m. Annette L., d/o Moses Webster, of Philadelphia. She is deceased. *MDC:214-15*

HEUISLER, JOSEPH ANTHONY, b. Munich, captial of Bavaria, Germany, to America at end of 18th century & settled in MD; horticulturist. He d. 1862. He m. Mary Parker, d/o an English gentleman, George W. Parker, who had settled in Baltimore. *MDC:525-26*

HEWELL, ---, to America from Germany at age of 11 months with his mother, his father having d. on the ocean enroute. His mother later m. John Reichstein, a fellow passenger. Desc. James Lewis Hewell, d. in Baltimore 1916, aged 91. *TR3:589-91*

HICKMAN, JOHN, one of company of emigrants from Germany to America & settled in Loudoun Co., VA early. He m. Catherine, d/o George Fawley, another early settler of Loudoun Co. They had 9 children, among them was William, farmer of Loudoun Co., b. 1814, who m. Eliza, d/o Philip & Laura Everhart. They had 10 children, among them: John P., farmer of Buckeystown District, Frederick Co., MD; Millard F., farmer near Boyds, MD; Ella, dec'd., m. to Benjamin F. Stouffer of Point of Rocks, MD. John P. Hickman d. Feb. 1863 & was bur. in the cemtery at Lovettsville; his widow d. 1898. Another of the sons of William was George H. C. Hickman, b. Loudoun Co., VA 6 July 1844, in 1863 enlisted in Co. B. of the Loudoun Rangers, attached to the 3rd WV Cavalry of the Union Army. Captured in 1864, he was at Libby & Pemberton prisons until the end of the war. Merchant at Taylorstown, Loudoun Co., & later removed to Point of Rocks, MD, where he opened a store & served as post master. *FR2:1098-1100 & 1107-8*

HIESTER, JOHN, with 2 brothers Joseph & Daniel, all b. village of Elsoff, duchy of Wiltzenstein, province of Westphalia, Germany. All to

America, John c. 1732 & Joseph & Daniel in 1738. John's desc., Joseph Hiester, Gov. of PA 1820-1823. Later descs. include Felix Vincent Goldsborough, b. Baltimore 1 Nov. 1882, s/o Henry Paul Goldsborough & Helena McManus. *TR4:796-7*

HIGGINBOTHAM, ANN, b. Ireland, m. Robert McCausland of Harford Co., MD. Son Thomas Jefferson McCausland b. 5 March 1834, in Harford Co. Robert's father, George McCausland, b. in Ireland, to America, general store in Dublin, MD; surveyor. George served in the War of 1812. *H/C:344-5*

HILD, MARGARET ANN, youngest d/o Georgius Hild, burgomaster of Soden, Germany. She m. John M. Frederick, bookseller, proprietor of Catholic book concern in Baltimore City. Son Rev. J. Alphonse Frederick, served parish of St. Ignatius, originally known as St. Joseph's Mission, Deer Creek. Joseph Alphonse b. 1 Aug. 1848 in Baltimore. *H/C:321*

HILDEBRAND, ---, & wife, both b. Germany, early settlers of Frederick Co., MD. Their son John, farmer of Tuscarora District, situated near Rocky Springs, 3 miles north of Frederick. John m. Lydia Albaugh & had: Amanda, m. Peter Eves; William; Lewis A.; Sophia, m. Hiram Hargett; Louisa m. Hiram Hargett, her brother- in-law; John of Myersville, MD; Lydia, m. Charles Orrison, farmer of the Tuscarora District, Frederick Co.; Laura A., m. Simon Best, farmer of Montgomery Co., MD; Joshua of Dayton, OH. *FR2:1020-1*

HILDT, JOHN, from Germany in 1794 to America. He m. Mary Weller, d/o a shipowner of Baltimore, MD. John served as Ensign in the 51st MD Infantry in the War of 1812. *TR3:852-3*

HILL, CLEMENT, to MD with Calvert family & obtained a patent of the estate now called "Woodlawn," in Prince George's Co. *MDC:291*

HILL, GEORGE, of Dumfermline, near Glasgow, Scotland, came to America in 1792, first locating in city of Philadelphia. Removed to Baltimore 2 years later; book store owner. Methodist. Desc. Thomas Gardner Hill m. Martha Bryant. Their son Thomas b. 31 Oct. 1834 in Baltimore, was pioneer real estate operator in the city. *TR3:585-6*

HILL, RALPH, to Plymouth MA from Devon, England before 1638. Desc. Charles E. Hill from Temple, Hillsboro Co., NH to MD where he d. 6 Sept. 1917. *GME:171*

HILLEARY, JOHN, settled in Prince George Co., MD, farmer & slave holder. Either this John or his father b. in England. John m. Miss Perry & had John Henry Hilleary who m. Cornelia Williams & had: Ann Perry, Thomas, Ellen McGill, John William, M.D. & Tilghman. Their son, Thomas Hilleary, b. near Jefferson, Frederick Co., MD 21 March 1827. He was aged 7 or 8 when his father died & before he was aged 12 his mother died. His aunt, Miss Elizabeth Hilleary, was appointed guaridan for the 5 children & cared for them at her home at Steiner's Mill. *FR2:1115-6*

HILLEARY, THOMAS, b. Suffolk, England, res. in MD 1683-1697. High sheriff of Prince George's Co. *TR4:721*

HILLIS, FRANK NORMAN, b. British Guiana, of Dublin, Ireland family. He was s/o the late John David Hillis, M.D., fellow of the Royal College of Surgeons. Dr. John Hillis d. in Dublin 18 Dec. 1908, aged 65. Frank is the next to youngest of 6 children. He came to the US in 1905; grad. Univ. of MD Medical School in Baltimore 1912. He m. Laura Susan Parker, d/o of Lewis B. & Virginia Lewis Parker. Members Emmanuel Protestant Episcopal church. *TR3:577-9*

HILTON, CLEMENT, b. England, to Frederick, MD when young; shoemaker. His dau. Susan m. Henry Young, b. Frederick 1805. German Reformed Church members. *6TH:347-48*

HILTON, THOMAS Sr., from England to St. Mary's Co., MD when a young man. For time lived in WV, but later located in Montgomery Co., MD. He m. Flavila Stewart. Son Thomas Jr. m. Sarah E., d/o John Scheckles. Their eldest son, Robert S. Hilton, b. Montgomery Co., MD 25 June 1831. *6TH:838*

HILTZ, PHILIP, b. Darmstadt, Hessen, Germany. At age 10 with parents to US, settled in Baltimore, MD, where he d. aged 53; stevedore. Lutheran. Son John b. Baltimore 28 April 1852. *TR3:129*

HINES, MATTHEW, to America from Ireland in 1720, was s/o Lord Matthew Hines, member of the Irish parliament 1697-1710. Matthew settled first at Whitemarsh, where he m. Mrs. Ann Simpson. His stepson, John Simpson, was the grandfather of Gen. Ulysses S. Grant. Matthew's dau., Sarah Hines, m. John[?] Eder & their son, William H. b. Montgomery Co., PA 24 July 1818, removed to Elkton, MD in 1848. *H/C:442-3*

HITCHINS, OWEN EATON, b. in the south of Wales 25 May 1831, to America & settled in Frostburg, MD in 1854. He was joined there by brother Adam E. *6TH:537-38*

HODGES, THOMAS, one of the "20 Gentleman of Good Fashion" who accompanied Leonard Calvert to St. Mary's, MD in 1634, when he was aged 19. He settled in Anne Arundel Co. in 1659, and served in many political offices. In 1689 he was of Baltimore Co., his home plantation being "Benjamine's Choice," in that county. *TR4:409*

HOEN, AUGUSTUS, b. Hoehn, Duchy of Warsaw, Germany 28 Dec. 1820, s/o Martin & Eliza (Schmidt) Hoen. His brother Berthold was one of the first settlers of county of Santa Rosa, CA & m. Mary Anderson, a Danish lady. A sister, Dora, m. Edmund Berger & settled in Burlington, WI. Sister Guida m. Maurice Lippman & settled in St. Louis, MO. Augustus' family to US with Schmidt & Weber families, landed in Baltimore in 1835. Augustus m. Mrs. Weber 28 Feb. 1849; she was d/o Philip Muth. *MDC:495-96*

HOFFMAN, ---, & wife, from Germany, settled in Germantown, PA in 1768, when their son Daniel was born. They removed to Baltimore, MD during the first years of the Revolution, when Daniel was 8. *MDC:351*

HOFFMAN, ALEXANDER, b. Wiesbaden, Hesse-Nassau, Germany, 11 March 1876, s/o Alexander. Alexander the father to America c. 1861. A sculptor, first settled in Chicago, later to Baltimore. He took out citizenship papers, but d. in Germany in 1882. His wife was Louise Wolff & now resides at Wiesbaden. Alexander the son, to Baltimore in the year his father died, later res. in VA & NC & established business in 1850 in Baltimore. He m. Rose Elizabeth Gunther, b. Baltimore, d/o the late John F. in 1905. *TR3:366-7*

HOFMANN, JULIUS KAYSER (REV.), b. 9 April 1865, in Friedberg, Hesse, Germany, a s/o Peter & Marie (Engelter) Hofmann. Peter was a decorated officer in the German army. Julius was raised in town of Giessen. He studied & taught at Johns Hopkins Univ. in Baltimore, MD.

Served at Zion [German Evangelical Lutheran] Church. He was an artist & member of the Bach choir & in 1893 founded the Choral Society. He m. 22 July 1890, Adele Louise Chatin of La Chaux-de-Fonds, Neuchatel, Switzerland, a lady of Huguenot ancestry. *TR3:749-50*

HOHING, CONRAD, b. 9 Feb. 1826 in Germany, s/o George, a blacksmith. Conrad was trained as a cooper & brewer. In 1854 to America & settled at Cumberland, MD. Member of the German Lutheran Church. He m. 22 April 1856, Christina Trott. *6TH:604-05*

HOKE, PETER, b. Germany, to America at an early date & received a deed for land in present-day York Co., PA from an Indian Chief, which grant was later confirmed by William Penn's heirs. His son Jacob spent his entire life on this land, as did his son Jacob who m. Anna Mary Grons. Their son Jacob m. Mary Link & their son Jacob was b. on family farm in York Co., PA. He was a hatter & broom-maker & mechanic in wood. After his m. he removed to Frederick Co., MD, where he engaged in milling & making brooms. Their son Jacob b. in Frederick Co. 21 Jan. 1848. *FR2:1023-4*

HOLBEIN, JACOB, b. Germany, to Baltimore as a young man. He m. in Baltimore, Sarah Nock of Isle of Wight Co., VA. Their son, Wesley A. J. Holbein, m. Kate M. Flynn & their only child was Edgar Allan Holbein, b. 2 Aug. 1881, in Baltimore. *TR3:804-7*

HOLLINGSHEAD, WILLIAM, b. Ireland & left for America c. 1798. He m. Martha Kerr & settled in Baltimore Co., MD. Martha d. c. 1821. *MDC:167*

HOLLINGSWORTH, HENRY, VALENTINE & THOMAS, from England to PA in the ship *Welcome* with William Penn in 1682. They were sons of Valentine Hollingsworth & Catherine d/o Henry Cornish, High Sheriff of London. Valentine, the immigrant, settled in Delaware Co. on the Brandywine &. Valentine was still living in 1710. He had a son Henry who m. Lydia Atkinson in 1688 in Ireland. They res. in DE & PA & removed to Elkton, MD c. 1712, surveyor of Cecil Co. They were founders of the family in Cecil Co. Quakers. Valentine's descs., Thomas Sr., Thomas Jr. & Nathaniel; the latter b. in Westtown, Center Co., PA in 4 Sept. 1755 m. Abigail Green in 1783 & removed from Chester Co., PA to Harford Co., MD. [H/C:413-14 states that Valentine

Sr. emigrated to America with William Penn in 1682 also & settled in what is now New Castle, DE. Although the family were Quakers, it is stated that many of his descs. served in the Rev. War.] *C:220-30; H/C:413-14; 519-20*

HOLLOWAY, RICHARD, b. England, to US & located near Darlington, Harford Co., MD. Farmer, 1850 purchased the old Hopkins farm in Harford Co. He d. 1868, aged 63; m. Hester N. Stump & had 5 children. *H/C:357-8*

HOLLYDAY, THOMAS (CAPT.), Englishman who came to America in 1654 with sons James, who became chief judge on the Eastern Shore of MD, & Col. Leonard of Prince George's Co. *TR4:670-73*

HOLMES, THOMAS, brought out from England by William Penn & given a tract of land on part of which the town of Holmesburg, a suburb where Philadalphia now stands. His grandau. Sarah Holmes m. Louis Dugan, of a Scotch family. Their dau. Sarah Dugan m. William D. Alexander, of an early Scotch-Irish family that settled in Cecil Co., MD. *TR4:332*

HOLTER, GEORGE, from Germany, settled in Frederick Co., MD c. 1768. He m. 4 Feb. 1776, Margaret Arnold & had: Jacob; Catharine; John; Daniel; Magdalene; Sarah; George: William & Margaret. About 1815 Jacob & Catharine went to Centre Co., PA. Son Jacob walked from Centre Co., PA & return, a round-trip distance of 440 miles, to visit his brothers & sisters in Frederick Co., MD. George & John settled in Meigs Co., OH c. 1817. Other members of the family remained in Frederick Co., MD. *FR2:1100-01*

HOLTHAUS, FRANCIS THEODORE, and wife Marie E., both b. near Osnabruck, Hanover, Prussia, m. in Baltimore, MD. Both had been brought to America at a young age. *GME:187*

HOLYLAND, ---, b. England, to US c. 1830. He was an engraver; Baptist. Son John b. Harsimus [sic] NJ 6 Oct. 1841; family at Baltimore, MD by 1861. John with photography gallery of M. Young in Baltimore & at age of 24 m. his cousin, Rebecca Hart of Middletown, Orange Co., NY 27 July 1865. His father died 3 months after his marriage. *MDC:222*

HOMER, CHRISTOPHER, b. Hanover, Germany, to Baltimore c. 1827. He was in the bacon business & retired in 1866. His wife was Dora Male, also from Germany. Both had immigrated to America at an early age. Their only child, Charles C., b. 1 Nov. 1847 in Baltimore, m. Fannie M. Holthaus, b. Baltimore 7 Sept. 1847, a d/o Francis Theodore & Marie E. Holthaus, natives of Hanover, Germany. *MDC:623; TR3:555-7*

HOOD, BENJAMIN, from Lancashire, England c. 1690 to America with brothers James & John. They were sons of Samuel Hood. James, Episcopal clergyman, settled in PA; John, a lawyer, settled in VA. Benjamin was a physician & settled on the Patapsco near what is now known as Hollofield Station on the B&O Railroad, where he built a mansion & large mill, calling his home "Hood's Haven." He was the first known settler upon the Patapsco that far west. He left two sons, James (b. c. 1755) & John. Desc. Benjamin Hood m. Hannah Mifflin Coulter, d/o Alexander Coulter of Baltimore. Their son, John Mifflin Hood b. Bowling Green, near Sykesville, Howard Co., MD 5 April 1843. *TR3:230-1, 466-73; AAH:476*

HOOD, JAMES, b. England, to Baltimore, m. Elizabeth Mifflin, a descendant of Gen. Thomas Mifflin, of PA. Son James Mifflin Hood b. 22 March 1821, Baltimore, d. 3 April 1894. James m. (1st) Sarah Ann Boggs, Quaker lady of Philadelphia. He m. 2d 21 Oct. 1873, Margaret Elizabeth, d/o Daniel Scholl & Maria Susan Thomas, of Frederick Co., MD. The Scholl family were originally from Switzerland. *6TH:415-16; FR2:1400-1*

HOOD, JOHN, JAMES & JOSHUA, in colonial days from England to America. One brother settled in MA & from him is desc. the Dr. Hood who compounded that famous proprietary remedy, Hood's Sarsaparilla. Another brother settled in LA. The remaining brother settled in Howard Co., MD. The son of this emigrant [not named here] served in the Continental army. His son, John Hood, was a farmer in the Woodville area of Frederick Co., MD. John m. (1) Tabitha Wolf & (2) Rachel Grimes. *FR2:1555-6*

HOOPER, HENRY, & wife Sarah & son Henry Jr. came into province of MD from England 1651 & first settled in Calvert Co. on the Patuxent River. Was justice of Calvert Co. 1658; later took up land in Dorchester Co. 1668. In 1684 his son Henry (II) lived on Hooper's Island. He was

b. in England in 1643 & was aged 8 years on his immigration with his parents. He was a justice of Dorchester Co. & was twice married: (1) Elizabeth, d/o Levin Denwood of Somerset Co. & (2) Mary ---. *TR4:433*

HOOPER. Three Hooper brothers from England in Colonial times; one settled in Dorchester Co., MD, one settled in SC & one in the West. Decs. Thomas Hooper, merchant & ship builder, b. Taylor's Island, Dorchester Co., MD 1803, s/o James, farmer. Thomas removed to Baltimore as young man. *MDC:263-4*

HOOTEN, JOHN (CAPT.), b. 27 day of 1st month 1752, of the English Army. He m. 7th day, 4th month, 1780 Rachel Mott, b. 11th day, 5th month, 1757, d/o Jacob & Keziah Mott, Orthodox Quakers of Hempstead, Long Island. Their son, John, b. 7th day, 6th month, 1700 & m. 21st day, 2d month, 1737 Sarah Key, d/o Thomas of Wigdon, Co. of Cumberland, England. Capt. John was s/o Thomas Hooten & Mary Lippincott of Shrewsbury, England, who settled in 1677 in Burlington and later settled in Mooretown, NJ. *MDC:101*

HOPE, JAMES, b. Scotland, early in life emigrated to America & settled in Bucks Co., PA. In 1771 he moved to Harford Co., MD, where he died. His son, Thomas Hope, b. Bucks Co., PA & also later a farmer in Harford Co., d. 20 March 1815, aged 72. *H/C:441*

HOPKINS, GERARD, in America as early as 1658. His will of 1691 names his children: Gerard, Anne, Thompsin & Mary. Thompsin m. Capt. John Welsh of South River. The 2d Gerard m. Margaret Johns & had: Joseph, Gerard, Philip, Samuel, Richard, William & Johns, all b. between 1706 & 1720. The founder of Johns Hopkins University was a desc. of this family. *AAH:318*

HOPKINS, JOHN, from Scotland & settled on the MD side of the Potomac c. 1775. He m. Eleanor Wallace, d/o James of Montgomery Co., MD. Children: Herbert, William, Richard, Alexander, James & John. *AAH:318*

HOPKINS, MATTHEW, of County of Ayr, Scotland to Rock Creek, now Montgomery Co., MD in 1742. His widow Mary m. Henry Thralkeld. *AAH:318*

HOPPER, JOHN, with 2 brothers from England to America in the 18th century & settled in NJ. John's son, Thomas Hopper, b. in Woodbury, NJ; wheelwright. 1838 removed to Delaware City, DE where he d. 1844, aged 52. John m. Keziah Hufsee, b. NJ & d. in Chesapeake City, MD, aged 98. Presbyterian. *H/C:377-8*

HORMAN, AUGUSTUS F. C., b. Hanover, Germany, tailor. Came to US in 1837. He m. in Germany Dorretta Barriger, also b. Hanover. His wife & dau. followed him to America in 1840. He located in Frederick, MD & later removed to Hyattstown, Montgomery Co., MD. When his health failed he removed to Urbana District, on land now owned by his son William. He farmed there from 1856 to 1869, when he retired. He d. 19 Sept. 1880, aged 71 years & is bur. at Hyattstown. He was m. 3 times. Dorretta d. c. 1850, aged 30. By her he had: Linetta, m. Albert C. Strauss of Washington, DC; Charles E., d. aged 60 years in Howard Co., MD, m. a Miss Kessler; William Henry; Augustus R. of Prince George's Co., MD, m. Violetta Haller. Augustus' 2d wife was a Miss Neikirk, of Washington Co., MD. His 3rd wife was Mrs. Ann Sebley, widow of Thomas Sebley, nee Fowler. No children by last two marriages. *FR2:1454-5*

HORN, JOHN WATT (GEN.), b. Dumfries, Aberdeenshire, Scotland 30 March 1834, s/o Alexander, a millwright & carpenter, & Isabella Watt, a lineal descendant of the discoverer of steam power. She still living in Baltimore; Alexander d. 1877. Alexander & Isabella to American when John was a child & settled in Baltimore, where Alexander had a relative named Yates. *MDC:411*

HORNER, JOAHUS, b. Co. Armaugh, Ireland 1 Jan. 1806, s/o William, of Scotch descent, & Mary Allen. *MDC:665-66*

HORNSTEIN, KALMON, b. Poland, wife Esther Bernstein (d. 1881), b. Germany. Kalmon to Baltimore, MD in 1874, aged 22. Once established he sent for his parents in Poland and moved them to Baltimore. *TR3:141*

HORWITZ, J. (DR.), b. near Berlin, the captial of Prussia, 6 July 1783. To America in the early part of the present century & settled in Baltimore, where he d. 30 June 1852. In 1817 he m. Debby Andrews, d/o Major John of NY. *MDC:648*

HOUCK, ---, b. Germany, to Frederick Co., MD c. 1773. His son George Houck, b. Frederick Co. 1775, d. 1867. George's son Ezra, b. Frederick City, 30 July 1802, d. 8 April 1878, judge; m. in 1826, Catharine Bentz, d/o Jacob. *FR2:1375-6*

HOUCK, PETER, of French & German extraction, a prominent man of Paltz Alsace, but owing to religious persecution he came to America & settled in Frederick Co., MD. Desc. Ezra Houck m. Catherine Bentz, b. Bentztown, MD, which was named in honor of the family. It is now included in the corporate limits of Frederick. *TR3:819-20*

HOUGHTON, RALPH, from England to New England in middle of the 17th century. First clerk of Lancaster, MA (1656-1682) & d. in Milton, MA, 15 April 1705. A desc., Elijah Houghton, had a son Thomas, b. 8 Jan. 1767. Thomas m. Betsy White, d/o Capt. John White, b. in Lancaster 1738. Thomas & Betsy had a son, Stedman, b. 1799 at Harvard, MA & d. 1880. He m. Ann Andrews Cragin & had a son b. in Harvard 24 Aug. 1827, Charles E. Houghton. Charles m. Caroline Selmann McMurray & had Ira Holden Houghton, real estate dealer of Baltimore, who was b. in Cincinnati, OH 7 May 1865. Charles E. lived in Harvard & New Ipswich, NH until the age of 17 when he went "out west" to OH. In 1866 he moved his family to Baltimore, where he d. 2 Jan. 1908, aged 81. *TR4:402-3*

HOUSE, ANDREW, wealthy nobleman from Germany to America 1760. Was a great friend of King George III of England & "was active in helping England in the Revolutionary War & was given a grant of land in MD." When King George & the hold of England on America failed, Andrew returned to Germany [England?], where he died before the end of the war. While living in America he had a son, John Valentine House, who later removed to KY, where he had six children. John Valentine House, a Tory, after the war refused to pay the US gov't. tax on his land & the land was confiscated. *FR2:916, 1182-2*

HOWARD, HENRY (SIR), to MD 1706 as an agent of the British crown; m. Sarah Dorsey; res. Anne Arundel Co., MD. Their dau. Honora m. Henry Davidge. *TR4:15*

HOWARD, JOHN (MAJ.), an English Catholic priest, who, eschewing celibacy, m. Miss --- Evans, a desc. of Gov. John Evans of PA. Major Howard d. at Valley Forge during the war of camp fever. His mother was the d/o Jacques' Casho, an Alsatian who came to America to serve in the American Revolution in the DE line. His grandau., Eliza Ann Howard m. Francis Asbury Ellis & had Charles M., b. at Elkton, MD 13 Dec. 1838. *H/C:551-3*

HOWARD, JOSHUA, b. near Manchester, Lancashire, England 1665; an officer in the army of the Duke of York during the Monmoutn Rebellion. To America 1667, c. 1685, res. Pikesville, Baltimore Co., MD where he d. 1738. His wife was Joanna O'Carroll. Their son Cornelius Howard, b. 1706/07 & d. 14 June 1777, m. 24 Jan. 1738, Ruth Eager, b. 23 May 1721 & d. 17 Nov. 1796. She was d/o John Eager & granddau. of George Eager. George Eager was immigrant who settled in Baltimore Co., MD where he d. 1705/06. George m. Mrs. Mary (Wheelock) Bucknall, twice a widow & John Eager, son of this m. b. 23 Feb. 1691 & d. 11 April 1722. John Eager m. Jemima Morray who d. 18 Sept. 1725. Jemima was d/o James & Jemima (Morgan) Morray; James an immigrant who settled in Baltimore Co., MD where he d. in 1704. Jemima Morgan was d/o Capt. Thomas Morgan, also an immigrant who settled in Baltimore Co., where he d. 1697. John Eager Howard, s/o Cornelius who was s/o Joshua the immigrant, was the 5th governor of MD & a hero of the Rev. War. *TR4:521-4; MDC:362; AAH:240; TR4:818-20*

HOWELL, JOHN BRAZIER, son of John b. 18 Nov. 1741, & wife Elizabeth Wells, who m. 24 May 1764 at St. Mary Le Bon Church. John Brazier Howell the immigrant, b. London in 1766, emigrated to America in 1793, bringing with him two daus. Agnes & Eliza. He m. as his 2d wife in 1802, Elizabeth Carpenter. The family resided in Philadelphia & Baltimore. The first American wallpaper manufacturers. *MDC:172-73*

HOWLETT, ---, b. Germany, to America & settled in York Co., PA. Had dau. Nancy b. York Co., who m. Jacob Enfield & settled in Harford Co., MD, where their son Jacob was b. in 1811. *H/C:207*

HOYE, PAUL, from Ireland in an early day & settled in Washington Co., MD, near Williamsport, where he had a grant of land from the English government. He had a son John, who resided in Cumberland. Another son, William Waller Hoye, resided near McHenry, MD & d. aged aged 60. *6TH:546-57*

119

HUBBARD, HUMPHREY, of the Parish of East Kirkby, Lincolnshire, England, settled in Dorchester Co., MD in 1674 & d. there in 1709. His eldest son was also Humphrey who d. 1742. Another son was John Hubbard, settled in what later became Caroline Co., MD & m. Elizabeth Scott of Somerset Co., MD. They had only one son, Solomon, who m. Margaret Mahoun. *TR3:597-8*

HUBER (HOOVER), ---, settled in PA, Manor Twp., Lancaster Co. His children settled in Frederick & Washington Cos., MD & York & Franklin Cos., PA. Desc. Daniel Hoover farmed near the town of Graceham, Frederick Co., MD & had 4 children. *FR2:929-30*

HUGHES, DANIEL (MAJOR), b. Montreal, Canada 3 Feb. 1773; to MD as a youth. Served in US Army; retired to Frederick Co., MD. *FRI:283*

HUGHES, FELIX, b. Ireland, Catholic. He settled in Loudon Co., VA 1732. One of his sons, James, m. a Miss Dunn of Jefferson Co., VA in 1772, & was among one of the first white settlers of Greene Co., PA (then a part of VA). One of his sons, Thomas, b. in what is now Greene Co., PA m. Mary Odenbaugh, of near Winchester, PA. They moved to Wheeling, VA. Thomas was a veteran of the War of 1812. The 7th child of Thomas & Mary was Alfred, b. Wheeling, VA 16 Sept. 1824. Alfred was a newspaper correspondent for the *Baltimore Exchange* during the Civil War. 18 Dec. 1865 he removed with his family to Baltimore. *MDC:333-34*

HUGHES, JOHN HALL, b. Scotland, to America where his son John was b. on homestead on Trap Farm, Harford Co., MD 21 Aug. 1772. *H/C:176*

HUMMER, ---, to America before the Revolution, settled in NJ. Desc. William, soldier of the Rev. under Washington; after war removed to VA. His son Washington Hummer m. Mortena B. Fox, b. Loudoun Co., VA; farmer & j.p. Mortena still living at age over 80. Their son, Dr. James Cephas Hummer, b. Louden Co., VA 10 Nov. 1833, Methodist Episcopal Minister & M.D., 1867 to Baltimore Conference & served several parishes & in 1873 to Baltimore. He m. 10 June 1886, Annie A., d/o James & A. M. Whaley of Loudoun Co., VA. *MDC:203*

HUNCHEN, EDWARD GAVEHART, b. Germany. To Baltimore & d. at an early age in 1852. He m. Mary E. Griffith. *6TH:819-20*

HUNNER, JOHN, emigrated from area of Strassburg, Germany to the US in 1834 & settled in Buffalo, NY. He was accompanied by his wife, Katharine Reichert (who was half French). Their son, also John, m. Eudora Cooke & their son, Guy LeRoy Hunner, b. Alma, Buffalo Co., WI, was physician of Baltimore. Eudora was desc. of Henry Cooke, res. of Plymouth, MA before 1640. *TR4:793-4*

HUNT, ---, & wife --- Jones, b. England, to America c. 1810. Their son, Col. Thomas H. Hunt, of Howard Co., MD, b. in Frederick City in 1832. *AAH:529*

HUNT, JOB SR., b. England, settled in MD at an early date, from Talbot Co. to Green Spring Valley, Baltimore Co. in 1761. His brother Samuel a farmer of Talbot Co. *6TH:251-52*

HUNTER, JOHN, b. Ireland. He m. Catherine Breathed, b. in MD. Their dau. Catherine m. Baltus Stigers, b. Fulton Co., MD, but removed to Washington Co., MD when young. *6TH:489-90*

HUSSEY, CHRISTOPHER (CAPT.), b. 1599 England, d. 1688. To America 1630, the first white settler in Hampton, NH. Was one of the purchasers of Nantucket Island. He m. Theodate Batchellor, d/o Rev. Stephen of Hampton, NH. Their son, John Hussey, b. Hampton 1635, d. 1707. He removed to New Castle, DE & m. Susanna Perkins. Desc. Miriam Rebecca (Grace) Hughes, b. 13 April 1872 in Easton, Talbot Co., MD, only child of Luther & Grace Hester (Pritchett) Grace. Grace d. at Bel Air, MD 7 Oct. 1883, aged 33. *TR4:190*

HUTCHINS, FRANCIS, to America in 1698 & descs. settled on estate known as Stoakley, near the Patuxent River. *TR4:410*

HUTZLER, ABRAM G., b. Hagenbach, Bavaria, 12 March 1836, eldest s/o Moses Hutzler & Caroline Neuberger. Caroline was d/o Eli Baer Neuberger of Furth, Bavaria. Moses b. in Hagenbach in 1800; tailor. At age 38 Moses brought his family to America, settled in Baltimore; moved to Frederick, MD & then back to Baltimore where he d. 1889, aged 89; retailer. Caoline d. 1866, aged 75. *TR3:352*

HYLAND, JOHN & NICHOLAS, brothers, b. Labadeen, England. John a col. in the English army, resigned his commission & emigrated to MD in colonial times & obtained a land grant. On account of a difficulty, he settled in PA & also acquired land in NY. He returned to MD in 'the early part of the last century,' after that province was restored to Lord Baltimore. His estate, part of St. John's Manor on Elk Neck, was called in honor of his wife, "John's & Mary's Highland." Their eldest son was Col. Stephen, b. Elk Neck, 23 Feb. 1743, d. 19 March 1806; served in the Rev. War from Cecil Co. & 1 Dec. 1774 m. Rebecca Tilden of Kent Co., MD. *C:522-4; H/C:504*

HYMES, HENRY, b. Germany, to PA, among the early settlers of that state. His son John, b. PA, to Frederick Co., MD during the Whiskey Insurrection soon after the Rev. War. John was the father of Samuel, who was b. in Frederick Co., MD. *FR2:1031-2*

HYNDMAN, HUGH, b. Ireland 1800, d. PA 1880. To America & settled in Carbon Co., PA & m. Catharine Huff, b. Carbon Co. 1806, d. 1899. She was d/o Capt. John Huff who served under Washington. Their son Edward K., b. Carbon Co., 25 July 1844, d. 27 June 1884. *FR2:813*

HYNSON, THOMAS, b. England, to America in 1650/1 with wife Grace, children & 7 servants. He settled in Kent Co., MD 1657 & served in political affairs & lt. of the militia. He d. c. 1669, leaving several daus. & sons: Thomas, Charles, Henry & John. He bore the arms of the Hynsons of Fordham, Cambridge co. England. Their son Charles m. Margaret Harris, d/o Major William Harris, b. England & early settler of Kent Co., MD. He was b. 1650 & d. 1772. Desc. W. G. Hynson, b. Kent Co , m. Anna Maria Dushane & he d. 4 May 1882, aged 42. Anna Maria was d/o Col. Nathan T. Dushane, col. of 1st MD Regt. in the Civil War & was killed in action at the battle of Weldon Railroad, near Petersburg, VA. Her mother was Mary Eliza Patterson, d/o William of Baltimore. Dushanes were French Huguenot family who settled in DE. *TR4:217, 438, 648-9*

 GLEHART, JOHN WILSON, & Matilda Davidson his wife, from Germany & located near Marlborough, Prince George's Co., MD in 1740. Their son, Dr. James Davidson Iglehart to PA from England in 1775 & served in the Rev.

War. He settled at Davidsonville, Anne Arundel Co., MD, d. there in 1841. *AAH:329*

IRELAND, JOSEPH, b. 17 June 1727 near Halifax, Yorkshire, England, settled in Shrewsbury Parish, Kent Co., MD & m. 10 July 1761, Alethea, d/o William & Ann (Cosden) Comegys. *MDC:422*

ISEKOFF, KARMON, to America with wife Elizabeth, both b. Russia. Son Thomas, attorney, b. 9 Oct. 1894 New Haven, CT; to Baltimore 1907. Karmon d. by 1925; merchant after coming to US. *TR2:8*

ACKSON, JOSEPH, b. Devonshire, England, c. 1855 to America with wife and 3 sons, settled in Prince George's Co., MD. *TR3:343*

JACKSON, THOMAS P., b. Scotland, s/o John, to America with his family at age of 15. Settled in Fall River, MA, where son Thomas' son William Joseph was b. 28 Dec. 1884. William Joseph Jackson, D.D.S., practices in Baltimore. *TR3:217*

JACOB, JOHN (CAPT.), to MD in 1665 & settled on South River in Anne Arundel Co., MD. He was a land owner in 10 MD counties. Desc. Acsah Wilhelmina Clark m. Roderick Octavius Shipley. *TR4:810-16*

JACQUES, LANCELOT, French Huguenot, to MD as refugee before 1776. *FRI:106*

JACQUETTE, JEAN PAUL, b. Neufchatel, Switzerland, to province of New Sweden in 1650. Was in 1676 justice of New Castle, DE. Miss Elizabeth Grant McIlvain of Baltimore, MD is a desc. *TR4:103*

JAMAR, HENRY, exiled from France & emigrated to America in early 18th century. Served in the Revolutinary War in a PA regiment & after the war settled in Alexanderia, VA, where he d. in his 44th year. His son Henry removed from VA c. 1800 to Newark, DE & later to Cecil Co., MD, where he d. 1844. A pioneer Methodist. Henry m. Rebecca, d/o James & Hannah MacCauley 9 April 1812. *MDC:358*

JANNEY, THOMAS, member of Society of Friends, to the colonies from Chester [Cheshire], England in 1683, arrived in the Delaware River on the ship *Endeavor* from London 7th mo., 29th day, 1683, accompanied by his wife Margery, 4 sons & 2 daus. He purchased land in Bucks Co., PA. His 4th son, Joseph, m. Rebecca Biles in 1703 & their son, Jacob Janney, m. Hannah Ingledue & moved to Loudoun Co., VA in 1745. For 3 generations Loudoun Co. remained the family seat. Jacob's son Israel m. Pleasant Hague & his son, Abijah, also spent his life in Loudoun Co. & m. Jane McPherson. Richard Mott Janney, s/o Abijah & Jane, lived in Baltimore, engaged in coal business. He m. Sarah Hopkins, sister of the famous Johns Hopkins & their son Johns Hopkins Janney was b. in Baltimore Co. & res. in the the City of Baltimore until his retirement in 1876, when he moved to Indian Spring farm in Deer Creek, Harford Co. He d. there 2 Aug. 1889, aged 54. His wife was Caroline, d/o Thomas Alexander & Angeline (Steuart) Symington of Baltimore. Caroline's uncle was William Steuart, mayor of Baltimore in 1830. Both the Steuarts & the Symingtons were of Scotch ancestry.

Thomas Janney Jr., another son of Thomas the immigrant, to American from England with his father & settled in Cecil Co., MD. Thomas' (II) son, Eli Janney m. Hester Lackland & had George W., who m. Elizabeth A. Nolan, d/o John Nolan. Methodist Episcopal Church at Bayview members.

Thomas the immigrant's great-granddau. Hannah Janney, d/o Amos of Loudoun Co., VA, m. at Fairfax Meeting, Loudoun Co., VA, 30 Oct 1759, James Brooke of MD. Quaker family. *TR3:951-2; TR4:449; H/C:582; GME:234*

JARBOE, ---, emigrant from France, landed in Southern MD & res. St. Mary's Co. His son, William, b. in St. Mary's Co., MD & removed to Middletown Valley of Frederick Co., MD in early life. William m. Margaret Schaffer of Frederick Co. *FR2:1034-5*

JENKINS, WILLIAM, b. Wales, to America in 1534 in the company of Lord Baltimore. He settled in St. Mary Co., MD, extensive land owner. His son, Ignatius Jenkins, b. MD & had son Oswald Jenkins. Oswald's son, Ignatius W. Jenkins, b. Baltimore Co., was later farmer in Harford Co. where he m. Anna M. Brown. *H/C:523*

JOHNS, RICHARD, b. "ye 29th day of the First month [March], 1649/50, being the 5th day of the week," at Bristol, England; removed to MD & settled at The Cliffs in Calvert Co. 1675. He m. 7 July 1676, Elizabeth, youngest d/o Hugh & Margaret Kensey & widow of Thomas Sparrow. Richard d. 16 Dec. 1717. He & Elizabeth left 9 children. *TR4:343, 760*

JOHNSON, ANTHONY & JOHN, from England in 1665 & settled in MD. 1695 Anthony received a grant of 360 acres of land on the north side of the Patapsco River. Many land transactions are recorded for Anthony & it is recorded in the registry of St. Paul's Parish, Baltimore that he m. Katherine Smith on 3 March 1699. They had 7 children, 5 sons & 2 daus. Son Thomas b. 3 July 17810, on 25 July 1752 was m. to Ann Risteau, d/o Edward, a Huguenot & they settled at Pleasant Green near Pikesville. Their second son, Horatio, b. 1755, d. 1811, m. (2d) Elizabeth Warfield & had 6 children. *TR4:447-8*

JOHNSON, HENRY EDWARD (REV.), b. Co. of Cork, Ireland 27 March 1838. With his family to the US in 1841 & settled near Richmond, VA. He entered the ministry of the Methodist Episcopal Church South at age 19 & served in VA & Baltimore. *MDC:568*

JOHNSON, JOHN, b. 24 June 1809, Co. of Derry, Ireland, s/o Patrick who was b. in Ireland of Scotch descent, & Alice, d/o Bernard Trainor, of Co. Derry Ireland. In 1847 John left Ireland & landed in NY; teacher in DE, NC & MD. Catholic. *MDC:509-10*

JOHNSON, THOMAS, b. in Porte Head, Yarmouth, England; eloped with and m. Mary Baker. To MD, settled at St. Leonards, Calvert Co. c. 1660. *FRI:101*

JOHNSON, THOMAS, of Yarmouth, England, to Anne Arundel Co., MD 1660, was a desc. of Sir Thomas Johnson of Great Yarmouth. Thomas was the first Governor of MD, b. in Calvert Co., 4 Nov. 1732. He removed to Frederick Co., MD. Because of ill health he declined a cabinet post in Washington's administration. His wife was Ann Jennings, only d/o Thomas of Annapolis. Thomas d. at his home at Rose Hill, Frederick Co., aged 87 & was bur. in the Episcopal burial ground of Frederick. *AAH:224-6*

JOHNSTON, CHRISTOPHER, b. Moffat, Scotland, m. Susan, d/o Griffin Stith of Northampton County, VA. Their son Christopher was a merchant of Baltimore & m. Eliza, d/o Major L. Gates of Keene, MA. *MDC:554-55*

JONES, CHARLES (MAJOR), b. 2 Feb. 1758 in Ireland, to America 1793. He d. Oct. 1811 & he & his wife, Prudence Hawkins, bur. in the Congressional Cemetery at Washington. Charles was s/o Thomas &

Hannah Jones, Thomas the s/o Robert Jones, b. Wales & removed to Ireland in 1690. *6TH:139-40*

JONES, DAVID, from Wales to America & settled in city of Baltimore, blacksmith & woodworker. Served in War of 1812 & m. a Miss Evans. *6TH:732-33*

JONES, HUGH (REV.), (1670-1760) England to MD in 1696; rector of St. Stephen's (North Sassafrass) Parish, Cecil Co., MD 1731-60. His sister, Abigail m. William Barroll (d. 1754) of Hereford, England. *TR4:75*

JONES, NATHAN, member of the English nobility, to MD & became land owner in Montgomery Co. Great-grandson, Sylvester C. Jones, b. 22 Sept. 1832, owner of farm in Potomac District, Montgomery Co. *6TH:828-29*

JONES, RICHARD, to America from Wales 1781, settled at Fells Point, Baltimore, manufacturer of paints & oils. Member of the Wesleyan Methodist Society. Dau. Jane m. William Baker, and their son Charles Joseph, b. 28 May 1821, Baltimore. *MDC:64*

JORDAN, DAVID, b. Wurttemberg, Germany 24 Dec. 1872, s/o Wolf & Erustina (Meiers) Jordan. Wolf was a butcher & d. 1904, aged 61; Erustina d. aged 49. David to US & settled in Baltimore in 1897. He m. 14 June 1903, Fannie Kahn, b. Saxony, Germany, a d/o Moses & Sarah (Hecht) Kahn. He became an American citizen in 1906. *TR3:545-6*

JORDY, ---, b. France, settled in LA in early days of its history. Descendant Numa Joseph Jordy m. Sophie Andrea Murr, settled in Baltimore. Their son Albert Stauffer Jordy, b. in New Orleans, LA 27 Nov. 1835. *TR3:272*

JOURDAN, CHARLES HENRY, professor of mathematics & science at Mt. St. Mary's College, Emmitsburg, MD. Born 24 Feb. 1830 in Forcalquier Province, France, youngest s/o Antoine Jourdan & Francoise Bremond. In 1871 his eldest brother Jerome to US with family & settled in NY. Charles settled in Montreal, Canada in 1861 & in 1854 removed to Emmitsburg. July 6, 1871 Charles H. m. Adelaide Young, d/o Dr. Henry Dielman, music composer & professor at Mount St. Mary's. *FR2:801, 6TH:361-2*

JOYCE, EUGENE T. (HON.), s/o Thomas (d. c. 1845) & Celia, b. Town of Clifden, Co. Galway, Ireland 28 March 1839. To Canada with mother, sister & brother. 1860-77 business in Baltimore; m. 29 Jan. 1859 Margaret C. Helsen, d/o Richard (dec'd.) of Baltimore. *MDC:99*

ABLE, JOHN, b. Germany, to America & settled at what is now Kabletown, Jefferson Co., VA, which was named after him. He m. Elizabeth Johnstone, b. Jefferson Co, a d/o David Johnstone of Irish desc. Their son, John James Kable, b. Kabletown, d. 1905; Presbyterian. He m. Ella V. Dudrear, d/o John. They had: Ida, m. Daniel Knight of Charlestown, WV; Clarence, res. Baltimore; William Hartman; Charles H. of near Kabletown; Helen A., never mar.; Elinor D., m. Edward Brown of Charlestown, WV; Mayme, m. T. J. Kniught of Morton, PA; Madge VF. Kable, never mar. Son William Hartman Kable, physician, res. VA, TX, WV & Woodsboro, Frederick Co., MD. *FR2:1333-4*

KARN, ADAM, b. Holland, m. an English lady & to US, settled in MD. His son Philip b. in the latter part of the last century, d. 1868, aged 84. Philip was a hero of the War of 1812 & m. Miss --- Abrake. *6TH:262-63*

KASTEN, FREDERICK, b. Germany, to US in 1839 & settled in Baltimore. His son Henry was aged 2 on their emigration. Henry served in the Civil War & was a broom manufacturer of Baltimore. He m. Katherine Fink, also b. Germany & their son William J. Kasten was a surgeon of Baltimore. *TR3:493-4*

KAY, ALEXANDER B., b. near Edenburgh, Scotland in 1823. To America 1844, located at Morristown, NJ & later settled Greenville SC; also res. Trenton, NJ, Manchester, NH, St. Johns' New Brunswick, Elwood, NJ & Cecil Co., MD. He m. 1869, Elizabeth Talmadge. *H/C:285-6*

KEALHOFER, THEOBALD, prior to the Rev. from Alsace, France to Hagerstown, MD. Son Henry b. Hagerstown 28 June 1776 & d. there 1851, Oct. 21. *GME:305*

KEARNEY, PATRICK, & wife Mary, both b. in Ireland, to America & settled in Baltimore Co., MD where son Michael J. was b. at Long Green.

Michael m. Margaret C. Nagle & had Francis X. Kearney, M.D. b. there 2 Oct. 1889. Catholic. *TR3:355*

KEATING, MICHAEL, from Ireland to Baltimore at age of 21. He m. Elizabeth Jane Palmer, d/o George. Michael was a teacher & resided chiefly on the MD Eastern Shore & DE. *MDC:508*

KEEDY, ---, from Germany to America & was a pioneer settler in Western MD. His son Jacob H. b. in the vicinity, farmer. To Keedysville, where he d. aged 75. Jacob's son John J., b. 1805, farmer. In 1834 built a grist mill in Keedysville (Centreville). He m. Mary Ann Middlekauff, d/o Christian M. She d. 1882, aged 82. *6TH:550-51*

KEFAUVER, NICHOLAS, b. Germany, to America & was an early settler near Middletown, Frederick Co., MD in 1782. Accompanied to America by his brother Philip who settled in PA [MD]. Nicholas' son, George m. Mary ---; members of Reformed Church, both bur. in Reformed graveyard at Middletown, Frederick Co., MD. George's children: Daniel; John res. Baltimore, flour inspector; Jonathan a miller, went to OH;, Henry, farmer; Jacob, farmer; Elizabeth, m. Hanson Flook; Mary Ann, m. Philip Coblentz; and Rebecca, m. a Mr. Young of PA [FR2:1429-31 adds dau. Sarah Ann, d. single]. Son Daniel d. 1876, aged 68 & had been twice married, (1) Sarah Bechtel, d/o Lewis & Catherine (Stemple), (2) Catherine Bechtel, a sister of his first wife. By 1st marriage he had Horatio B. (only surviving child) & by his 2d marriage had Richard C., Daniel Edward, William D., Lewis F., Joseph H., Samuel M., Amanda C., Mahalia & Martha E. *FR2:791, 908-9, 921-2, 1296-7, 1356-7, 1361-2, 1374-5, 1429-31; 6TH:505-6*

KEHUE, FREDERICK, and wife Christina, from Germany to America with children, including Henrietta, who m. Elias Grove and resided at Frederick, MD. Their child John Henry Grove b. 1862. Other children of Frederick & Christina: Emma M., m. John J. Joy, farmer of Mechanicstown District, Frederick Co.; Rosa B., m. John J. Putnam, farmer of Shookstown; Charles W., farmer of Bradock; Benjamin F., grocer of Frederick; Christina V., m. Charles W. Harrison, merchant of Baltimore; twins, Francis H. & Marshall L., the former a carpenter of Braddock & the latter a farmer near that place; Grace, m. Gracen Mercer & res. near Braddock. Elias d. 7 July 1896 & was bur. in Mt. Olivet Cemetery, Frederick. *TR3:110*

KEITH, JAMES, from Scotland in 1662 settled at Bridgewater, MD, where he d. 1719, aged 76. His descendant, Enoch Pratt, b. North Middleborough, MA 10 Sept. 1808, removed to Baltimore in 1831. *MDC:493*

KELLER, ---, b. Germany, to America in early manhood & settled 4 miles north of Middletown, [Frederick Co.] MD & later took up land 1 mile south of Myersville. He is bur. in the cemetery of the Reformed Church at Middletown. His son David inherited his estate & m. Hannah Bussard. They also bur. at Middletown. Their 4th son, Henry, b. near Myersville 13 Dec. 1819 & m. at age 30 Sarah, d/o Daniel & Elizabeth (Routzahn) Biser of Middletown. Daniel Keller, another, or the same son of the immigrant but misnamed in one of these entries, inherited the family farm, m. Hannah --- & their son H. Melvin Keller b. near Myersville 13 Dec. 1812. *FR2:790, 967-8,*

KELLY, ---, b. Ireland, to America at age 7; stonecutter. He d. aged 55 in Oct. 1905. His wife was Mary McClean, of an Eastern Shore, MD family. Their son, Bernard Vincent Kelly, M.D., b. Baltimore 26 July 1882. *TR3:510-11*

KELLY, CATHERINE MAY, d/o James, who was a lifelong resident of Athy, Ireland, m. John Joseph Roberts & resides in Baltimore, the home of their son Dr. Joseph J., who was born in 1889. *TR3:245*

KELLY, DANIEL, immigrated from Isle of Skye to America in early 19th century, settled in NC, where his descs. have since resided. Desc. Evander Kelly m. Eliza McIver & had son John E. Kelly, b. Carthage, NC, who m. Penelope Kelly. John E. had an only son, Evander Francis Kelly, b. 2 July 1879, near Carthage, Moore Co., NC. Evander Francis Kelly now dean of the Univ. of MD School of Pharmacy. On 11 Oct. 1906, at Green Cove Springs, FL, he m. Marian Low, b. FL & d/o John E. & Emma (Heiberger) Low. John E. Low was of an old MA family & Emma Heiberger of a family of Washington, DC. *TR3:744-6*

KELSO, THOMAS, b. 28 Aug. 1784 in Clonis, a market town in the North of Ireland. He d. on East Baltimore Street, where he had lived for many years, 26 July 1878, in his 94th year. His brother John also to the US & resided near Baltimore about the year of Thomas' birth. Seven years later another brother, George, came to Baltimore, bringing Thomas with him. The Kelso brothers went into the butchering business in

Baltimore. George never married & d. in 1807. John retired early to Clover Hill near Baltimore, where he lived for 30 years. Member of the Methodist Episcopal Church. Thomas founded the Kelso Home for Orphan Children of the Methodist Episcopal Church. In 1807 he m. Ellen Cross, d/o John & Jane, of Cecil Co, MD; Presbyterian. *MDC:571-72*

KEMP, CONRAD, b. in Germany upon the Rhine. To America with his 3 brothers & settled on "Peace & Plentiful," later known as Rocky Springs, 1 mile northwest of Frederick, MD. His son Gilbert had a son Frederick, b. on the family homestead. Frederick m. Dorothy Hershberger. *6TH:468-69*

KEMP, JOHN CONRAD, of German family, b. "on the River Rhine." He came from the Palatinate to this country, sailing from Roterdam in 1733 on the ship *Samuel*, landing at Philadelphia. Original spelling was Kaempf. He settled 1st in Lancaster Co., PA & later in the New Market District, Frederick Co., MD. He was founder of the present town of Kemptown. The immigrant had at least two sons, Frederick & Gilbert. John's son Frederick Kemp, was also b. in Germany & came to America with his father. His son, Peter Kemp, b. in Frederick Co., 1749, was bapt. in the Lutheran Church at Frederick 29 July 1749. *FR2:791-2, 1253-4*

KENNEDY, JOHN, from Londonderry, Ireland to Phildelphia, PA with his elder brothers before the Revolution; m. a dau. of Philip Pendleton of VA. Their first child b. Baltimore 1811. They had four sons, all b. in Baltimore, only John, the eldest (1795-1870) & Anthony, the youngest, named here. Anthony in 1851 m. a d/o Christopher Hughes of Baltimore. He d. 4 July 1892 in Annapolis. [TR4:879-80 gives the immigrant's name as William Kennedy.] *TR4:14, 879-80*

KENNEDY, JOHN, m. Amelia Fitzgerald and sailed from Dublin in the ship *Neptune* 30 April 1784, landed at Baltimore. Amelia d. Salisbury, MD 1790. John d. St. Croix, West Indies on a visit to his brother James. Their dau. Bridget A. m. Jacob Poe 4 Jan. 1803 in Baltimore. *GME:194*

KENNEDY, JOHN, from north of Ireland to settled in Harford Co., MD some time in the 18th century. His son James b. in Harford Co., large land & slave owner of Harford Co. served in War of 1812. His son,

Silas Baldwin Kennedy, b. in Harford Co., 1834 apptd. capt. of the state militia; m. Eliza Cory, d/o James & Hannah. *H/C:564*

KEOUGH, ---, d/o Patrick & Ella (Mannion), all of Co. Galway, Ireland; m. Dr. Thomas K. Galvin. She d. 5 Jan. 1903, aged 38, in Baltimore. *TR3:305*

KER, WALTER, banished from Scotland in reign of James II, settled in Monmouth Co., NJ. His son William W. b. there 21 Feb. 1802 at "Handy Hall," near Salisbury. William studied at Snow Hill, MD & m. Anne D. Huston, d/o Dr. John Huston of Salisbury. He removed to Princess Anne, MD to practice law. *MDC:515*

KETZKY, WILLIAM, b. in Poland, to America at age of 12, resided in NY & AL, merchant; m. Annie Finkelstein, b. NY. Their only child, Dr. Joseph William Ketzky, b. Bessemer, Jefferson Co., AL 14 June 1882, practices medicine in Baltimore, MD. *TR3:207*

KEY, PHILIP, from England to MD early in the 18th century. Grandson John Ross Key, Lt. in the 2d Rifle Co. of MD in the Rev. War. John's only sister m. Roger Brooke Taney & his only son was Francis Scott Key, author of the Star Spangled Banner. *TR4:844-6*

KIEFFNER, CHARLES J., b. Germany, to America as a youth, settled Baltimore, where he d. 1920; m. Elizabeth Herrmann, b. Baltimore, d. 1917. Their son, George E., b. 23 Feb. 1894 in Baltimore. *TR3:193*

KILGOUR, WILLIAM (BISHOP), from England for the purpose of ordaining Bishop Seabury, of CT, the first Episcopal bishop in this country. He then returned to Scotland. His son, also William, to America c. 1730 & settled in St. Mary's Co., MD. *6TH:758-59*

KIMMEL, ANTHONY (GEN.), b. 17 March 1746, Manheim, Germany, from which place his father, Anthony Z. Kimmel, with 6 brothers, emigrated in 1750, to America. The brothers all settled in Lancaster Co., PA & probably gave its name to the town of Manheim. Descs. scattered throughout PA & other parts of the country. Anthony, son of Anthony the immigrant, settled in Baltimore City; many of the family members of the old Church of the Disciples of Christ at Paca & Lombard Sts. When the church graveyard was closed, family members removed to Loudon Park Cemetery. Family is of Saxon ancestry. *FR2:846-7*

131

KINDLEY, FREDERICK, from Germany to America as young man, settled near Ijamsville, Frederick Co., MD & later near Monrovia, MD. Frederick's son William, had son George F. b. 22 Nov. 1806. *FR2:795*

KING, WILLIAM, American progenitor, was a desc. of Roger King, b. in Devonshire, England in 1639. William settled in Philadelphia, where he was a silk importer, a member of the firm of King & Lowry. His son John was b. there 1783 & later removed to Baltimore. John served as an officer in Harris' Artillery in War of 1812 & m. Hester Stauffer who was b. 22 Nov. 1798, d. 22 Nov. 1868. John King d. 22 Nov. 1872. *TR4:447-9*

KINNEMON, JOHN, ANDREW & AMBROSE, Scotchmen, to NJ in early settlement of America & soon afterwards removed to Talbot Co., MD, where they bought tract "the Trappe." *MDC:429-30*

KIRECOFE, ---, from Germany to VA "about a century and a-half ago." His son Henry had grandson Rev. John Wesley Kirecofe, pastor in charge of the Centennial Memorial United Brethren Church of Frederick City, MD. Rev. John b. Staunton, Augusta Co., VA 25 Aug. 1841, one of 12 children, s/o John & Mary (Sowalter) Kirecofe. Rev. Kirecofe m. (1) Oct. 1863, Catharine V. Snyder who d. at Walkersville, MD 1870, leaving 2 children. He m. (2) Susan P. Buxton of Washington Co., MD. *FR2:893-4*

KIRK, JOHN, s/o Godfrey, b. 14 June 1660, at Alfreton, Derbyshire, England; to America c. 1682/3, settled in Darby twp., in what is now Delaware Co., PA. He d. 8th mo. (Oct.) 1705; m. 1688, Joan, d/o Peter Ellet, who survived him. John, 2d s/o John and Joan, b. 29 March 1692 in Darby, PA; m. at Abington Meeting, 17 Oct. 1722, Sarah Tyson, d/o Reynear Tyson & Mary Roberts of Abington. Isaac Kirk, 3d s/o John and Sarah (Tyson) Kirk, b. 30 Sept. 1735, d. 17 June 1826; m. 20 June 1756, Mary Tyson, d/o John and Priscilla (Naylor) Tyson. Mary b. 28 April 1733, d. 1 June 1828. Samuel, grandson of Isaac & Mary (Tyson) Kirk and 3d s/o Joseph & Grace (Child) Kirk, b. 15 Feb. 1793 Doylestown, d. 5 July 1872 in Baltimore, MD. *GME:274*

KIRK, ROGER, emigrated from Ireland 1712 & settled in Chester Co., PA & later removed to the banks of North East Creek, Cecil Co., MD. His son, Elisha Kirk, was the father of Allen Kirk, who was b. in Cecil

Co., MD in 1789, m. Martha McCullough & had 14 children. *H/C:472,
487-8*

KIRKPATRICK, JEREMIAH, b. 10 March 1785, County Antrim, Ireland, d. 3 March 1814. His dau. m. Dugold Carmichael, who d. in 1812. Jeremiah's grandson William Carmichael b. Old Town, Baltimore, MD 5 Feb. 1810. *MDC:109*

KIRKWOOD, ROBERT, b. Ireland, to America with his mother c. 1730 & settled in DE; farmer. He & an uncle, William Kirkwood, served in the Rev. *H/C:538-9*

KISSNER,. WALBURGER, d/o a burgomaster in Baden Baden, [Germany] m. Michael France, settled in Baltimore where their son John Caspar France was b. 14 May 1860. *TR3:267*

KLEE, JOHN, b. Germany, to America & m. Mary Opitz; they both d. 1914. She was b. MD. Their surviving children: John Peter, m. 16 Nov. 1898, in Carroll Co., Jennie Carroll Hering, d/o Granville T. & Mary Lucinda (Miller) Hering of Carroll Co.; Charles W., res. in Westminster, MD; George, res. Liberty Heights; Harry, res. Eastview; Henry who res. with John Peter's widow in the vicinity of Gamber; Margaret (Mrs. Green), res. in Bird Hill; Clara (Mrs. Crumbine), res. Westminster; & Elizabeth, res. Eastview (all in present day Carroll Co., MD). *TR3:854-7, 864-7*

KLEES, HENRY, b. 12 April 1813 at Hesse Darmstadt, Germany, s/o Conrad, also b. that place. At age 20 he went to England where he was a tanner & currier. Settled in Baltimore, MD in 1839, worked on the railroad & at tannery of James Carrigan. He started his own tanning business in Frederick Co., MD & later in Baltimore. German Methodist Church member. *MDC:590*

KLEIN, E. FREDERICK, b. Wurtemberg, Germany 5 Oct. 1790; d. Frederick Co., MD 21 Aug. 1873; baker, served in German Army. His four brothers all killed in Battle of Moscow, 1817. He m. Anna R. Lillich, d/o Frederick & Anna (Frizen) Lillich & had: Elizabeth, m. Adam Kahler; Louisa C., m. Thomas Sappington of Frederick City; Harriet, m. Rev. Enoch Frey of Madison Co., IN; Charles S.; E. Frederick, dec'd. of Woodville district; & George J., res. Marshall Co., IA. *FR2:797*

KLIPP, JOHN, b. Germany c. 1813. Sailed with his parents for America, landing at Baltimore in 1841. Tailor of Frederick, MD & later a farmer & huckster in the same county. He m. Elizabeth Smith, also b. in Germany. They had: Annie, dec'd.; Paul, farmer of Braddock District, Frederick Co.; Elizabeth, m. Frederick Mosser of Braddock District; Henry of Frederick City; John, farmer of Tuscarora District; Charles, dec'd. *FR2:1363-4*

KNABE, WILLIAM, b. Kreusburg, Duchy of Saxe Weimar [Germany] 3 June 1803. He m. 1833 Christiana Ritz of Saxe Meiningen & soon after emigrated to America with her family & settled in MO. He later removed to Baltimore. Piano manufacturer. He d. 21 May 1864 in Baltimore. *MDC:403*

KNAPP, FREDERICK, b. Wurtemberg, Germany 26 April 1821. Left Reutlingen 26 May 1850 & landed in Baltimore, MD 8 Aug. 1850. Teacher. He m. 4 May 1851 Louisa Anne Grossinger of Germany. *MDC:354*

KOEBER, LENA, b. Germany, m. Frank Barton, who was killed during the Civil War serving in 20th NY Volunteer Infantry. Son George C. Barton merchant of Annapolis, MD, b. New York City 30 July 1857. George m. 1884 to Annie E. Brooks, d/o William E. of Baltimore. *TR3:183*

KOENIG, WILLIAM, from Saxony to America in 1831 & settled in Baltimore. After 7 years removed to Lonaconing, MD & later settled on a farm in Garrett Co., MD near the present site of Deerpark. He d. there aged 73. He m. Henrietta Houper, b. in Germany, d. in MD aged 67. *6TH:189*

KOLIOPULOS, DEMETRIOS S., b. in Tripolis, Greece, 25 June 1881, his parents being Stratis & Sophia. His father, a farmer, still res. in Greece. Demetrious to US in 1901, first locating in NY. In 1907 he arrived in Hagerstown, MD, where he established a restaurant & later purchased the Hotel Maryland, which he remains proprietor. 22 June 1921 he m. Margaret Boyle, d/o Dr. Charles B., of prominent family of Hagerstown. *TR3:570-3*

KOONS, HENRY, to America from the Netherlands in 1730 & after a stay in NJ came to Frederick Co., MD. He was a blacksmith & had 5 sons. Son John Koons settled near Sugar Loaf Mountain & he changed the spelling of his name to Koontz, while other branches of the family retained the spelling of Koons. John m. Georgiana C. Miller. Other sons of the immigrant: Abraham lived near Keysville; Henry near Bruceville; and George, also a blacksmith, served in the Revolutionary War & in 1780 farmed near the Double Pipe Creek bridge, 1 mile from Middleburg, then Frederick Co., now Carroll Co. George m. Susannah Shroyer (1760-1848) of near Emmitsburg. They had 11 children & he d. 1817. *FR2:1613-14*

KORN, CHARLES, to America from Hesse, Germany at age of 18. Settled in Buffalo, NY, shoe business, d. at age 94. Dau. Elizabeth Anna m. William Weinbach, educated in Buffalo & graduated Martin Luther Seminary in 1864. Elizabeth Anna d. Sebringville in 1902, aged 58. Rev. Otto Frank Paul Weinbach, their son, is pastor of St. Paul's Evangelical Lutheran church of Baltimore. *TR3:239*

KORRELL, JOHN, b. Germany, from Hesse Darmstadt to America as a young man, landing at Baltimore in 1835. Removed to Frederick Co., MD, where he d. 1895. Tanner in the employ of the old John Louts tannery. He m. Elizabeth Sherman who d. 1 March 1907, aged 75. They had: Mary, m. Paul Klipp; Elizabeth, m. George B. Hanshew & d. 1908; John A.; Charles, d. in Abilene, KS & Frank of Frederick City. *FR2:1317-18*

KRAFT, FREDERICK, b. near Bremen, Germany, to America at an early age & settled in Baltimore Co., MD. He d. c. 1846. *MDC:666*

KRANTZ, JOHN D., b. Germany, to America as young man, settled in Frederick Co., MD; shoemaker. He m. Catharine Arter & had son Frederick J., b. 3 May 1820 in New Market District of Frederick Co. When Frederick was àged 6, John D. died. At age 21 Frederick opened a mill on the trail farm on Carroll Creek. Another son of John D. & Catharine (Arter) Krantz was William H. Krantz, who res. for a time in VA & later removed to Frederick Co., MD, miller. He bought the Old Flag Pond Mill, situated at Flag Pond, MD, which was built by Michael Late in 1773. William m. Julia Ann Beavers of Loudoun Co., VA. *FR2:796, 1414-15, 1419-20*

KREH, JOHN, b. Frankfort, & wife Christiana, b. Berlin, Germany. John to US as a young man; he d. 1894. His children settled in Western MD, Baltimore, Washington DC & Philadelphia. *6TH:290-91*

KREH, PETER, b. Schafheim, Hesse Darmstadt, Germany, to US as a young man & settled in Frederick City, MD, where he d. 1888. Stone & brick mason; Lutheran. He m. Elizabeth Hax & had: Mary, m. George Yost of Baltimore; Lewis T., cigar maker of Frederick City; John F. (b. 1861); William H. of Frederick & Charles, mason & builder of Frederick. *FR2:1315*

KUHLMAN, JOHN FREDERICK, b. Germany, s/o Henry. To America at age 8 with his parents & located in Somerset Co., PA. John Frederick minister of the Lutheran Church & has been located in NE. He m. Louisa, d/o Garrison Smith of PA & later served at Jennerstown, PA & Baltimore, MD until 1888, when he removed to Frederick, MD. *6TH:507-09*

KUNKOWSKI, FRANK, b. Poland, s/o Frank; shoemaker. To America at age of 22 & located in Fall River, MA for one year & then he removed to Baltimore, MD. He m. Viola Glenka & had son Andrew b. 10 Nov. 1897 in Baltimore, now physician & surgeon. Other children of Viola & Frank were Joseph, m. Matilda Levinska; Mitchell; and Catherine. *TR3:874-5*

KURTZ, JOHN NICOLAS (REV.), b. in Kingdom of Nassau, Germany, of a German Protestant family. To America in 1745, located at Philadelphia & later at Germantown. His son John Daniel Kurtz b. in Germantown, PA 1763, served the Lutheran Church in Baltimore for 50 years. Edward Kurtz, s/o John Daniel, b. in Baltimore 24 Sept. 1796. *MDC:712-13*

KYLE, SAMUEL A. S., b. of Scotch-Irish family in Ireland, s/o George Kyle, a Lt. in the royal navy. He came alone to the US at the age of 14 & joined his uncle, Adam Kyle, a merchant in Baltimore, a member of firm of Dinsmore & Kyle, established in 1805. He m. (1) at age 28 to Anna E. Fendall, who died childless in 1876. Three years later he m. (2) Ella V. Harward, d/o C. W. Harward of Harford Co., MD. Episcopalian. *H/C:395-6, 540*

A BARRE, GEORGE ROYAL, to America with his brother as soldiers under Gen. Lafayette in 1776. Desc. res. Frederick Co., MD. Granddaughter Angeline LaBarre m. Christopher M. Riggs. *FR2:845*

LAMB, PEARCE, b. in England, Quaker, settled in MD. He had 2 sons, Francis & Pearce, & several daughters. Pierce settled first in Frederick Co., MD & later moved to KY. Francis settled in Kent Co., MD. *MDC:462*

LAMBDIN, ROBERT, to MD in 1663. His widow Sarah m. William Thomas & they administered Robert's estate (1687). Their son, William Lamdin m. (1) Mary & (2) Sarah Elliott. Res. Talbot Co. *TR4:831-3*

LAMORE (LAMAR), THOMAS, PETER & JOHN (DR.), originally from Wicres, a small village not farm from Lille in France, emigrated with other French Huguenot families that came to MD & VA c. 1660. Thomas & Peter settled in VA & later removed to MD, where they appear in records at Annapolis in 1663. In 1674 Dr. John Lamore, subject of France, was naturalized in MD & located in Charles County. Peter & John left no sons, so the family traces its roots to the brother Thomas. *FR2:1183-4, TR4:783-4*

LAMPE, JULIUS, b. Germany 1801, d. Frederick, MD 1881; with wife Christine & family in 1854, emigrated & settled in Frederick Co., MD. Son John Henry Lampe, b. Brunswick, Germany 7 May 1841, to America with parents. John Henry learned trade of painting, frescoeing & sign-writing. He worked on many churches, halls & prominent buildings in the area. He m. in 1863, Elizabeth M. Ross; Reformed Church members. *FR2:907-8*

LANASA, ANTONIO, b. Italy in 1871, s/o Michael Lanasa, merchant. Antonio to America in 1884 & sent for his father and brother Michael, the latter a businessman of Baltimore. Antonio was a fruit importer. In 1894 to Italy where he m. his childhood sweetheart, Guiseppa Sansone. *TR3:504-5*

LAUGHLIN, HUGH, of Scotch-Irish descent, emigrated via Cuba to PA & was one of the earliest settlers of Fayette Co. Descendant Adam Laughlan, farmer, had one son, Rev. Robert Laughlin, a minister of the Methodist Episcopal Church. He served in the 7th WV Infantry in the

Civil War. Robert m. Elizabeth Chalfant, d/o James, b. Brownsville, Fayette Co., PA. She now lives in Greene Co., PA, aged 83 years. Son James W., M.D., b. Harrison Co., WV, 29 April 1845, reared in Greene Co., PA. He has practiced medicine at Mt. Morris, PA, Oak Forest, Greene Co., PA and Deer Park, MD. He & brothers Adam and George enlisted in Co. I, 8th PA Reserve Infantry. *6TH:596-97*

LAWRENCE, JACOB, with wife Elizabeth, both b. Germany, to US with 2 children: Laura, who m. --- Matthias & Rebecca, m. --- Little. Son William b. Washington Co., MD; blacksmith, Mennonite, d. aged 26 in 1867. William's wife was Annie, d/o George & Mary (Drill) Lantz of Washington Co. Elizabeth m. (2) Elias Stottlemeyer & removed to Caveton, Washington Co. *TR3:437*

LAWSON, THOMAS, came at an early period to VA with Capt. John Smith. Descendant Courtney Cordelia Barrand, b. 1 July 1836 in Norfolk, VA, d. 4 Aug. 1871, bur. Chester Cemetery, near Chestertown, MD. She was d/o Dr. Daniel Cary Barrand & Mary Lawson Chandler of Norfolk, and she m. Col. George Adolphus Hanson, b. 30 Dec. 1830 at "Woodbury" at head of Sassafras River, Kent Co., MD, on his father's estate. *MDC:311*

LE FEVRE, ABRAHAM, of French-Huguenot family, to America in 1707 & settled in what is now Kingston, NY. Later removed to Lancaster Co., PA, where his son David b. 1719. Before the Rev. David to Washington Co., MD, where his son John b. 1770. Son John m. Cristianna Householder, a granddau. of Maj. Otho Zwingley, hero of the Rev. *6TH:220-22*

LE GRAND, SAMUEL D., grandson of Gen. le Compte Claudius Just Alexandre Le Grand, count of the empire, peer of France, chevalier Grand Cross Double Eagle, &c. Samuel emigrated to MD in 1780 & his son, John Carroll LeGrand b. Baltimore 1814. *TR4:854-5*

LEASE, WILLIAM, to America from Germany with 2 brothers. Brother George located in Frederick City, MD & another brother to PA. William settled in vicinity of McKaig, Frederick Co. His children: William; George, lived & d. in Frederick City; a dau. who m. a Mr. Rhoderick & another dau. m. a Mr. Sheldon. Son William b. c. 1775 at Mt. Pleasant, d. 1845. Ran cooper shop on home farm, m. 24 May 1825, Mary Riner. *FR2:1142-3*

LEATHERMAN, ---, from Germany in 1725 & settled in Lancaster Co., PA, whence his descs. went to Frederick Co., MD. Desc. Godfrey Leatherman m. Miss A. Miller & had son Daniel b. 9 April 1797, d. 4 March 1859, res. Middletown Valley, Frederick Co. & m. Christine Warrenfeltz. *FR2:882, 1588-9, 1616-17*

LEATHERMAN, DANIEL, b. Germany, to America & settled at Germantown, PA. His son Peter, minister of the German Baptist Church, m. Annie Swigard & had a son Jacob, also a minister. Jacob m. Catharine Harp & had (among others) son Peter b. 27 Oct. 1831 & d. 27 Dec. 1904, farmer of Frederick Co., MD. *FR2:993-4*

LEATHERMAN, DANIEL, b. Germany, to America & settled at Germantown, PA. Member of the German Baptist Church, m. & had son Peter, who was minister of the church. Peter m. Annie Swigard & he d. 29 Nov. 1845; bur. on the graveyard on the home farm. *FR2:1147-8*

LEE, FRANCIS, to the island of Barbadoes from England at end of the 17th century & later removed to SC. His son, Thomas Lee, b. 6 Feb. 1710, d. 8 Aug. 1769, had a son Stephen Lee, b. 21 July 1750. Stephen's eldest son, Paul S. H. Lee, b. 22 Sept. 1784, had son Col. Stephen States Lee, b. SC; engineer. Col. Stephen m. Sarah F. Mallett, d/o Gen. E. J. Mallett, a descendant of David Mallett, A Huguenot refugee. Stephen was a world traveler who settled in Baltimore, MD in 1843. *MDC:595-96*

LEE, RICHARD (COL.), to Colony of VA in 1640 as Lt. Gov. under the British crown. Philip Lee, grandson [given as the son of the immigrant in the 2d named reference below] of the immigrant, founded the MD branch of the Lee family in 1700. His grandson [son?], Thomas Sim Lee, was 7 times Gov. of MD & a friend of Washington, Lafayette & other distinguished men of the Rev. period. After the Rev. War he retired to his estate of Needwood in the Middletown Valley, Frederick Co., MD, where he d. 1819. *FR2:1444-5; TR4:75*

LEGG, WILLIAM, an Englishman who settled at Kent Island on a warrant obtained in 1717. *MDC:499*

LEGGET, JAMES (SR.), to America from England c. 1760, settled in Lisburn, Cumberland Co., PA. He was a soldier in George Washington's army during the Rev. Operated an iron furnace at Lisburn along the

Yellow Breeches Creek. His son James Jr., surveyor of Cumberland Co., PA & school teacher. James Jr. to MD 1800 & was teacher at Sharpsburg, Creagerstown & Woodsboro in MD & in Shepherdstown, WV. He d. near Middleburg, Carroll Co., MD in 1848. Through his mother, Catharine Vaines, James Jr. was a great-grandson of Sir William Keith, gov. of PA (1717-1726). *FR2:1387-9*

LEHMAN, ISAAC L., b. 7 Feb. 1831, Lembach, Alsace, France, s/o Henry & Caroline (Culman) Lehman, both b. in that province. 1852 Isaac to US, located in Louisville, KY where he d. 13 June 1885. Distiller & wholesale liquor dealer. Hebrew, served with Confederate forces during Civil War. Son Clarence Morton Lehman removed to Baltimore, MD merchant. *TR3:121*

LEIPER, THOMAS, b. Strathaven, Lanark, Scotland, 15 Dec. 1745, to Philadelphia in 1763; served as an officer of the Rev. War and d. in Delaware Co., PA, 6 July 1825. His granddau., Mary T. Leiper, d/o Judge George Gray Leiper, m. 1851, John Henry Thomas, b. St. Mary's Co., 4 July 1824, d. Baltimore, MD 14 July 1898. *GME:243*

LEITZ, ---, from Germany to Baltimore 1812. His son, Thomas Leitz, m. Mary Kern. Thomas served in the Civil War in the Union Army as a private. Jacob F. Leitz was s/o Thomas & Mary, merchant & now retired. He m. Mary Schuman, whose parents were b. Germany. They have 3 living children: T. Frederick, b. 29 Oct. 1882; Margaret, m. Howard Bucher, jeweler of Baltimore & Alice May, m. E. S. Roberts, canner of Baltimore. Family connected with Oheb Shalom congregation. *TR3:766-7*

LEONARD, ROBERT, British soldier, founder of family in America, settled in MD; d. in Rev. War. Grandson Griffith Jeems Leonard m. Nancy Emmett Porter, a desc. of Robert Emmett, the Irish patriot & dau. of William Emmett of Emmitsburg, MD. *TR3:49*

LESER, FREDERICK, of Prussia, a compatriot & friend of Carl Schurz & Franz Siegel in the uprising of 1848 against Prussia. Fought with American forces in the first World War. In 1880 he removed to Philadelphia, PA. His son, Oscar Leser, a twin, b. St. Louis, MO 16 Oct. 1870, was educated in Philadephia, PA. In 1898 took up res. in Baltimore, attorney & editorial work for the *Baltimore American* newspapers on questions dealing with law, finance & government. In

1896 he m. Annette Angus, d/o Gen. Felix Angus of Baltimore. *TR3:579-80*

LESLIE, ROBERT, to America from Scotland c. 1645. In 1758 he purchased a farm north of the town of North East, Cecil Co., MD. Sometime before 1786 he moved his family to Elkton; clock & watch maker & later they removed to Philadelphia. *C:520-1*

LETHER (LEATHER), JOHN, b. Germany. To America as a soldier in War of the Rev. He settled on Carroll's Manor, Frederick Co., MD, west of Buckeystown; farmer. His son John, b. in MD Jan. 1790, farmer; served in the War of 1812, Lutheran. He removed to what is now known as Flint Hill Church, in Urbana District, Frederick Co. & d. in 1865. John's (2d) wife was Mary Leather, d/o George Leather. She d. 1839. *FR2:1469-70*

LEVERING, WIGARD, and brother Gerhard to America in 1658 & settled in Germantown, PA. They were descs. of Robert Levering, b. France c. 1600, fled to Holland or Germany. Wigard, b. c. 1648 in Gamen, Westphalia, Germany, m. Magdaline Boker in 1671. Brought family of wife & 4 children to America in 1685 and settled at Germantown, near Philadelphia PA; in 1692 Wigard bought 500 acres of land at Roxborough. Son William, b. at Mulheim on the River Rhine 4 May 1675, was 8 years of age when his parents brought him to America. William d. in 1746, aged 75. His son William, b. Roxborough (PA), Aug. 1705, m. Hannah (nee Harden) Clements, widow of Robert Clements, 2 May 1732. Hannah d. 23 May 1768, aged 49 years. William d. 30 March 1774, aged 49. A s/o of William & Hannah, Enoch Levering, b. Roxborough 21 Feb. 1742, tanner. Enoch removed to Baltimore 1773/75 and m. Hannah Richter 10 April 1765. Hannah was a sister of his brother Aaron's wife. Aaron was a Rev. War veteran who removed to Baltimore c. 1780. *MDC:139, H/C:275*

LEVIN, HYMAN LOPUIS, s/o Abbe Asher Levin, was b. in Russia, to US 1881, settled in Baltimore, MD, where he d. at the age of 63. He m. Fannie Block, d/o Jacob & Mary Block of Baltimore. *TR3:271*

LEVIN, MAX, b. Jacobstadt, Province of Courland, Russia, where he lived until 1896, when he came to America with his family, settling in Baltimore, MD. Retail shoe business. He m. Celia Miller in Russia & they had 2 children, their son Ellis, being 3 years of age on immigration, was b. Riga, Russia, 4 July 1893. Ellis, practicing attorney of Baltimore, m. 25 Dec. 1921, Annette D. Alter, d/o Abraham, of Baltimore. *TR3:730-33*

LEWIS, ABSALOM, from England prior to the Rev. & served on the American side in that war. Settled near Darnestown, m. a Miss Dudley, who was descended of Lord Dudley, of England. *6TH:746*

LIEBIG, GUSTAV ADOLPH, b. 18 Aug. 1824 in Hayda, Austria, s/o Frantz, an artist. To America in 1856, landing in New York, where he stayed 2 years & then on to Baltimore, MD. He m. Elizabeth S. Holland of Baltimore. *MDC:168*

LIEUTAND, DENNIS CLAUDE, one of the largest sugar & coffee planters on the Island of San Domingo before the insurrection. He was driven from the island with his family. He d. in Baltimore a year two after reaching that city. His grandau., Emily C. Hoffman m. Thomas A. Healey of Cumberland, MD, before 1842. *MDC:306-07*

LIMERICK, THOMAS KERR, b. Co. Clare, Ireland, to America at age 14, settled Philadelphia; m. Maria Hunter b. Philadelphia, PA; son J. Arthur b. Philadelphia 19 July 1870, settled Baltimore. Protestant-Episcopal. *TR3:61-3*

LIND, EDMUND GEORGE, b. Islington, near London, England, 18 June 1829, s/o William Alexander Lind, an engraver of Swedish descent, & Elizabeth Violet Lind, of an old English family. Edmund m. Margaret, 6th d/o William T. Murdoch of Baltimore, 23 April 1863. *MDC:708*

LINDSAY, WILLIAM, with wife Elizabeth Griffith, both b. Fintaugh, Ireland, to America 1825, settled Baltimore; grocery business. He d. here in 1849, aged 52. Son George W. (Judge) b. Baltimore 10 May 1826. Episcopal. *MDC:66*

LINTHICUM FAMILY,, Natives of Wales, where the name was spelled Lynthicum, & when they removed to Liverpool, England the spelling was changed. There were 5 brothers; one remained in England & 4 emigrated to America--1 settled in KY, 1 in VA & 2 in MD. One of these 2 on a farm in the lower part of Frederick Co. A desc., Slingsberry Linthicum, settled in what is now Howard, then Frederick Co., MD. *FR2:1227-8*

LITCHENBERG, ISADOR, b. Austria, to US at age 12; merchant of Baltimore; m. Ethel Pollack. First child, Joseph, b. 31 Jan. 1898, Baltimore. *TR2:48*

LITCHFIELD, LAWRENCE, founder of the family in America, of English desc., for whom the town of Litchfield was named. Desc. Francese H. Litchfield, d/o the late Edwin C. & Grace (Hubbard) Litchfield, b. 24 Jan. 1871, m. Lawrence Turnbull, res. Baltimore. *TR4:257*

LIVENGOOD, CHRISTIAN, from Switzerland to America & settled in Somerset Co., PA, where he d. His son Christian b. in Somerset Co., & removed to Salisbury, Lancaster Co. His son Christian M. b. in Somerset Co., PA 1835, removed 1868 to Grantsville, MD & m. 1884, Jennie Ulery, d/o Frederick of PA. *6TH:398*

LLEWELLYN, JOHN, a lineal desc. of Prince Daird ap Llewellyn the Great, whose mother was Princess Joan, a natural dau. of King John of England, by Agatha, d/o Ferrars, 4th Earl of Derby, was among the early settlers of St. Mary's Co., MD. His dau., Jane, m. (1) Philip Key & (2) John Hanson Briscoe. *TR4:203*

LLOYD, EDWARD, founder of the family in MD, was b. on the banks of the Wye River in Wales early in the 17th century. He accompanied the Puritan colony which settled in Isle of Wight Co., VA in 1619 & in 1649/50 [1640?] settled on the banks of the Severn River, near what is the city of Annapolis, MD. He was Surveyor-General & Gov. of a part of the Province under Lord Baltimore. Edward I returned to London, where he d. 1695. His son Col. Philemon Lloyd m. Henrietta Maria Neale & their eldest son, Edward Lloyd II, was president of the provincial council & acting gov. of MD 1709-1714. Henrietta was the widow of Richard Bennett, the Puritan leader in the province. She was the d/o Capt. James Neale, agent in Spain of the Duke of York & had been maid of honor to Queen Henrietta Maria, wife of Charles I of England. Edward II m. Sarah Covington in 1703. She was a Quakeress. One source here says that Edward, the founder, outlived his son Philemon. Eight Edward Lloyds have, in succession, owned this historic estate, located on Wye River in Talbot Co. Edward Lloyd (1779-1834) was the 5th of the name & the 14th gov. of the State of MD. *TR4:53, 865 & 869-70; MDC:523*

LOATS, HENRY, & wife Elizabeth from Germany to America c. 1800. Henry was a horticulturist. He d. 1817. Son John b. in Baltimore 7 Oct. 1814. Evangelical Lutheran Church member. *MDC:639*

LOCHER, AUGUST, German tailor, to America in early 1850's & settled in Portsmouth, OH, where he d. His son Charles A., b. in Portsmouth, manufacturer & Methodist. Charles m. Mary Adena Blomeyer & their son Roy W. Locher is physician of Baltimore, MD. Roy m. 23 April 1923, in Portsmouth, OH, Mazie Dickey b. PA. *TR3:689-90*

LOCKWOOD, ---, brothers Edward & Rober from England, settled Watertown, MA c. 1630. Lockwood descendants settled in DE & Cecil Co., MD. *H/C:181*

LODEN, DENNIS, & wife Mary Lanahan, both b. Ireland. Dennis to America at young age, worked for B&O Railroad for 25 years. Dennis' father [not named here] was a stone mason in the city of Baltimore for many years. Dennis & Mary had a son, Daniel J. Loden, b. Baltimore 1868, m. Delia J. Stivers in Baltimore in 1889. She was d/o Joseph. *TR3:603-4*

LOGAN, ROBERT, b. Ireland, settled Cecil Co., MD. His dau. Sophia m. John Christie, their son George M. b. Cecil Co. in 1844. *H/C:283*

LOMAS, ARTHUR J., M.D., b. Montreal, Canada 17 Sept. 1879, s/o Henry Stephen & Jane (Walton) Lomas, both b. England; Henry at Maidstone, Kent Co., a s/o Stephen & Beatrice (North) Lomas. Henry served in the British navy & after Crimean War to Canada (c. 1865). Arthur was one of 5 surviving children of 10. He served in WWI and after the war became connected with the Johns Hopkins Hospital in Baltimore, MD. He m. in St. Johns, Newfoundland, 27 April 1911, Elena Maria Perez, d/o Jose, Spanish consul general at that place. *TR3:370-1*

LONG, JAMES, b. Ireland, to US as a small boy, settling in VA. Later a resident of Baltimore, MD. He m. Miss --- Mahoney, also b. Ireland. Son Patrick E., b. Richmond, VA Feb. 1861, proprietor of the Carlin Hotel in Frederick, MD. He m. 1st, in Baltimore, Winifred Boland; m. 2d. Margaret Harvey of Washington, DC. Catholic. *6TH:362-63*

LONG, JOHN, b. Germany & came to the US while a young man. He settled near what is now Littlestown, Adams Co., PA. Veterinary surgeon & farmer. He m. in PA Sarah Keller, also of German birth, who immigrated to America in early life. Their children: Mary, m. Jacob Hahn, farmer of Adams Co., PA; Edward, miller; Philip, farmer of Emmitsburg District, Frederick Co.; Barbara, m. Henry Raughter; Sarah, d. unm.; & Abraham, farmer of Carroll Co., MD. Members German Reformed Church. *FR2:787, 1599-1600*

LONGBOTHUM, NATHANIEL, settled on Long Island, NY, where his eldest son, Nathaniel Jr. was b. 22 Jan. 1735 & m. Annie Yarrington of NY. Desc. Rev. Louis St. Clair Allen, leading divine of Baltimore, MD, minister in Methodist Episcopal church, was b. in Brooklyn, NY 11 July 1883, s/o George Hanford Allen & Lillian May Price. *TR4:274-5*

LOOS, ALEXANDER, b. German Silesia, 11 Aug. 1822, with wife Julia Frommann, d/o a Prussian army captain, & their year old son, George W., landed at Staten Island NY in 1853. Their 2d son, August J. Loos, was b. there that same year. Alexander located in Claverack, NY, where he was a music & language teacher. Removed to Hudson, NY, where hhis wife d. in 1863. May 1865 Alexander m. Marion Elizabeth Mead of Hudson, d/o William & Polly (Hover) Mead. Family removed to Petersburg, VA & later to Lewisburg, PA. In Jan. 1869 to Philadelphia, PA; Alexander d. in Germantown, PA Sept. 1877. Dau. Julia Clara Loos, practicing physician of Baltimore was b. Philadelphia. *TR4:786-8*

LORAINE, TOWARD, & wife Catherine (Lodge) to America when Toward was age 30, machinist, b. England. He was employed first in Philadelphia; 1854 to Chesapeake City (Cecil Co., MD), where son Toward N. was b. 7 Sept. 1862. Toward N. m. Willie R. Cavender, born in MD. *H/C:258-60*

LOUGH,---, from Germany to settled in Adams Co., PA. Had son George who had son John b. Adams Co., PA 1817. John was a farmer in PA & m. Christianna Flickinger, b. Adams Co. Both are bur. at New Oxford Cemetery, New Oxford, PA. They had 7 children. Son Uriah A. was a teacher in Adams Co. & removed to Woodsboro, MD, stone cutter & marble business with elder brother John Q. Lough. Eventually settled at Emmitsburg, MD & in 1883 to Frederick City near Mt. Olivet Cemetery. Uriah m. Jan. 1874, Margaret Reifsnider, d/o David of Carroll Co., MD. *FR2:945-50*

LOVELACE, RICHARD (SIR), knight of Woolwich, Kent, England, member of the VA Company who d. 1648. Desc. Mrs. Fillmore Beall was d/o James T. Perkins, b. 25 Dec. 1824, at "Catalpha View," in Prince George's Co., MD, & wife Susan Margaret Travers, they m. 2 June 1853. *TR4:431-2*

LOVELACE, WILLIAM (SIR), Knight of Bethersden, Kent, m. Anne Barne, d/o Edwin Sandys, archbiship of York. They had Anne, Richard Cavalier poet, & Col. Francis, gov. of province of NY. Anne b. 1610 m. Rev. John Gorsuch of England at age of 18 & d. in 1652. Rev. John was a Roylaist, killed during the Parliamentary wars. After his death she came to VA with 7 of her children. Her son Charles took up a 50-acre tract of land, Whetstone Point, in 1661, now known as Locust Point, South Baltimore & is occupied by Fort McHenry. Upon this site the town of Whetstone Neck was laid out in 1706, 22 years before the founding of Baltimore. Charles m. Sarah Cole, dau. & sole heir of Thomas Cole. *TR4:337*

LOW, HULO, b. England, to America with 5 brothers, resided in colony of PA in what is now York County. Hulo had a son John, b. PA, farmer; John had a son Jeremiah who served in the War of 1812 & m. Rebecca Fifer, both b. PA. Rufus, b. 3 Dec. 1826, Harford Co., MD, was s/o Jeremiah & Rebecca. Methodist Episcopal. *H/C:245*

LOWBER, PETER, from Amsterdam to settle on farm 7 miles below Dover, DE in 1684. Family spread through DE & the eastern shore of MD. The Lowbers were connected with the Gilders of Philadelphia & NY. Desc. Samuel B. Cooper and Catherine his wife had a son, Samuel B. Jr., who m. Mary Cooper. Their son John W. Cooper b. in Kent Co., DE in 1813, m. Susan Dill, d/o John. From the age of 18 John W. made his home on his share of the estate, in Caroline Co., MD & Kent Co., DE until his death in March 1891, aged 73. *H/C:493-4*

LOWE, JOSHUA R., probably from England, settled in Cecil Co., MD; son Joshua m. Sarah Ales in Harford Co. and their son, Silas J., b. there 27 Feb. 1842. *H/C:291-92*

LOWENSTEIN, DAVID, b. 26 Nov. 1845 in Germany, brought to America by his parents in 1853 & settled in Baltimore. David was one of five children. When he was 13 his father died. In 1863 he removed to Frederick, MD with his mother & opened a small store. David &

brother Isaac opened clothing house in Hagerstown in 1882. Large manufacturer of clothing & shoes in Baltimore & Western MD. David m. 1 May 1870, Clara Stern of Frederick City. They have no children. *FR2:1368-9*

LOWERY, WILLIAM (COL.), b. Ireland, to Baltimore early & was Port Surveyor. *MDC:290*

LOWREY (LOWRY), THOMAS, from the north of Ireland c. 1740, with his wife Anna (nee Lowery), b. Scotland. They were not related. Landed at Boston & proceeded to West Hartford, CT & later to Farmington. He d. 16 May 1788, aged 87; she d. 31 Dec. 1790, aged 84. Both bur. in old cemetery in eastern part of Farmington (now Plainfield). Their 2d child, Thomas, b. 17 Aug. 1734 & m. 20 Nov. 1760 Phoebe Benedict, b. 16 Dec. 1742. They removed to VT, where Thomas d. 1800/01 & was bur. at Jericho. One of their sons, Oliver, married 1st Sophia Holenbeck, b. Canaan, CT 18 Dec. 1781 & d. 23 April 1839. Oliver d. at Jericho March 1868. Their son Abner B., b. at Jericho, VT 6 Feb. 1808, 1824 to Burlington where he d. 12 Jan. 1883, aged 75. Unitarian Church member, he m. 1825 Olivia S., d/o the late Luther Moore, early settler of Burlington, who was b. 22 Oct. 1818 & d. there 13 Oct. 1897. Their son, Horatio Barnard Lowry of the US Marine Corps, retired, resided at Rockville, Montgomery Co., MD. Horatio was b. in Burlington VT 10 Nov. 1837. *6TH:525-27*

LUDY, NICHOLAS, b. 1 Jan. 1776, Germany, d. 25 Aug. 1863. To America. His son Nicholas, b. 8 Nov. 1779, d. 22 March 1847; farmer of Jackson District, Frederick Co., MD & m. Ann Smeltzer. *FR2:781*

LYNCH, JOHN, b. Ireland, his son William, b. at Principio Furnace, Cecil Co., MD. Methodist Episcopal church members. William's son, William H. Lynch, b. 30 Sept. 1836 in Cecil Co. *H/C:375*

AC CUBBIN, JOHN, of the Lowlands of Scotland, claiming descent from Kennith II, first king of Scotland. John to Anne Arundel Co., MD with the Howards & m. (1) Susan, d/o Samuel Howard. He m. (2) Elinor --- & d. in 1686. Children named in his will: Samuel, William, Zachariah & Moses. *AAH:177*

147

MAC GILL, JAMES (REV.), b. Perth, Scotland, in 1727 to MD. In 1730 appointed first minister of Queen Caroline parish (Christ Church), Anne Arundel Co., MD. Oct. 1730 he m. Sarah Hilleary of Prince George's Co., d/o Thomas Hilleary. He d. Dec. 1779, aged 78, leaving a widow, one son John & 5 daus. *FR2:1154-5*

MAC RAE, RHODERICK, & wife Jane Parker, both b. Scotland; Rhoderick in Inverness & Jane in Ayr. They m. in Scotland in 1840. Their son George Parker MacRae of Philadelphia, PA m. Margaret Jane Maxwell of Baltimore, MD & had Mary Maxwell MacRae, b. 11 Nov. 1881. *TR4:372*

MACKALL, JAMES, b. Scotland c. 1630, emigrated to MD & settled at the "Cliffs," Calvert Co. before 1660. His will dated 30 Nov. 1693, names his wife Mary executrix & son Col. John Mackall (1669-1739). John m. Susannah (Parrot) Parker, d/o Gabriel and Elizabeth Parrot of Anne Arundel Co., MD. *TR4:575-8*

MACKLEM, JOHN, b. Scotland, to America in early life. Served in War of 1812 & lived to an advanced age. His son William m. Mary Thompson & grandson John M. b. 17 Oct. 1837. Both William & John were stone masons. Mary Thompson d/o Andrew & Elizabeth Thompson, b. Belfast Co., Ireland; to America & settled in Newcastle Co., DE. John M. ran a meat market in Wilmington, DE for 15 years, then settled on as farm in Harford Co., MD.; "Quaker Bottom Farm." *H/C:177*

MADDOX, JOHN, b. Wales, m. Mary ---, settled in Charles Co., MD. Family intermarried with the Harris family, who came from Wales with them. John Jr., their eldest son, m. Elizabeth Jenifer & their eldest son, also named John. m. Martha Harris. 5th generation descendant, Charles J. Maddox, M.D., s/o William T. & Anna Maria King, d/o Charles. William T. & Maria m. 1818 & her father a merchant of Georgetown. *6TH:724-25*

MAGRAW, JOHN, b. Kilkenny, Ireland, to Gilbratar & then America, settled in PA. Served in a PA regiment during the Rev. War. He m. Jane Kerr, of Middle Octorara, [MD] & d. 22 Dec. 1818, aged 68. Their son James studied theology & was licensed by the Presbytery of Middletown, PA. He accepted a call to West Nottingham, Cecil Co., MD & 4 April 1804 was ordained & installed. In 1822 he organized a church at Charlestown & d. there. James m. on 6 Dec. 1803 Rebekah, d/o

Stephen & Jane Cochran of Cochranville, Chester Co., PA. He d. 20 Oct. 1835, aged 60; she d. 1 Dec. 1834, aged 54. *MDC:359-60*

MAGRUDER, ALEXANDER, into MD in 1651 & in 1668 received patent of 600 acres in Calvert Co. Desc. [son?] Samuel Magruder (1654-1711), b. Calvert Co., military & civil officer of Prince George's Co. *TR4:825-7*

MAHON, JAMES, & wife Ann Larkin, from Ireland to Baltimore, MD c. 1840 & were married in this country. Son John J. b. in Baltimore 13 Aug. 1851. *MDC:305*

MAIN FAMILY,, American progenitor first settled in the New England states & later removed to Baltimore City & still later to the Middletown Valley, Frederick Co., MD, where desc. remain today. *FR2:1575-6*

MAISCH, JOHN M. (PROFESSOR), & wife Charlotte J. Kuhl, both b. in Germany & from the same small town, to America, but did not become acquainted until after their arrival in the US. John, b. 1831, to America at age 18 in 1849 & settled in Baltimore. He became a drug clerk & worked in Washington, New York & Philadelphia. Teacher of chemistry & pharmacy. Their son, Dr. Augustus Carl Maisch, b. Philadelphia 1 July 1872. In 1900 he opened an office for practice of general medicine & surgery in Hagerstown, MD. 21 June 1905, in Philadelphia, he m. Elda Katherine Thompson, d/o Jacob George & Samantha J. (Hilbert) Thompson, natives of MO & OH, respectively. *TR3:898-901*

MARCILLY, FRANCIS, b. Paris, France, coffee planter in the island of San Domingo. To MD & resided in Harford Co. & later took position as professor in Mt. St. Mary's College. He d. at his farm, the Hermitage, & buried in the Catholic Cemetery. *6TH:307-09*

MAREEN, MILLESON, Huguenot, first settler of the Eastern Shore family of this name in MD. He was s/o Alexandre Marien or Marin, registered among Huguenot records of Canterbury & Threadneedle St., London. Alexandre d. in London aged 73 & left Jacob & Alexander. Milleson, b. c. 1634 in France, Quaker, settled in MD in 1655 & d. in 1679 in DE. *TR4:719*

149

MARKELL, CONRAD, officer in the Prussian army, emigrated to America & settled in MD. He was father of William Markell, who was the father of John, b. Frederick City 1781 & d. 1860. *FR2:1141-2*

MARKEY, JOHANN DAVID, from the Palatinate 1736 & settled in Frederick Co., MD. His son, also Johann David, capt. of the 16th Regt. of the MD Militia in 1809 & served in the War of 1812. His son, David John Markey of Frederick. *TR4:385*

MARONEY, MICHAEL, b. Ireland 1848, to America at age of 15, landing in NY. He then went to St. Louis & made his home with an uncle until he removed to Oakland, MD in 1858. He served in the 3d VA Cavalry during the Civil War. In 1860 he m. Bridget Keefe, d/o James & Rose, from Ireland to MD in 1851, settling in Oakland. *6TH:180*

MARSHALL, JOHN (CAPT.), capt. in the battle at Edgehill during the reign of Charles I, immigrated to America c. 1650 & settled at Jamestown, VA & later to Westmoreland Co., VA. Served in the Indian wars & d. near Dumfries, leaving 2 sons, one of whom was Thomas. Thomas was b. 1655 & d. 1704, was the father of Capt. John Marshall, b. Westmoreland Co., VA c. 1700 & d. 1752. About 1722 he m. Elizabeth Markham, d/o of Lewis of England & VA & their second child was Thomas Marshall. Thomas was b. in Washington Parish, Westmoreland Co., VA 2 April 1730 & d. in Washington, Mason Co., KY 22 June 1802. He served in the French & Indian war. In Fauquier Co., VA in 1754, he m. Mary Randolph Keith, d/o Rev. James & Mary Isham (Randolph) Keith & had 14 children. A desc. Thomas Marshall m. Margaret Wardrop Lewis & they res. Oak Hill, Fauquier Co., VA. Margaret was b. 29 Oct. 1823, d. 23 Oct. 1907 in Baltimore. Son Dr. Henry Lee Smith, b. 23 March 1868 in Ashland, Hanover Co., VA, was a physician of Baltimore. *TR4:194-5*

MARSHALL, THEOPHILUS, American progenitor, was of French Huguenot origin. He settled in the James River Country c. 1700. Desc. John E. Marshall res. Baltimore & m. Susan Arringdale Dorritee. Their son, William Arringdale Marshall m. Emma M. Dilworth. The Dilworth family is of English & Irish ancestry. Emma is the d/o Peter & Emma Dilworth of VA & Baltimore. *TR3:829*

MARTENET, JONAS, b. St. Blaise, near Neufchatel, Switzerland, to America as young man & resided in Baltimore. He d. 1835, leaving widow Catharine (Johannes) & 6 sons. *MDC:447*

MARTIN, JOSEPH, and wife Betsy Jamison, both b. Ireland, married there. With family to America in 1856 & settled in Oneida Co., NY & shortly to Oakland, MD, where Joseph d. 1874. He had m. again, his 2d wife being Mary A. Dare. Joseph's son, Thomas, b. in Co. Down, Ireland in 1833, was 23 years of age when he came to America. He & brother George settled in NY. Thomas m. in 1870 Ellen, d/o John Graham. *6TH:530-31*

MARTIN, WILLIAM, b. England, farmer, m. Mary Gurley, b. Frederick Co., MD. She m. (2) after William's death, George W. Yourtee of Washington County, MD & she d. 1884, age 64. John, only s/o William & Mary, b. in Frederick Co. in 1845, was age 9 when his father died. He was employed by the B&O Railroad, first at Martinsburg, WV & later at Brunswick, MD. He m. 1868 Margaret C. Conway, d/o William of Martinsburg, formerly of Staffordshire, England. *FR2:954-5; 6TH:593-4*

MARTINDALE, AMOS, Englishman, settled in Bucks Co., PA where his son Ross R. Martindale was born. Son Ross removed to Cecil Co., MD & d. there as the result of a railroad accident in North East, MD at age of 52. He m. Ellen S. Singley of Bucks Co. & they had 7 children. *H/C:417*

MARTZ, GEORGE (MAJOR), officer in US Army in War of 1812, to America from Germany as young man, accompanied by a brother who settled in PA. George settled in Frederick Co., MD & m. Catherine Reece. They had 6 children, including David S. *FR2:1010-11 & FR2:1021-2*

MASON, SAMSON, a Dragoon of the Republican Army of Oliver Cromwell, came to America in 1650 & settled at Rehobath, MA, where as an Anabaptist he was allowed to buy land. He m. Sarah Robinson. Many descendants through generations were pastors of the Baptist Church in Swansy, MA. Seventh generation Rev. Auguste Frencke Mason served in NY & MA & as pastor of the Calvary Baptist Church in Washington, DC. *MDC:37*

MASSEY, JAMES, from England to America 1627. His son Peter had son Col. Elijah Massey, who d. as a soldier of the Rev. Army & was bur. at Fort Mifflin, PA. Col. Elijah m. Hannah Parson & their son, Benjamin Massey, m. Elizabeth Massey. Their son, Ebenezer Thomas m. 1821 Emily Ann Massey. *TR4:609-10*

MATHIOT, JEAN, & wife, with other Huguenot families, to America c. 1752 & settled in Lancaster, Lancaster Co., PA. His eldest son removed to Baltimore c. 1794 & d. there when his son Augustus was aged 12. Augustus was b. in Baltimore 4 Aug. 1799. He m. 1826 Mary Hodges, her paternal ancestors of a Kent Co., MD family. *MDC:608-09*

MATTHAI, JOHN C., from Germany to US in young manhood & settled in Baltimore. Manufacturer of horseshoes, carriages, buggies & other vehicles. His wife was Theresa Jackins, a member of the family who came from France to America. Their dau., Mary A., m. James Edmondson Ingram of Baltimore & the Eastern Shore of MD. *TR3:803-4*

MATTHEWS, WILLIAM (DR.), from Ireland & settled in America "at the close of the 1st century" & m. Ann Penrose of Philadelphia. After her death he removed to Baltimore & m. Eliza Sterrett, d/o John, merchant of Baltimore. *MDC:538-39*

MAUGHT, JOHN, Hessian soldier brought to America during the Rev. War, taken prisoner at Yorktown, VA & marched to Fredericktown, MD. He was a weaver & m. in Middletown Valley [Frederick Co., MD] & had children: John, Samuel, Daniel, William, Henry, Mary Ann & Katy. *FR2:994-5*

MAULDIN, FRANCIS, & wife Mary, both b. Wales, settled in Elk Neck, Cecil Co., MD in 1684. Francis' will proved 1762 & he names his children: Francis, Benjamin, William, Henry, Rebecca, Elizabeth & Mary. *C:510-11*

MAXWELL, ELIZABETH, niece of Daniel Defore the author, came from England 1718 at age 18. Down to the present day all of the family have resided within 2 miles of Brick Meetinghouse, Cecil Co., MD. All were Quakers. Elizabeth, an indentured servant, was sold on her landing at Philadelphia, to Andrew Job, res. of Nottingham, now in Ceci Co., MD. In 1725 she was m. to Thomas Job, son of Andrew. *C:526-34*

MAY, LOUIS, & wife Rose Lensh, both b. Russia. Rose to US with her parents who settled in NY state, where she m. Louis. Louis to America at age of 20 & in 1890 grad. from NY College of Pharmacy. Their only surviving child, William T. May, b. NY City 7 Feb. 1891. William grad. College of Physicians & Surgeons in Baltimore in 1913. He was connected with the Hebrew Hospital at that place until 1916, when he joined the MD National Guard. *TR3:1020-1*

MAYER, CHRISTIAN, one of the first Germans to settle in Baltimore shortly after the Rev. War. His son Charles F. was b. in Baltimore 15 Oct. 1795 & d. 4 Jan. 1864. *MDC:711*

MAYER, JOHN, b. Germany & settled in Baltimore in 1854. He worked in Wheeling, WV, in 1856 moved to Cumberland, MD, brewer. His son Henry b. there 15 March 1860. In 1865 John to Frostburg, MD & d. there 12 April 1888. He m. Elizabeth Herwig 17 May 1859. *6TH:506-07*

MAYNADIER, DANIEL (REV.), clergyman sent to MD by the Bishop of London to take charge of the White Marsh Church, Talbot Co., near Easton. Daniel was a French Huguenot, b. near Languedoc. Descendants resided in MD. *TR3:274*

MAYNARD, HENRY, merchant of England, settled in Proctor's Park, Anne Arundel Co., MD before 1702. He may have come to America with his brothers James & Thomas, of the line of the Lords Maynard of St. Albans, in Herefordshire & Little Easton in Essex. Thomas, s/o Henry & Sarah & others left Anne Arundel Co. & patented 1000 acres in Frederick Co., MD soon after it was formed. *FR2:782*

MAYO, WILLIAM, b. England, to America in 1690 by way of the Barbados, settled at Powhatan, VA. His son, Major William Mayo, laid out the city of Richmond. Desc. Dr. John C. Mayo m. Mary Stovin. John was grad. from College at Baltimore & served as surgeon in Confederate Army during the Civil War. Their son, Rev. Charles J. S. Mayo, m. Mary R. Webber, b. Fauquier Co., VA. Their son, Dr. Robert W. B. Mayo, b. Hampton, Elizabeth City Co., VA 23 Dec. 1882, grad. Johns Hopkins Univ. with M.D. degree. He was connected with the Church Home & Infirmary and Women's Hospital at Biloxi, MS. He m. 6 Nov. 1922 in NY City, Florence Stabler, d/o Jordan & Caroline

(Semple) Stabler. Jordan Stabler is of a MD line; Caroline Semple is of a Philadelphia line. *TR4:589*

MC BRIDE, ---, b. Ireland, settled Middletown Valley, Frederick Co., MD as early settler. His son Philip had son Henry, farmer & member of Church of God. Henry's son William b. Frederick Co. 21 Aug. 1822, d. 1908. William's wife was Elizabeth House. *FR2:953-4*

MC CARDELL, THOMAS, one of 3 brothers who emigrated from Ireland at an early date. One brother west to MO & one located in NJ. Thomas m. Annie Nogle & settled in Williamsport District, [Frederick Co.], MD. Their children: Richard P.; Wilfred D.; Courtney; Upton; Willoughby; Rebecca, m. Frank Dugan & Annie, m. John French. *FR2:1248-9*

MC CART, JOHN, b. County Tyrone, Ireland, 18 June 1828; in 1830 with parents Lawrence & Ann (Owens) McCart to Baltimore, MD. John m. 1 April 1856, Bridget Ann Riley, of Baltimore. Catholic. *MDC:250-51*

MC CAULEY, JOHN, b. Dublin, Ireland, to America & settled in PA. His dau. Catherine m. Michael Sentman, b. Chester Co., PA. Their son Eli S. Sentman, b. near New London, Chester Co., PA 23 April 1833. [In the same article her name is given as McMillan, not McCauley.] *H/C:434-5*

MC CAY, JOHN, b. Scotland, a desc. of the Scottish nobility, came to America c. 1775, locating near Rowlandsville. Veteran of the Rev. War; large slave owner. His son, John Jr. had a son James McCay b. in Baltimore who served in the War of 1812 in the 27th Regt. of MD with the rank of major. James m. Mary Broughton & they had 11 chldren. His desc., James McCay was b. MD, veteran of War of 1812, with rank of major; d. 1881, aged 88. *H/C:379, 481*

MC CLEARY, JOHN, b. Ireland, shoemaker; to America & eventually settled in Cecil Co., MD in 1817. He m. Ann Robinson & had 9 children. *H/C:354-5*

MC CLEARY, WILLIAM JOHN, b. Co. Tyrone, Ireland, to America with parents at age 7 in 1853, settled Baltimore. William m. Anna

Rebecca Coleman, d/o Noah of Baltimore; she d. in Baltimore July 1921, aged 71. William d. 1907, aged 61, civil engineer. *TR3:317*

MC CLENAHAN, SAMUEL, Scotch-Irish, m. Ellen ---, to America & settled in Cecil Co., MD. c. 1750. *MDC:268-69, 620*

MC CLUNG, ---, from Ireland & located in Baltimore Co., MD. His son, Joseph McClung, b. Baltimore Co., had son Robert, b. on family homestead, veteran of War of 1812; m. Mary Payne, b. Harford Co., where they subsequently removed. *H/C:389-90*

MC CLURG, JOHN, s/o James of Scotland, b. in County Kirkcudbirght (Kirouchtrie), Scotland 14 Nov. 1726. In 1752 joined his brother Dr. Walter McClurg, who had emigrated to VA before 1746 & settled at Hampton. John to PA in 1752 where he was granted 100 acres of land in Londonderry (now Lower Oxford) twp., Chester Co. He m. Eliza Jackson in 1753, d/o Samuel Jackson of Londonderry. John d. 12 July 1799 & Eliza 16 April 1782. Their eldest son Samuel, b. 9 July 1754, m. Agnes Foulis of Lower Oxford, d/o Archibald & Mary Foulis. He removed to York Co., PA & d. at Slateridge 4 April 1810. Mary d. near Oxford 8 Dec. 1849. Archibald McClurg, elder s/o Samuel & Agnes, b. 25 March 1794, m. Sarah Russell, d/o John Russell & Margaret McNeil of Russellville, Chester Co., PA. Removed to West Nottingham Twp., Chester Co., PA, where he died. One son, James Hervey McClurg, b. 1 June 1832 at Lower Oxford Twp., served in the 124th PA Vol. Infantry in the Civil War. He m. 26 Jan. 1869, Elizabeth Helen Grier of Chester Co. Their son, James Patterson McClurg, b. 11 Nov. 1880 in Oxford, PA, was admitted to the bar in Baltimore in 1909 & res. there. *TR4:650-4*

MC COMBS, WILLIAM, b. city of Armagh, Ireland 1765, of Scotch-Irish origins. He m. Elizabeth ---, of the same place, b. 1769. 1787, at that time unmarried, they came to the US & settled at Newcastle, DE, where they were married the following year. Son George T. McCombs, b. 19 July 1797 near Newark, DE, m. Ellen Prizer of Chester Co., PA 19 July 1823. He was assassinated near Allentown, PA in Oct. 1836. He was veteran of War of 1812 & Methodist preacher, as were his brothers, James & William. George's son, Abram [Abraham] P. McCombs, b. Coventry, Chester Co., PA 16 June 1824; removed to Baltimore Co. & later to Havre de Grace, MD. He m. 29 March 1849, Maria C., d/o Louis Schott of Lebanon, PA. In 1865 Abraham took a position at Ashland

Iron Works, Baltimore Co. He later worked at Havre de Grace, MD. Ironworker & newspaperman. *H/C:341-2; MDC:370-1*

MC CRACKEN, WILLIAM, from Ireland to America & settled in Cecil Co., MD, shipowner. He m. Ruth Richardson & after his death she became owner of the "North Star," a large sloop that was captured near North East by the British fleet. Their son John was b. on the Shawner farm in Cecil Co., farmer & member of ME Church of North East. John m. Martha J. Cazier, b. Cecil Co., who died there in 1873. Their son, John H. McCarcken was b. in North East 11 Jan. 1840. *H/C:398-99*

MC CURDY, ALEXANDER C. (REV.), b. Scotland, to America at age 16 & landed at Castle Garden, NY. He was a Baptist preacher & officiated at the first baptism by immersion ever administered in Peach Bottom Twp., York Co., PA. He res. York Co., PA & had 14 children. His son, Dr. Alexander C. McCurdy became physician, grad. Baltimore & res. Harford Co., MD. Presbyterian. He m. Hannah Stansbury. *H/C:505*

MC CURDY, JAMES, JOHN & CHARLES, Scotch Covenanters who emigrated to America. Their descs. res. Western PA. Desc. George McCurdy, b. Westmoreland Co., PA, farmer & coal miner, left son James Crawford McCudey, b. Westmoreland Co., PA 1837, where he d. 1871. James served in the Union Army during the Civil War, Capt. of Co. E, 11th PA Vol. Inf. His wife was Jennie Eyler & they had one son, Ira J. McCurdy, who was raised in Woodsboro, MD. Ira is a physician of Frederick Co., MD & has never married. *FR2:1549-50*

MC DEVITT, EDWARD, b. County Donegal, Ireland, to America in 1840 & settled in Philadelphia, where he remained for seven years, and then removed to Baltimore, MD. *MDC:156*

MC DONAL, WILLIAM, b. Soctland & settled in Minneapolis, MN. His wife was Hattie Redman & their son William was b. there 28 Oct. 1888. When son William was 5 the family moved to Talbot Co., MD. Son Wiliam was in employ of Morris Iron & Steel Co. of Frederick, MD. He m. at McVeytown, PA, 18 Dec. 1915, Leona Vera Lantz, a d/o E. O. Lantz. She d. Oct. 1918. Episcopal & member of Holy Innocence Church in Talbot Co. *TR3:786-7*

MC DONALD, JOHN, b. Ireland & of "good old Protestant Celtic stock," b. 24 May 1837, s/o Thomas & Katherine (Hoar) McDonald. To America at age 18 & enlisted in the US Army. He served in AZ & CA & later was assigned to the Army of the Potomac. He retired to a farm in Montgomery Co., MD. He m. 7 May 1865, Mary J. Benton, d/o Horace. *6TH:215-17*

MC DONOUGH, STEPHEN J., b. 23 Dec. 1875, Clifden, Co. Gallway, Ireland, s/o John & Mary (King), settled Baltimore, MD. John King, a great uncle settled in Gloucester, MA. Stephen J. m. Mary A. Sweiger, b. Baltimore d/o Joseph A. and Caroline (VonSheer). Roman Catholic. *TR3:71-2*

MC DOWELL, ALEXANDER, to America from the north of Ireland, his ancestors having been among those Scotch families who sought refuge there in days of religious persecution. He was a veteran of the Rev. War. Samuel Smith, general in the American army, is named as his brother-in-law. Alexander's son James, b. Bucks Co., PA, a soldier in War of 1812 and James' son, David McDowell was b. also in Bucks Co., m. Susan d/o Samuel Runner of Philadelphia. James d. Jan. 1857. David's son Henry C. McDowell farmer of Prospect Hill farm in Cecil Co., MD. *H/C:392-3*

MC ELFRESH, DAVID, from Scotland "at an early date" & settled in Anne Arundel Co. His son John H. to Frederick Co., MD. *FRI:313*

MC GAGA, ---, b. Ireland, to America & settled in Loudoun Co., VA. His son David b. in Loudoun Co., distiller. David m. Dorcas Chaney, desc. of old MD & VA families. They had: William, m. Sophia Cooper, d. in Burkittsville District, Frederick Co., MD; John, m. Savilla Cooper, sister of Mrs. William McGaga, d. in Montgomery Co., MD; Joseph, m. Mary Mauabam, d. near Brunswick, MD 1905; Mary, m. Henry Adams, d. near Point of Rocks, MD; Duenna, m. her brother-in-law, Henry Adams; Leanna, d. in early womanhood; Thomas, machinist, m. Annie Lawrence, removed to OH. *FR2:1434-5*

MC GANN, JOHN H. (M.D.), b. Ireland 1853, s/o Bernard & Winifred (Cunningham) McGann. To America with parents in 1859 & settled in Baltimore, MD. There were 9 other children in the family; those still living, Kate, Mary, Nora & John H. *6TH:456-57*

MC GAW, ROBERT, b. Scotland, to America & settled in Harford Co., MD. His son, Robert Jr. b. on Red Hill, Harford Co., miller. Res. in town of Bush & ran Bush Tavern beginning in 1830 for 25 years. Presbyterian. Robert Jr. d. 1877, aged 72. He m. Elizabeth Henson, a d/o Thomas of Harford Co., she d. 1878. *H/C:520-1*

MC GILL, JAMES (REV.), of Scotland, appointed to a parish in Prince George's Co., MD by the bishop of London. His grandson, Dr. Thomas J. McGill, had dau. Eleanor West McGill who m. J. Alleine Williamson & their son J. Alleine Williamson b. in Frederick, MD 9 Sept. 1876. The Williamson family in America was founded by Joseph Alleine Williamson, young Scotchman who came to America to visit a former schoolmate in the law school of Edinburgh University, who lived in Philadelphia. Joseph was so ill from seasickness he decided to remain in America. He was member of Scot Presbyterian family & served as a minister in that denomination. He established a church in the "valley of VA." He m. Sarah North Newton, b. Clarke Co., VA & they named their oldest son Joseph Alleine Williamson. *TR3:995-6*

MC HENRY, JAMES, b. Ireland 16 Nov. 1753, arrived in Philadelphia c. 1771. He induced his father [not named here] to settle in America also. Was secretary of war in the cabinet of Pres. Washington. James became a res. of Baltimore in 1781. Fort McHenry in the Baltimore harbor was named for him. *TR4:884*

MC ILVAIN, DONALD, b. Invernesshire, Scotland, s/o William McIlvain, Gent. & Christiana Campbell, 31 Jan. 1800. On his father's death when he was aged 11, he came to America at invitation of maternal uncle, James Campbell, Baltimore merchant. He m. Sarah Beatty, widow of David Telfair McKim 5 Nov. 1849. *TR4:102*

MC KANNA, JAMES, b. Co. Tyrone, Ireland, to America on sailing vessel at age 18. On this trip he was shipwrecked 3 times. Res. Baltimore where he d. 25 Oct. 1879; m. Catherine Bowes, d/o William & Mary, who died in their native Queens Co., Ireland. *TR2:49*

MC KIM, JOHN JR., Gent., b. 23 March 1766. From Londonderry, Ireland to US in 1780, settled in Baltimore. One of the founders of the B&O Railroad, pres. of the Merchants National Bank of Baltimore. In 1793 he m. Margaret Telfair, d/o Rev. David & Margaret (Duncan) Telfair. *TR4:98*

MC KIM, THOMAS (JUDGE), b. Londonderry, Ireland 10 Oct. 1710; d. Brandywine, DE, Sept. 1784. To America 3 Oct. 1734. His son John b. DE 1742, to Baltimore, MD 1785, where he d. 1819. *GME:161*

MC KINNEY, M. M. (REV.), Presbyterian minister, emigrated from the Isles of Skye, off the northwest coast of Scotland to America & located in NJ about the time William Penn settled there. His son, Mathew McKinney, res. near Harrisburg, PA, farmer & miller. Matthew's son, James Harris McKinney, b. Dauphin Co., PA 1794, later removed with parents to Northumberland Co., PA & later to Clinton Co., PA, where he d. 1881. He m. Ruth Ferguson & they had (among others) David Ferguson McKinney, b. PA. David served in the Civil War in the Union Army & in 1865 settled in Frederick Co., MD; physician. He m. 22 Feb. 1865, Mary E. Trego, d/o William Trego of Baltimore City. *FR2:1552-3*

MC KINSEY, ---, b. Scotland, his son James b. MD & James' son Folger McKinsey, former newspaper editor of Frederick City, MD, b. in Elkton, Cecil Co., MD 29 Aug. 1866. *6TH:867*

MC LAIN, DANIEL, to America from Ireland, 1840. Of family of Scotch Covenanters driven from Scotland & settled in town of Coleraine, on the river Bann, near Giants' Causeway in Northern Ireland. Daniel settled in Carbon Co., PA. The 3rd of his 5 sons, also named Daniel, when a young man mined coal with his father in Carbon Co., but removed to Berks Co., PA, where he farmed. His wife was Elizabeth Brewster & they had 4 children: James, Samuel, Daniel (physician) & John (a teacher) who d. 1886. Son James b. at Summit Hill, Carbon Co., PA 9 Sept. 1843. At a young age with his father to Amity Twp., Berks Co. Member St. Paul's Church, Amityville, PA. He m. Mary Amanda Lorah in 1866 & had Eugene L. McLean, b. Berks Co., preacher of the Reformed Church, ordained in 1893. Served in Everett, Bedford Co., PA & in 1898 received a call from Grace Reformed Church of Frederick Co., MD. 15 Nov. 1905 he m. Mary Harnish Neff, d/o William & Cordelia Neff of Alexandria, PA. *FR2:1041-2*

MC LAUGHLIN, GEORGE, b. Londonderry, Ireland 1796. He m. at age 21 to Mary A. McCadden & the next year they settled in Baltimore. Shoe manufacturer. He d. in 1851; his wife in 1853. *MDC:481*

MC NABB, THOMAS, b. Scotland, banished as a participant in the rebellion of 1716 & came to America as a prisoner on the ship *Speedwell*.

Settled Harford Co., MD; his son James served in the Rev. War. *H/C:203*

MC NAMEE, FRANCIS, b. Ireland. He was a shoemaker, married & came to America. Son Frederick, weaver, m. Sarah A. Hollowell of Chester Co., PA & had 5 children, one of which was Merritt S. McNamee, b. 8 Sept. 1836, b. at Farmington, MD. *H/C:327*

MC NEAL, ARCHIBALD, b. County Antrim, Ireland, emigrated to Talbot Co., MD 1774. There, shortly after his arrival, he m. Mary Harrison of VA. His father, Hector, is supposed to have been b. Scotland, a resident of Leith. *MDC:335-36*

MC PHERSON, ROBERT, b. northern Ireland 1687; d. Adams Co., PA 23 Sept. 1767; wife Janet --- b. Ireland 1689, d. Adams Co. 25 Dec. 1749. Their son John McPherson, b. Adams Co., PA, an officer in the Rev. After the war he located in Frederick Co., MD. His wife was Sarah Smith of Frederick Co. *FR2:765*

MC SHERRY, PATRICK, b. 1725, from Ireland to US & m. Catherine Gartland, of Armagh. Patrick d. 1795. His son James resided in Adams Co., PA, was a Congressman & d. Feb. 1849. His son James Jr. was b. in City of Frederick, MD 30 Dec. 1842. In 1866 he m. Clara Louise, d/o the late Hugh McAleer of Frederick Co. Edward, son of the immigrant Patrick, served in PA Regt. during Rev. War. Descs. settled in Frederick Co., MD. *6TH:129-30, FRI:316*

MC SHERRY, PATRICK, b. Ireland 1725, to America accompanied by his wife, formerly Catherine Gartland, of Co. Armagh. Settled in PA, where Patrick d. 1795. They had 12 children. Eleventh child, son James, b. Adams Co., PA 28 July 1776. He served in the War of 1812 & later was elected to congress. He d. Feb. 1849 [1846?]. James' wife was Ann Ridgley (Sappington). James Jr., s/o James, b. Libertytown, Frederick Co., MD, 29 July 1819, d. in Frederick 13 July 1869. He m. Eliza Spurrier, b. Anne Arundel Co., d/o William, of English descent. [This entry and the one just above are confusing, but not necessarily conflicting if you consider that James Jr. could have married more than one time. Both entries have been left intact to forestall further confusion.] *6TH:650-51, FR2:693*

MC VEY, JOHN, b. Ireland. His dau. Nancy m. William H. Andrew and their son John W., b. 1820 near Hall's Cross Roads, Harford Co., MD. *H/C:238*

MC WILLIAMS, JOHN, b. Londonderry, Ireland, to America in 1831 & was m. in Baltimore, MD in 1835 to Mary Mullin. Son John b. in Baltimore 10 Jan. 1836. *MDC:233*

MEAKIN, EMMA LOUISA, d/o Samuel Meakin of Derby, Derbyshire, England, m. James Preston, of Irish desc., res. Baltimore, MD. Their son, James Oscar Preston, b. Baltimore 23 Dec. 1879. *TR4:328-9*

MEARNS, ANDREW, b. Ireland, later a farmer of Cecil Co., MD; m. Mary, d/o Robert Cameron. Their son Abel d. 1848, aged 51. *H/C:432*

MEDFORD, MACALL, of Hanover Square, London, England & Kent Co., MD. He m. Anna Maria Parr & had dau. Anna Maria who m. Nathaniel Thornton Hynson of Colebrook Vale, MD. Their son Henry Parr Hynson b. 27 May 1855. *TR4:648-9*

MEHRLING, JOHN LEWIS, b. Ostheim, Germany 1814, to America & settled Frederick City, MD c. 1839, where he d. 1893. Their children: Henry, b. Germany, res. Baltimore; August of Frederick City, also b. in Germany, with brother Henry served in Union Army during the Civil War; George W.; Margaret Elizabeth, unm.; Philipina, m. John T. Crouse of Frederick; Anna Mary, unm.; & Lewis William. *FR2:777*

MEID, CONRAD, b. 15 Aug. 1840, Hesse Darmstadt, Germany; at age 17 with father to America, at Baltimore, MD 10 Oct. 1857. He m. 12 May 1864, Elizabeth, d/o Lewis Schmick of Baltimore. German Reformed. *MDC:113*

MEIER, AUGUST H. F., b. Brunswick, Germany 18 July 1867, was s/o August, b. 3 June 1824, d. 10 Sept. 1879. He was s/o Henry C. A. & Christina (Celecker) Meier. Henry was in the pottery business. August m. Rosina Hennecke of Germany. August & Rosina had: Gustav, Herman, William all dec'd.; Mary, dec:d. & Henry C. A. August H. F. Meier learned trade of banker in Hanover, Germany & sailed for America in 1891, landing at Baltimore. Res. Baltimore, Washington DC, Cleveland OH, Fredericksburg VA & eventually purchased the old Blumenour bakery & later that of E. J. Hudson, of the same place. He

m. Charlotte Schnebel, d/o William & Caroline of Washington, DC. Mr. & Mrs. Meier have no children at this time. *FR2:1290*

MELVILLE, JOHN GRAHAM, b. Bar Head, Scotland, brought to US by his parents, James & Elizabeth (Taylor) Melville, when he was 3. Family settled in Ellicott City, MD. James murdered at Point of Rocks, MD & son John taken at age 7 as apprentice by Weatherhead Bros., woolen manufacturers. Res. Carroll Co., MD & Fredericksburg, VA. John Graham d. at his farm at Oakland Mills, Carroll Co. Methodist Episcopal. He had m. the d/o Samuel & Elizabeth (Boden) Moore, both b. in Ireland & to America in early life. Elizabeth, d/o Samuel Boden, res. of Baltimore. John, s/o John G. Melville & --- Moore, b. at Weathersville, now known as Hillsdale, Baltimore Co., 3 Jan. 1862. *TR3:404*

MERCER, JOHN, of Dublin, Ireland, s/o John & Grace Fenton Mercer, to VA in 1720, was Secretary of the Ohio Company & a noted crown lawyer. He m. (2) Ann Roy, had a son John Francis Mercer, b. at "Marlboro," Stafford Co., VA 17 May 1759. John Francis served in the Rev. War & m. 3 Feb. 1785, Sophia, d/o Richard Sprigg of "Cedar Park," West River, Anne Arundel Co., MD & wife Margaret Caile, d/o John & Rebecca (Ennalls) Caile of England. John Francis Mercer removed to his wife's estate at "Cedar Park." *AAH:250*

MERCER, ROBERT, England to VA 1740; his grandson John Francis Mercer, b. 1759, Stafford Co., VA, was the first non-native Marylander elected Governor of MD. John m. Sophia Sprigg of Anne Arundel Co., MD & res. at her family estate on West River. John d. 1821. *TR4:56*

MERCIER, ---, 3 brothers, b. France, to America. One settled in VA & his son, John William Mercier, farmer, m. Betsey ---. Their children: Nancy, lived to be 96 years, m. in VA Ezra Fidler; Fanny, m. in VA John W. Kadle; & John William. John William Mercier was b. at Smithfield, Jefferson Co., WV. Butchering business at Smithfield. He m. Susan Custard, who d. aged 81 years. Members of the Methodist Protestant Church. Their son William F., served in the Civil War in Co. A, 12th VA Regt. After the war he went to Frederick Co., MD where he was employed on farm of E. L. Derr, near Frederick City. Later went to the Charles Shultz place near Mt. Pleasant for 9 years. Studied veterinary surgery. William m. (1) Jemima Barthelow, d/o Elisha. She d. in 1904.

He m. (2) Alice Wagner, d/o John of Mt. Pleasant. Mollie, a sister of William, m. Jacob D. Hessen of Mt. Pleasant. *FR2:1533-5*

MERCIER, RICHARD, emigrated from France to America when a young man & settled at Hood's Mills, Carroll Co., MD. His brother, John Mercier, settled in NY City, silk merchant. Richard was a planter. He m. Miss Tivis & some of their children: Archibald, farmer & hotel keeper, d. in Howard Co., MD; Richard, d. in Carroll Co., MD; Tivis, d. in Carroll Co.; Cornelius; Robert; Cordelia m. --- Dorsey; Keturah, m. Joseph Sims & res. IL; Rachel, m. Eli Bennett. All are now dec'd. *FR2:1180-1*

MEREDITH, NORRIS, "four generations ago left the rugged hills of his native Wales & journeyed to Frederick Co., MD, where he lived & died." Norris' son Simon was b. Unionville, Frederick Co., 12 July 1811 & to Hagerstown in 1859, where he d. 1887. His son, Veniah T., m. Catherine Mentzer. Their son, Harry Lionel Meredith, b. in Mercersburg, PA 28 Sept. 1874, grad. Philadelphia College of Pharmacy in 1900 & he returned to Hagerstown to enter the drug business in partnership with H. R. Rudy. Presbyterian. *TR3:902-5*

MERRIMAN, JOHN, from England to VA with wife Audrey in 1649, settled in Lancaster Co., PA. Their son Charles to Baltimore Co., MD with other noncomformists of VA by 1682. His home, built in the beginning of the 18th century, now occupied by Bishop Murray of the Episcopal diocese of MD & the site of the pro-Cathedral is part of the original lawn (Baltimore City). *TR4:432*

MERRITT, WILLIAM, of family of Wiltshire, England & he arrived in America in March 1676 & took up land in Cecil Co., MD. His great-grandson, WIlliam Merritt, b. 1738, served in the Rev. War as a member of the First Company of the 27th Battalion & was high sheriff of Kent Co., MD, 1778-79. William m. (1) Mrs. Martha Bergan, who d. 1773 & (2) in 1776 Martha Van Sant, d/o Benjamin who d. 1808. *TR4:659-61*

MERRYMAN, ---, b. England, to Baltimore Co., farmer. His son, Joseph, b. there & at age of 26 he m. S. Alice Gemmill, b. PA. *H/C:547*

MESSNER, JACOB, b. Switzerland, to America before Rev. His son David d. Lewistown, MD c. 1854, m. Elizabeth d/o Henry Wilhide. Their children: Josiah G.; Ann Rebecca, m. Abraham Hahn; Jacob H., farmer near Mountain Dale, Frederick Co., MD; & Sophia, m. Tobias Weddle. *FR2:771-2*

METZGER, GEORGE, b. Germany, to America in early manhood & settled York Co., PA; farmer, buried near Manchester, PA. Son J. William, farmer & distiller near Manchester, York Co., m. Eva Baker. Their son William b. York Co. 17 July 1809; removed to Myersville, MD after college, school teacher. William m. Lydia, d/o Samuel of W. [sic] & Mary (Hoover) Toms of Jackson District, Frederick Co., MD. *FR2:767*

METZGER, MARCUS, b. Germany, to America c. 1770, settled in Bedford Co., PA. His son John accompanied him to America. His wife was Elizabeth Treadwell. Their son Daniel b. Bedford Co. 26 July 1818. Lutheran Church member, he m. Elizabeth B. Hinchman, b. 9 June 1820, d/o John G. & Harriet, both b. CT, but for many years residents of Bedford Co. Son John S., b. Bedford Co. 30 Aug. 1847, to Frostburg, MD 1871. *6TH:509-10*

MEYERHOFF, JOSEPH, b. Paltova, Russia, 8 April 1899, s/o Oscar & Anna (Gurwitz) Meyerhoff. Oscar was s/o Alexander & Rebecca & came to the US in 1906 with his family & made his home in Baltimore, MD. In real estate business & construction work. Joseph was Baltimore attorney & builder of homes & apartments. In 1921 he m. Rebecca Witten, d/o Rubin & Sarah. *TR3:667-8*

MEZWICK, JEWEL (JULIN), French Huguenot, settled in Somerset Co., MD & m. 29 April 1674 to Sarah Covington, widow of Abraham Covington. *TR4:719*

MICHAEL, ANDREW, in 1773 from Germany to MD & settled in Frederick Co., one of the first settlers of the area; m. Jennie Grisbert. Their children: Henry S., dec'd., farmer of Buckeystown District; Samuel A., dec'd., farmer on St. Mary's, Vego Co., IN; Ezra; Daniel of IL; Eliza, dec'd., m. Elias Delashmutt, retired farmer of Frederick City; Sarah, dec'd., m. Arthur Delashmutt, merchant of Buckeystown, MD. *FR2:930-1*

MICHAEL, BALCHIOR, b. Germany, purchased property near Aberdeen, MD. Had sons Jacob & Daniel. *H/C:148*

MILLER, EDWARD, b. in England, woolen manufacturer of MD. His dau. Adeline, b. Harford Co., m. Dr. Richard N. Allen, also b. Harford Co. Their son, E. M. Allen m. Sallie E. Wilson. E. M. in 1881 elected to the state senate. *H/C:417-19*

MILLER, FREDERICK, s/o John Henry Miller, b. Darmstadt, Germany. He m. --- Laudenbach & in 1853 came to America in company with his 2 brothers, J. Henry & August Miller. They located in Baltimore, MD & was joined 2 years later by his father. Frederick was a farmer & res. in Baltimore Co. until his death in 1872. He served in the Baltimore Battery of Alexander's Light Infantry during the Civil War. Lutheran. Their son, J. Henry Miller, b. Baltimore 6 Oct. 1864. *TR3:647-8*

MILLER, GUION, & wife Margaret (known as Moggy), to America from Wales. They settled in East Culm Twp., Chester Co., PA. The homestead stayed in the family until 1858. Grandson Warwick was b. 1735 (old style), son of Robert, and Warwick m. Elizabeth Price. Their 2d son, Mordecai, b. 1764, went to VA & m. Rebecca, d/o William & Susanna (Saunders) Hartshorne, 8 Nov. 1792. He was a clockmaker & carried on business in Alexandria & Leesburg, VA. Rebecca d. 19 Dec. 1810; Warwick d. 2 March 1832, both at Alexandria. Son Robert H. Miller, b. 10 Aug. 1798, d. 10 March 1874. He m. Anna Janney, b. 25 Sept. 1802, d/o Elisha & Mary Janney of Hillsboro, VA. They were m. at Waterford, VA 23 April 1823 & she d. 23 Feb. 1885, having survived him for 11 years. Son Francis resided in Sandy Spring, MD. Other children Sarah, Benjamin H. & Caroline resided in Montgomery Co., MD. Another son, Robert H., businessman of Alexandria, VA, Quaker. also resided in Sandy Spring. *6TH:838-40*

MILLER, JOHN, from Germany & settled on the South Mountain in Frederick Co., MD. Keeper of South Mountain Tavern. His children were John, Catherine & Jane. John, farmer & miller, m. Susan Koogle & had: Jane, Daniel, Henry, George, John D. & several who d. in youth. He d. c. 1870. *FR2:1157-8*

MILLER, JOHN, "of German descent." To America with the older Cramers, Shanks, DeLaplaines, Woods & others, the founders of Woodsboro. He came before the Rev. War, which he served in. Was accidentally killed by being thrown by a horse in 1793. He left a family of 3 children, 2 daus. & son George. George, b. on homestead 1791 &

d. 14 Jan 1861. George served in the War of 1812 & was member of the Lutheran Church; 1825 m. Catharine Harbaugh. *FR2:1264-5*

MILLER, NATHAN, and wife Lena Caplan, both b. Latvia, to US 1885 & settled first in Philadelphia then Baltimore; furniture dealer. *TR3:299*

MILLER, THOMAS, b. Ireland, to America & settled in Cecil Co., MD. His son, Thomas Miller, Methodist Episcopal Minister who in 1813 purchased tract of land in Cecil Co. *H/C:355-6*

MILLER, WILLIAM, b. Germany, butcher & farmer, settled near Boonsboro, Washington Co., MD; m. Louisa Hagenbrouzer. William d. at his home in Boonsboro, July 1889. *FR2:779*

MILLS, NATHAN, & wife Sarah Melzer, both b. Russia, where they were married; to US in early 1880's, settled NY City. Nathan manufacturer of ladies' clothing & he d. 14 Jan. 1899, aged 35; Sarah d. there 1902, aged 32. Son Meyer left an orphan at age of 6; educated in Jersey City, NJ & m. in Baltimore 2 April 1922 Rose Lee Block d/o Israel & Kate (Dunn) Block of Baltimore. *TR3:323*

MINIFIE, WILLIAM, s/o James & Elizabeth Hyne Minifie, b. Devonshire, England 14 Aug. 1805. His parents belonged to the National Episcopal Church. He m. Mary White 14 Jan. 1828, of Torquay. Immediately after their wedding they started for London & soon sailed for Baltimore. *MDC:510-11*

MITCHELL, GEORGE EDWARD (COL.), & wife Mary Hooper, from Scotland & settled in Lancaster Co., PA c. 1770. Son Arthur Whiteley Mitchell, pharmacist, b. Elkton, Cecil Co., MD. Practiced along with his brother Dr. Henry Hooper Mitchell. Arthur d. 23 Nov. 1885, aged 61. *TR4:382-3*

MITTEN, WILLIAM, and wife Susan ---, both b. England. William to US in early manhood with parents who settled in Westminster, now Carroll Co., MD. William's father conducted a saddlery business. William & Susan's son Henry G., b. 12 Sept. 1844, m. Catherine Ebaugh. *TR3:255*

MOALE, ---, b. Devonshire, England, the first of the name to America; settled in MD. *MDC:358*

MOALE, JOHN, English merchant, settled early in Province of MD. In 1723 purchased a tract of land in what is now Baltimore City. He m. the d/o Capt. Robert North. John d. 1740. *MDC:277*

MOHLHENRICH, JOHANNES, b. 1818 in Allendorf, Hesse-Cassel, Germany, to America 1848; m. Gretchen Schaberg, b. Bramsche, Hanover, Germany in 1825. Their son, J. George, was b. in Baltimore 25 March 1865. *TR3:252*

MOLESWORTH, SAMUEL, one of 3 English brothers to America; m. Miss West and farmed in Woodville District, Frederick Co., MD. Methodist. Their children: Joseph, Thomas (b. 1818), William, George & Matthew. *FR2:768*

MONDAY, BERNARD, b. Germany 6 July 1828, s/o John & Barbara. Learned blacksmith trade from his brother. At age 20 to US, landing in Philadelphia & went to Baltimore, MD. In 1853 he rented a blacksmith shop on the road to Frederick; having married he removed to Rockville. His 1st wife was Catherine Dove. *6TH:816-17*

MONKS, JOHN, b. in England & emigrated to US, settling in Abingdon, MD, opened a store. His son, James P. Monks, m. Mary A. Treadway, was a farmer. James d. 1873, aged 73; Mary d. aged 67. They had 16 children. *H/C:400-1*

MONTGOMERY, THOMAS, from Ireland to America & settled in the capital of the MD Colony. *MDC:655*

MOONEY, LAWRENCE, and wife Julia (Quinn), both b. Ireland. Julia at County Kildare, Parish of Manstreven & c. 1855 to Baltimore, MD where they married. Lawrence b. in Co. Kildare in 1837, s/o Patrick. To Baltimore at the age of 15; d. 1900. Their son, John H., b. in Baltimore 21 Nov. 1870. Catholic. *TR3:378*

MOORE, ROBERT, from the north of Ireland, s/o William Moore, b. Scotland. Robert to America c. 1760 & settled in Talbot Co., MD, physician; he d. in Philadelphia. Robert's son, Benjamin P. Moore, b. 1791, m. (1) Mary Hopkins 21 May 1817, she d. 29 July 1834 & he m. on 24 June 1840 Mary G. Jones, who d. 13 Aug. 1896, age 90. Benjamin b. Caroline Co., MD & when a few months old taken to Talbot

Co., MD; later to Baltimore where he had grocery business with Johns Hopkins; 1842 to Harford Co. *H/C:510-11; MDC:571*

MORCELL, JAMES, French Huguenot, to MD 1675, settled at "Plum Point," Calvert Co., MD. *TR4:345*

MORRIS, JOHN, and wife Johanna Colbert, both of Youghal, Ireland, to America. John descended from a Welsh family who settled in South of Ireland c. 300 years ago. John d. when son Martin was young, Johanna d. 1877. Son Martin Ferdinand b. near Youghal, Ireland 3 Dec., 1835 to America with his parents. Martin resided in MD & Washington, DC. Catholic. *MDC:371-72*

MORRIS, WIENER, M.D., b. Berlin, Prussia, 15 Jan. 1812, s/o Jasper Weiser, banker & --- Morris of Glasgow, Scotland. He traveled extensively; 1849 to Baltimore, MD. *MDC:268*

MORRISON, JOSEPH, b. Ireland, to US & settled in Wheeling [W]VA; iron dealer. He m. Elizabeth, d/o Rev. Richard Tydings, a Methodist Episcopal divine & author. Joseph d. aged 42 & left 8 children. Son Robert to Baltimore. *MDC:519*

MOSHER, CALVIN S., b. Newport, Nova Scotia 6 Aug. 1825, s/o James & Mary Mosher, both b. Nova Scotia & both d. at Windsor, in that colony, within a few days of each other in 1858. Calvin S. m. Augusta Wilde, only d/o John & Mary of Baltimore, MD. Soon after he removed to Selma, AL & in 1870 returned to Baltimore. *MDC:355*

MOSS, RICHARD, to America in 1655, settled in VA, "and at an early period in the colonization of Maryland representatives of the name came to this state . . ." Desc. James E. Moss m. Adelaide S. Melthorn of Carroll Co., MD & they res. near Annapolis. *TR3:735-6*

MOTT, ADAM, b. Cambridge, England 1695, with wife & children to America in 1635 & settled in Roxbury, MA & later moved to Portsmouth RI area. His son Jacob, b. 13 Dec. 1661 in Portsmouth, was Quaker minister & a proprietor of town of Dartmouth, MA. Jacob m. Joanna Slocum, d/o Rev. Giles & had son Adam, b. 12 April 1692 in Portsmouth. Adam m. 18 Dec. 1718 in Portsmouth, Apphia Hathaway, a lineal desc. of Francis Looke, *Mayflower* passenger in 1620. Their son Adam m. Rachel Rider 23 Feb. 1762 & they were parents of a dau.,

Apphia, who m. Abner Shepherd 29 May 1788. Their dau. Meribath Shepherd m. Elihu Mosher & had Rachel Mosher of New Bedford, MA who m. Ichabod Eddy Clark. Their dau., Sarah Wilcox Clark, m. John William Sills, jeweler of Baltimore. *TR4:501-2*

MOTTER, ---, family originally of Alsace; during reign of Louis XIV to German side of the Rhine. Ancestor of family in America was George Motter who m. Anna Maria Eber & in 1751 to America to settle in York Co., PA. They had 6 children. Later generations to MD & settled in Baltimore City & Frederick Co. *FR2:815*

MOWBRAY, ---, two brothers accompanied Lord Baltimore & settled at Dorchester Co. Desc. Levin Mowbray, b. Dorchester Co., merchant. His son, William H., b. Dorchester Co., MD & later removed to Denton; carpenter. William H. m. Anna Sparklin, d/o Daniel of Caroline Co., of Scotch ancestry. Their son, Rev. Alpheus S. Mowbray, b. in Denton 30 Dec. 1858. His brothers, like himself, are Methodist minsiters: Rev. W. R. stationed at Smyrna, DE & Rev. E. T., educated at Westminster MD. *H/C:543-4*

MUELLER, JUSTUS, b. Germany, to America in 1872. Justus was a builder & d. in 1889, aged 49. His wife. Wilhelmina Hammel, also b. Germany, had come to Baltimore, MD in the early 1870's as a young woman & they married at St. Matthew's German Lutheran Church. Their son, William, b. Baltimore 5 Sept. 1877; 30 May 1904 he m. Mary Minerva Miller in Baltimore. She was b. Berkeley Springs, WV. *TR3:724-5*

MULLIKIN, JAMES, from Scotland in train of Lord Baltimore & 18 April 1665 patented a 300 acre tract of land in Dorchester Co. called "Mullikin's Orchard." He also held land in Anne Arundel Co. & d. 16 Oct. 1669, a large landowner. *TR4:755-7*

MULLIKIN, PATRICK, from Scotland to America 1647 & settled in Calvert Co., MD & later in Talbot Co. on estate known as Patrick's Plan & still in possession of the family. Desc. Capt. Charles B. Mullikin, b. MD, register of wills of Talbot Co., veteran of the Union Army. *TR4:518-19*

MURDOCH, ALEXANDER, b. Scotland. His wife Susan, d/o William Trumbull, also b. Scotland. Their son Thomas F. Murdoch, M.D. b. 9 May 1829 in Baltimore, MD. *MDC:687-88*

MURDOCH, BENJAMIN, Englishman, one of the very eartlist settlers in Western MD, where he settled in Urbana District [Frederick Co.] as early as 1730. His son, William Bouy Murdoch, was veteran of War of 1812. William's son, Richard Howard Murdoch, b. Frederick Co. 14 March 1826. *FR2:1280-1*

MURGATROYD, EDWARD HILTON, res. of Manchester, England who came to America & settled in Baltimore, MD where he d. 11 Nov. 1900, aged 76. His son, George Washington Murgatroyd, res. in Baltimore all his life, merchant, Episcopal. He d. 2 June 1921, aged 69 & was survived by his wife the former Mary Elizabeth Mettee. *TR3:896-7*

MURPHY, JOHN, b. Omagh, Co. Tyrone, Ireland, 12 March 1812; to America with his parents at the age of 10 & they settled in New Castle, DE. He was an apprentice to the printing business in Philadelphia & later removed to Baltimore. 17 June 1852 he m. Margaret E. O'Donnoghue, d/o Timothy of Georgetown, D.C. She d. 1869. *MDC:653-54*

MURRAY, JAMES, b. Glasgow, Scotland, m. Ann Kirkwood Murray b. Larkhill, Scotland. Son Rt. Rev. John Gardner Murray, D.D., Bishop Coadjator of the Diocese of MD b. Lonaconing, Allegany Co., MD 31 Aug. 1857. In 1881 he m. Harriet M. Sprague of Osage City, KS. James the immigrant d. 4 July 1876, KS. Widow Ann res. in MD after James' death. Family lived in MD, KS, CO & AL. *FR2:773-4; TR2:11*

MUSGROVE, ----, b. Scotland, to America, an early settler of Western MD. The immigrant's grandson, James L. Musgrove, m. Angeline Brewer. James b. Jefferson Co., WV 27 Sept. 1823 & d. Montgomery Co., MD 6 Aug. 1890. Member Methodist Episcopal Church South. James & Angeline had: Walper G.; Zacharias, farmer of Montgomery Co., MD; Eliza, m. Andrew Easton; Mary, m. Joseph Swartz; Amy, m. Hicks King; & Francis M., carpenter of Montgomery Co. *FR2:1564-5*

MUSSETTER, CHRISTIAN, b. Germany, to America with parents as a child. They took up land between Roger's Mill & New Market, MD.

Christian & wife d. on their homestead in Frederick Co., MD. His son Christopher served in the War of 1812. *FR2:975-6*

AGLE, PATRICK, & wife Bridget (McCarthy), both b. Ireland; to America & settled in Philadelphia, PA & later in Baltimore Co., MD. Bridget d. in Baltimore, 1910. Their dau., Margaret C. Nagle, m. Michael J. Kearney of Baltimore. He d. 1903. *TR3:355*

NAYLOR, HENRY RODLEY (REV.), b. England 27 Feb. 1837, s/o Henry & Mary, descended from two of the oldest families in the West Riding of Yorkshire. Henry to America in his infancy & settled in Buffalo, NY. Methodist. Served in Baltimore, MD from March 1875. He m. Oct. 1855 to Laura E., only d/o Benjamin T. & Jane Adams, of Clarence, Erie Co., NY. *MDC:514*

NEALE, JAMES (CAPT.), b. 1615, s/o Raphael & Jane (Forman) Neale of Wollaston, Northampton & Drury Lane, London. To MD between 1635-1638 & settled in what is now Charles Co., on a grant which he named Wollaston Manor. He m. Ann [Anna] Gill & beginning 1646 lived for 14 years in England & Spain. Returned to MD 1660 & applied for naturalizaton for his children, Henrietta, Maria, James, Dorothy & Anthony, all b. in Spain. He represented Charles Co., MD in the House of Burgesses in 1666; d. in Charles Co. 1684. [NOTE: Daughter Henrietta Marie m. Richard Bennett, Jr. AAH.] *TR4:87-8; AAH:41*

NEEDLE, SIMON, & wife Lena (Baer), both b. Russia, m. 1881 and to US on their honeymoon. Settled in Baltimore, MD. Their son Sidney b. in Baltimore 5 Sept. 1895. *TR3:361*

NEIDHART, JOSEPH WILLIAM, b. Germany, with wife Louisa & children emigrated in 1844, & settled in Frederick, MD. Members St. John's Catholic Church. Children: Augustus, dec'd.; Lena, dec'd.; Rudolph; & Mary E., m. Frank E. Crouse of Frederick. *FR2:1560-1*

NEIGHBORS, NATHAN O., b. England, to America 'over a hundred years ago,' & settled in Montgomery Co., MD. Member of the Reformed Church. His children: John T.; Elizabeth, m. Charles H. Burkhart; Nathan O.; William; Sarah, m. Michael Zimmerman; & Martha, d. young. Nathan O. Neighbors, s/o Nathan, was b. in Montgomery Co. in 1801 & d. in Frederick Co. 1879. He m. Elia Ann Christ. *FR2:1606-7*

NEISTADT, CHARLES S., b. Kiev, Russia 5 April 1892 s/o Maurice and Rosa (Reihenstein); to US age 43 with family, arrived Baltimore, MD 1898. *TR3:68.*

NELSON, THOMAS, & wife Margaret Reid, progenitor of the Nelson family in VA from England 1700 & settled in Yorktown. Son William, president of the Dominion of VA, m. Elizabeth Burwell & had son Thomas Nelson b. 1711. This Thomas was Gov. of VA & signer of the Declaration of Independence & served in the Rev. War. [This Thomas given as son of the immigrant "Scotch Tom" in MDC.] He m. Lucy Grimes, d/o Philip & Mary (Randolph) Grimes of Middlesex Co., VA. Their son, Francis Nelson m. Lucy Page, d/o Hon. John of Gloucester Co., VA & their dau., Sallie Page Nelson of Hanover Co., VA, m. Dr. Samuel Scollay. Dr. Scollay had come to VA from Boston, MA. Harriet Lorones Scollay, dau. of Sallie Page Nelson & Samuel Scollay, m. Dr. A. M. Evans, b. Lee Town, WV, served in Confederate Army. Harriet d. in Baltimore, MD 26 Feb. 1911, age 65. Dr. A. M. Evans & wife Harriet had Alexander Mason Evans, M.D., b. Middleway, VA 5 April 1885, studied medicine & practiced in Baltimore, served in WWI.

Another son of Thomas the "Signer" was Hugh Nelson, saw government service & had a son, Keating S. Nelson, who m. Julia Rogers. Their son Hugh Nelson, physician & surgeon, b. Albermarle Co., VA, 7 Oct. 1842, removed to Baltimore after the Civil War, in which he served in the Confederate Army. *TR4:433-4; MDC:283*

NEWBOLD, THOMAS, from Derbyshire, England, before 1665, settled in Somerset, MD. He received land for transporting his wife Adriana, their two children, Murphy and Sarah Newbold, and five servants. Thomas 2d wife was Jane ---. *GME:320*

NEWCOMER, WOLFGANG, with parents from Switzerland c. 1720, landed and settled at Philadelphia; later to Lancaster Co., PA. His son Henry had 13 children. John, son of Henry Newcomer, b. 18 Dec. 1797, large real estate holder in Washington Co. MD, and founded the flour and grain commission firm of Newcomer & Stonebraker in Baltimore. John m. his cousin Catherine, b. 18 Dec. 1802, d/o Samuel Newcomer. She d. 3 Feb. 1883, aged 81 and John d. 21 April 1861. *GME:378*

NEWELL, M. A., b. 7 Sept. 1824 in Belfast, Ireland, s/o John, an Irish educator, & Agnes Johnson. He m. 1846, Susanna Rippard of Liverpool, England, d/o George. In 1848 M. A. to Baltimore, MD to visit relatives

& decided to settle there. He served as Professor at Baltimore City College & later at Madison College, Uniontown, PA. He returned to Baltimore & established a college in connection with his brother-in-law, James Rippard. *MDC:564-65*

NEWMAN, JOHN NICHOLAS, b. Rhenish Prussia, to America c. 1753 & settled near the town of Hanover, York Co., PA. Farmer on farm which has remained in possession of the family for c. 135 years. His son, Jacob, b. near Hanover 1789 & d. 1873; farmer. Jacob's son, Jacob M. Newman, b. Hanover 1843; 1866 removed from York to town of Woodsborough, Frederick Co., MD; merchant. He removed to Frederick City in 1893 & had coal business. Jacob M. m. Feb. 1868 to Catharine E. Shaw, d/o Francis of Woodsboro. *FR2:856-7*

NICHOLS, JOHN, German by desc., one of the first settlers of Montgomery Co., MD, one of the original land owners of the county, receiving his tract from Lord Baltimore. One of his sons was Jacob, merchant of Montgomery Co., Md, b. on homestead near Barnesville, MD. Farmer & store keeper. Jacob m. Sarah Rowlings. *FR2:1302-3*

NICHOLSON, WILLIAM, b. c. 1675, emigrated to America from Berwick-on-Tweed. Settled at Annapolis, MD soon after 1700, where he d. 1719. He m. Elizabeth Burgess & had 5 sons: William, Joseph (res. Kent Co., MD), & 3 sons living in England. Elizabeth was d/o Col. William Burgess who was b. 1622 & d. 14 Jan. 1684. Col. Burgess was m. 3 times & his will names 7 sons & 4 daus. One wife, the mother of Elizabeth, was Elizabeth Robbins, d/o Edwards Robbins, emigrant & member of the VA colony in 1621-35 & settled in Northampton Co. Edwards was s/o Thomas Robins of Brakeley, Northamptonshire, England. Elizabeth Burgess, wife of William Nicholson, b. 1682, d. prior to 1719. *TR4:560-2*

NICODEMUS, HENRY, one of four [three] brothers to America from the south of Germany & first settled in Philadelphia in 1720. [One source says they initially settled in Lancaster Co., PA.] One brother settled in Franklin Co., PA, one in Washington Co., MD & the third was a minister of the Lutheran Church, the first of that denomination to preach in Middletown Valley, Frederick Co., MD. Henry [one of the immigrant brothers] removed from Philadelphia to what is now Carroll Co., MD, where he took up land before the Rev., where he d. aged 60 &

is bur. on the homestead. He had a sister, Mrs. Baile, whose son was named Nicodemus. Henry's son John L. Nicodemus, b. on the homestead [Carroll Co., MD], farmer & miller, member of Reformed Church. John L. m. Ann March Neff of Swiss descent.

One source says that one brother [not named] had 2 sons, Valentine & Conrad, who came to what was then Frederick Co., MD at the close of the Rev. War. From these two are desc. the Nicodemus family of MD. *FR2:970-1, 1065-6, 1509-10, 1534-5; 6TH463-5*

NIEDENTHOHL, JACOB, b. province of Darmstadt, Germany & left home at age of 12. He lived on the Rhine & became a successful hotel manager. At the age of about 35 years he immigrated to the US. His wife was a member of the English Sinclair family. Their son, Henry Andrew Niedenthol, b. Seven Valleys, York Co., PA; machinist & dancing master. Henry A. m. Emma Kathryn Piper, d/o Jeremiah & Mary Elizabeth (Douglass) Piper of Waynesboro, Franklin Co., PA. Their son Norman Leslie Niedentohl was b. 11 Dec. 1885 in Waynesboro. Norman was a grad. of the dental dept. of Univ. of MD in 1913. He m. in Baltimore, 10 June 1915, Helen Virginia Waidner, d/o Charles W. & Sarah Jane (Frew) Waidner. Her maternal grandparents were Alexander & Esther (Scott) Frew, both b. Ireland. Dr. Jacob Niedenthohl is associated with the Methodist Episcopal Church. *TR3:1008-11*

NIXDORFF, JOHN GEORGE, b. Schiefer, Silesia, Province of Bohemia, Germany 22 Feb. 1700, to America in 1730 [1740?], settled in Bethlehem, PA, where he d. 22 Sept. 1785. His wife was Miss --- Karns. They immigrated together with the Moravian immigration in 1730. Son Samuel, and several of his brothers, settled in MD shortly after the Rev. War. Samuel b. 18 April 1745, d. 1 March 1824; m. Barbara Medtard. Samuel served in Rev. in Capt. John Nelson's Co. of Independent Riflemen. Wagon manufacturer & blacksmith in Frederick Co., MD after the war.

Henry, another son of the immigrant John George, b. Frederick Co., MD 1789 & d. 1859. [Could this Henry be s/o Samuel instead?] Veteran of War of 1812, merchant of Frederick Co. His wife was Susan Medtart. *6TH:485-86; FR2:764, 832*

NOBLE, MARK, located near Aberdeen, MD; desc. James Noble, b. near Havre de Grace. His son, Benjamin Noble, b. at Swansburg, near Havre de Grace, had son William S. Noble, b. in Stafford in 1853. Member of Harmony Presbyterian Church. *H/C:568*

NORRIS, JOHN, b. England, as a young man came with his brother George to America & they settled in Harford Co., MD, where they purchased 1800 acres of land of Lord Baltimore, the first governor of the colony. The town of Norrisville is named for Vincent Norris, one of their descs. *H/C:469-70*

NORRIS, JOHN HAMMOND, to America from Scotland in early 18th century & settled in St. Mary's Co., MD. He was accompanied by 3 brothers, one settled near Norristown, PA, one in VA & the 3d in one of the New England states. *MDC:649-50*

NORRIS, JONATHAN, b. England, to America with two brothers. One brother settled on Eastern Shore of MD & Jonathan settled in Frederick Co., MD. Jonathan had a son, Amos, first of the family to live on the "Locust Grove" farm in Johnsville District of Frederick Co. Member of the Methodist Episcopal Church, m. Elizabeth Hoy. They had: Israel, Basil, Nicholas (b. 1804, m. Mary Ann McKinstry, d/o Evan & Joanna (Lyons) McKinstry & d. 1866), Susan who m. Samuel Urner, Tabitha who m. Jonas Urner, Mary who m. John Phillips, Elizabeth who d. unm., and another [unnamed here] who d. aged 20. *FR2:1075-7*

NORTHERN, ---, and wife, both b. in England, to America & settled in Boston, MA. Their dau. Esta V., b. Boston, m. Dr. William Joseph Jackson, 1 May 1904, dentist of Baltimore, MD. *TR3:217*

NORTON, JOHN CONDON, b. Ireland, to Baltimore, MD at age 25, blacksmith; d. 17 May 1899, aged 45. He m. in US Catherine A. St. Leger, d/o Patrick and now a resident of Baltimore aged 68. *TR3:228*

NORWOOD, JAMES, b. England, settled in vicinity of Kemptown, on border of Frederick & Montgomery Counties, MD c. 1772. *6TH:739-40*

NORWOOD, JOHN, from England to America & in 1650 settled near Annapolis. *FR2:1216-17*

NOTNAGLE, LEONARD, b. Bavaria, Germany 8 Dec. 1822; d. Frederick City, MD 8 Jan. 1893, where he settled in 1848. He was a butcher & member of the Lutheran Church. He m. in Frederick, 1851, Mary Stephen, b. Wertburg, Germany, Sept. 1824 & d. in Frederick 9 May 1901. She came to America in 1851. *FR2:1561*

NOURSE, JAMES, s/o John, m. Sarah Fonace & to America & settled in VA in 1764; d. 1784. Descendant Charles H., b. 1 Dec. 1816 & reared in Washington, DC. He resided in Culpeper, VA; Washington, Rockville, Seneca, Leesburg, VA, West River, MD & Georgetown. Presbyterian minister. *6TH:794-96*

NOURSE, JOSEPH, emigrated from England & was the 1st treasurer of the US. *6TH:768-69*

NUMSEN, WILLIAM, b. 3 Dec. 1803, town of Delmhorst, Dukedom of Oldenberg, Germany, s/o Peter & Sophia (Mendsen). Sophia joined her brother, a Lutheran minister, in Philadelphia, PA & was joined by her husband. William to America at age of 17 & landed in Baltimore, MD & apprenticed to a baker (Muth). In 1823 he m. Mary Schneider, d/o Rev. John, 3d pastor of the Otterbein Church on Conway St. in Baltimore. *MDC:229-30*

NUSBAUM, ABRAM W., b. Germany, served in their army & as a young man emigrated to the US, settled on a farm in Liberty District, Frederick Co., MD, where he purchased 137 acres on Linganore Creek, where & his wife (Rachel Baumgardner) both died & are bur. at Union Chapel. They left two sons, Adam who m. Rachel Baumgardner is the only one named here. They are bur. at Union Chapel. Their son Abram Washington Nusbaum m. 15 Nov. 1859 to Margaret Cashour, d/o William & Martha (Albaugh) Cashour, who d. 2 Dec. 1870. Abram m. (2) Feb. 1873, Henrietta Molesworth, d/o William & Ruth (Condon) Molesworth of near Woodville, Frederick Co. *FR2:1297, 1546-7*

NUSBAUM, JACOB, emigrant from Germany, settled in what is now Linganore District, Frederick Co. & later removed to Wakefield Valley, Carroll Co., MD. He m. Miss Hyde, b. Ireland, & had: Isaiah; Harvey; Elizabeth, m. Jacob Nail; Mary, m. David Franklin; Laura, m. Frank Barnes; Fanny, m. William Baker; Susan, m Thomas Bond. Mrs. Nusbaum d. previous to Jacob, who d. at his home in Westminster in 1879, agd 79. *FR2;1278-9*

NUSBAUM, MATHILDA (GOLDSMITH), of Erdmanrode, Kur-Hessen, Germany, widow of Aaron; to Baltimore 1865, age 74, with eldest son and family; d. aged 83. Her dau., Mrs. Violet Rothschild, to Baltimore 1863. *TR3:79*

NYBERG, --- (REV.), of Sweden, served Evangelical Lutheran Church in Frederick, MD c. 1745/6. *FR1:420*

'NEILL, JOHN, b. Ireland, 22 [23?] Nov. 1768, to Havre de Grace, MD in 1805. Nail factory. Served in the military under Gen. Henry Lee in 1794 & 1798 served in the American Navy against the French. Captured by the British in the War of 1812. John, the immigrant, d. 26 Jan. 1838. His son, John O'Neill, b. & raised in Havre de Grace, 1861 appointed keeper of the light house; he m. Esther Mullen, b. in Fulton, NY. John d. 1863 & wife appointed keeper of the lighthouse, which position she held for 18 years, when impaired eyesight caused her to resign in favor of her son, Henry E. She d. age 86. Member St. John's Episcopal Church. *H/C:358-60; TR4:858-9*

OBENDERFER, JOHN L., b. Germany in Oct. 1815, d. in Frederick City, MD 1891. He was a cabinetmaker & in 1851 founded furniture & undertaking business now conducted by his son. Member of the Reformed Church; m. (1) Miss Sabean --- of Germany & had: Catharine, dec'd.; Caroline; Christina, m. William Walsh of St. Louis, MO; Mary, dec'd.; John L. of CA; Augustus, dec'd., was soldier of the Confederate Army as was his brother John L.; & Frederick W. John L., the immigrant, m. (2) Margaret Vennegn, b. Germany. All children of 2d m. d. young. *FR2:1559*

OGLE, SAMUEL, b. c. 1694, s/o Samuel of Northumberland, England, was appointed governor by Lord Baltimore in 1732 & served 1731-2, 1735-42 & 1747-52. He was founder of a family prominent in southern MD for a number of generations. He m. Ann, d/o Benjamin Tasker who succeded him as governor on his death. One of their descs., Benjamin Ogle, became gov. of MD 1798. *AAH:209; TR4:899*

OLAND, FREDERICK, b. Hanover, Germany 9 Dec. 1821. To America in 1830 with his parents. Landed in Baltimore & settled in Frederick, MD. Frederick's father [not named here] d. shortly after their arrival in America. Frederick was a shoemaker & m. Annie, d/o Peter Schaffer of Frederick Co. & had: Frances m. John Karney; Carlton E. farmer of Montgomery Co., MD; Alice E. m. Parker Devilbiss, res. near Frederick; Lucretia m. Edward Stull, res. Frederick Co.; Charles F., farmer of Buckeystown Dist.; David P. of Licksville, MD; Jacob L.

farmer of Montgomery Co.; Virginia m. John A. Geesey of Walkersville Dist., Frederick Co., MD. *FR2:989, 1049*

OLER. Three Oler brothers from Germany to America in early 18th century; one settled PA, one to the West & one to Frederick Co., MD & one of his sons to Baltimore before the Rev., carpenter, had 4 sons: Peter, John, Jacob & George. *MDC:284*

OLIVER, THOMAS, gentleman, b. Bristol, England early in the 16th century. His grandson, Thomas Oliver, to Boston, MA in 1632 on the ship *William & Frances*; surgeon. Desc. Dr. John Rathbone Oliver, 11th in desc. from the immigrant, is s/o Gen. Robert Shaw & Marion (Rathbone) Oliver & was b. 4 Jan. 1872 in Albany, NY. Dr. John studied abroad & grad. Harvard College in 1894. He is a member of the dispensary staff of Johns Hopkins Hospital & in private practice with Dr. Llewellys F. Barker. *TR3:895-6*

ORDEMAN, HERMAN (CAPT.), b. Bremen, Germany 28 Nov. 1812. Seaman for 32 years. He res. in Baltimore for some time & later removed to Park Mills, MD [Frederick Co], built a distillery. He m. Catherine Schmaul, b. in Paris France in March of 1816. Children: John H. of Philadelphia, PA, now dec'd.; Charles O., sergeant in the Confederate Army, killed at Perryville, KY; Georgiana, d. unm.; Daniel T., merchant of Frederick, now dec'd.; Mary C., widow of the late John E. Price; Emma C., widow of the late Eugene Hughes of Washington, D.C.; Frederick A. Members of the Reformed Church.

　　　　Daniel T. Ordeman (son of the immigrant Herman), farmer in Frederick Co. until 1882 when he formed partnership with John E. Price, hardware & implement business in Frederick, MD. Member of the Protestant Church of Frederick. He m. 1887, Edith Best, d/o William H. & Elizabeth (Haller) Best, of Frederick. *FR2:1439, 1459-60; 6TH:310*

OTTE, LEWIS, b. Hanover, Germany 10 June 1870, s/o Theodore (1838-1906) & Augusta Otte. Lewis' siblings are Charlotte of Hanover Germany; Robert Adolph, of Washington, DC; Minnie and Louise of Germany & William of Memphis, TN. Lewis sailed for US on the *Elba*, landed in NY in 1886. He res. in Fredericksburg, VA until 1888, when he went to Washington, DC. Baker, cook & waiter. Later res. in NJ & NY & Washington again. In 1903 he removed to Frederick, MD & opened the Buffalo Cafe. Presbyterian. He m. 1896, Pauline Kunkle of Philadelphia, PA. *FR2:1138*

OTTERBEIN, PHILIP G. (REV.), of Nassau, Dillenberg, Germany. To America, served at Lancaster & Tulpenhocken, PA and served as pastor of the Reformed Church of Frederick, MD, 1760-1765. *FRI:408*

OTTO, JACOB J., & wife Maria Shetler, both b. Germany. To America, settled in Somerset Co., PA & after two years removed to Bittinger, Garrett Co., MD. He d. 1870, aged 69. Amish. Wife d. at age 84 at home of son Christian J. *6TH:475-76*

OULD, HENRY LONGITUDE SEAL, s/o Henry & Jane Ould, b. 2 Feb. 1793, in Devonshire, England; d. Georgetown, District of Columbia. To Georgetown with his brother Robert, both became naturalized Americans. Robert m. Pauline Riggs Gaithe. Henry m. Elizabeth Cloud Peirce. *GME:250*

OWEN, JOHN (REV.), clergyman of Church of England, & wife Eliza Sophia Spry, both b. Scotland, to MD c. 1833. *TR4:359*

OWENS, JOHN E., b. Liverpool, England 2 April 1823. His father, Owen Griffith Owens, b. Wales. With his parents to US, resided 10 years in Baltimore & then settled in Philadelphia. *MDC:675*

OWINGS, RICHARD, from Wales to MD prior to 1659. He was of ancient & noble house of Owains Glendower, a desc. of the last ruling house of Llewellyn in Wales before its final annexation to England. Richard (Owains, Owings, Owens), was justice of Calvert Co., res. also in Dorchester Co. & later in Anne Arundel Co. In 1692 he m. Rachel Beale (Beall), d/o Col. Ninian Beall & Ruth Moore & removed with other families to Baltimore Co., where they bought large tracts of land now known as the Green Spring Valley. They had four sons: Isaac, Samuel, Joshua & Richard & 1 dau., Rebecca Owings, who m. Sir Henry Howard, s/o Joshua. *TR4:767-8*

ACKARD, SAMUEL, with wife & 1 child to America on ship *Dilligence* in 1629. Desc. Amos Packard m. Lydia S. Herrick & had 28 May 1858 in West Paris, Oxford Co., ME, Morrill Nathaniel Packard. Morrill is atty. & inventor, res. Baltimore, MD; m. 1906 Lenora Virginia Terrier, nee Seltzer, of Baltimore, d/o the late William H. D. Seltzer. *TR4:493-5*

PAGELS, CHRISTOPHER, burgemaster & manufacturer of Hesse Cassel, to America with his family in 1833 & settled in Baltimore County, MD. Second son, George H., b. 22 March 1816, Hesse Cassel. Christopher still living in Baltimore County at age 93. Another son, Edward, named. Family in blacksmithing & iron railing business, E. & G. H. Pagels. Edward went to CA. George H. member of United Brethern in Christ (Otterbein Church) in Baltimore City. George m. in 1841 Rosina, dau. of Michael Zimmer of Baltimore; she d. 1862. He m. 2d, 1865, Barbara, dau. of Christian F. Hailer of Baden, Germany. *MDC:121-22*

PAGON FAMILY, settled in St. Mary's Co., MD c. 1665. Descs. res. in Baltimore City. *TR4:788-9*

PAPIN, JOSEPH MARIE, from Canada & m. Marie Louis de Laclede, youngest d/o Pierre de Laclede, founder of St. Louis, MO. Ancestor Pierre Papin came from Brittany with the famous 20 or 30 founders of Montreal. Desc. Minnie Lucile Nash, d/o Charles Henry & Isabel (Tracy) Nash of St. Louis, MO m. at Prospect Hall, Frederick, MD 26 Jan. 1910, Dr. Benjamin C. Perry, b. Kensington, Montgomery Co., MD 7 Jan. 1881, s/o Richard Humphrey & Margaret (Waters) Perry. *TR4:464-5*

PARROTT, AUGUSTIN, to America "in the boat that brought hither the father of George Washington." He settled in Westmoreland Co., VA but later to Mathews Co., where his son John H. Parrott, Sr. was b. in 1809. John H. resided at Petersburg, Richmond & Alexandria, VA & later in Fauquier Co. Member of the Presbyterian Church & d. aged 75. He m. in 1832 Elizabeth E., d/o Capt. Elias & Sarah B. (Fitzhugh) Edmunds. Elias served in the War of 1812. Sarah was d/o Col. Fitzhugh of Prospect Hill. The son of John H. & Elizabeth Edmunds was John H., b. Fauquier Co., VA 1849; worked for the American Coal Co. in Lonaconing, MD. *6TH:487-88*

PASCAULT, LOUIS CHARLES, [or Jean Charles Marie Louis Pascault, Marquis de Poleon], to America with his family when he escaped during the massacre of St. Domingo, France. His children: Josephine Marie Henriette, m. James Gallatin, s/o Albert; Louis Charles, m. 1811, Anne E. Goldsborough (b. 1787, d. 1855 on Kent Island, both bur. St. Joseph's Church, Talbot Co., MD); Sarah Rebecca, m. William Goldsborough (s/o Howles & Rebecca); dau. m. Columbus O'Donnell;

dau. m. Gen. Reubel of Paris, who came to America on the staff of the brother of Napoleon Bonaparte. *TR4:796*

PATERSON, HENRY, & wife Elizabeth Hoag, both b. Cumbernauld, Scotland. Henry to US in 1869 & settled in Tioga Co., PA, where he d. aged 70. Merchant; Presbyterian. Elizabeth was the d/o Henry Hoag, who brought his wife & 3 children to US. Alexander H. Paterson, s/o Henry & Elizabeth, b. in Arnot, Tioga Co., PA 11 May 1878. Grad. Univ. of MD with DDS in 1911 & practices dentistry in Baltimore. He m. 2 June 1913 Caroline Elizabeth Haas of Baltimore, a d/o John F. Haas. *TR3:560*

PATTERSON, GEORGE, of Scotland, to America at an early day & settled in PA, near Emmitsburg, MD. His son George M. m. Louisa Wolford, d/o John, a PA farmer. Their son Albert M., b. on the homestead served as sheriff of Frederick Co., MD & m. in 1893 Miss Bruce Shoemaker of Frederick Co. *6TH:337-38*

PATTERSON, GEORGE FREDERICK, s/o William of Bristol, England, to Baltimore 1880 at age 40. President of Great Western Steamship Co. of Bristol. George F. b. Bristol May 24, 1840, d. Baltimore Feb. 13, 1914. *GME:86*

PATTISON FAMILY, arrived at St. Marys City, MD, soon after it was established. Desc. enlisted in American army during the Rev. War from SC. Descs. res. in MD. *TR4:788*

PAUL, ALEXANDER, & wife Agnes Haig, both b. Scotland. Father to US as a young man of 19. He owned a factory in South Paterson, NJ & was the maker of the first locomotive built in NJ in 1832. In 1838 to Baltimore, MD & he d. there in 1851, aged 62. Agnes d. aged 94. *6TH:664-65*

PAYNE, JOHN, b. England, to America at an early age, veteran of the Rev. War. His dau. Mary Payne m. Ezekiel Slade, both b. Harford Co., MD. This Slade family from Ireland. Ezekiel Slade a veteran of the War of 1812. Mary & Ezekiel's dau., Rachel Slade, b. Harford Co., m. Joseph W. Strong, b. NY & they settled in Harford Co., where they had 4 children. *H/C:507-8*

PEALE, CHARLES, (1709-1750), b. County Rutland, England, m. Margaret Triggs at St. Margaret's, Westminster. In 1742 emigrated to Chestertown, MD, master of the Kent Co. school, where he remained until his death in 1750. His eldest son, Charles Willson Peale, one of the most notable painters of America, b. Parish of St. Paul's, Queen Anne Co., 15 April 1741. Charles m. 12 Jan. 1762, Rachel, d/o John & Eleanor (Maccubbin) Brewer of West River. *TR4:855-7*

PEARCE, WILLIAM, b. England, settled in MD c. 1660; high sheriff of Cecil Co. Desc. Gideon Pearce of Kent Co. m. Julia, d/o Dr. Elisha Cullen Dick of VA. Their son, James Alfred Pearce, b. Alexandria, VA 8 Dec. 1804, studied law with Judge John Glenn in Baltimore. *TR4:870*

PEARCE, WILLIAM, Welshman who settled in Kent Co., MD 1660. Desc. Thomas Pearce erected home on "My Lady's Manor" in 1808. *TR4:546-7*

PEARRES, JAMES, of France, obtained from George III of England a patent for land in what is now Frederick & Montgomery Counties, MD. Desc. William T. was large slave & land owner of Montgomery Co., & left 3 sons: George A., Charles B. of Waco, TX and James, farmer of Montgomery Co., MD. *FR2:944-5*

PEAT, WILLIAM, b. Lanarkshire, Scotland, 13 Oct. 1829, s/o John & Elizabeth (Cadzow) Peat. Elizabeth m. 2d. William King. William 1853 to America, settled NY; 1858 m. Christine Riddell who d. 1861. To Baltimore. He m. 2d 1864, Feb. 16, Mary Virginia, only d/o Capt. William & Martha (Lennox) Patterson. Presbyterian. *MDC:112*

PEIRCE, GEORGE, (or PEARCE), from the parish of Winscomb, Somerset Co., England; m. Ann Gainer of Thornbury, Gloucestershire, 1st day 12th month (Feb.) 1679. With wife & 3 small children left Bristol, England 1684 & settled in Chester Co.,PA, Thornbury twp. Quakers. To East Marlboro twp., where he d. 1734. Their 2d son, Joshua, b. 5 Jan. 1684 in England, d. 15 Sept. 1752 East Marlboro Twp. Joshua (2), 2d s/o Joshua & 2d wife, Rachel Gilpin, b. 22 Jan. 1724, m. Ann Bailey. Their son Isaac was the ancestor of the MD branch of the Peirce family. He settled on large tract of land in present DC, now known as Rock Creek Park, in 1760. *GME:252*

PELCZAR, MICHAEL, b. 12 Sept. 1885, Krosno, Poland, s/o Frank Pelczar & Katharine Zajdel. Michael m. in Baltimore Josephine Polek, d/o Jacob. *TR2:19.*

PELS, SIMON M., and wife Jette Koopman, from Germany to US, settled in Baltimore in early 1860's. Their son, Moses, b. in Weenar, Prussia, to America as a boy of 13 with his younger brother Edward, arriving in Charlotte, SC in 1859; four years later to Baltimore, MD. Jewish. *TR3:349*

PENDERGAST, CHARLES (CAPT.), b. Dublin, Ireland, in 1794, at age c. 15, settled in Havre de Grace, MD, where son Jerome Aloysius was b. 25 Oct. 1831. Charles was a mariner & then a quarry businessman at Port Deposit; 1838 removed to Baltimore as shipping merchant. *MDC:193-4*

PERCY, DOUGLAS, noted Scotch geologist, to America & was an early developer of coal mines of Allegany Co., MD. His dau., Eleanor Maria, m. 15 Dec. 1863, W. H. LeFevre. *6TH:220-22*

PERINE FAMILY, French Huguenots to America and settled at Staten Island, NY in late 1600's. William (1710-1768) to Baltimore Co., MD Oct. 1760; wife was Jane ---. They had 6 children; only one named here was the eldest son, Peter (1735-1775), who m. Hannah Amos of Baltimore 13 Nov. 1760. Quaker. *TR4:64*

PERKINS, DANIEL, Welshman, arrived in America c. 1700 & settled in Kent Co., MD. His son is named as Col. Isaac Perkins, but another Col. Isaac Perkins is named in the writeup, b. 1743, & named as son Ebenezer Perkins and wife Sarah Barney. Ebenezer's will dated 14th day of 5th month, 1750. Quakers. *TR4:659-61*

PETER, ROBERT, Scotsman to America about middle of the last century & d. at his residence in Georgetown, DC 1806. He was first mayor of Georgetown, 1789-1798. He was one of the younger sons of Thomas Peter, Esq., Laird of Crossbasket, Lanarkshire, Scotland. Thomas' wife was Jane Dunlop, d/o James, Laird of Garnkirke & wife who was a Campbell of Blytheswood & descendant of Lord Napier. Robert, the immigrant, m. Elizabeth Scott, d/o George, deputy commissary-general of Lord Baltimore. George Scott was a son of Sir Thomas Scott of Malenie, in Midlothianshire, a cousin of Sir Walter Scott, and a descendant of the Dukes of Buccleugh. The wife of Sir Thomas was Elizabeth, d/o Lord Fountainhall. George Peter, s/o Robert, b. Georgetown, now in DC, 28 Sept. 1779. He was a member of the US Army. He m. 3 times: 1st, Ann Plater of MD; 2d, Agnes Freeland; 3d, Sarah Norfleet Freeland, of Petersburg, VA. *6TH:639-41*

PHALEN, DANIEL, b. Kilkenny Co., Ireland. As young man emigrated to America & settled at Harper's Ferry, WV. Was gatekeeper at the Harper's Ferry US Arnsenal the night John Brown & confederates captured the place. Daniel was Catholic, married twice & by 1st wife had dau. Mary, who is now a widow & res. in NY. His second wife was Mary Rooch, b. County Cork, Ireland. His children by 2d marriage: Ella, m. Patrick Reily, now dec:d.; Martin W.; Thomas H.; John dec'd.; and Maria who m. Samuel Kenny, of Brunswick. *FR2:1274-5*

PHELPS, ELISHA, emigrated with his father & brothers from England & settled in VA in the last century, where he m. Rachel Payne, d/o Henry Payne of Shenandoah Valley, and Elizabeth Kurtz, a German emigrant who settled in PA. Elisha's dau., Mary E., m. Rev. N. J. Brown Morgan, & their son, Wilbur P. Morgan, M.D. b. 25 Feb. 1841 in Jefferson Co., VA, settled in Baltimore, MD. *MDC:648-49*

PHELPS, WILLIAM, from England to Dorchester, MA in 1630 & founded the town of Windsor. Eighth generation descendant Charles Edward Phelps, s/o John & Almira (Hart [Lincoln?]) Phelps, b. 1 May 1833, in Guilford, VT, was raised in Baltimore, MD. He m. Martha E. Woodward, d/o William (b. 1801) & Virginia (Burneston), early settlers of Baltimore & Anne Arundel Cos. & they had son John b. Baltimore 23 July 1873. Another s/o Charles & Martha was Rear Admiral William Woodward Phelps, also b. in Baltimore, 26 Nov. 1869 & grad. from the US Naval Academy in 1889. *MDC:293; TR4:441*

PIEPER, FRANZ AUGUST OTTO (REV.), b. Carwitz, Pomerania, Germany 27 June 1852, s/o Augustus & Bertha. At age 18 in 1870 to US & 2 years later graduated from Northwestern College in WI; 1875 graduated from Concordia Seminary & ordained to the Lutheran ministry. Has served in WI, MO, OH & other states. Dr. Pieper m. Minnie Koehn of Sheboygan, WI, reside in St. Louis, MO. Their dau. m. 4 Aug. 1915, in St. Louis, the Rev. Mr. Rudolph Stang Ressmeyer; they reside in Baltimore. *TR3:227*

PINKNEY, JONATHAN, an Englishman whose son Wiliam was b. 17 March 1764 at Annapolis, MD. Jonathan was m. twice, to sisters [not named here]. His children: Margaret, Nancy, Jonathan, William & Ninian. William was an attorney and practiced law in Harford Co. This family is said to be distantly related to the Pinckneys of SC. *MDC:133; AAH:127; TR4:19*

PITSNOGLE, ADAM, from Germany to the US in early manhood & settled in MD near the PA line, later removing to WV & settled near Little Georgetown. He served in the War of 1812 & m. Miss Miller, b. in MD. He d. at the age of 53. His son, Levi, b. & reared at Little Georgetown, Berkeley Co., WV. Episcopal. He d. aged 73 in Berkeley Co. His wife was Matilda Long, b. near Greencastle, PA, and accompanied her parents to Washington Co. MD at an early age. She d. aged 69. Their son Jeptha E. b. in Bedington, Berkeley Co., 11 Jan. 1863. *6TH:201-02*

PITTS, WILLIAM, from England to visit friends in Baltimore Co., MD, where he stayed & married. He had two sons, William & Thomas. Son William remained in Baltimore Co. & Thomas removed to Anne Arundel Co. & m. Susannah Lusby. Their son Thomas m. Sarah Sewell in 1782. *AAH:142*

PLACIDE, PAUL, b. Bordeaux, France, m. Louisa --- of Paris, France. To America at the time of the French revolution. Paul was a cooper & settled in Baltimore, MD, serving in the War of 1812 at the Battle of North Point. Son Henry S. b. Baltimore 28 Oct. 1800. *MDC:178*

PLACK, LOUIS, b. Germany, his dau. Amanda M. m. Robert E. Strange of Annapolis, MD after 1885. *TR3:199*

PLUMB, ALANSAN, & wife Nancy Guy, both b. England. Nancy Guy had 2 brothers, Richard & Robert Guy, who attained considerable prominence as physicians of London. Son [name not given] b. Albany NY, attorney, m. Katharine Branden, d/o John & Mary (Baird) of VA. Their dau. Amy Eleta Plumb is a physician, was b. Auburn, DeKalb Co., IN, 20 Dec. 1867; practices in Baltimore. *TR3:238*

PLUMMER, SAMUEL, Quaker & Welshman who settled on a land grant in Frederick, MD in 1743. 4th generation desc. William Walker Plummer m. Harriet French. *TR4:384*

POE, DAVID, in 1743 with his parents to America from Londonderry, Ireland, at age of 2. He served in the MD Line during the American Rev. His son, David Jr., was disowned by the family when he m. Mrs. Elizabeth Hopkins, an English actress of some repute. She d. of pneumonia 8 Dec. 1811 at Richmond & David was one of the 70 victims that perished in the burning theatre in the same month. Their eldest son was Edgar Allan Poe. *MDC:629-30*

POE, JOHN, m. Sept. 1741 Jane McBride of Ballymony, County Antrim; brought wife and 2 sons to America, set. Lancaster Co., PA and later in Cecil and then Baltimore Co., MD where John d. 1756. Sons David & George m. in Cecil Co. and later moved to Baltimore Co. George d. at home of his son Jacob in Frederick Co., MD 20 Aug. 1823. Daughter Jane d. in Baltimore 17 July 1802, at age 96, and is bur. Westminster Churchyard. *GME:193*

POFFENBERGER FAMILY, left Germany for America in 1740 & settled in Lancaster Co., PA. In 1766 removed to Frederick, now Washington Co., MD. Simon Poffenberger, one of the original MD settlers, m. a Miss Todd, a lady of English birth. Simon b. 1806, d. 1890. He is bur. at cemetery in Boonsboro, MD. His wife was Mary Ann Thomas & they had: Lawson, now dec'd.; Sarah, wife of the late Urias Gross, now dec'd.; John H. retired farmer of Rohrersville, Washington Co., MD; George W. of CA, dec'd.; Josiah, retired farmer of Washington Co.; Thomas L., now dec'd.; Ann Maria, m. Josephus Alsip of KS; William H., now dec'd.; Susan, m. John L. Smith of Locust Grove, Washington Co., MD. Mary Ann d. 1876 & Simon m. 2d. Mary C. Gouff of Washington Co. They had one child, Maud, who m. John Eichelberger, res. Hagerstown, MD. *FR2:1496*

PORTER, JAMES, b. Ireland, settled Peach Bottom, Lancaster Co., PA in latter part of the 18th century & in 1753 removed to Cecil Co., MD. *H/C:293-4*

PORTER, JOHN, b. Gloucester, near Bristol, England. "Made himself obnoxious to the party in power by singing a song of his own composition at a gathering of his neighbors, in which he made an uncomplimentary allusion to the reigning monarch, George I." To America 1715 & settled in Baltimore Co., MD, where his son John Jr. was b. & was the first of the name to settled in Allegany Co., MD in 1782, settling first near the PA line, but later in Mt. Savage, & thence near Eckhart Mines, wher he d. 1810. He m. a Miss McKenzie. *6TH:518-20*

POSS, JACOB, b. Prussia near the castled Rhine, 1 Aug. 1839, s/o Henry Jacob & Apolonia (Emrich) Poss, farmers. To America at age 12 with an aunt & resided in Washington, MD. Later opened a hotel at Brightwood, DC until 1864. Resided in DC, Prince George Co. & Montgomery Counties, MD. In Feb. 1862 m. Mary Ellen Dobson of DC. She d. 21 Feb. 1887, aged 40 years, 10 months & 16 days. *6TH:772-73*

POTEE, ---, b. France & came to America on the *Mayflower*, settling in what is now Washington, DC. Desc. --- Potee was a plasterer in that city & his son, George Needham Potee, b. in Baltimore, MD; manufacturer of brick in Brooklyn. George m. Sara May Roach, a d/o James Roach of Brooklyn, MD & a granddau. of James Roach, Sr. who immigrated from Ireland to America & settled in Brooklyn, a well digger. James Roach Sr. is bur. in the Cedar Hill Cemetery. George Potee d. 27 Aug. 1895, aged 65; Sara d. 30 Dec. 1909, aged 65. They had a large family of 16 children; 13 sons & 3 daus. *TR3:740-3*

POTTS, JOHN, of Llanidoss, Wales; his dau. Mary m. at Abingdon, MD Mathias Tyson. *GME:223*

POTTS, WILLIAM, from King's County, Ireland to the Island of Barbadoes c. 1700. He & wife Rebecca had several children, including William, who settled at Bridgetown, Island of Barbadoes. He d. 1721. His wife's name was Rebecca --- & they had a son William (3d), b. Barbadoes in 1718. William (3) removed to MD & took up land on Choptank River & c. 1740/41 & he m. Sarah Lee, d/o Philip Lee of Prince George's Co., MD. He returned to Barbadoes in 1775 & d. at Gaudeloupe, West Indies in 1761, where he died. Sarah d. 1790 at the home of her son Richard at Frederick City, MD. Richard to MD, settled at Annapolis & was Rev. War veteran. Descendants settled Frederick Co., MD. *FR1:127, FR2:1342-3*

POUDER (POUNDER), JACOB, of a French family who settled first in Germany & then in Ireland, to America 1730. His wife d. on ship leaving an infant son, Jacob Leonard Pouder. They landed in PA & located in Frederick Co., MD--that part which is now Carroll Co. *TR4:317-20*

PRATHER, ---, 3 brothers, missionaries came from England to America & settled in St. Mary's Co., MD. Descendants to Washington Co., MD in 1838. Samuel Prather, b. 1763, spent his life as a farmer on land on which was situated the old Fort Frederick. He d. 1818, aged 54. *6TH:821-22*

PRATT, PHINEAS, arrived at Plymouth, MA in ship *Ann* from England 1623 & d. at Charlestown, MA 19 April 1680. Desc. Isaac Pratt b. in North Middleborough, Plymouth Co., MA 6 March 1776 m. Naomi Keith, b. Bridgewater, MA 11 Sept. 1785. Their son Enoch Pratt b. North Middleborough 10 Sept. 1808 removed to Baltimore, MD 1 Jan. 1831; commission merchant. He m. Louisa Hyde, b. Baltimore 22 Sept., 1818 on 1 Aug. 1839. *MDC:493-94*

PREISS, HIRSCH, to America 1830. His dau. Mina m. Moses Cohen in Baltimore. Jewish. *TR3:367*

PRESTON, RICHARD (COL.), arrived in VA c. 1642; removed to MD in 1649 & settled in Anne Arundel Co. *AAH:112*

PRESTON, THOMAS, from England (?), appears in MD rent rolls (1650-1710) had a son James Preston Sr., who was the father of James Jr. who m. Clemency Bond 31 March 1749. James Jr. was owner of Vineyard, in Hartford Co., MD, which is still in the family. His son, Bernard Preston, b. 2 Aug. 1786, m. Sarah Fell Bond, d/o Jacob, s/o Thomas. The Bond family were large landowners in Harford & Baltimore Counties. *TR4:96*

PRICE, THOMAS, b. England, sailed on *The Ark & The Dove*, landed at St. Mary's, MD in March 1634. He m. Elizabeth Phillips, d/o Robert of Calvert Co., MD & they had Mordecai Price, large landowner res. in West River, MD who m. Mary Parsons, d/o Thomas & Isabel. They were parents of Mordecai Price II of Anne Arundel & Gunpowder Forest, Baltimore Co., MD. *TR4:516-18*

PRICHARD, HENRY, b. Wales, to America & settled in Shenandoah Valley, VA & later to Clarksburg, VA. In 1866 to Will Co., IL as superintendent of the Wilmington coal mines, later worked in Bloomington, next in Lincoln, IL. He later removed to Frostburg, MD. He m. Elizabeth Bevan. Son Enoch H. B., b. Monmouthsire, Wales 8 May

1840, to America with father, resides in Frostburg. Enoch m. Mary A., d/o Henry & Joanna (Jones) Harris, of Morganshire, Wales. *6TH:401-02*

PRIOR, EDWARD A., b. in village of Oldendorf, near Osnabruck, in the late Kingdom of Hanover, Germany, March, 1841, s/o Christian Frederick & Louisa (Schrader) Prior. To America, landing in NY, Aug. 1859. He was employed by a Baltimore firm as a traveling salesman. He m. twice; 1st 4 April 1868 to Bertha, d/o Dr. Pape, who died after 7 years; his 2d wife was a cousin of his former wife & they married 8 May 1877. *MDC:329*

PRY, PHILIP, of French descent, b. in Germany, to America at age of 6 with his parents. Name originally BRYNE, later changed to BRY & after coming to MD altered to Pry. His parents died on the trip to America & he was taken by a Mr. Rohrer, who settled near York in Franklin Co., PA. In 1810 he came to MD & settled in Washington Co. Philip d. there in 1828, aged 65. *6TH:859-60*

PURCELL, JOHN JAMES, b. Dublin, Ireland, 13 Nov. 1817, s/o Matthew, of a family of Staplestown, County Wicklow, & Julia (McDermott) of County Kildare. John James was a mariner & eventually settled in Baltimore, MD, where he was apprenticed to John Swartz, a house carpenter, in "Old Town" in 1832. In Oct. 1840 he m. Ann Kemp, who d. Dec. 1845; in 1848 he m. Rebecca A. Easter. *MDC:208*

PURNELL, THOMAS, from Berkeley [Beckley], Northamptonshire, England in 1635 & settled Northampton, VA [Worcester Co., MD]. Descendant William T. Purnell, b. in DE, educated in Worcester Co., MD, settled in Port Gibson, MS. He later settled in Worcester Co., MD & was prominent in public life. He d. near Cambridge, MD in 1873. His wife was Henrietta Spence, d/o John S. of Worcester Co. *6TH:519-20; MDC:431*

PURVIANCE, ROBERT, b. at Castle Finn, Ireland, s/o Huguenot refugees; to America 1763. Appointed by Gen. Washington as a naval officer of the port of Baltimore. He d. Oct. 1806. *MDC:96*

PUSHKIN, BENJAMIN (M.D.), b. in province of Vitebsk, Russia, 1 April 1886, a s/o Israel & Gussie (Stam) Pushkin, who immigrated to the US in 1905, settling in Baltimore, MD. Benjamin to US in 1906, grad. Univ. of MD 1914. Specialized in mental diseases. He m. in Alexandria,

VA, 4 Sept. 1914, Gussie Duke, b. Moscow, Russia, a d/o Abraham & Sophie (Rossett) Duke. Her parents settled in Baltimore during her childhood. Dr. Pushkin became a citizen in Baltimore in 1912. *TR3:488*

PUTMAN, ---, to America from Germany & settled in Middletown Valley. His son, John J. Putman, farmer of the Middletown Valley, Frederick Co., MD, res. near what is now Harmony. John m. Annie E. Summers & had: Amanda, m. Henry Coblentz; Samuel, farmer of Woodsboro District, now dec'd.; John Jr.; Annie E., dec'd. wife of the late Leander Stull of Creagerstown District; Julia, m. Lewis P. Ramsburg of Walkersville, both dec'd.; & Hezekiah, dec'd. of Frederick City. Family were members of the Lutheran Church. *FR2:1446-7*

 UARLES, ROGER, of England & VA. Desc. Dicie Pemberton Quarles, b. 1805, d. 1845, m. John King. John was desc. of Miles King, first mayor of Norfolk, VA & wife Lady Mary, d/o Lord Bailey of Benalnd. Their son, Lucian Minor King, b. in old Quarles mansion "Woodbury," built by Roger Quarles in King William Co., VA, 5 May 1842. Lucian served in Confederacy in Civil War & was captured at Gettysburg. Lucian m. Henriette Octava Gibson & had Hartwell M. King, b. Ellerson, Hanover Co., VA 2 Feb. 1879. Hartwell studied law in Ohio & Baltimore & practiced in Baltimore. 9 Jan. 1920 he m. Ida C. Brown, d/o George W., formerly of Winchester, VA, but now of Baltimore. *TR4:436-7*

 ABERG, ANDREW, b. Hanover, Germany, 26 Sept. 1761, m. 30 Nov. 1786 in Baltimore, Sarah York, b. Baltimore. He served in the Rev. War as a private in the PA Continental Line. He was s/o George William (b. Hanover, Germany 1730, and Anna Maria Lucy Raberg. *TR4:245*

RABORG, GEORGE WILLIAM, b. Hanover, Germany; 11 Sept. 1753 sailed for America with wife Anna Marie Lucy & settled in Lancaster, PA. Their son Christopher, b. Hanover 3 May 1750, was 3 years at immigration. Christopher res. Philadelphia & Lancaser, PA, & later Baltimore, MD; coppersmith. Christopher m. at Lancaster, PA Catherine Barbara de Ormand 1 March 1772. *TR4:553-5*

RADCLIFFE, RICHARD, in 1687 to Talbot Co., MD, via PA, from Rosendale, Lancashire, England. Quaker; m. Fannie LeCompte. (RATCLIFFE, RADCLIFFE) *GME:257*

190

RAILING, HENRY, s/o Adam of Hesse Darmstadt, Germany, b. there in 1810. To America 1831 & landed at Baltimore. He was a shoemaker, as was Adam, but went to work as a laborer on the Chesapeake & Ohio Canal & later settled in Frederick Co., MD. Member of the Bethel Lutheran Church. Henry m. Catharine B. Smith, also b. Germany, who had come to America with her parents while a young woman. Their children: Catharine, m. Samuel Keyser of Hagerstown; Adam of Frederick City; George H. of Frederick City; Christian; Peter Z. dec'd. & Lewis D. dec'd., res. in Baltimore. *FR2:1156-7*

RAINE, WILLIAM, to America & located in Baltimore, MD, where he was joined by his son (Col.) Frederick Raine, who was b. in the Fortress of Minden, in Prussia, 13 May 1821. Newspaper editor. *MDC:27*

RAITH, CHARLES, b. Hesse-Darmstadt, Germany, 1866, to America at age of 8 with his uncle, Christian Brill, who located in Richmond, VA. Charles to Baltimore, MD in 1887, at age of 21, meat packing business. Lutheran, he d. 1913, aged 47 & is survived by his mother, who makes her home in Baltimore. Charles m. Susan Binner, b. Baltimore. Her maternal grandparents, Adam & Margaret (Spuck) Binner, were early settlers. *TR3:669-70*

RAMAGE, JAMES, b. Scotland, when not long in America he & his wife were captured by the British during the Rev. War at raid on Elk Forge, Cecil Co., MD. They were grandparents of Mrs. Agatha Scott, wife of David Scott, Esq. of the 4th district of Cecil Co. *C:331*

RAMPLEY, JAMES, from England to Harford Co., MD. His son, Capt. James Rampley, farmer, veteran of War of 1812, m. Elizabeth Nelson, also b. Harford Co., MD. Their son Robert N. Rampley b. there 25 June, 1817, as were Sarah, James & William. *H/C:468/9*

RAMSBERG, GEORGE, b. Germany 1730-35. He m. 20 Dec. 1756, Maria Elizabeth Brunner. They had 11 children, among them a son named George P. Ramsberg. George was b. 16 March 1770, farmer. He m. Catherine Culler & had: Sebastian, Elizabeth, Jacob (b. c. 1802), Susanna, Catherine & Anna. *FR2:1415-16*

RAMSBURG, ---, first from Germany & located in PA, but later removed to near Charlesville, Frederick Co., MD; pioneer settlers. A member of the 3rd generation of the family was Frederick Ramsburg, m.

Lydia A. Snook. Their son Urias D. b. 27 April 1825, d. 1 Sept. 1903; farmer near Charlesville in Tuscarora District. Member Reformed congregation at Bethel; m. Ann S. Staley, d/o Peter S. & Margaret E. (Albaugh) Staley. *FR2:901-2*

RAMSEY, JAMES, emigrated from Ireland & settled in Drumore Township, Lancaster Co., PA at an early age. He m. Jane Montgomery. William, eldest of their 3 sons, graduated at Princeton College in 1754. He was received at into the Abingdon Presbytery & ordained & settled as pastor of the Fairfield Church in 1756. He d. 5 Nov. 1771. Nathaniel, second s/o James & Jane, was graduate of Princeton, attorney of Cecil Co., MD & served in the Revolution. In 1771 m. Margaret Jane Peale, sister of Charles Wilson Peale, the portrait painter. David, youngest s/o James & Jane Ramsey, also graduated Princeton, 1765. He settled in Cecil Co., MD, but later removed to Charleston, SC. *C:537*

RANDALL, THOMAS, from England in early 1700's & settled in Westmoreland Co., VA; m. Jane Davis of VA. His youngest son John, b. in what is now Richmond Co., (then Westmoreland) VA in 1750; to Annapolis, MD in 1770. He served as an officer of the MD Line during the war; m. Deborah Knapp of Annapolis & d. there in 1852, aged 90. *AAH:116*

RANDOLPH, EDWARD FITZ, & wife Elizabeth Blossom, m. 1646, both having come from Nottingham, England, in the *May Flower*. Desc. of the 4th generation, Thomas Randolph, resided in Elkton, Cecil Co., MD, where his 2d son Andrew Jackson Randolph was b. 13 March 1815. *MDC:622-23*

RANDOLPH, WILLIAM, to America in the 16th century & settled in VA. Descendant Robert Lee Randolph was a planter in Frederick Co., VA, where his son Alfred Magill Randolph was b. in 1836. Alfred was rector of Emanuel Church, Baltimore, MD in 1867. In 1858 he m. Sallie Griffith Hoxton, d/o William of the US Army & granddau. of Rev. Mr. Griffith, the first Episcopal Bishop-elect of VA. *MDC:694*

RANKIN, ALEXANDER, b. Ayrshire, Scotland in 1823, m. Jessie Gracie. In 1852 to America & settled in MD, miner. His son Alexander b. Frostburg, MD 7 March 1863. *6TH:822*

RANSOM, SAMUEL (CAPT.), b. 1737 near Ipswich, England, m. 6 May 1756, Esther Lawrence at Canaan Town, now Norfolk, Litchfield Co., CT. In 1773 he moved to Wyoming valley in PA. Samuel was soldier in the Rev. War. During the Wyoming Indian Massacre his family suffered great hardship. Desc. Charles Edmund Ransom, b. 7 Dec. 1835 at Tioga Centre, NY, m. Georgiana Anderson of Port Deposit, Cecil Co., MD on 21 Oct. 1862. She was b. Port Deposit 19 April 1836, d/o Allen & Esther (McCullough) Anderson. The Anderson family was from Scotland & settled in St. Mary's & Charles Cos. in colonial days. The emigrant was John Anderson who arrived in MD in 1658. *TR4:741-6*

RAPHEL, STEPHEN JOSEPH, & wife Mary E. McAtee, both b. France, immigrated to America. Their son, Eugene F., b. 6 Oct. 1845, d. 14 March 1907, retired farmer, Civil War veteran & member of the Roman Catholic church. Eugene m. Jeannette Theresa Braden, of VA desc. & the d/o Noble S. & Mary E. Braden. William Pusey, the grandfather of Mrs. Mary E. Braden, came to America with William Penn. *TR3:661*

RASIN, WILLIAM, from France to Kent Co., MD in early 17th century. *MDC:482*

RAWLINGS, GREENBERRY, from either Scotland or Ireland, settled in the Cecil Co., MD area at what is now known as Battle Swamp. His son John had a son Robert b. in Cecil Co., farmer, where he died aged 64. He m. Mary McVey and had 5 children. Son Z. Taylor Rawlings was b. 1848. *H/C:455-6*

REA, DAVIS, b. Bangor, County Down, Ireland, 14 June 1809; in 1830 to NY City, where he learned the slater's trade. In 1835 to New Orleans for 20 years. 1855 to Cecil Co., MD. 1838 m. Mary Graham, b. NY City in 1822, a d/o Robert Graham, a native of Scotland who came to America in 1821. *H/C:469*

REABURG, GEORGE WILLIAM, of Hanover, Germany, with his family to America & settled in PA. His son, Andrew, served in Rev. War. Desc. Dora Reaberg m. William Henry Peters of Baltimore, MD. *TR4:644-7*

READING, JOHN, with wife Elizabeth, & two children, John & Elsie, settled at NJ at what is now Gloucester. He was one of the pioneer settlers of that place & in 1687 represented the County. He d. 1713 & was bur. across the river in Bucks Co., PA. His son John m. Mary, d/o George Ryerson of Passaic Co., NJ. Their son John b. 1722 m. Isabella, d/o William Montgomery of Ayr, Scotland. Their son John b. 1751 m. Elizabeth, d/o Joseph Hankinson. Their youngest son, Joseph, d. 1820, aged 69 years. Joseph m. Eleanor, d/o Dr. John Grandin of Hamburg, Hunterdon Co., NJ. Son William, b. in Hunterdon Co., farmer, in 1853 removed to Washington, DC & purchased land in Montgomery Co., MD, where he removed to in 1860. In 1886 he moved to Rockville, where he d. 29 Dec. 1897. He was a Methodist & m. 28 May 1845 Sarah Matilda, d/o Hugh Capner of Flemington, NJ. *6TH:565-66*

REAMER, MEYER, b. Russia 9 Feb. 1895, brought to US by his parents in 1906. His parents not named here, both now dec'd. Jan. 1921 he m. Minnie Isaacs of Syracuse, NY & has since res. in Baltimore. *TR3:620*

REDUE, ISAAC, Frenchman, to America before the Rev. War, which he served in, & settled in Kent Co., MD, where descs. for many generations resided. One was John H. Redue who m. Louise Seymour, of another old MD family. *TR4:637-8*

REED, JOHN, 4th s/o Thomas and Mary (Cornwall) Reed; to America in 1630 with brother Thomas; was granted land at Salem in 1640. Res. New London 1650, then to Barbadoes. His son Joseph settled with sons at what is now Trenton, NJ. Joseph m. in England Esther de Berdt, d/o Dennis de Berdt, London merchant, old Huguenot family May 22, 1770; bride & groom to America,. settled Philadelphia. Joseph's eldest son William Bradford Reed, b. 1806; his son, also William, b. June 7, 1838 in Philadelphia, to Baltimore 1868. *GME:119*

REEDER, CHARLES, b. England, settled in Baltimore, MD 1813 & established Reeder shipyard. Son Charles M. m. Katie Dawson of MD & had a son, J. Dawson Reeder, b. Dorcheser Co., MD, 16 July 1880. *TR3:142*

REESE, JOHN, to MD with early colonists from England. Desc. still res. in MD. Desc. Harry S. Reese m. Ida Belle Lippincott & had son, Gordon L. Reese, b. 11 Jan. 1879 in Baltimore, the oldest of 3 children. *TR3:861-2*

REIK, HENRY A., b. in Rudisheim, on the Rhine River in Germany, s/o Henry Reik, a German revolutionist who sought refuge in America, settling in Baltimore Co., MD; dairy farmer. Son Henry A. was 6 months of age on immigration. He settled in Delaware, served in the Union Army during the Civil War & d. 1913, aged 62. *TR3:345*

REINEWALD, JOSEPH LEWIS, b. Darmstadt, Germany 24 Oct. 1834. 1852 from Havre, France to NY; m. 1855, Hollidaysburg, PA, Catherine Sommer of that place. Catherine b. Stuttgardt, Germany 1833 and sailed from Havre to NY to reside with her uncle Frederick Weidler. Their son Charles, Lutheran minister, at Braddock, PA & Emmitsburg, MD (1892), m. at Gettysburg, PA 1890, Irene, d/o Hon. Joel B. Danner of Gettysburg. *FR2:751*

REINHARD, JOHN ANDREW (DR.), b. Germany & d. 1864, aged 47. He practiced medicine in Cumberland, MD for many years. His wife was Emma Doerner, b. Germany, who became a resident of Cumberland at age 7. *6TH:562-63*

REMBOLD, CHARLES, s/o Henry who was b. 26 March 1820 at Wartemberg, Germany & wife Victoria Neff also b. Wartemberg & d. 1839. Charles to US 1847, settled Harford Co., MD, where he m. 1848 Fredericka Pleching, b. Baden, Germany. *H/C:233*

REMSBERG[ER], GEORGE, from Wurtemberg, Germany to Philadelphia with his brother (nephews of Stephen Remsburg of Lancaster Co., PA & Frederick, MD). George, b. 19 Feb. 1836 in Wurtemberg, d. 24 Nov. 1820 near Frederick, MD. He m. 1st Marai Elizabeth Brunner on 20 Dec. 1756 & 2d Catharine Susler on 27 March 1789. He had 11 children, all by his first wife: Anna Maria b. 1758; John b. 1760; Catharine b. 1762; Elizabeth b. 1764; Anna Margaret b. 1767; George Peter b. 1770; Charlotte b. 1772; Stephen b. 1774; Barbara b. 1777; Sebastian b. 1779; Susanna b. 1782. *FR2:1877-80*

REMSBURG, STEPHEN, first of the name found in America. He res. in Lancaster Co., PA as early as 1719. He was b. 11 Oct. 1711, but his birthplace is unknown. He removed to Frederick Co., MD as early as 1732 & settled on part of "Tasker's Chance." He m. Anna Katherine, youngest d/o Joseph Brunner. Their children: John, Christian, Katherine (Mrs. Steiner), Jacob, Elias, Margaret (Mrs. Myers), Henry. Stephen d.

7 March 1789. Member of Reformed church. The Brunner family came from Schiefferstadt, Manheim, Germany. *FR2:1422-4, 1425-6*

RENNER, WILLIAM, with others from the family to America from Germany; m. Miss Hafer. Their children: John, m. Polly Kuch; William, d. unm.; Abraham; Kate & Annie. Abraham m. Elizabeth Overhultz & left children: William, Annie, Noah, Joseph, John, Sophia, Susan, Eliza & Isaac. Isaac in 1835 removed from home place in vicinity of Haugh's Church, Frederick Co., MD to Smithsburg, Washington Co., MD. *FR2:749*

RESLEY, ---, b. Switzerland, to America before the Revolutionary War & settled in Lebanon Co., PA. His son Jacob, b. Lebanon Co., to MD at his majority & located in Washington Co., in the vicinity of Hagerstown. He fought in the continental army & was one of the heroes of Valley Forge. *6TH:598-99*

RESSMEYER, HENRY F., s/o Henry & Meta (Bruening) Ressmeyer, b. Schwarme, Hanover, Germany, to US, settled in NY City; m. Felicitas, d/o Frederick & Anna (Wollschlager) Stang of NY City. Son Rev. Rudolph Stang Ressmeyer, b. NY City 26 June 1891, since 1921 served as pastor of the Emmanuel English Evangelical Lutheran church of Baltimore, MD. *TR3:227*

REVELL, THOMAS, of family of Ogston Hall, Derbyshire, England. Thomas to America & settled first in West Jersey, became member of Lord Cornbury's Council & had a plantation known as "Baythorpe," now Burlington, NJ. Randall Revell settled in MD in the 17th century. *TR4:408-9*

REYNOLDS, HENRY, b. c. 1655, with wife from Nottingham, England & settled in Nottingham in Cecil County, MD in the 18th century; Quakers. Henry's brother William later to America & settled in NY. Another brother, John, settled in Carolina. Henry m. 2d a Mrs. Haines & he had 12 sons. His son Jacob b. 1727, was father of Jonathan b. in Cecil Co. 9 April 1755. Family res. near Rising Sun; later generations were Quakers. *MDC:556-57, H/C:282*

REYNOLDS, JOHN, one of 3 brothers to American from England, settled in PA. Samuel Reynolds, desc. of John, to Lancaster Co., PA; his son Josiah & wife, Mary Swagert also b. there. Their son, Joseph W.

Reynolds, M.D., b. Lancaster Co., in 1834; removed to Cecil Co., MD. Cancer specialist. *H/C:337-8*

RICE, DANIEL, to the colonies before the Revolutionary War, settled in Hardwick, MA. Rev. War veteran. In 1776 moved to Somerset, now known as Dover, in VT. His son, Ephraim, had a son, George E., who d. aged 77 in 1898. Ephraim m. Eliza Mills, of an old MA family. Their youngest son, Lewis C. Rice, b. 7 Oct. 1858 in Dover, VT. At age 19 he removed to Baltimore, MD where he worked for his brother Duane H. Rice, wholesale baker. Lewis m. in Baltimore, 20 Sept. 1888, Atlanta T. McCubbin, d/o Oliver McCubbin & Amanda Shipley. *TR3:680-3*

RICE, WILLIAM, of Scotch-Irish ancestry, to America c. 1700 & settled on the MD Track. His wife was a native of the north of England. Son George b. in Frederick Co., MD 4 Jan. 1774 & m. Dec. 1800 Elizabeth Dofler, d/o Peter & --- Schley, d/o Thomas. Elizabeth b. 1780, d. 25 March 1856. Reformed Church members. *6TH:279-80*

RICHARDSON, ---, 3 brothers came during the Rev. War from England to America. One settled on the Elk River, another near Wilmington, DE & the 3d in Kent Co., MD. Desc. of the Elk River settler, D. H. Richardson, M.D. of Cecil Co., MD was b. there in 1851. He was s/o Joseph Richardson & Margaret McCullough of Cecil Co. *H/C:574-5*

RICHARDSON, WILLIAM, a friend of William Penn, he came to VA in the *Paul* of London in 1634. Removed to MD in 1666 & m. Elizabeth Talbot, widow of Richard, & d/o Matthias Scarborough. William's will names children: Sarah (m. Joshua Dorsey of "Hockley"); John & Lawrence. *AAH:174-5*

RICHARDSON FAMILY, of Talbot Co., MD, originally of White Haven, Cumberland Co., England. *TR4:509*

RICHTER, JOHN L., b. in Germany 1847, s/o Henry who emigrated from Germany to US in 1850, landing in NY. After 2 years to Cumberland, MD & in 1853 to Piedmont, WV & in 1856 to Allegany Co., MD. He resided in Accident, MD, a manufacturer of shoes. Henry m. Elizabeth Krouse, of near Hoff, Bavaria, Germany. Her brother John H. was educated in Additon, IL & resided in Paterson, NJ & later in Chicago, IL. *6TH:590-91*

RIDDELL, JOSEPH, & wife Katherine, b. Canada, settled in Sharon, PA where son William Alan Riddell was b. 13 Oct. 1883. William a steel manufacturer, res. in Cleveland, OH & western PA; 1916 to Frederick, MD. He m. 16 April 1915, Mary Josephine Berlin of Columbiana, OH, d/o E. H. Berlin who now reside in DE. *TR3:403*

RIDDLE, HUMPHREY, b. Ireland 1732, c. 1750 to America; m. Bridget Shannon, b. 1737. Descs. res. Cecil Co., MD. *H/C:296*

RIDER, --- (COL.), England to MD early 1700's; his dau. m. Col. John Henry of Dorchester Co., MD. Their son was John Henry (1750-1798), 9th gov. of the state of MD. *TR4:57*

RIDGELY, HENRY, of Devonshire, England, settled in MD in 1659 on a royal grant. Was vestryman of the Parish Church of St. Anne's, Anne Arundel, Co., MD. His wife was Elizabeth Howard. Henry's brother, William Ridgely, to province of MD in 1672. *AAH:77-8, 81*

RIDGELY, ROBERT, landed from England on ship *Assurance* at St. Inigoes Creek, MD at an early time when the land was yet undeveloped (1635). He was a large landowner in counties of St. Mary's, Prince George's & Somerset. His wife was Martha --- & they had: Robert, Charles, William, Martha who m. Lewis Duvall. Son Robert left no desc.; Charles m. Deborah Dorsey, d/o Hon. John & left 2 sons, Charles & William. Charles d. c. 1715 & his son, Col. Charles, m. 1721, Rachel, d/o John Howard. *FR2:1072-3; TR4:809-10, 818-21*

RIGGS, JOHN, s/o Ralph & Mary (Blake) Riggs of Southampton, England, to this country 1716 & settled in Anne Arundel Co., MD. He m. Mary, d/o Thomas Davis of neighboring family at St. John's Church, Annapolis, 16 Jan. 1721. Lived in Montgomery Co., MD. Their 12th son, was Capt. Amon Riggs of the Continental Army, b. 21 April 1748, m. Ruth Griffith, d/o Henry & Elizabeth (Dorsey) Griffith. *FR2:845*

RINEHART, PHILIP, b. Germany, to America with 2 brothers, landing at Philadelphia. One brother remained in Philadelphia & one settled in Carroll Co., MD. Philip settled in Frederick Co., MD, farmer. His wife was Susanna Smith & they had: William, David, Frederick, George, Andrew & one dau. d. young. *FR2:1163*

RINGGOLD, THOMAS, Lord of Huntingfield, emigrated from England to VA & removed to Kent Island, MD in 1650, at which time he was a widower with 2 children, James & John. Rent Roll for Queen Annes Co. in 1707 show his property held by Dr. Thomas Godman for his heirs. He is recorded in court records in Nov. 1652 as a witness, aged 43. His son James was a Major & freeholder planter in Kent Co. By his first wife James had a son Thomas & his second wife was Mary Vaughan, d/o Capt. Robert of Kent. By this 2d m. he had 4 more sons: James, William, John & Charles, & a dau. Barbara. James d. 1686. *TR4:194; MDC:159*

RISTEAU, JOHN, French Huguenot from province of Ghent to American colonies in 1688. He took up a lot in Baltimore Town in 1730 & he & father-in-law George Ogg largest subscribers in erection of St. Thomas Protestant Episcopal Church. He m. Catherine (Ogg) Talbot, widow of William Talbot. His will dated 1760. *TR4:122-3*

ROACH, JOHN, b. Plymouth, England, had dau. Mary Matilda who m. Marcus Denison, merchant of Baltimore. Their son John Marcus Denison b. Baltimore 14 June 1828. *MDC:171*

ROBBINS,, --- b. England, to America in early part of the 17th century & settled in Plymouth, MA. Descendant Orlando Douglas Robbins, s/o Isaac, b. Alexandria, VA, removed to MD prior to the Civil War & served in the Union Army; mining engineer. He m. Fannie Schley (Magruder) Robbins, of Scotch lineage. Son Jonathan M. Robbins b. 18 March 1863 in Cumberland, MD. Episcopal. *TR3:329*

ROBBINS, JOHN, b. England, settled in CT 1638. Descendant Henry Russell Robbins, b. Hartford, CT, removed to Baltimore, MD & engaged in stove business under name of Robbins & Bibb. His son Henry Russell Jr. b. Baltimore 23 April 1848. *MDC:633-34*

ROBBINS, OBEDIENCE, & brother George, settled in VA on James River in 1621. Obedience later removed to Northampton Co., VA & his grandson Thomas came to Worcester Co., MD at close of the 17th century. *MDC:431*

ROBERTS, ALFRED, b. England, res. on the Eastern Shore of MD & m. Mary Elizabeth Bowdle of MD. Their dau. Clara m. William F. Stone, b. Baltimore. *TR4:450*

ROBERTS, JOHN JOSEPH, b. Athy, Ireland, educated in Ireland & England; m. Catherine May Kelly. John to America at age of 18, settled in CT, where he d. 1902. Dr. Joseph John Roberts, s/o John & Catherine, b. Naugatuck, CT 28 March 1889, resides in Baltimore & is on the staff of several local hospitals. *TR3:245*

ROBERTS, ROBERT, & wife Elizabeth Williams, both of Wales, to PA with William Penn. Their son, Hugh Roberts, Quaker divine & member of the PA colonial assembly, d. in Merion, PA 1702. Hugh's wife was Jane Owen, a desc. of Owen Glendower. Their son, Robert Roberts appears in Quaker records of The Cliffs, Calvert Co., MD in 1702. He on "ye 31st of ye 10th month, 1703" filed intention of marriage with Priscilla Johns at the Cliffs meeting. Robert remained in the area & became a prominent elder & minister. [First source says Robert Roberts, grandson of the immigrant, m. Temperance --- & their dau., Anne Maria Roberts m. Major Joshua Dryden, s/o Sewell Dryden of Snow Hill, Worcester Co., MD, where he was b. 1803. Anne Maria & Joshua m. 9 Feb. 1813.] *TR4:342-3, 767.*

ROBERTS, WILLIAM M., b. Brazil, South America 21 Jan. 1865, s/o William M. of Carlisle, PA, now a resident of Cumberland, MD. William M., s/o William M., was a civil engineer. William M. of Carlisle m. Elizabeth Humbird, d/o Jacob of PA. *6TH:138-39*

ROBINS, EDWARD, b. England 1602, to VA in bark *Thomas* in 1615. He was of Northampton (now Accomac Co.), VA; his dau. Elizabeth m. William Burgess of MD. His dau. Rachel m. Richard Beard, who later removed to MD. *AAH:49-53*

ROBINSON, CHRISTOPHER, Bishop of London & ambassador to Sweden, given first land grant in Feb. 1652, and to America & settled in 1666. His brother John had previously settled on MD's Eastern Shore. *TR4:241*

ROBINSON, JOHN, b. Scotland, in early manhood to America. His son, Joseph, b. in DE, to Harford Co., MD c. 1808; miller & farmer. His son, William Robinson, m. Mary Kirkwood, both b. Harford Co., MD. *H/C:511-12*

ROBINSON, MAXIMILLIAN, b. England, to US in 1882 & first located in Cincinnati, OH & later in NY City; drug business. He m.

Rose Band, b. Austria, who came to America as a young girl. They had 4 children; 3 now survive. Their son Harry M. Robinson, b. Cincinnati 14 Sept. 1884, was their eldest child. He grad. Univ. of MD School of Medicine in 1909 & practices in Baltimore. Harry m. in NY City, 4 Sept. 1922, Mary V. Ryan, b. Baltimore & d/o Ambrose A. & Katherine (Moran) Ryan. Presbyterian. *TR3:842-5*

RODDY, HIGH, to America from County Kildare, Ireland in 1780 & settled near Littlestown, Adams Co., PA. About 1820 removed to a place near Mount St. Mary's, Frederick Co., MD: farmer. He m. Margaret Philips; members of Mt. St. Mary's Roman Catholic Church. Children: Abramah, John, William, Daniel, Catherine (Mrs. McCallion), Mary (Mrs. Mullen), Martha (Mrs. Foreman). *FR2:1013*

RODERICK FAMILY, desc. from 1 of 3 brothers from Germany; one settled in VA, another in PA and the 3rd in MD. *FR2:1577*

ROELKE, CHRISTIAN FREDERICK WILLIAM, b. Germany, to US with his parents at the age of 12. He m. Sarah Ann Glass & res. in Frederick Co., MD. Their dau., Christina, m. Benjamin Franklin Chew & their son, William F. Chew, now of Baltimore, b. in Frederick, MD 14 May 1879. *TR3:645-6*

ROELKE, JOHN, b. Hesse Cassel, Germany, to America with wife & 8 children in 1827; weaver & member of the Reformed Communion. Landed in Baltimore & settled in Frederick Co., MD. He was weaver of carpets & woolen goods. Children: William, cabinet maker in Middletown, later tobacconist [undertaker] in Frederick, m. Sarah Slake, d. in Frederick; Augustus, coffee merchant in Baltimore; Peter; Harmon, enlisted at age 18 for the Mexican War, in 1849 went to seek gold in CA, where he married, res. Sacramento; Chrissie, m. Mr. Kester, a baker, d. in Frederick; Sophia, m. John Berger, baker, d. in Frederick; Eliza, m. David Haller [Miller], machinist; d. in Frederick. John the immigrant d. in Frederick in 1861, aged 70. Son Peter, b. Hesse Cassel 5 May 1821, was 6 years old on emigration, was a blacksmith, huckster & farmer. He eventually settled near Burkittsville & m. in Frederick, 28 Feb. 1850, Mary Ellen, d/o Robert Anderson. *FR2:1095-6, 1542-3*

ROHDE, CHARLES L., and wife Agnes M. Wolsch, both b. Germany. Charles to US at age of 19 & located in East Baltimore. Agnes to US as young girl with her parents. Their son Theodore H. b. in Baltimore 15 Sept. 1874. *TR3:312*

ROSE, JOHN (DR.), of Huguenot ancestry, b. on the Island of Guernsey, England & came to America in 1817. Methodist lay preacher. He m. Harriet Bennett of Baltimore & d. 1874. *MDC:545*

ROSEBAUM, ISAAC, b. Bavaria, Germany, as was his wife Rebecca Steinhart. Dau. Helen b. in Philadelphia, PA m. Moses Pels, who had settled in Baltimore, MD in 1863; shoe merchant. *TR3:349*

ROSS, ---, b. England, a major on the staff of Cornwallis, sold his commission & emigrated to America in 1804. He settled in Baltimore, MD & m. Mary Bradenbaugh. He was the brother of the English Gen. H. L. Ross of the Battle of North Point fame. *MDC:178*

ROSS, ADAM, from Ireland in latter part of the 17th century & settled in PA. Adam's brother William had preceded him to America & settled at Elkridge Landing, Howard Co., MD & later removed to Baltimore in 1785. William d. 1820, aged 60. *MDC:590-91*

ROTHSCHILD, MOSES, b. Erksdorf, province of Hesse, Germany 17 July 1863, s/o Zadok and Violet (Nusbaum), landed NY City 1882; resided in VA & NC where he worked with brother Israel, 1889 to Baltimore. *TR3:79*

ROUSE, JOHN, to America in early manhood & settled in MD & opened a hotel on the road between Havre de Grace & Baltimore. His homestead still occupied by desc. in late 1800's. *H/C:460-2*

ROUSTON, HENRY, b. Germany, to America in early manhood. He landed at Baltimore & settled in Uniontown, Carroll Co., MD, then a part of Frederick Co. Tailor & merchant & m. Mary Garner & had 11 childern, 3 reached maturity: Thomas H., George H. & John. *FR2:1040-1, 1106-7*

ROUTZAHN, FREDERICK, b. Germany, to America & settled Littlestown, PA where his son Ludwick was b. 13 Aug. 1767. Ludwick later settled in Middletown Valley (MD); m. Esther Sheffer, b. Middletown, 1 Jan. 1767. Ludwick d. 15 Aug. 1856, Esther d. 8 March 1815; bur. at Church Hill. *FR2:756*

ROUTZHAN, WOLFGANG, from Maintz, Germany with his family to America in 1727, landed at Philadelphia, PA. He settled north of that city & desc. now res. Buffalo & Rochester, NY. Johannes Ludwig Routzahn, left city of Maintz on the Rhine, with his wife & two children early in 1750, and went to Cowes, England, from which place they took passage on ship *Brothers* & landed in Philadelphia 30 Aug. 1750. He worked at a hat-makers shop until his passage was paid. Removed to Lancaster, PA & was employed transporting supplies to Braddock's army at Frederick, MD in 1755. In 1756 he moved to Frederick Co., MD with his family & settled near where the present village of Ellerton now stands. Served in the Rev. War. Johannes had 2 sons: Adam, who was the father of Ludwig 2d & Benjamin who was the father of John. *FR2:1427-9*

ROWLAND, JOHN, b. in Germany, to MD. Son Jacob b. near Hagerstown & a farmer who d. aged c. 45. Jacob's son was Jonas, b. Washington Co., a Dunkard. Jacob's son, Lewis B., was b. at Long Meadows, Washington Co., MD 19 June 1843 & m. Ann Gilbert of Washington Co. who d. 1888, aged 77. Also a Dunkard. *6TH:189*

ROWLAND, JOHN, b. Wales, to America 1640 & settled at the site of Philadelphia more than 40 years before the Quaker city was founded. Later removed to Lancaster Co., PA & descs. in the 18th century settled in MD. Desc. Samuel Rowland, b. 28 Feb. 1780 on the family homestead, near Port Deposit, MD, s/o William & Sarah (Latham) Rowland, was in the lumber industry. He m. Mary Black of Geneva, Ontario Co., NY & they res. at his farm on Octoraro Heights until she d. 1856 & he went to live with his dau. Mrs. Steel, at whose home he d. 1864. *TR4:395*

ROWLAND, WILLIAM, & wife Sarah Latham, emigrated to America in latter part of the 18th century & settled in DE & later removed to Cecil Co., MD, where son Samuel was b. 28 Feb. 1780 near Liberty Grove. Sons Robert & John to OH, James remained in Cecil Co. Samuel businessman of Port Deposit. *MDC:421-22*

RUMSEY, CHARLES, from Wales to America c. 1665. He landed at Charleston, SC & after some years removed to NY, later to Philadelphia & before 1678 settled at the head of Bohemia River in Cecil Co., MD, where he married. His will was probated in 1717. His children Charles

(d. 1761), William (surveyor, will proved 1742) & Edward (d. 1770). *C:508-10; FRI:338*

RUNKLE, HENRY, from Ireland to America. His dau. Agnes, who was 6 months old on coming to America, m. William Bittinger in Allegany Co., MD. She d. in Garrett Co., aged 58. *6TH:180-81*

RUNKLES, ---, from Germany & landed at Baltimore. Their son Joseph was b. on the voyage to America. Joseph settled on farm near Mt. Airy, in what is now Woodville District, Frederick Co., MD (1864). He m. Susan Bussard & had: John; Joseph; Samuel; William; Basil; Daniel; Brice & Nancy who m. Levi Van Fossen of Frederick. *FR2:1343-4*

RUTLEDGE, ABRAHAM, settled on 2000 acres of land of My Lady's Manor in Baltimore & Harford Cos. under Lord Baltimore. His son, Jacob, b. in MD, m. Monica Wheeler, d/o Col. Ignatius Wheeler, officer of the Revolution. Jacob's son, John W., b. in Harford Co. m. Julia A. Ward; members of St. James' Church. *H/C:537*

RUTTER, JOHN, b. Ireland, early settler of Cecil Co., MD. His dau. Elizabeth (d. 1873) m. Jesse Foster (d. 1845) & had Washington Foster, b. 22 Jan. 1842, Cecil Co. Methodist Episcopal. *H/C:218*

RYAN, TIMOTHY, to America from Ireland in 1840 on the ship *Arabella* & located in NJ, where he farmed. In 1848 to Baltimore, manufacturer of lime from oyster shells. He d. 1888. His wife was Mary Shortall & they had son Augustine Joseph Ryan b. Baltimore 24 May 1868. Augustine is at this time unmarried & lived with his mother until her death in 1923 at age of 87 years. Timothy & Mary had 14 children; 7 daus. & 7 sons; Roman Catholic family. *TR3:818*

ADLER, RICHARD, b. England, to America c. 1700 & settled in Adams Co., PA. Descendant Nancy m. John Appleman, b. Washington Co., MD, of German descent. Alpheus R. Appleman, s/o John & Nancy was b. at Middletown, MD 19 July 1836. *MDC:149*

SADTLER, PHILIP B. (CAPT.), from Germany to Baltimore & in 1812 participated in the Battle of North Point. He m. --- Sauerwein & their dau. Elizabeth J. m. Charles E. Dickey in 1854 in Baltimore. *TR4:707-8*

SAGER, MATHIAS, from Germany to NY at age 14 with brother & sisters who went West to Frederick Co., MD. He d. near New Midway & is bur. Rocky Hill Cemetery. Was member of the Rocky Hill Lutheran Church. He m. Catharine Fogle & had: George; John; Elizabeth, m. George T. Koons; Harvey of WV; Charles of Washington, DC: & Tacie Idella, at home with her mother. *FR2:945-6*

SAMUEL, MARGARET, b. Cardiff, Wales 1796; with father to NY in 1810. She m. John Nowood & son Summerfield N. b. 5 May 1823, Baltimore. Baptist. *MDC:114*

SAMUELS, SAMUEL, b. London, England, in early 1840's to US & settled in Baltimore, MD; leather business. He m. Sarah Bernheimer, of Hartford, CT, of German desc. Son Abraham Samuels, M.D., b. Baltimore 27 Aug. 1876, is their only surviving child. He m. in NY City, 31 March 1903, Rose Leah Bloomberg, a d/o Aaron & Sarah of NY City. *TR3:189-90*

SANDYS, GEORGE, poet & member of VA Company, at Jamestown, VA 1621-22. His sister Anne m. Sir William Barn, also member of VA Company & they were ancestors of Mrs. Fillmore Beall of MD. Anne Barn & brothers were children of Edwin Sandys, Archbishop of York, b. at Hawkshead in Lancashire 1519 & d. at Southwell 1588. *TR4:432*

SAPPINGTON, FRANCIS, from Wales to America. He m. Frances Brown & had four sons. One settled in KY, one in MO & one in Harford Co., MD. The 4th son was Francis, physician of Liberty, Frederick Co., MD. He m. Ann Ridgely. Dr. Sappington was an Episcopalian & d. in Liberty. His children: Harriet, m. Perrigrene Warfield & settled in Georgetown, DC; Francis; Greenberry Ridgely; Thomas; Ann Ridgely, m. a Mr. McSherry & settled at Littlestown, Adams Co., PA; Matilda, m. Dr. John Dorsey & located in Frederick; & Lydia Ridgely, m. Dr. Abdiel Unkefer & res. Liberty. [Note: No dates are given anywhere on early members of this family. Thomas, s/o Francis & Ann, d. in 1857. His 6th of 9 sons was b. in 1827. Later members of the family were Roman Catholic.] *FR2:1449-50*

SAPPINGTON, MARK, M.D., b. England, res. of MD from early manhood. He was one of the men who went on board the ship *Peggy Stewart* at Annapolis in the Rev. War period. His son, Richard Sappington, M.D. was a surgeon in the Rev. War. Richard's son John b. near Havre de Grace, 1801. *H/C:331*

SAUNDES, JOHN, gentleman, came with a colony & settled in VA. Descendant James Saunders was a planter in Loudoun Co., VA. He served in the War of 1812 & m. Lucy H., d/o Richard Henry Lee. His son John b. at Norfolk, VA 29 Dec. 1816. Protestant Episcopal. He m. 17 Nov. 1852 Emily Catherine White, d/o Nathan S., who d. at his home near Dawsonville aged 84. John d. 2 May 1883. Son Richard Lee Saunders settled in Potomac District of Montgomery Co., MD. *6TH:836-37*

SAVAGE, MOSES M. (M.D.), b. Riga, Russia, 18 Dec. 1871, s/o Bernard M. & Hannah (Goldberg) Savage. Moses to US 1892 & joined his parents in Baltimore, MD. His paternal grandparents were Harry & Sophie Savage; farmers. Bernard was b. in Russia & in 1891 immigrated to US, settled in Baltimore; capmaker. He d. aged 60; Sophie d. 7 March 1893, aged 80. Jewish. *TR3:344*

SCHAEFFER (VON SCHAEFFER), ---, family of Berlin, Germany. A family member [not named here] to America 1776. His son, Jacob Schaeffer, in 1785, at the age of 25, m. Ann Catharine Uttz. They had: John, Jacob, Peter (b. 1798), Sophia who m. Peter Brunner & Elizabeth. *FR2:1254-5*

SCHAIDT, JOHN G., b. Bavaria, Germany to US in 1837. In 1842 he sent for his brothers, Casper & Peter. All settled in Allegany Co., in or near Cumberland, MD. Peter m. Catherine Gehauf, b. Germany. Their 3 living children: John; Harmon now in NJ; Christina m. Matthew Muir & resides in Rock Springs, WY; & George, resident of Britich Columbia. Peter settled in Lonaconing, where he d. aged 66. Son John b. in Cumberland 22 Dec. 1850. *6TH:588-89*

SCHANBERGER, FREDERICK C., b. Germany, to US in early 19th century & settled in Baltimore. His son, Henry M., lifelong res. of Baltimore, manufacturer of shoes. Henry was Roman Catholic & d. 2 March 1922, aged 84. He m. Mary Elizabeth Debring, of Scotch desc., who still res. in Baltimore. They had 11 children; 10 sons & 1 dau., but 5 of the sons are now dec'd. Their 3d child, Frederick C., b. 9 Aug. 1872, from the age of 11 has been connected with the theatrical business.

7 Feb. 1893 he m. Hannah Marie McGinnis, b. Baltimore & d/o Henry M. McGinnis, now dec'd. *TR3:980-3*

SCHEIB, HENRY (REV.), b. 8 July 1808 at Bacharach, a small town on the Rhine under French jurisdiction at the time of his birth. To NY in April 1835 & in the same year he went to Baltimore, MD. 1835 pastor of Zion German Church in Baltimore. *MDC:169-70*

SCHEU, WILLIAM, b. 21 April 1845, Hamburg, Germany. Left orphaned when very young; to Baltimore landing from a clipper ship. Was a sailor at age 19. Died 27 May 1913, Baltimore; m. Barbara, b. 1 Oct. 1850, d/o Thomas & Louisa (Helm) Hormes. *TR2:31*

SCHIAFFINO, GIOVANNI (CHEVALIER), b. Camogil, near Genoa, Italy 10 July 1853, s/o James & Frances (Ferro) Schiaffino. Giovanni to America c. 1880 with his wife, Paulina Mortola; his brother Amicare res. for a time in Baltimore, but now makes his home in Genoa, Italy. Chevalier captain & ship-chandler, located his business in Fells Point, Baltimore City. Catholic. *TR3:358-9*

SCHILDKNECHT, ---, & wife, both b. Germany, were early settlers of the Middletown Valley, Frederick Co., MD. Their son Jacob, b. Frederick Co. 1798, d. 11 May 1882. Jacob was a farmer, m. Maria Routzahn & had 9 children. *FR2:1019*

SCHILLING, CHARLES L., & wife Louisa Billings, b. Germany, where they married & had 5 children, 2 of whom died there. Their children who came to America with them: Henry C. Schilling, b. 30 June 1832, farmer of Baltimore Co. & later had woolen mill in Harford Co. He m. in 1857 Emma Lawton, b. England & brought to this country at an early age. William H., another son of Charles & Louisa, served in the Union Army, was captured & d. in Andersonville prison in 1864 at the age of 30. Caroline is the only dau. of Charles L. & Louisa Schilling & m. Dr. Charles Krause of Cedar Creek, WI. *H/C:490*

SCHLATTER, MICHAEL (REV.), of St. Gall, Switzerland, sent to America 1746 by the Reformed Churches of Holland, arrived Philadelphia 1747; to Frederick Co., MD. *FRI:407*

SCHLEY, JOHN JACOB, b. Germany, settled in Frederick Co., MD early. He was progenitor of the Schley family in MD & GA, where his son afterward lived & reared a family. *TR4:443*

SCHLEY, JOHN THOMAS, to America from Germany 1739, son Thomas, lawyer, merchant & farmer. Thomas' son, Admiral Winfield Scott Schley, b. at Richfields, near town of Frederick, MD 9 Oct. 1839. *FR2:700*

SCHMID, JOHN, b. Germany, to America 1730, settled MD in southwest part of Monocacy Valley on grants from Charles Calvert, Lord Baltimore. Naturalized 1761. Revolutionary soldier, sgt. in Capt. William Blair's Co. from Frederick Co. He d. 1785. His son John, b. 1776, in Monocacy Valley. Another son, George Smith, b. 12 June 1776, d. 26 Oct. 1832; Lutheran. George m. (1) Lydia Baugher & (2) Mary Nixdorff, d/o Henry. *FR2:703, 832; 6TH:485-6*

SCHNAUFFER, CARL H. & WILLIAM, family of Frederick Co., MD that originated from Saxony on the border of Prussia, salt mine owners. They intermarried with the Hasemeyers of Wurtemburg. Earliest American ancestor Carl H. & younger brother William, s/o Johan Heinrich Schnauffer & wife Caroline Hasenmeyer. The family settled in Baltimore, MD in 1851 as German exile of the revolution of 1848. Carl H. founded a German daily newspaper. He d. 1854 of typhoid fever, was the husband of Lise W. Moos, d/o John Adam & Caroline (Hays) Moos, a merchant of Baden. Family later resided Brunswick, Frederick Co., MD. William Schnauffer to Baltimore City Spring of 1854 & assoc. with his brother in the newspaper until his death in 1889. *FR2:840*

SCHNEBLY, HENRY, b. Zurich, Switzerland 7 Dec. 1728, to America 1750 & settling in what is now Washington Co., MD. He m. Elizabeth Shafer & had 4 sons & 1 dau. *TR4:489*

SCHNEPFE, CHARLES H., a 'native European,' lived in Baltimore from his 9th year & d. in his 79th year. His wife was Emma Morsberger & they had 8 children, 5 sons & 3 daus. Their son, Charles H. Jr., b. 14 Aug. 1872 in Baltimore. He m. 20 April 1898, Bertie B. Auld, a d/o Harry & Sarah (Legar) Auld. Bertie b. VA. *TR3:549-51*

SCHOENEIS, ADOLPH, b. Iserlohn, Westphalia, Germany, 26 June 1881, s/o Adolph & Sophia (Borghoff) Schoeneis. To US where he entered Baltimore Law School, grad. 1912. He m. Carrie K. Miller, d/o Martin Miller of Baltimore. Reformed Lutheran. *TR3:185-6*

SCHOENWOLF, CHRISTOPHER, b. in Hesse-Darmstadt, Germany; in early 1840's to America & settled in Baltimore. Lutheran, he d. 1884 at age 56. His wife was Christina Obrecht, also b. in Germany. Their son, John, b. in Baltimore 21 Aug. 1860, m. Aug. 1888 Henrietta Frances Joeckel, d/o Martin. *TR3:398-400*

SCHOFIELD, ALLEN, and wife Ann Bradley, both b. England. Ann (d. 22 April 1923, aged 76) d/o Henry & Amelia (Crowe) Bradley of Haddersfield, England. Mitchel Crowe, brother of Mrs. Bradley established pioneer woolen manufacture in Moosup, CT c. 1855. Allen b. Marsden, s/o Samuel & --- (Hunt) Schofield of Marsden, England. He settled 1871, Providence, RI, where he still resides. Frank M., s/o Allen & Ann (Bradley) Schofield, silversmith, 29 June 1899 to Baltimore; m. 25 June 1913 Bertha Kline Tarbeau, b. Providence RI 1885. *TR3:103*

SCHUERMAN, CARL C., to US from Germany & for many years connected with the Smithsonian Institution. He m. Rose Calvert, of the famous MD Calvert family of MD. Their dau., Nancy C., m. Preston Blair Ray, clerk of court at Rockville, MD who was b. near Kensington, Montgomery Co., 22 Feb. 1876, s/o the late Alfred & Eleanor M. (Gatch) Ray. *TR3:718-21*

SCHULER, HANS, b. 25 May 1874 in Morange, province of Lorraine, Germany, s/o Otto & Amalia (Arndt) Schuler. Amilia still resides in Baltimore. Hans' maternal grandfather lived in Pirmansen, Germany and his paternal grandfather, Julius Schuler, made his home in Zweibrucken. Otto emigrated in 1878 to Baltimore, where he died; caterer. Hans is a sculptor of international reputation. *TR3:333*

SCHWARTZ, GERSON A., to US in early 1880's and settled in Baltimore. His son, Harry, b. Russia, came to America in early 1890's, settled in Baltimore, where he d. 21 July 1916, aged 49. Harry's wife was Mary R. Kline, d/o Lester M. who d. abroad. Her mother d. in Baltimore. *TR3:333*

SCOTT, JOHN, b. Belfast, Ireland, to America 1841 & soon afterwards married a wealthy young lady of Bruceville, Elizabeth T., d/o Norman Bruce, a native of Scotland. Norman Bruce settled in Carroll Co., MD;

the town of Bruceville named in his honor. Elizabeth d. aged 83, in the faith of the Episcopal Church. *6TH:646-47*

SCOTT, WILLIAM GIFFORD, b. Scotland, to America before Rev., settled DE. Desc. William G. Scott m. Mary Rebecca Christopher, b. Baltimore. Methodist. *TR3:77*

SCRIVENER, MATTHEW, to America in the year 1608, helped forward the building of James Town. [From Burke's *History of VA.*] Desc. John Scrivener m. Mary Boswell & had son William Boswell Scrivener, b. Anne Arundel Co., MD. John m. Sallie Jane Kent Barber in 1861, a d/o Jonathan Yates & Mary Wheeler (Kent) Barber of Silver Stone, Calvert Co., MD. John & Sallie res. at "Rose Valley," near Friendship, MD, where he d. as a result of a fall from his horse in 1898, aged 68. *TR3:933-4*

SEBOLD, PETER, emigrated from the Rhine Country to PA in 1822. He res. a number of years at Reading, PA & removed to MD, settling near Taneytown; cooper. He later removed to a place near Emmitsburg. He m. (1) Miss --- Deitrick & had 4 children; m. (2) --- & had 5 more children. He m. a third time, but this wife's name is not recorded here. His son Samuel, b. Frederick Co. c. 1820, m. at the age of 30 to Ann Miller of near Bruceville, MD & settled near Sabillasville, MD. Ann b. Carroll Co., MD & d. near Emmitsburg in 1889.

Nicholas, another s/o the immigrant, b. 1812 in MD, m. Apelonia, d/o David & Rebecca (Reider) Hoover, who was b. in Emmitsburg, MD in 1790. She d. at the same place aged 99. *FR2:968-9, 1554-5; 6TH:297*

SEFF, ROBERT, b. Russia 14 Oct. 1884 & to America at age of 6 with parents Israel & Bessie. The family settled in Baltimore where Israel, coal dealer, d. 1918, aged 68. Israel & Bessie had 5 sons & 4 daus., Robert was the 8th in order of birth & their youngest son. Their other living children are Samuel & Hyman; Anna, m. Max Levitt; & Marie, m. Joseph F. Sandler. In Baltimore 25 March 1917, Robert m. Freda Silberman, d/o Tenchum & Anna (Bronson) Silberman, also of Russian ancestry. *TR3:992-5*

SEGWICK, THOMAS, to MD 1670. Had son Joshua who m. Elizabeth Fisher, d/o John of Calvert Co., who came into MD 1651. *TR4:345*

SEIDEL, HERMAN, b. 15 April 1884, near Waski, Ponieves County, Lithuania, which was at that time a Russian province. He was s/o Joshua Seidel, b. Waski & d. there 1886, aged 36; shoemaker, left a widow & 3 children. Joshua's wife was Hennie Berlin, d/o Latvian Jewish parents. Hennie now makes her home in Baltimore, as do her children Moses, Rose & Herman. Herman came to America as a young boy & studied medicine in Baltimore. He m. Rose Finkelstein, also b. Lithuania. She came to America with her parents c. 1902. *TR3:593-5*

SELFE, JAMES, b. Chilcompton, England; to US in 1855 & settled in Havre de Grace, MD. He m. Catharine Moon, also b. Chilcompton, she d. in MD 5 Jan. 1897, age 67. James a machinist employed as an engineer on the railroad, d. aged 32. Son, William B., b. Havre de Grace in 1857, hardware store & blacksmith shop at Darlington. *H/C:238, 526-7*

SEMMES, BENEDICT JOSEPH, of Normandy, France, in 1640 settled in MD. Desc. Raphael Semmes, admiral of the Navy of the Confederate States of America, b. Charles Co., MD, 27 Sept. 1809. His father was Richard Thompson Semmes & his mother, Catherine Hooe Middleton, was desc. from Arthur Middleton, a signer of the Declaration of Independence. Raphel's parents d. when he was young & he was raised by an uncle, Raphael Semmes, of Georgetown, DC. *TR4:909-13*

SENTMAN, LAWRENCE, b. Lorraine, Germany, aged 18 to America with a brother & settled in Berks Co., PA, farmer. Served in the Rev. War & d. at age 56. His son, Michael, b. Berks Co., PA, farmer until 1838 & then to Cecil Co., MD, where he d. aged 82. *H/C:434-5*

SEWARD, ---, Englishman, to America & settled in Dorchester Co., MD. His son, Solomon Seward, b. & grew up in Baltimore. Solomon was in business as a cooper in partnership with his brother Joseph. The brothers are now retired & res. in Baltimore on Patterson Ave. Solomon m. in Baltimore Louisa Baker, & had: Margaret m. William Higgins, now dec'd.; Isabel, m. William Holland, res. Baltimore; Mary, m. Samuel Rose, res. Baltimore; Emma Jane, m. William Crawford, now dec'd.; James C. res. Baltimore; William Joseph; Charles H., merchant of Rosedale, Baltimore Co. Louisa d. 1869 & Solomon m. 2d. Mrs. Hutchin. Son William Joseph Seward, at his mother's death aged 9, went to live in home of Joseph Shaffer in Jefferson District, Frederick Co.,

MD. He m. in 1882, Manada, d/o Joseph & Caroline (Brown) Babington of Jackson District, Frederick Co. *FR2:1471*

SEWELL, HENRY, to VA from England before 1632. His wife was Alice Willoughby, d/o Thomas, who came to VA in 1610 & was in Elizabeth City in 1628. They had Anne b. 1634, m. Lemuel Mason, s/o Francis & Henry Sewell the younger, b. 1639. Henry the elder d. 20 Feb. 1644 at Lower Norfolk Co., VA. By 1662 Henry the younger settled in Anne Arundel Co., MD, where he m. Johanna Warner, d/o James, of a neighboring VA family. *AAH:135-7*

SEWELL, MARK, to St. Michael's, Talbot Co., MD in 1709 from Coventry, England. Also named is Henry Sewell, to MD in 1661 as secretary to Lord Baltimore. He was nephew to Henry Sewell who settled in Marblehead, MA in 1634. *TR4:644-7*

SEXTON, GEORGE, "the first colonial ancestor of the Sexton family in America," b. 1630, d. 1690. With his wife Catherine he settled at Windsor, CT & later removed to Westfield, MA. Their son Daniel m. Sarah Bancroft, d/o John & Jane, who emigrated to America from London, England in 1632 & settled at Lynn, MA & later removed to Westfield, MA. Desc. Samuel Budd Sexton m. Elizabeth Anne Elbert. Elizabeth was desc. of Hugh Elbert of Kent Island who came to America prior to 1687 & d. 1703. His son, William, of "Lloyd Costin," Wye Mills Talbot Co., MD d. 1736. Children of Samuel Budd Sexton & wife res. Baltimore. *TR4:773-4*

SHAFER, HENRY, & wife Mary Catherine Grove, both b. Burkittsville District, Frederick Co., MD, both were children of parents b. in Germany who settled in Middletown Valley, Frederick Co., MD. *FR2:1144-5*

SHAFER, JOHN SR., b. Germany, settled in Frederick Co., MD. His son John Jr. d. aged 51 & bur. in the Reformed Church Cemetery, Frederick. He m. Elizabeth Leinbach, b. in Middletown Valley & d. age 80 in 1876. *6TH:375-77*

SHANNON, ---, b. Ireland of Irish family, to America & settled in Ohio, among the early settlers. William, son of the immigrant, was b. Ohio & was the father of L. C. Shannon, b. Allegany Co., MD 1847. L. C. was a farmer & res. of Doddridge Co., WV & member of the United Brethren

Church. L.C. m. Maria L. Duckworth, b. Alleganey Co., MD.
FR2:1294-5

SHAPIRO, MORITZ, b. Vienna, Austria; in 1879 to America, teacher at Boston & eventually coming to Baltimore, MD, where he d. 15 Nov. 1915. Teacher of foreign languages & mathematics. Member Baltimore Hebrew congregation. His father was Wolf Shaprio. Moritz m. Anna Rosen, d/o Morris & Minna (Blum) Rosen. The Rosen family is of German extraction, both the Rosens & the Blums coming to the US c. 1881. Samuel, s/o Moritz & Anna was b. in Baltimore 8 June 1895. *TR3:705-6*

SHARPE, HORATIO, Governor of the Province of MD, arrived in 1753 on the ship *Molly* of London. His office was held during the French & Indian War. He was a bachelor. *AAH:213*

SHEARER, THOMAS (M.D.), b. 1 Aug. 1825, at Stonehouse, c. 15 miles above Glasgow, on the Clyde, Scotland. His mother's maiden name was Bruce. He arrived at New York in 1849 & resided a brief time in Philadelphia, PA. 1856 he m. Harriet Fox, d/o George of Philadelphia. He resided for some time in Charleston, SC & later located in Baltimore, MD. *MDC:197-98*

SHEFFER, ---, b. Germany, farmer in Middletown Valley at early date. His son, Philip, farmer at close of the Rev. War. Philip's children: Catherine who m. Hanson Remsburg; Kittie m. Jonathan Routzahn; Betty m. Enos Daub; Jonas; Philip; Daniel; Sallie who d. young & a dau. [unnamed] who m. Joseph Smith. *FR2:1077-8*

SHEFFIELD, ANDREW, b. Saxony, Germany in 1832. C. 1844 to America & settled in Frederick City, where he d. 1895. Member of St. John's Catholic Church of Frederick. His wife was named Crescent & she d. 1904, aged 71 years. Their children: Frank E.; John, res. Frederick; Joseph, d. aged 26 & Edward, d. aged 23. *FR2:1357-8*

SHELBY, EVAN (GEN.), from Wales early, settled at Valley of the Antietam in Western MD 1750. *FRI:124*

SHELLMAN, JOHN (COL.), from Germany to America in 1745 & settled in Fredericktown, MD. He carried the chain when the town was marked out. He m. & left 3 sons. *FR2:1313-4*

SHEMWELL, ELIAS, of England, had deeded to him in 1656 a large tract of land called Chaptico Manor, located in St. Maryh's Co., MD. Joseph & William Shemwell, brothers, (no direct relationship to Elias stated) served in the Rev. War & these brothers were prominent in affairs of All Faith church in St. Mary's Co. Joseph Shemwell m. Mary Hanson Briscoe of St. Mary's Co. William Shemwell m. Anne Billingsley of the same place. *TR4:196, 770-1*

SHEPSLE, CHARLES ABRAHAM (D.D.S.), b. Riga, Russia 6 Nov. 1891, s/o Elijah & Deborah (Shindel) Shepsle, both b. in the Baltic province of Riga. The father is at present in missionary work in Cape Town, South Africa; the mother & other family members res. in Montreal, Canada. Charles to Chicago & later to Washington, DC. Settled in Hagerstown, MD after 1916. He m. in Washington, DC, 2 March 1919, Yetta Dana Coonin, d/o Nathan & Cecilia (Caplin), both b. MD. *TR3:439-40*

SHRINER (SCHREINER), HANS ADAM, JOHAN MICHAEL & JOHAN MARTIN, from Wurtemburg, Germany in 1738, sailing from Rotterdam & landing at Germantown PA 5 Sept. 1738, from ship *Winter Galley*. Johan Michael had 2 sons, Michael & Pieter. Michael, b. 1749, emigrated to York, PA with brother Pieter, & later went to MD. Michael was veteran of Rev. War, serving in 8th Battalion, Capt. William Weybright, commanded by Col. Ross. Peiter was appointed "Commissary Aid," to assist in feeding soldiers camped near Germantown, PA. The 2 brothers opened a tavern on the Westminster Rd. & later a tailor shop. Michael d. in 1827 & left a son Michael, b. near Unionville, Frederick Co., MD where he d. in 1837. He m. Anna Elizabeth Worman of Unionville. *FR2:1352-4*

SHULENBERGER, BENJAMIN, b. Germany, settled early in what is now York, PA. Revolutionary War veteran. His son Benjamin Jr. was a farmer of Adams & Franklin Cos., PA. Member of the old Dunkard Church. Benjamin's son John m. Jeannette Beaty, both b. Franklin Co., PA. Jeannette's parents b. & raised in Scotland, subsequently located in Belfast, Ireland & later in the Cumberland Valley [PA] in America. John to Franklin Co., PA in boyhood. Member of the Reformed Church. He d. 1878, at age 66. John's son, William C. B., b. near Newburg, Cumberland Co., PA 7 Aug. 1838. He studied at Mercersburg Theological Seminary & served in Franklin Co., PA, Middleburg, VA, Scottdale, PA, St. Petersburg, PA, West Alexandria OH, Shelby OH, Lancaster City,

OH. In 1895 pastor of the Reformed Church of Emmitsburg, Frederick Co., MD. 23 Nov. 1876 he m. Sallie N. Martin, d/o S. H. & Rachel Martin of Martinsburg, WV.

Other children of John & Jeannette: Benjamin, Samuel & Elizabeth; Anthony pastor of Reformed Church in Mt.Pleasant, MD & at present in charged of same in China Grove, NC; Robert, veterinary surgeon near Newburg, Cumberland Co., PA; Adam, farmer in MO; Elizabeth m. Adam Heberlig, now dec'd. Members Reformed Church. *6TH:35051; FR2:1279-80*

SIEDLING, GEORGE C., b. Salzderhelden, formerly kingdom of Hanover, Germany in 1829. Merchant tailor of Frederick Co., MD. Emigrated to America in early manhood, landed at Baltimore, where he res. two years. After his marriage removed to Frederick, MD, where he worked with Mr. Hartman as foreman of the cutting dept. & later started his own business. He m. in Baltimore, 22 June 1854, to Joahanna Christina Schade, b. also in Salzderhelden. She arrived in Baltimore 2 years after George. They had: Julia H. F., unm., b. in Baltimore; George F. C., Frederick merchant now dec'd. Members Evangelical Lutheran Church in Frederick. *FR2:1277-8*

SIEGWART, CHARLES, b. in Swiss village of Ems in 1863, s/o Andrew Siegwart, Swiss glass blower who came to America in 1883 & d. in Baltimore, MD 4 years later. Charles to America at the age of 21, also glass blower & horticulturist. He m. in Baltimore to Carrie Lohr, d/o the late Henry, of Baltimore. *TR3:887-9*

SIGGERS, GEORGE W., b. England, to US from Colchester & settled first in Troy, NY, later in Brooklyn & still later in Alexandria, VA & then Washington, D.C., where he d. 1894. His wife was Mary Eleanor Gregory, d/o Andrew & Eleanor (Chidester) Gregory of Catskill, NY. The progenitor of the Gregory framily in the US was Henry who settled in Boston, MA c. 1639 & Judah Gregory, early settler of Danbury, CT. Harriet Elizabeth Siggers m. John Edwin Simms, b. Baltimore 14 Jan. 1853; she b. Brooklyn, NY 29 March 1855. Mr. Simms was s/o Robert Alexander Simms & Margaret J. Mitchell, d/o John & Margaret (McLaughlin) Mitchell of Baltimore, MD. *TR4:407-8*

SILLS, JOSEPH, s/o Edward Pracey Sills of Walbrook, England & Barbara Beard of Rollingdean, England. Joseph was a grad. of Oxford Univ. who migrated to America c. 1827 & m. Ann Morehead. He d. of yellow fever in Charlestown, SC, when his son John William Sills was aged 4. John William Sills m. Sarah Wilcox Clark & was president of James R. Arvinger Co., jewelers of Baltimore, MD. Sarah was d/o Ichabod Eddy & Rachel (Mosher) Clark of New Bedford, MA. She d. at New Bedford c. 1897, aged 82. *TR4:501-2*

SILVER, JOHN, with two brothers from England to NY or NJ, time unknown. Son Gershom m. Mellicent Silver of NJ & they emigrated from near Burlington to Harford (then Baltimore) Co., MD, c. 1760, with their son Benjamin, aged 10. Gershom d. 1775. *MDC:280*

SILVERWOOD, WILLIAM (HON.), b. Croxton, Kerrial, Leicestershire, England, 13 Jan. 1826, s/o William Sr. who d. at Croxton Kerrial 8 Feb. 1873, aged 85, farmer. William m. 6 March 1848 Mary Sadler, d/o David & Elizabeth of Waltham, Leicestershire and the following 4th April they sailed on the *Thomas Bennett* and landed at NY 27 May 1848. Settled in Baltimore, MD, June 4th, same year. *MDC:38*

SIMCOE, GEORGE, felt-maker of Scotland, first Simcoe to America. Res. Queen Anne Co., MD & after 1720 a farmer of Cecil Co., settling on Bay View Farm at Carpenter's Point. Methodist Episcopal church member. His son William m. Rebecca Cazier, b. Cecil Co., of Irish desc., a d/o Capt. Thomas Cazier, who served in the War of 1812. Their son, John S., b. at Carpenters Point, Cecil Co., 18 May 1831; Episcopal. *H/C:382-3; 578*

SIMMONS, ABRAM, from England with Leonard Calvert in 1634. Tobacco planter of Southern MD. *TR4:543-4*

SIMON, WILLIAM, b. Eberstadt, Hessen, Germany 20 Feb. 1844, s/o William, a Lutheran clergyman. In 1870 to Baltimore, MD to work at the Baltimore Chrome Works. He m. 13 May 1873 Pemla, d/o F. Driver of Oldenburg, Germany. William is a professor of chemistry at the MD College of Pharmacy, Baltimore. *MDC:466-67*

SINCHELL, HENRY, b. Germany, to US in 1810 & settled in Frederick, MD. *6TH:644-45*

SINCLAIR, DUNCAN, b. City of Glasgow, Scotland, 15 Nov. 1852, s/o Peter & Jane (Clark) Sinclair. He joined an uncle in the US, Malcolm Sinclair, at Cumberland, MD. He m. 20 March 1879 Josephine Gerstell, d/o Dr. Arnold Gerstell of Keyser, WV. She b. in Western Port, Allegany Co., MD. Her mother was Fannie Cresap, a lineal descendant of Col. Michael Cresap. She was member of Presbyterian Church. *6TH:589-90*

SISK, JOSEPH, to MD in the first half of the 18th century & settled in what is now the southern part of Caroline Co. Desc. William Sisk, b. Caroline Co., m. Lucetta Dean; he d. 1899, she d. 1908. *TR3:250*

SKANE, ---, barrister of Co. Cork, Ireland, his son Thomas H., b. Baltimore, MD; grandson Thomas J. Skane b. Baltimore 22 March 1894, attorney. Catholic. *TR3:178*

SKILLMAN, THOMAS (SIR), from England to America in the 17th century, arriving here at the time when Gov. Nichol took New Amsterdam from the Dutch. Desc. George R. Skillman, b. Baltimore, MD, m. Mary E. Pearce. Their son, Wilbur F. Skillman, M.D., b. there 6 April 1878. The Pearce family is of English origin & were in America prior to the Rev. *TR3:829-30*

SKUTCH, DAVID, b. Munich, Bavaria, Germany, to America & settled in GA. His son Max was b. & reared in Savannah, GA, where he res. until 1860 when he came to Baltimore, MD, where he died 10 Nov. 1919, aged 73. Clothing manufacturer; member of the Baltimore Hebrew Congregation. Max m. Fannie, d/o David Frank, of an old Baltimore family. *TR3:795-6*

SLICER, JOHN T., b. Germany, one of 3 brothers who came to America in early manhood & settled near Baltimore, MD. His son Thomas had son John T., who m. Martha J. Read of Cecil Co. & their son John B. Slicer, M.D., b. 1858. *H/C:553-4*

SLOAN, ALEXANDER, b. Scotland, to America c. 1841. He d. 6 Sept. 1874, aged 55. He m. Sarah Percy, b. Scotland, to Allegany Co., MD in girlhood. She was d/o David Percy, who with two brothers, James & Dougles, were pioneers in coal operations at Jackson Mine at Lonaconing. Sarah d. Jan. 1894, aged 67. *6TH:156-58*

SLOAN, MATTHEW, b. Muirkirk, Ayrshire, Scotland, s/o David. Brothers of Matthew were James, killed by the Indians during the early days of CA; Duncan resided in Pomeroy, OH; John, d. in Frostburg, MD; Margaret m. Hugh Sampson of Frostburg, MD. David & John served in the 2d Potomac House Brigade during the Civil War. C. 1830 Matthew to America & settled in PA, later settled in Mount Savage, MD. He m. Anna Muir, b. Ayrshire, who accompanied the family of George Tennant to Frostburg, MD. *6TH:140-41*

SMITH, ---, b. England, to America, veteran of the American Revolution. The emigrant's son, Isaac Smith, b. NY; businessman & farmer. His son Buell J. Smith, b. in NY, m. Sarah Field, b. CT. Baptist Church members. Their son, Milton E. Smith, grad. MD Univ. of Law school class of 1891; educator, res. Harford Co., MD. *H/C:540-1*

SMITH, CHARLES, b. Lorraine, France came to America in the French service as a Sub-Lt. of Marines under Count Rochambeau. He returned to America in 1785 & settled in VA with his wife, where his son Frederick was born. Frederick m. Mary A. Cover & had son Washington Augustus Smith, M.D., b. there 20 Dec. 1820. Washington Augustus m. 1847 Jane L., eldest d/o the late Samuel K. Travers & settled on Taylor's Island, Dorchester Co., MD. *MDC:591*

SMITH, CHRISTIAN, & Elizabeth Burkely, wife, both b. Germany, to America 1850 & settled in Harford Co., MD; mason & farmer. He d. 1872; Elizabeth still living at age 66. Lutheran. *H/C:161*

SMITH, CONRAD, b. Hesse Darmstadt, Germany. His wife was Elizabeth --- & they had son Conrad & a dau. In 1835 the family emigrated to America & landed in Baltimore. They later located in Middletown Valley, Frederick Co., MD. Their son Conrad was b. in Hesse Darmstadt 6 March 1819; shoemaker. He m. Elizabeth Suman, member of the Lutheran Church of Middletown. *FR2:1334-5*

SMITH, HENRY, b. London, England, m. Josephine V. Tilyard, settled in Baltimore at age 20; son Edward A. (M.D.) b. Baltimore 4 April 1862. *TR3:58*

SMITH, HENRY, s/o Rev. Alexander Smith, Scotch-Irish by parentage, & Presbyterian minister, of County Donegal, Ireland, where Henry was born. Henry to the US at age 18, locating in Howard Co., MD. Mar.

Sarah Ayler, b. on the eastern shore of MD, who d. in Baltimore, aged 45, d/o Henry. *GME:283*

SMITH, HENRY, b. 3 Oct. 1831 at Hesse Darmstadt, Germany. In 1846 with his parents to reside in Baltimore, where he served apprenticeships with John Meiser & W. Robinson in the carpenter business. He m. Elizabeth C. Dietz, d/o George W. of Germany, 26 July 1852. *MDC:621*

SMITH, JOHN, b. Ulster, to America from the north of Ireland in the middle of the 18th century & settled in PA, later removing to Baltimore; merchant. Two young sons came with him: Samuel & Robert. Robert, b. in Lancaster, PA Nov. 1757, served as secretary of the navy & attorney general under Pres. Jefferson. He d. in Baltimore 26 Nov. 1842. Samuel, b. 27 July 1752, served as capt. in Smallwood's regt. during the Rev. *TR4:885-6, 888-9*

SMITH, JOHN, from England during the Revolution & joined the American Army. His dau. Mary Ann, b. 20 Dec. 1782, m. Levi Wayson of Anne Arundel County, MD, where their son George Washington Wayson was b. 18 Nov. 1819. *MDC:390-91*

SMITH, JOHN, b. Germany, to America & settled in Frederick, MD c. 1829-30. He was a miller & member of the Lutheran Church. He m. Ellen Blake, also b. Germany. They had 11 children, only one of whom is yet living: Christian, reared in Frederick Co., MD. He later went to Frederick Co., VA, miller. In 1873 he returned to Frederick Co., MD. *FR2:1590-1*

SMITH, JOHN, from Ireland & settled in Chester Co., PA. His son, William, reared in Chester Co., stone mason. In 1832 William removed with his family to DE. He had m. Mary DeHaven, b. Chester Co., PA, d/o Jesse DeHaven. Their sons George I., Winfield S. & James P. reside in Cecil Co., MD. *H/C:393-4*

SMITH, JOHN, b. England, emigrated & settled in what is now Calvert Co., MD 1660-1666. He m. Dorothy Brooke, d/o Rev. Robert Brooke, minister of the Episcopal Church & then res. in Calvert Co. Their son, John Smith, b. Calvert Co., m. Jane Brooke, d/o Leonard & Ann (Boarman) Brooke. Leonard was the s/o Baker Brooke of "De La Brooke Manor" & his wife Ann Calvert, d/o Leonard Calvert, 1st gov. of the Province. *FR2:1215-16*

SMITH, JOSEPH, b. Germany, to America in early manhood; manufacturer of paper, pasteboard & paper boxes. His parents located in PA & Joseph to MD where he d. aged 84. Had a large trade in Baltimore, MD. Joseph had 5 children who survived to adulthood: all now dec'd., William, Joseph, Edward, Perry Green (b. 1 Dec. 1820, Frederick Co., MD & m. Susannah Rebecca Geesey, 1824-1907), Margaret (m. the late George Washington Fink). Members Lutheran Church. Son William, b. Jefferson District, Frederick Co., MD Feb. 1814. He res. in Jefferson & Doubs, where he d. William m. Ann Mariah, d/o the late George Zimmerman, retired farmer of Frederick Co. *FR2:735, 1307*

SMITH, NOAH J., b. Germany, to America & settled near Smithsburg, Washington Co., MD, farmer. His wife was Dorothy --- & they had: Lena, m. Christian Kline of Washington Co.; Malinda, m. David Smith, Solomon, dec'd., m. 1st Susan Null & 2d Miss --- Kline; John C.; Lizzie, widow of Jacob Williams, res. near Waynesboro, PA; Saville, to VA & d. there; Nancy, m. Mr. --- Kline; Jonathan, m. 3 times 1: Nancy J. Himes, 2: Mrs. Frances Baker, nee Harting, 3: Elizabeth Kline; and Isaac, res. Waynesboro, PA. *FR2:1220-2*

SMITH, RICHARD, lawyer, b. & m. in England, to Calvert Co., MD (c. 1649) & in 1657 was commissioned attorney general of the province. He d. in MD at Hall's Croft in 1667. His wife Eleanor to America c. 1651. Their son Richard Jr.'s 2d wife was Barbara Rousby, widow of J. Rousby of Calvert Co. [a wife in TR4:344 is named as Barbara Morgan, d/o Henry & Frances. Could be this Barbara Rouseby or could be his 1st wife.] & his 3d wife was Mrs. Maria Johanna Lawther, widow of Mr. Lawther of the Queen's Life Guards & a d/o Charles Somerset & granddau. of Lord John Somerset, Marquis of Worcester. *H/C:571-3; TR4:344, 760*

SMITH, ROBERT V., b. 14 Feb. 1870, St. Mary's, Province of Ontario, Canada, s/o Martin Smith. Family name originally Smythe & the American ancestor was Thomas Smith, b. Ireland. "Over 100 years ago" he emigrated from Belfast to Ontario, Canada. Martin, father of Robert V., was s/o Thomas the immigrant. Other children of Martin were: C. P., who d. in Hagerstown, MD 1907, veterinary surgeon; Jennie L. m. William McIntire of British Columbia; R. H., veterinary surgeon of Hagerstown, MD; Robert V., also a veterinary surgeon in Frederick Co., MD; and Lula--Robert V. & Lula have never married. *FR2:1302*

SMITH, SAMUEL, from Ireland in 1728 & settled in PA at age 35. His son John of Carlisle, PA & in 1760 to Baltimore, MD merchant; member Constitutional Convention of MD 1776. His son, Major-General Samuel Smith, b. Carlisle, PA 27 July 1752, of Rev. War fame. *MDC:237-8*

SMITH, THOMAS HENRY, b. England, to America as young man, farmer in Prince George's Co., MD; m. Emily Watson of Prince George's Co. Episcopal Church members. Their children: Thomas L., m. Lenora Horman, d/o William H.; Johanna Rebecca, m. George Curtis & d. 3 days after her marriage; William Frances of Prince George's Co., m. twice to sisters by the name of Perry. *FR2:737*

SNOOK, ---, b. Germany, emigrated to America & settled in Frederick Co., MD before the Rev. War. His son Simon, farmer, had a son Daniel Snook, also a farmer. Member Utica Reformed Church. Daniel m. Margaret Ann Hill & they had: Julia, m. Andrew Gernard; Margaret M., m. Henry Johnson; Daniel J., dec'd.; Jacob, dec'd.; John A., dec'd.; Susan M., dec'd., wife of Augustus Shaffer & Lewis A. *FR2:1399-1400*

SNOUFFER, GEORGE, b. Germany, was early settler of Frederick Co., MD. He with 2 of his brothers emigrated to America. One settled in Westminster, MD, one in Emmitsburg, MD & George in southern Frederick Co. He m. & had 6 children, one of whom was Benjamin, Frederick Co. farmer, b. 24 Jan. 1816. Benjamin m. Ellen, d/o Benjamin Moffett of Jefferson District, Frederick Co., MD. *FR2:1322-3*

SNOWDEN, RICHARD, b. Wales, held commission in Cromwell's army, came to MD & purchased land in Anne Arundel Co. in 1669. Richard m. Elizabeth Grosse, d/o Roger of Anne Arundel Co., MD; he d. 20 May 1711 in Anne Arundel Co. He was known as "the iron-master," had a son Thomas who m. Ann Ridgely. Richard, son of Richard the immigrant, was large landowner & built first iron works on the Patuxent River in Prince George's Co., MD. Richard Jr. m. before 1691 to Mary, d/o Thomas Linthicum. He res. in Anne Arundel Co. & the family owned the town of Laurel. Richard (II) m. Mary Waters. *TR4:227, 697-700; GME:103*
　　　This source states that this Richard Snowden is assumed, though not proved to be, the progenitor of the Snowdens of Anne Arundel Co., MD. *AAH:361*

SNYDER, JOHN GEORGE, s/o Michael & Barbara (Weimer) Snyder, b. Alsace Lorraine, Germany, then a province of France, 13 Jan. 1827. In 1838 settled in Stark Co., OH. John George m. Susannah Kelper & had 10 children. One son, Rev. George A. Snyder, b. Summit Co., OH, 10 Aug. 1863, pastor of the Christ Reformed Church at Hagerstown for 16 years & in 1904 was called to Catawba College at Newton, NC. *FR2:917-18*

SNYDER, LEONARD, b. Germany in the State of Saxony. Stonecutter & served in he Germany army. Emigrated to US & served in the American army under Gen. Scott in the war with Mexico. After the war he located in Washington, DC. At outbreak of Civil War again enlisted. His first wife was Mary Catherine Sueor & his second was Mrs. Eva Rosina Snyder, a widow, nee Long. They res. near Boyd's Station in Mongtomery Co., MD & later res. Urbana & later still near Browingsville, Montgomery Co. & finally at Linganore, Frederick Co., where he d. Nov. 1892. He is bur. Locust Grove Cem. Roman Catholic. No surviving children by 1st marriage. Children of 2d marriage: Catharine Margaret, m. John Dehoff & res. near Belair, MD; Charles Augustus, farmer of Woodville, m. Louisa Kline; Mary Theresa, missionary worker in the Dunkard Church; Christian Guttlieb of Baltimore, m. Amy E. Nusbaum & James Albert. *FR2:1308-9*

SOPER, JOHN, planter, from England to America in late 17th century & settled in what is now Prince George's Co., MD. *MDC:683*

SORENSON, ANTON CHRISTIAN, b. in Aarhuus, on the peninsula of Jutland, Denmark, 24 April 1868, s/o Orsen & Naren (Rasmussen) Sorensen. Orsen was b. in Ensler, near Aarhuus, s/o Nels & Karen Sorensen. In 1880 the family came to the US & settled in CO, ranchers. Anton went to Provo, UT at age 17 & later removed to Washington, DC & studied medicine in the George Washington University, grad. 1911. Interned Mercy Hospital & then opened an office in Baltimore, MD. He served in the Medical Corps of the US Army in WWI. He m. in Denver, CO 17 June 1912, Mae K. Guilford, b. Washington, DC & d/o William F. & Charlotte (Kerby) Guilford. William Guilford b. OH; Charlotte b. England. Lutheran family. *TR3:685-6*

SPEAR, MARY, b. Germany, m. John K. Klinkhart of NY state. Their son, Ames John Klinkhart, b. 21 Dec. 1876, Canajoharie, NY, is an architect of Hagerstown, MD. *TR3:494-5*

SPEELMAN, DAVID, b. Germany, s/o Sylvester, to US in early manhood & d. near Cumberland, MD. Son J. Peter, b. Allegany Co., MD, resided near Frostburg till 1850 &then to Selbysport. He m. Sarah Myers; they are both deceased. Son Otho b. near Frostburg 1832. Members of Methodist Episcopal Church South. *6TH:392-93*

SPENCE, WILLIAM WALLACE, b. Edinburgh, 18 Oct. 1815, from Scotland to VA, set. Baltimore, MD 1840, where he d. Was a resident of Baltimore 73 years and d. there 3 Nov. 1915. *GME:154*

SPENCE FAMILY,, from Scotland to MD c. 1680. Desc., John Selby Spence, b. near Snow Hill, Worcester Co., MD 29 Feb. 1788, served as US senator & member of the house of representatives. *TR4:876*

SPENGLER, HENRY, s/o Hans Rudolph, b. 8 June 1704 & m. Susanne Mueller 17 Jan. 1730. In 1732 they sailed to America on the ship Pleasant & settled in York Co., PA. He d. 6 July 1776. Their eldest child, Henry, was a member of the York Co. militia, 3d Battalion, in the Revolution. The youngest son, Rudolph, weaver, m. 5 Aug. 1759, Maria Catherine, d/o Henry Bahn. Son Henry b. at York, PA 2 Jan. 1761, m. Susannah Lightner of Lancaster, PA. They moved to Mercersburg, Franklin Co., PA. He d. 17 Aug. 1837 & his wife subsequently carried on the hotel business on the road from Baltimore to Wheeling & Pittsburgh. She d. aged 87 years, 8 months. The eldest son George, b. York, 25 July 1789. He served in th War of 1812. In 1818 removed to Williamsport, MD, wagon maker. Member of the Lutheran Church until 1840, when he & his wife joined the Methodist Church. 4 Sept. 1817 George m. Mary, d/o William & Elizabeth Fields, of Martinsburg, WV. *6TH:699-702*

SPITZER, ---, to VA from Germany. His son Eli G., b. Rockingham Co,. VA, m. Mary Carr. Members German Baptist Church. Eli's son, Joseph R., shoemaker & farmer, res. Broadway, VA & m. Amanda Rader. Their son, Alonzo Rader Spitzer, b. Rockingham Co., VA 3 Nov. 1867, to Brunswick, MD 1893, postmaster. Alonzo m. in VA 27 Dec. 1888, Julia Minick of Broadway. *FR2:933-4*

SPRIGG, THOMAS, b. 1630 in England. He settled in Northampton Co., VA & then moved to "Resurrection Manor" in Calvert Co., MD (later part of Prince George's Co.) 1661; later removed to Prince George's Co., MD, where he d. 1704. Desc. Samuel Sprigg (1782-1855), whose father d. in 1800, was raised by his uncle, Osborn Sprigg of Prince George's Co. *TR4:50, 378*

SPURRIER, MARY THOMAS, b. Bristol, England; m. 1835, John Yost of Lancaster Co., PA, b. 1800, lumber merchant. To Baltimore, MD 1850. Their son, William Franklin Yost, b. Baltimore 1856. *TR3:104*

ST. LEGER, PATRICK, b. France, emigrated to Ireland where he m. Nora Cusak; to Baltimore, MD with his wife & her brother & sister. His dau. Catherine A. b. c. 1857. *TR3:228*

STABLER, GEORGE, of Yorkshire, England, b. c. 1732, to America 1753 & m. Mary Robinson of Chester Co., PA. Resided a time in Philadelphia, removed to Petersburg, VA, where he d. He & wife buried at Gravelly Run, Friends' Cemetery, Nansemond Co., VA. Their son William m. Deborah, d/o Thomas & Elizabeth (Brooke) Pleasants of Beaver Dam, Goochland Co., VA & settled in Leesburg. They later removed to Sandy Spring, MD on a place she had inherited from ther mother. *6TH:838-40; GME:81*

STALEY, JOSEPH & JOHN, from Switzerland to America at an early date & both took up land from Lord Baltimore. This land was part of a tract four miles west of Frederick City, MD now called Rocky Springs. *FR2:1158-9*

STANLEY, JOHN, youngest son of the Earl of Derby, to MD in 1653 & was the first surveyor-general of the province. His son Dacy m. Elizabeth Wright of VA & their son, John Stanley, was the father of John Wright Stanley, b. Charles City, VA 1742. John Wright Stanley went to Philadelphia, PA early in life, where he organized the first insurance company in that city. He m. Anne Cogsdell of New Bern, NC in 1772 & established a business in that place. Their son, James Green Stanley, m. Elizabeth Harvey of NC. Their son, Harvey Stanley, b. New Bern 22 Sept. 1809. Harvey was a Protestant Episcopal minister & served in Elizabeth City, NC & Saybrook, CT. In 1843 Harvey to MD to take charge first of Princess Ann Parish in Somerset Co. & later other MD parishes. He m. Mary Anne Kinney, d/o Charles of Elizabeth City, NC. She d. in Laurel, MD 24 March 1893, aged 75. Their son, Charles Harvey Stanley, b. in Saybrook, CT 20 Oct. 1842, atty. of MD. *TR4:697-700; GME:246*

STAPLETON, JOHN, b. Co. of Roscommon, Ireland, settled in Cumberland, MD in 1858 & in 1884 removed to Bedford Co., PA. He m. Margaret May. Son, John J., b. at Vale Summit, Allegany Co., MD, 29 Aug. 1859. *6TH:622*

STAUFFER, MATTHICS [sic], of Wurttemberg, Germany, immigrated to PA & in 1735 rec'd. a grant from the Penn heirs in East Earl Twp., Lancaster Co., PA. His son, Peter, acquired an estate of 1,000 acres in the same twp., much of which is still owned by his descs. Desc. Isaac Weaver Stauffer, b. Goodville, Lancaster Co., PA 12 March 1817, farmer, d. 4 Sept. 1901. Isaac m. Evaline Kurtz, b. 13 Aug. 1822, d. 8 June 1881, & had 10 children. Their son Alvin Packer Stauffer, b. Goodville 27 Dec. 1856, was next to the youngest child. Alvin studied medicine in OH & in 1885 practiced in Shippensburg, PA until he removed to Hagerstown, MD in 1887. He is a member of St. John's Lutheran Church in Hagerstown. 11 Nov. 1891 he m. Elizabeth M. Hoffman, d/o Joseph L. & Mary Hoffman of Hagerstown. *TR3:979-80*

STAUP, JOHN, b. Germany & to America as a child. Basket maker & early settler of Creagerstown area of Frederick Co., MD. His son, John W. Staup, b. 1817, was aged 14 when John the immigrant died. *FR2:1277*

STEEDMAN, ANNIE FRANCES, b. Scotland, m. George Yost, b. Baltimore, MD of German ancestry. Son George Steedman Yost b. Baltimore 25 March 1890. *TR3:300*

STEGMAN, JOHN HENRY, b. Bremen, Germany, 6 Dec. 1848 to US with wife Anna S. & settled in Baltimore, MD, accountant. Lutheran; d. 24 Dec. 1920; left widow & 6 children. *TR3:114*

STEHL, JOHN, b. Ellenrode, near Cassel, 1816, m. Marie Bonciene, d/o French immigrants who had settled in the area in 1785. To US in 1843, settled in Baltimore, MD; druggist. He d. aged 57 at his home in Roland Park. His dau., Elberta, b. Baltimore 31 July 1890. *TR4:151*

STEINER, JOHN CONRAD (REV.), of Switzerland, to America 1749 & served in Philadelphia & Germantown, PA. Pastor Reformed Church of Frederick, MD, 1756-59. *FR1:408*

STEPHENS, JOHN, emigrated from England to colonies at end of 17th century & settled near Backtown, Dorchester Co., MD. *MDC:382*

STEPHENSON, WILLIAM, b. Scotland; to America in young manhood & settled in Harford or Cecil Co.; m. Rachel Barnes, b. MD. During the Rev. he was proprietor of a hotel at Perryville, after the war purchased large tract of land in Harford Co. He d. aged 74; his wife, one of the first Methodist in the neighborhood. *H/C:374-5*

STEVENSON, JOHN, b. Ireland, to America in 1815 & settled in KY. He d. an octogenerian in 1857. His father, Henry Stevenson, was b. Scotland. John's son, James M., was a physician of Baltimore, MD. His son John M., also a physician, was b. in Baltimore 30 Nov. 1840. *MDC:671-72*

STEWART, JOHN, b. Roxburghshire, Scotland 17 Feb. 1779. He m. & came to Baltimore, MD in 1817. Inventor & kept livery stable. He later retired to his farm near Bel Air, Harford Co., where he d. 8 March 1876. *MDC:395*

STIEFEL, JULIUS, b. Bavaria, resided in Wurtzberg, Germany until age 18 in 1833 he immigrated to America, settled in Baltimore, MD where he died in 1905, aged 90. Served in the Union Army during the Civil War. Shirt manufacturer. His wife, b. Bavaria [not named here], d. in Baltimore 1892, aged 51. *TR3:283*

STIEFF, CHARLES MAXIMILIAN, b. Kingdom of Wurtemberg, 19 July 1805. In 1830 m. Catharine R. Roesch, of the same place & they came to the US, settled in Lebanon Co., PA, but shortly removed to Baltimore, MD. Piano manufacturer. *MDC:686-87*

STIER, HENRY J. D'AERTZLAER, of Antwerp, Belgium, to America with his wife and only dau. in 1794. He returned to Belgium in 1805 and left behind his dau., Rosalie Eugenia, who m. George Calvert, of Riverdale, Prince George's Co., MD. *MDC:135*

STIRLING, JAMES, from parish of Stirling, Scotland, settled in Baltimore 1774, MD. Was of the family Keir & Cawder. [Family tree included in entry.] *TR2:38-41*

STOCKBRIDGE, --- (DR.), of England to Plymouth Co., MA in 1628. Descendant Henry, son of Jason who was b. 1780 & 2d wife Abigail Montague, to Baltimore, MD in 1845, attorney. Henry m. 1852, Fanny Montague of MA. *MDC:190*

STOCKETT, ---, family of Kent, England, loyal to King Charles & after his defeat at Worcester in 1651, came to MD. In 1668, all 3 brothers removed to Anne Arundel Co., MD near Birdsville: Thomas, Francis & Henry, and an older brother, Lewis is named. Thomas m. Mary Wells, d/o Richard of Herring Creek & on his death in 1671 she m. George Yate, surveyor. *AHH:93-6*

STOCKSDALE, ---, b. England; he & several brothers to Annapolis, MD as early settler. His son Edward, miller & left children: John, Solomon, Noah, Nellie & Mary. Noah was farmer in Carroll Co., MD & m. Catharine Haines. *FR2:798.*

STODDERT, JAMES (MAJOR), b. Scotland, settled MD c. 1675. Desc. Capt. Thomas Stoddert fought in the French & Indian War & was slain when part of Gen. Braddock's army in 1755. Thomas' son, Benjamin (1751-1812), b. Charles Co., MD, served as secretary of the Navy, 1798-1802. *FR4:17*

STONE, GREGORY (CAPT.), American progenitor of the family, served in the Rev. War & settled in MA. His descs. migrated to MD & 5 generations of the family have resided there. Desc. James Harvey Stone m. Harriet Newell of MD & became collector of the port of Baltimore. Their son William F. Jr. b. 19 Jan. 1890. *TR4:450*

STONE, WILLIAM, b. Northamptonshire, England 1605, emigrated to Northampton Co., VA. He served as 3rd proprietary gov. of MD & was progenitor of one of the most notable families in MD. He d. c. 1660. Among descs. were Thomas Stone, signer of the Declaration of Independence & several political office holders. *TR4:900-1; MDC:425*

STONE FAMILY,, English family that came to America before 1776. Daniel Edward Stone settled on the Eastern Shore of MD. William Stone settled in VA & is the ancestor of Stone family in Western MD. A Thomas Stone lived & d. on the Eastern Shore of MD. An early member of the family went to live in PA & was the ancestor of William Stone, late gov. of that State. A William Stone, planter of VA, was a Quaker

& did not own slaves. His son, Daniel Stone, b. Waterford, Loudoun Co., VA, m. Sarah Huff. They d. at Milford, Loudoun Co. & left a son William Huff Stone, among others. William Huff Stone b. Waterford, Loudoun Co., VA 1801, in 1847 removed to MD & settled near Monrovia, Frederick Co. & later removed to Fayette Co., VA & still later to Montgomery Co., MD. In 1861 he settled near Burnt Mill, Frederick Co. & retired to Mt. Pleasant, MD where he d. 18767. Bur. at Monrovia Quaker Church. He m. Cordelia Norris of New Market, Frederick Co., d/o Joel & Rachel (Plummer) Norris. She d. Feb. 1897, aged 84. *FR2:1547-8*

STORR, JOHN, of Liverpool, England, to America in 1852, landed at NY & settled in Mount Pleasant District, Frederick Co., MD, farmer. His son, Henry C., b. Liverpool 1836, to America with parents, farmer in Mount Pleasant District. In 1864 purchased Albert Ramsburg farm near Bethel, where he d. 1895. Henry m. Elizabeth, d/o David Glaze of Frederick. They had 8 children. *FR2:1022*

STOTTLEMYER, DAVID, b. Munich, Germany, to America in early manhood & settled in the southwest part of Middletown Valley, Frederick Co., MD. His wife's name was Margaret ---, & they had 5 children, one son was David Jr. who settled near Wolfsville, MD & m. Margaret Maugruter. *FR2:748*

STRANGE, WILLIAM FRENCH, b. Glasgow, Scotland, to US in 1823, landed in NY. Resided in Charlotte, NC, where he d. 1867. Son Robert Ellis Strange, b. Charlotte, NC 3 March 1846, to Annapolis, MD 1869, merchant; m. Caroline Yewell, d/o Thomas E. of Anne Arundel Co., MD. Episcopal. *TR3:199*

STRAUS, LEVI, b. Germany, to America in the 1840's, settled in Baltimore, MD where he died. His son Solomon b. & reared in Baltimore, in malt & grain business. *TR3:338*

STRAWSBURG, JOSIAH, b. England, to US with his mother 2 brothers & 1 sister. His father had accidentally been drowned in England when Josiah was 14 years of age. His mother's maiden name was Coppersmith. She took up res. in Clemsonville, Frederick Co., MD. One of Josiah's brothers, Jacob, went to MO; another brother, William, went to IL. His sister, Cassie, m. a Mr. Gilbert & went west. Josiah d. Nov.

1882 & is bur. in Beaver Dam Church Cemetery. His wife was Susan Engle & she is still living, being c. 75 years of age. *FR2:1501*

STREET, JOHN (COL.), b. England, to America before Revolution; farmer of Harford Co., served in Revolution & War of 1812. *H/C:162*

STREETT FAMILY,, one of the oldest in Harford Co., MD, was founded in America by 3 brothers: David, Thomas & John, who made the voyage from London, England early in the 18th century. Thomas settled in Harford (then Baltimore) county. He took out a patent on land above the Rocks of Deer Park, called Streett's Hunting Grounds, part of which is yet in possession of his descs. His son, Col. John Streett, b. 1762 in Harford Co. & d. there in 1837. He was politically active & served as colonel in the 7th Cavalry during the War of 1812. 11 Dec. 1784 he m. Martha St. Clair & had: James; Mary, m. Henry Amos; John; William; Shadrach, m. (1) Elizabeth Watkins & (2) Ann Harper; Thomas, m. Catherine Merryman; St. Clair, m. a member of the Jarrett family; Abraham, physician & m. Elizabeth Streett; & Charlotte who m. Silas Baldwin. *TR3:706-7*

STROMEYER, WILLIAM FRANCIS, b. Bremen, Germany, to US in boyhood & spent most of his life in CT. His son Francis William, musician, member of the Naval Academy Band, m. 21 Jan. 1890, Alice Clark, d/o George, who was b. in St. Mary's, MD. Mr. Clark, retired printer, now res. in Annapolis. Francis William Stromeyer d. 25 Nov. 1921, aged 51. *TR3:400-01*

STUART, WILLIAM, b. Scotland, to DE where his son, David T., b. 8 June 1828 & d. 6 May 1886. David T. m. Elizabeth Jane Davis, of Welsh desc., from family of early VA settlers. Their son, Samuel Ellicott Davis Stuart m. 27 Nov. 1895, Emma Robinson in Baltimore, MD. *TR4:88*

STUART, WILLIAM (MISS), of the Firth of Solway. Named William because her father had wanted a son. She m. 'abroad' John Beale Davidge of Baltimore, MD & they resided in Baltimore. *TR4:15*

STUDD, CHRISTINA, b. Germany, to America at age 3 with parents; m. Philip Hiltz, son John b. Baltimore, MD, 28 April 1852. *TR3:129*

229

STUMP, JOHN, & wife Mary, Prussians who emigrated to MD c. 1700, & settled on tract near present town of Perryville, Cecil County, where he d. 1747. They had 2 surviving children, John & Henry. Henry removed to the valley of Deer Creek in Harford Co. (then Baltimore Co.) & m. Rachel Perkins. John m. Hannah, d/o William Husbands, on the female side a descendant of Augustine Herman of Bohemia Manor. He removed to Harford Co. in 1796 & d. 1797. *MDC:547*

STUMPF, JOHN JOSEPH, b. Baden-Baden, Germany, brewmaster, settled in Baltimore, where he d. at the age of 56. Roman Catholic. His wife was Sophie Decker of Hessen, Germany & had 4 children. Two d. in childhood & their son, William E. Stumppf, b. in Baltimore, MD, 27 Sept. 1879 & a surviving dau., Sophie Marie. *TR3:521-2*

SUDSBURY, JOSEPH M. (COL.), s/o Peter & Clarissa (Weaver) Sudsbury, b. in Nymphenburg, Bavaria 17 March 1827. Peter d. 1854, aged 65. Joseph M. a soldier & later a carver. To US in 1851 & settled in NY; 1854 to Baltimore, MD, carver. Served 2d MD Regt. during the Civil War; m. 1855 Mary Rankin of Baltimore. *MDC:416-17*

SULIVANE, JAMES (MAJOR), an Irish officer in a regiment of King James, removed to America & settled in Dorchester Co., MD in 1693. *MDC:433*

SUMMERS, ---, from Germany & settled in upper part of the Middletown Valley, Frederick Co., MD. His son, Jacob Summers, farmer, m. Elizabeth Horine. He d. 1848 & wife d. 1847. Both bur. in graveyard at Church Hill, near Myersville, Jackson Dist. *FR2:985-6*

SUMMERS, JACOB, b. Germany, to America c. the time of the American Rev. He was accompanied by 2 brothers who settled in PA. Jacob settled in Middletown Valley, Frederick Co., MD. He served in the War of 1812. His son, George W. Summers, b. MD, March 1802, was a miller, farmer & wagoneer; Lutheran. He m. Catharine E. Michael, d/o Henry. She was member of Reformed Church at Middletown. Their children: Henry W.; Jacob V. of Tuscarora District; John T., dec'd.; Samuel M., retired farmer; David W. of Jackson District; Joshua of Myersville. Son George W. Summers above, wagoneer, hauler of freight between Baltimore & Wheeling, WV, later farmer in Jackson District. George d. 1885. His wife was Catharine E. Michael, d/o Henry. She was member of the Reformed Church at Middletown. *FR2:964-5, 1140-1, 1571-2*

SUTER, WILLIAM, Englishman who settled in Hagerstown, MD in 1811; undertaker. He d. there 1897. His son, Charles M., served in Co. I, 7th MD Union Army , 1861-1864, as Lt. Charles m. Laura Witzenbacher, who d. 1914. Laura was the d/o William & Catherine (Rauth) Witzenbacher, both b. Germany. William to Washington Co., MD in 1848, Catherine in 1851. *TR3:455-6*

SWEENEY, PETER, left England at the age of 20 and came to Baltimore, MD. He b. Ireland in 1820, but taken to England by his parents at a young age. To US in 1840, landed and stayed for a time in New York City; later established a wholesale pork packing house in Baltimore. Catholic. He m. Miss Chatterton, who d. in England & he later m. Margaret Hart 4 May 1853. *GME:303*

SWINDELL, JOHN, EDWARD & WILLIAM, to America from Tralee, Ireland. William came c. 1815. John, the eldest, lived & d. in Cambridge, MA & left no male issue. Edward also came c. 1815. His sons, John & William, changed their name to Swinden. John ran iron foundry in Philadelphia; William was a Baptist minister. Neither left male issue.

William (the immigrant) d. 1835. In America for many years superintendent of the Union Glass Works of Philadelphia. He m., sortly after coming to America, Lydia, d/o William Emmitt who was b. Bristol, England, to America c. 1812 from the town of Nalesy near the city of Bristol, England. William d. 1835. Families connected with glass manufacture. William & Lydia had 5 sons: William, Richard, John, James & Edward, and 1 dau., Maria. William, s/o William & Lydia, b. Cambridge, MA, 19 Feb. 1821, in 1827 to Philadelphia with father and maternal grandfather to originate Union Glass Co.. At age 23 he removed to Camden, NJ as journeyman, where he m. Henrietta Mullard, Quakeress who was adoped d/o Hughby Hatch, a farmer. In 1847 William arrived in Baltimore, MD with F. & L. Schaum for 5 years & then with William Gorten, David L. Lawson & Jacob Lye he built Spring Garden Bottle Works of Baltimore & other enterprises. Methodist. *TR4:386; MDC:258*

SYKES, JAMES, an Englishman who converted a flour mill into a cotton mill. Had an estate in Howard Co., MD & was the first to petition for the erection of the Howard District into a county in 1850. The town of Sykesville in present-day Carroll Co. named for him. *AAH:485*

SZOLD, BENJAMIN (REV.), b. in Hungarian village of Nemeskurt, 15 Nov. 1831. In 1859 he received a call to become Rabbi of the Oheb Shalom Congregation of Baltimore, MD and came to the US. In 1859, before settling in Baltimore, he m. Sophia Shaas, of Hungary. *MDC:155*

ALBOTT, RICHARD, b. England, member of Society of Friends, settled in MD on West River before 1659, where he received land from his father-in-law. Richard m. Elizabeth, d/o Major Richard Ewen [Evans], & settled on West River, Anne Arundel Co. His will is dated 2 April 1663 & he left sons Edward & John.

Major Richard Evans & wife Sophia immigrated to MD in 1649. Major Evans was with provincial forces in MD.

"Following him [Richard Talbott the immigrant] in the line of descent . . . were Edward, Edward Jr., Richard, John L., Richard & Edward A." Family later became Episcopalians & later still some Methodists. Descendant Hattersly Worthington Talbott, s/o Edward A. & Mary J. (Wareham), grandson of Richard & Sarah A. (Fairall) b. in Howard Co. 26 Aug. 1842. *6TH:719-20; TR4:827-9*

TALBOTT FAMILY, descs. of the Shrewsburys of England, a noted titled family of that country & the first of the name came to America prior to the Revolutionary War. Desc. Edward J. Talbott m. Sarah Jane Soper & their son, James E., b. in Calvert Co., MD 18 Aug. 1888. *TR3:766*

TALCOTT, JOHN, s/o John of Braintree, England, to America on the ship *Lion* in 1632 & in 1636 built the first house in Hartford, CT, where he d. March 1660. He m. in England, Dorothy, d/o Mark Mott. They landed in Boston & settled in Newton, now Cambridge, MA, where he was admitted freeman 6 Nov. 1632.

Desc. Hope Maria Talcott was grandmother of Cornelia Talcott Ransom, b. Tioga Centre, NY 26 June 1864, who m. Samuel Carson Rowland & res. Baltimore, MD. Mrs. Rowland is also desc. from emigrant John Hollister who settled in Wethersfield CT in 1642 and m. Johanna, d/o Richard Treat Sr. In 1644 John was in Weymouth, MA & the same year returned to Wethersfield where he d. in 1665. She is also desc. from Thomas Wright who came from England & was in Wethersfield in 1639.

Desc. [of immigrant John Talcott] Cornelia Talcott Ransom, d/o Charles E. & Georgia (Anderson) Ransom, former of NY & latter of MD. *TR4:395, 741-6*

TANEY, MICHAEL, to MD c. 1660, high sheriff of Calvert Co. 1675, had son Michael of Calvert Co., who m. Dorothy Brooke, d/o Roger Brooke & wife Dorothy Neale. She was d/o Capt. James Neale & wife Anne Gill, d/o Benjamin of Charles Co. Capt. Neale immigrated to MD 1638-45 & d. 1684. Michael (II) d. 1702. *TR4:575-8*

TAPPAN, ABRAHAM (TOPPAN), of Yorkshire, England to America in 1637 & settled in Newburyport, MA. Paul Tappen, 12th in line from Robert Topham of Linton, Yorkshire, England & 7th in line from Abraham the immigrant m. 11 Sept. 1909 in Washington, DC, Laura Maryland Carpenter, b. St. Mary's Co., MD, d/o James Walter & Mary Alice Llewellyn (Bunting) Carpenter. They res. at Ardmore, PA. [See Toppan entry] *TR4:196-212*

TAYLOR, DAVID C., b. Scotland, to America as an infant with his parents, who settled in VA. He m. Margaret S. Dalby & son David Bayley Taylor b. in Accomac Co., VA 8 Feb. 1840. David B. served in Co. I of the Chesapeake Cavalry during the Civil War, Army of Northern VA. After the war he moved to Baltimore, MD & 2 Oct. 1872 m. Agnes H. Montgomery of Augusta Co., VA. *MDC:185*

TAYLOR, HENRY, b. Dec. 1823 in Stirling, Stirlingshire, Scotland, s/o John & Elizabeth (Ronald) Taylor, Presbyterians. John was a carpet weaver & d. when Henry was 14 months old. In 1843, he followed his brother William, a weaver who had come to this country in 1825, to Baltimore, MD. Henry m. Mary A. Thorne, d/o Rev. Francis, Baptist clergyman of Devonshire, England. *MDC:201-02*

TAYLOR, RICHARD, res. of Long Sutton, Lincolnshire, England, in 1790 to America. He m. Elizabeth Calvert, d/o Capt. John Calvert, Rev. War veteran & a s/o Cornelius Calvert. *TR4:621-2*

THOM, ALEXANDER, adherent to the Jacobite cause in Scotland, after battle of Culloden in 1746, in which he was an officer, fled to America & settled in VA, eventually in Culpeper Co. His eldest son, Col. John

Watson Triplett Tom, was state senator, officer in the War of 1812, high sheriff of his county & a large slave holder. John's youngest son, Major Joseph Pembroke Thom, served as surgeon in US Navy & with the Confederate Army. After the war res. in Baltimore, MD; m. Ella L. Wright & son W. H. DeCourcy Wright Thom b. there in 1858. *TR4:126*

THOMAS, CHRISTOPHER, 1635 left Gravesend, England & settled in MD. His only son, Tristram, came to America & joined his father in MD & is cited as "gentleman of Talbot Co." Tristram left at least one son, William Thomas, member of the house of burgesses 1738-1748. *TR4:833-4*

THOMAS, HUGH, from Wales c. 1702 to PA & later to MD. *FRI:257*

THOMAS, JAMES, of Ware, Chester Co., [sic] MD, b. England before 1651. Will 1701, s/o Thomas Thomas, who also settled in MD in 1656. James m. Teretia ---. *GME:143*

THOMAS, JAMES, from Wales to America in 1651 & settled in MD. Desc. Major William Thomas was soldier of the Rev. War & his son James Thomas was gov. of MD 1832-35. *TR4:732-4*

THOMAS, JAMES & THOMAS, from Wales, emigrated during the reign of Queen Anne, settling in Kent Co., MD. Samuel d. unmarried; James married twice, the first time in England and she came to America with him. His 2d wife was Elizabeth Bellican, whose ancestors came from Holland. *6TH:721-24*

THOMAS, JOHN, b. Germany 1731, to America with 3 of his brothers in 1754, settled near Frederick, MD. He had: Mary, m. George Gear; Catherine, m. Christopher Widegan; Barbara & Henry (b. 18 Oct. 1765). Henry, of Buckeystown District, Frederick Co. m. 22 Nov. 1790, Ann Margaret, d/o George Ramsberg. Henry's son, George Thomas, b. 1798, member of the Reformed Church, d. at age of 86 & is bur. in the Buckeystown District cemetery. He m. 3 times: 1. Miss Roban of TN; 2. Miss Thomas; 3. Julia Ann Hargett, d/o John, farmer of Feagaville area. *TR4:284-5; FR2:1365; 1431-2, 1528-9*

THOMAS, PHILIP, s/o Evan Thomas of Swansea, Glamorganshire, Wales, to America 1651 & set. in MD. He m. in England Sarah Harrison. Also brought children Philip, Sarah & Elizabeth with them to

America. They settled in Anne Arundel Co. in 1651, where he was granted 500 acres, "Beckley." Later became a Quaker. Dau. Sarah m. John Meeres, Elizabeth 3d wife of William Coale & later wife of Edward Talbott. *GME:96; AAH:46*

THOMAS, THOMAS, of Co. Sussex, England, one of the early settlers in St. Mary's Co., on the Patuxent River in MD in 1651. On 1 June 1652 he demanded a warrant for 600 acres for transporting himself, wife Elizabeth, son James and Robert & Eleanor Paterson & Matthew Smith, his servants, into the province in 1651. His son James Thomas of "Ware," Charles Co., MD, was b. in England before 1651, m. Teretia --- & had 2 sons: John, (b. 1682 in Charles Co., MD, d. 1757 & left a son, William Thomas, b. in Charles Co. in 1714) & Thomas who d. before 20 Feb. 1723/24 & m. Susanna ---. James d. in St. Mary's Co., MD 1701. *TR4:779-81, 801-2*

THOMAS, VALENTINE, one of 3 brothers from Germany to America. Valentine settled c. 9 miles south of Frederick, MD; farmer. His eldest son was Gabriel Thomas, b. 24 Sept. 1752 in MD. He was a farmer of Buckeystown District. *FR2:1364-5*

THOMPSON, ---, from Ireland to the US, landed in Philadelphia in 1792. He m. a Miss Harrison, of Caroline Co., MD & settled in Easton, MD. This Thompson immigrant d. c. 1828. His youngest son, Walter Harrison Thompson was b. Easton 1823 and m. Susan A. Mills of Dorchester Co., MD. *MDC:257-58*

THOMPSON, ADAM (DR.), b. Scotland & organizer of the St. Andrew's Society. He m. the widow Lettice (Lee) Wardrop, d/o Philip Lee & great-granddau. of Col. Richard Lee. His decs., Dr. Henry Lee Smith, Baltimore physician, b. 23 March 1868 in Ashland, Hanover Co., VA. Dr. Smith m. Elise Garr Henry of Morristown, NJ, d/o Rev. Francis A. & Helen (Garr) Henry. *TR4:194-5*

THOMPSON, GEORGE, to America from Ireland & settled in Cecil Co., MD. He m. Elizabeth Lyon, d/o Hugh & Margaret of Cecil Co. *MDC:301*

THOMPSON, HENRY, to America from England in 1792 & settled in City of Baltimore, MD, where he d. in 1838. He m. Ann L. Bowly, eldest d/o Daniel of Furley Hall, MD. *MDC:344*

THOMPSON, JAMES, b. Lanarkshire, Scotland 14 Oct. 1836, s/o Robert & grandson of Thomas Thompson, one of the retainers of the house of Douglas. Another son of Robert, Thomas, resides in IL. James to America at age 20 to join his two uncles in Canada but changed his plans & to IL, settling near Peoria. From there to St. Louis & did much traveling. He joined the 2d MD regiment under Capt. Shaw during the Civil War. After the war he removed to Lonaconing, MD. James m. Elizabeth Rohm, d/o Conrad, b. Bedford, PA, but a resident of Cumberland, MD. *6TH:573-74*

THOMPSON, JOHN JACOB, b. North Germany, to America c. 1807 & settled in Baltimore, MD. For a time he farmed near York, PA. Returned to Baltimore where he d. aged 62. His son John Jacob b. Baltimore 23 May 1823. *MDC:660*

THOMPSON, JOSEPH, & wife Mary A. Early, from County Tyrone, Ireland in 1829 & settled in Baltimore, MD. Son Joseph b. in Baltimore City 19 Sept. 1836. *MDC:641-42*

THOMPSON, WILLIAM, b. Montreal, Canada. Orphaned young & at age 11 with his brother, John W., to Burlington, VT, where their grandfather lived. 3 years later to Washington, DC. William m., "near the beginning of the war," Helen L. Nourse, d/o John R., b. DC. *6TH:768-69*

THRASHER, THOMAS, b. in Wales in 1725. Emigrated from British Isles to America & in 1745 was chain-carrier for surveyors. He settled in what is now the Lewis Whipp farm, Frederick Co., MD. Thomas m. Maria Lee, a cousin of Gov. Thomas Lee of MD. She was from what is now the Petersville District. Episcopal. Their son Benjamin m. Martha Ridgely, d/o a planter of Frederick Co. *FR2:879*

TIERNAN, LUKE, s/o Paul who was b. County Meath, Ireland in 1728 & d. near Dublin aged 91. Luke was b. on the River Boyne, County Meath in 1757. Luke to America c. 1783 [1787] & settled in Hagerstown, MD; m. 6 Jan. 1793, Nancy [Ann], d/o Robert & Rebecca (Swearington) Owen of Hagerstown. Nancy [Ann] was desc. of Col. Cresap, whose family was from Yorkshire, England & who was a MD pioneer. Luke & family 1795 to Baltimore, MD, commission agent. Catholic. *FR2:824; MDC:497; 6TH:306-7*

TILDEN, MARMADUKE, of Great Oak Manor, Kent Co., MD, to Kent at an early period & d. Sept. 1671, leaving 3 sons: Marmaduke, Charles & John. Marmaduke m. Rebecca Wilmer, d/o Lambert & Ann; d. 20 June 1726. Charles, served as judge of Kent Co. *MDC:597*

TILGHMAN, RICHARD (DR.), s/o Oswald & Abigail (Taylor) Tilghman, b. 3 Sept. 1626 in England. With wife Mary Foxley, from London, England to America & settled in Talbot Co., MD 1660. Dr. Richard d. 7 Jan. 1675. Their dau. Rebecca m. Simon Wilmer, a burgess of Kent Co., MD 1698/9. Rebecca d. 1825. *TR4:50-3, 217, 575-8*

TOADVIN (TAUDVEINE/TOWDIN), NICHOLAS, French Huguenot who immigrated with the Brereton & Gardy families to America in 1675. Desc. Purnell Toadvin m. Amanda Parsons, d/o Jehu of Salisbury & had son Edwin Stanley Toadvin, atty. of Wicomico Co., MD, where he was b. 3 Dec. 1848. *TR4:495*

TODD, THOMAS, b. in England, to Elizabeth City, VA in 1647. He res. in MD 1657, an appointed justice of Anne Arundel Co., MD. He also took up lands in Fells Point, Baltimore Co. & the Eastern Shore of MD. *AAH:48*

TODD, THOMAS, to American from Denton, Co. Durham, England, settled in Gloucester Co., VA [Elizabeth City] c. 1637 [1647]. He res. in MD 1657, an appointed justice of Anne Arundel Co. He is supposed to have been the son of Robert Todd of York Co., VA & "passed his youth in England." Robert m. Ann Gorsuch, d/o Rev. John, rector of Walkham, Herfordshire, England and his wife Ann, d/o Sir William Lovelace. Thomas brought up the Puritan settlement to Annapolis in 1650, for which he was granted the land upon which Annapolis now stands. In 1669 he bought 300 acres at North Point. He is described as a merchant of the Patapsco River & d. in London, while on a visit in 1677. He m. Anne Lovelace, d/o Sir Thomas Lovelace of England. One dau., Elizabeth Frances m. Capt. North & was the mother of Mrs. Ellen (North) Moale, first white child b. in Baltimore. *TR4:420; AAH:48*

TOMLINSON, BENJAMIN, from England to America & settled on Wills Creek, Allegany Co., MD c. 1795. *6TH:817-19*

TOMS, JACOB, b. Germany, early settler of Middletown Valley, Frederick Co., MD. He had a large family, among them a son Jacob.

Jacob Toms Sr. is bur. in the old graveyard at Jerusalem, MD, near his farm. Jacob Toms Jr. farmer, res. 1 1/2 miles north of Myersville, where he was b. 1792. Jacob Jr. m. Mary Fioyd of Frederick Co. *FR2:958-9; 1521-2, 1523-4*

TONRY, WILLIAM P., b. City of Sligo, Ireland, 16 April 1840, eldest son of William & Catharie (Brennan) Tonry. With parents in infancy to St. John, New Brunswick; family later removed to Boston, MA. William P. studied at St. Charles College, Howard Co., MD & after further schooling he worked as a chemist in the Surgeon-General of the US Army in DC. He m. Annie E. Suratt of Prince George's Co. *MDC:177*

TOPPAN (TAPPAN), ABRAHAM, s/o William Topham of Calbridge, parish of Coverham, England, bapt. 10 April 1606. Res. for some time in Yarmouth, Norfolk Co., England, & in 1637 with wife & 2 children sailed for New England on the *Mary Ann*. He d. 5 Nov. 1672, aged 66 & she d. 20 March 1689, aged 82 years. Their son, Dr. Peter Toppan, b. England 1634, m. Jane, d/o Christopher & Anne (Toppan) Batt, 3 April 1661. Practiced at Newbury [MA] & d. 3 Nov. 1707. Desc. Benjamin Tappan, b. Manchester, MA, 21 Oct. 1747, m. 2 Nov. 1770, Sarah, d/o Lt. William & Rebecca (Dawes) Homes. Benjamin d. 1831, aged 83. Their second child, Benjamin, b. 25 May 1773, served as US senator from Steubenville, OH. He m. 20 March 1801, Anne Wright of Farmington, CT & had Dr. Benjamin Tappan, pioneer physician of Steubenville & veteran of the Civil War. Their son, William, b. Steubenville m. Sarah Elizabeth Buchanan. Their son Benjamin Tappan, b. 9 March 1890 in Rochester, Beaver Co., PA, educated at Johns Jopkins Univ. (1911/15), m. 18 Nov. 1916, Elise Gail, d/o George William & Helen C. (Baugh) Gail, of MD. [See Tappan entry] *TR4:558-60*

TORMEY, PATRICK, b. Roscommon, Ireland, emigrated to US in company of Father James Curley, S.J., a friend. About 1850 he removed from Frederick Co., MD to Baltimore, where he d. aged 55. His wife was Jane Jamison, b. 1797, d. 1876. Their son, Leonard Jamison Tormey, b. Frederick, Frederick Co., MD 26 Jan. 1730. He established his home in Baltimore c. 1850, where he d. 23 July 1883. Leonard was m. by Archbishop Kenrick to Ellen Mary Jenkins, of Baltimore, where she was b. 26 Dec. 1838 & d. 8 Feb. 1923. She was d/o Alfred & Elizabeth Cecilia (Hickley) Jenkins. *TR4:145, 414*

TOULSON, JOHN, to America 1671 & settled on Eastern Shore in MD. His son Andrew had 2 sons, Nathan & Patrick, soldiers of the Rev. War. *TR4:615-16*

TOWNSEND, JOSEPH, to colonies from England with William Penn & settled in West Chester, PA; merchant. Removed to Baltimore, MD & founded the first fire insurance company in America. Joseph m. 3 times & had 23 children, but only 2 of the sons married & the family died out rapidly. His first wife was Esther Hallet, 2d was Hannah Painter & the name of his 3d wife is not known. One of his sons who married was Richard Hallet Townsend, b. 1804, d. 1879. Quaker; was pres. of the Union Mills Manufacturing Co. of Elk Ridge. He M. Lydia Hallet Shotwell, of a NJ family. Their son, John Shotwell Townsend, b. Baltimore & d. 12 Oct. 1909, aged 60. 12 Oct. 1881, at Font Hill, Howard Co., MD John S. m. Adelia Conant Atkinson, d/o Joseph Townsend & Mary Isabelle (Conant) Atkinson. They have an only child, John, who is not married. *TR4:805-6*

TOWNSHEND, SAMUEL, b. London, England Nov. 1714, to America as a young man & m. Anne Pyles of Prince George's Co., MD. Their son William b. Prince George's Co. 1 April 1768. William had a son, William Belt Townshend, b. in the same place in 1816, m. Rose Dent. *TR3:867-8*

TRAIL FAMILY, Charles E. & Arianna (McElfresh) Trail had son Charles Bayard Trail, b. 1847 in Frederick, MD. He is given as desc. from: Lydia C. Ramsburg, of German family who originally settled Frederick c. 1735 (his father's mother); the Trail family of Belbo, in Co. Fife Scotland; the McElfresh family, settled in Western MD for over 150 years. *FR2:1336-7*

TRAPNELL, JOSEPH (DR.), b. England 19 June 1814, family of Staffordshire, England, to America at age 5 with his parents, landing in Baltimore. Later removed to Urbana in Frederick Co., & 2 years later settled in Frederick City. He was ordained & served the pastorate of St. Michael's Church in Bristol, RI, in 1857 to St. John's Church in Keokuk, IA. 4 years later to St. Mark's parish in Frederick Co., MD & at St. Paul's until 1883 when he retired & settled in Middletown with son-in-law Dr. J. E. Beatty, where he d. 3 Oct. 1887. *6TH:751-55*

TRAPNELL, JOSEPH (REV.), b. England, to America early in life. His dau., Sarah m. Affordby Philip Beatty, b. Frederick, MD, of Scotch descent. Episcopal. *6TH:237-38*

TRAVERS, HENRY, from England & settled in Dorchester Co., teacher. Served in the Colonial Legislature 1750-1770. *MDC:332-33*

TRAVERS, SHADRACH, MESHACH & ABEDNEGO, brothers from Ireland to US. One settled in Accomac Co., VA, another in Calvert Co., MD & the third in Washington, DC. Desc. of one of the brothers, William Hicks Travers, res. Dorchester Co., MD, s/o John, a sea captain & resident of the same county. William H. m. Mary Philips. John was s/o Capt. Samuel Hicks Travis, b. 23 Jan. 1811 near Cambridge, Dorchester Co., MD. *MDC:200*

TRAVERS, WILLIAM, & wife Catherine, from England before 1668 & settled in Dorchester Co., MD, where descs. were farmers for several generations. *TR4:367*

TRIPPE, HENRY (LT. COL.), b. Canterbury, England 1632, d. in Dorchester Co., MD March 1698. He fought in Flanders under the Prince of Orange (William III) & to America 1663. He m. Frances, widow of Michael Brooke of St. Leonard's Creek, Calvert Co., 1665. He was married a second time & his second wife d. April 1698. One of his sons was Henry who served as capt. of the Dorchester Co. Militia & d. 1724. He m. Susannah Heron & had 6 children. *TR4:172; GME:53*

TRITAPOE, JOHN, b. Germany & settled in early manhood in Loudoun Co., VA. His son Michael, b. Loudoun Co., VA, Aug. 1799, m. 1st Miss Fry, who d. shortly after their marriage. His 2d wife was Margaret, dau. of Henry & Christina (Spring) Fawley, of Loudoun Co. Their son Samuel served in Co. A of the Loudoun Rangers in the Civil War. After the war he farmed in VA & in 1882 removed to Frederick Co., MD. He m. Sarah E., d/o George & Susan (Frey) Vincel of Loudoun Co. Their children: Ada Va., at home; Edward H. of Petersville District; Gertrude A. m. David C. Sulcer of Jefferson, MD; Alvira E. m. Arthur Poffenberger of Jefferson District; Harry G. of Frederick City and Earl E., at home. *FR2:1172-3*

TROTTER, JOHN REYNOLDS, b. Glasgow, Scotland 17 Feb. 1879, s/o James Trotter and Catherine Loan. Father James b. Scotland 1848, master plumber, d. aged 56. Son John Reynolds Trotter to US 1899, located to NY City, later to Summit, NJ; 1904 to Baltimore, plumber. He m. 1 July 1909, Anna Louise Schuchardt at St. Michael's & All Angels Episcopal Church. Anna d/o Henry & Catherine (Wills) Schuchardt, of German descent. *TR3:234*

TROTTER, PETER, b. Mid Lothian, Scotland in 1813, s/o William who d. 1858 & Jean Fogry, d/o John of Mid Lothian. Jean d. in Scotland in 1872. Peter was 9th of their 11 children. He came to America in 1853, landed in NY & was indentured to William Oliver, of Lone Head, Haddingtonshire, Scotland. He removed to Tipperary Co., Ireland & engaged in agricultural blacksmithing for 4 years. In 1855 located in Bryantown, Chalres Co., MD, blacksmith, carriage & wagon maker. Protestant Episcopal. He m. in 1852, in Ireland, Harriet Quarman, d/o Henry of England. *MDC:455*

TRUNDLE, JOHN, s/o David of Suffolk, England who was b. 1574, d. 1671, to America in 1649 & settled at Herring Creek, Anne Arundel Co., MD. He was b. in Suffolk, England in 1624, d. 3 Aug. 1699 at Herring Creek. He m. Mary [Ross?] & had at least one son, John Trundle II (1687-1771). *TR4:770; GME:26*

TRUOG, GEORGE, b. Verona, Italy in 1861. Resided in various counties of Europe, set sail in Dec. 1883 for America. He spent 4 years in Wheeling, WV, employed at the Central Glass Works & in 1887 to Cumberland, MD. In 1892 organized the Seneca Glass Co. at Morgantown, WV & in 1893 started the MD Glass Etching Works. He was the s/o George & Mary (G'Frey) Truog, both b. Switzerland. George m. Barbara Wegman in 1888. *6TH:642-43*

TUERKE, GEORGE, from Harz Mt. district of Prussia to US before Civil War; m. Miss Appel, settled Newark, NJ. Their son Otto Tuerke, b. Newark, NJ, res. in NJ until 1865, when he came to Baltimore. Trunk manufacturer, retired in 1912. Lutheran. Otto m. Elizabeth Fessman, of an old MD family. Her grandfather was b. Germany & his son, Philip Fessman, b. in MD. Philip m. a Miss Potzer, who was b. in France, & they res. in Baltimore. *TR3:28*

TUNSTALL, ALEXANDER, b. England, m. Anne McCauley Walke. Became American citizen after the Rev. War made president of Farmers Bank of Norfolk, VA. Their son was Dr. Robert Taylor Tunstall. Desc.

Robert Tunstall Taylor, physician of Kernan Hospital in Baltimore, MD. *TR4:621-2*

TURNER, ---, of Scotch-Irish ancestry, to America before the Rev. War & owned an estate in Wicomico Co., MD. His son, John, m. Alice Anderson & they had John W. Turner, b. Nanticoke, MD. In 1860 John W. removed to VA. He was Methodist & d. in Baltimore 20 July 1902 from the effects of a sunstroke at the age of 48. *TR4:463*

TURNER, ROBERT, of English family, to MD 1687 & became one of the proprietors of Easton, NJ. His great-grandson, Capt. Daniel Turner, was soldier in the Rev. War. "From this Daniel, through another Robert, a Benjamin & John Duffield, came Leonidas Grant Turner, who has not only materially assisted in the upbuilding of Baltimore, but who is the father of a family whose male members have offered their lives in defense of their country." Leonidas was b. in NJ, s/o John Street & Ruth L. (Charlesworth) Turner. He m. Amelia Archer in Harford Co., MD, d/o Roland Dutton Archer, of a pre-Rev. family in MD. *TR4:837-8*

TWEED, ROBERT, b. Scotland, to America 1841, at age of 16, located in New Orleans, LA. His last years were spent in NY City. He served in the Civil War in the commissary dept. of the Army of the Confederacy & d. 1897, aged 72. Desc. Robert Tweed m. Virginia Vanuxem & their dau. Mary Virginia Tweed, b. Charleston, SC, m. Rev. James J. Chisolm. Their son, Dr. J. Julian Chisolm, b. Winchester, Clark Co., KY, 24 Dec. 1889, raised in Natchez, MS, now practicing physician of Baltimore. The Chisolm family was founded in America by Alexander Chisolm, who settled in Charleston, SC in 1746. *TR3:825-6*

TYLER, JOHN, b. England 11 April 1784, d. 24 April 1872. His son William Tyler, b. Prince George's Co., MD. About 1798 William removed to Fredericktown, MD, where his elder brother, Dr. John Tyler had preceded him. He studied medicine under his brother & completed his studies in 1807. William served in various political offices. He m. Mary Addison & had sons Samuel & William. *FR2:-1398-9*

TYSON, REYNEAR, emigrated to PA at the request of Wiliam Penn. Reynear arrived on ship *Concord* at PA 6 Oct. 1683 & settled at Germantown in 1689, where he served as burgess & other public offices. He was a Quaker, member of the Abingdon Friends' Meeting, & d. 27 July 1745, aged c. 86. His wife was Margaret Kunders. Their grandson (s/o Mathias & Mary (Potts) Tyson) b. in Philadelphia 1718, to Baltimore Co. 1789. *TR4:734-6; GME:221*

ULMAN, BENJAMIN F., b. city of Lombheim, on the Danube, near Ulm, Germany, 28 Jan. 1836. To America at age 15, landed at Philadelphia, where he had relatives. After a year he went to Snow Hill, MD & then to New Town, MD. Later, in connection with his brother, Alfred I. Ulman, he entered into the wholesale liquor business in Baltimore. 23 Nov. 1856 he m. Henrietta Benjamin, dau. of the late Levi & Rachel Benjamin, of Baltimore. Benjamin & Alfred were the sons of Jacob Ulman, b. in the City of Ulm, Wurtemberg, and Bertha Laubheimer. When the parents died all six of their children emigrated to America. The other children were: Beber, Matilda, Henrietta & Solomon. All are married & living in Baltimore with the exception of Solomon, who d. several years ago in Chicago. *MDC:154*

UNDERHILL, JOHN (CAPT.), arrived in America with Gov. Winthrop in 1630 & settled in MA Colony. He was closely associated with Roger Williams & was driven from the colony owing to political & religious views. Desc. Joshua James Underhill, b. Somerset Co., MD, in 1865 to Baltimore until 1900, when he went to Los Angeles, CA, where he d. aged 62. Joshua's parents were William J. & Nancy (McCready) Underhill of Albermarle Co., VA. Nancy's father was a German immigrant who settled in Baltimore. She res. Los Angeles. *TR4:740-1*

UNVERZAGT, HENRY, s/o John & Caroline (Pabst), b. near Hesse Darmstadt, Germany 28 May 1833. To America 1852, landed in NY, to Philadelphia, PA and later to Baltimore, MD. Later settled near Harmony (then Bellsville) Frederick Co., MD; shoemaker; m. Magdaline E., d/o Ludwig & Magdaline E. (Bent) Ropp, who had emigrated from Germany to America in early life. Ropps later resided in IN. *FR2:732*

UPSHUR, ARTHUR, from Warwickshire, England during the 17th century. Descendant George M. Upshur, M.D., b. Northampton Co., VA, s/o James & Susan (Martin), m. Priscilla A. Townsend in 1839. She is d/o Levin Townsend of Snow Hill, Worcester Co., MD. Their son George M. Upshur, b. Snow Hill, Worcester Co., MD 14 Dec. 1847. *MDC:270*

URIE, THOMAS, of Glasgow, Scotland, b. 1725 & d. in Kent Co., MD 1794, where he had settled c. 1747. Manufacturer of tobacco hogsheads, flour barrels, etc. Member of Old St. Paul's Episcopal Church. In 1751 he m. Martha Clark. *TR4:504*

URNER, ---, of canton of Uri in Switzerland, settled in Chester Co., PA. Jonas Urner from Chester Co. to MD & located in what was then Frederick Co. (now Carroll Co.), MD, on Sam's Creek. Jonas had ten children, one was Samuel, b. Chester Co., PA 1797 & d. Frederick Co., MD 1872. Samuel m. twice, (1) Elizabeth Snader, d/o Jacob of Frederick Co. & (2) Susannah Norris, d/o Amos. *FR2:990-2*

UTZ, DANIEL, b. Amsterdam, Germany 22 Oct. 1728. German Baptist minister. He & 2 brothers to America at early date. One brother to OH and one to VA. Daniel settled near Hanover, York Co., PA, where he d. 15 Nov. 1818, aged 90; buried in Hanover. Son Daniel, b. near Hanover 1769, m. Eve Bolinger, Dunkard Church member; son John b. York Co. 12 Nov. 1801 and after marriage settled near Gettysburg, Adams Co., PA. Later removed to MD. John Utz m. Elizabeth Hohf. *FR2:730*

ALLIANT, JOHN, of an old French Huguenot family. During the reign of Louis XIV his father Jean fled to London. John to America at an early age. He obtained by patent land in Talbot Co., MD, Tred Avon River. *MDC:382*

VAN BIBBER, JACOB ISAACS, a Hollander, one of the first settlers of Germantown, PA (1680), came with William Penn. Jacob to Cecil Co., MD in 1700. His sons, Isaac & Matthias, b. Holland, were naturalized in MD in 1702. They res. for a time in Philadelphia before coming to MD. Isaac's will, proved in 1723, names his children: Jacob, Peter, Isaac, Hester, Christiana & Veronica. Matthias' will was proved in 1739 & names children: Jacob, Adam, Matthias, Henry, Sarah, Rebecca, Christiana & Hester. Another son of the immigrant was Henry, who came to Cecil Co., MD c. 1720. *C:136-8; H/C:164*

VAN DORSNER, ---, d/o Gen. Franz van Dorser, b. Hungary, m. Jesse Slingluff, b. Baltimore, MD. Son Charles Bohn Slingluff, b. Baltimore, attorney had son Jesse b. Baltimore 7 June 1870. *TR3:289*

VAN SWEARINGEN, GARRETT, a desc. of an old Bavarian family, b. in Holland in 1636 & d. 1712. He m. Barbara De Barrett, of Norman-

French lineage in 1660 & settled in Anne Arundel Co., MD. Their son Thomas, b. 1665, m. Jane --- & had son Van (1695-1785), m. Elizabeth Walker of Patuxent, MD. *AAH:320*

VANDERWEIR, JACOB, to America from Holland c. 1655 & settled near what is now Wilmington, DE (Christianna). Many descendants settled DE & MD. *H/C:311-14*

VEAZEY, JOHN, planter of Cecil Co., MD, of the family of Vesey of "Wickes," in co. of Essex, England. He was a member of North Sassafras (St. Stephens) parish. In 1697 his family consisted of his wife Martha & 5 sons. He d. c. 1700. His eldest son William m. Rossamond & had one child, Susanna, b. 20 Jan. 1696, m. John Ward 25 March 1717. *TR4:258*

VICKERS, EDWARD, from England to New Haven, CT 1670, d. 1684. His son George served in King Philip's War & m. Rebecca, d/o David Phippeny of Hull, MA. Their son George also had a son George b. 14 Aug. 1688 & m. Elizabeth Binney 12 Nov. 1713. Their son, also George Vickers, m. Lydia Tower in 1730 & soon afterward he & his wife moved to the Eastern Shore of MD. Their third son, George, b. 26 Jan. 1742, m. Rachel Roberts & had a son in Kent Co., MD 14 Aug. 1744, Joel. *TR4:132*

VOCKE, CLAAS, b. 18 Nov. 1815, at Emden, then kingdom of Hanover, Germany, s/o G. L. Charles Vocke, who d. at Emen 1869, aged 86 & --- Tholen. To Baltimore, MD in 1837. He later returned to his native city & m. Johanna E., d/o William L. Abegg; she d. 1852. In 1846 he & wife left Bremerhaven for Baltimore. *MDC:364*

ACHTER, ----, to America with one or more brothers, & located in PA & later moved to Frederick Co., MD in what is now the Tuscarora District, near Bethel. He had a son Philip, b. c. 1785, who m. Anna M. McCormac. *FR2:1593-4*

WACHTER, ---, from Wurtemberg, Germany in 1749 on ship *Speedwell*, landing at Philadelphia. One year later he moved to Frederick Co., MD. Desc. Henry Wachter (1816-1851) m. Sarah Kiser. *TR4:638-40*

WACHTER, MICHAEL, b. Germany, with wife Maria to America & settled in PA. Later removed to Frederick Co., MD, where he was among other early settlers. His son Jacob was b. 27 Dec. 1789. Jacob's son Michael, b. 9 May 1821, now living at the age of 88 at Utica Mills, Frederick Co. Blacksmith & farmer, Michael m. Rebecca Reese, b. 1823. Members of St. Paul's Lutheran Church. *FR2:724, 1225-6*

WAESCHE, HENRY, b. 1801 Germany, to America with uncle, raised in Baltimore City, later resided Carroll Co., MD; d. 1849 in Panama on way to gold fields of CA. He was Methodist, m. Catharine Castle, d/o Leonard of Carroll Co., MD. Children: George, dec'd.; William, farmer of Montgomery Co., MD; John, farmer of Montgomery Co.; Joseph, merchant at Westminster, MD; Rapold, dec'd.; Leonard Randolph; James Theodore of Thurmont; Charles of Baltimore & Catharine, dec'd. *FR2:727*

WAGNER, DANIEL (REV.), b. in Eibelshausen, Germany 11 Jan. 1750; to America at age of 2 with parents. Served at Tulpenhocken and York, PA and to Frederick, MD 1802-1810. *FR1:411*

WALKER, FRANCIS, of English desc. from family that in the 16th century fled to Holland. Francis left Holland in 1732 & settled in Prince George, now Frederick Co., MD. He was accompanied by 3 sons: Jacob who eventually settled in Somerset Co., PA (c. 1771); and George, who settled in Frederick Co., where he d. of hydrophobia. Francis was Protestant & his wife was Roman Catholic [not named here]. *FR2:1271-2*

WALKER, GEORGE, b. Scotland, from early manhood a resident of what is now Harford Co., MD. His son, George, b. Harford Co., d. aged 86. His son, George, b. Churchville, MD, was farmer near Perryman all his life; m. Susan Co. Their son, also George Walker, b. in Aberdeen, Presbyterian & living at the time the book was published. *H/C:363*

WALKER, ROBERT, b. Ireland, to America as young man, settled Portland, ME & after War of 1812 to Harford Co., MD where he m. d/o Christian Hoopman. Robert d. c. age 70. Methodist Protestant. *H/C:281*

WALLACE, ANDREW, b. Scotland 1672, settled Cecil Co., MD before 1700. Andrew m. Ellinor Wallace, his cousin, she d. 8 Dec. 1753, aged 78; he d. 3 March 1751, aged 79 years. *H/C:236*

WALLACE, JOHN LECOMPTE, Huguenot refugee, emigrated to America & settled on the Choptank River, in what is now Dorchester Co. *MDC:524*

WALLACE, OATES CHARLES SYMONDS, b. 28 Nov. 1856, Canaan, Kings Co., Nova Scotia, s/o William John & Rachel Louise (Witter) Wallace. William Wallace was b. in Halifax, & d. in Canaan Jan. 1906, aged 81. He was s/o Robert Wallace & Christina McClellan & grandson of William Wallace who migrated from Scotland to the North of Ireland & thence to NC, a Tory who after the Rev. War had his estate confiscated & removed to Rawdon, Hants Co., Nova Scotia. Two of the immigrant's sons returned to NC, but one settled permanently in IN & the other in Ontario. Rev. Oates C. S. Wallace served in Lawrence MA, Toronto Canada, Lowell MA, Montreal Canada & was pastor of Eutaw Place Baptist Church of Baltimore (1921). He m. Helen Moore, d/o Rev. John Wright & Louisa (Fish) Moore of New Brunswick, 2 March 1919. *TR4:478-80*

WALLIS, ALBERT, b. Wales, to MD "more than a century ago." He had at least one son, Samuel, who had Albert E. Wallis, b. Harford Co., MD 1844 & d. Frederick City in 1891. Member of the ME Church, Albert E. m. (1) Mrs. Columbia Duvall, nee Dutrow. They had one child, Albert A., & after her death he m. (2) her sister, Rebecca E., d/o Samuel & Elizabeth Ann (Geisbert) Dutrow, of an old Frederick Co. family. *FR2:1282-3*

WALSH, JOHN, b. Ireland, settled in Baltimore, MD; lumber business. His son John Carroll Walsh, b. in Baltimore; at age of 17 went to Ft. Madison, IA where he bought land & stayed 4 years. Returned to MD & settled in Harford Co., where he d. 1 Dec. 1894. Catholic. John Carroll Walsh m. Amanda Lee, d/o Dr. Ralph Lee, physician of Washington, DC. *H/C:578-9*

WALSH, MICHAEL, s/o Thomas & Catherine Walsh of Glynn, Co. Limerick, Ireland. Michael m. Mary Houck, d/o George & Elizabeth (Brown) Houck in 1860 & settled in the Hampstead District of Carroll Co., MD. *TR4:323*

WALSH, RABUCK, m. Ellen Carey, both b. Ireland. Their son Michael m. Margaret Mansfield & their dau. May Ellen Walsh m. Judge Joseph Baptist Mannix. Their dau. Margaret Mary Mannix of Cincinnati, OH m.

in San Diego, CA 1 June 1910, William Joseph Gough of Sacramento, CA, b. 20 Feb. 1883, near Leonardtown, St. Mary's Co., MD. Catholic family. *TR4:533-4*

WALSH, WILLIAM, b. 1 May 1828 in Ireland, to America at age 14 & located in VA. Later removed to MD & eventually resided in Cumberland. Lawyer. In 1853 he m. Marian Shane. Catholic. *MDC:690*

WALTER, ---, Dutch baron, to America with Lord Baltimore & built first house on the site of the City of Baltimore. His son was robbed & murdered on the Hookstown Rd. near Baltimore. Son John Walter, b. Baltimore 1799, shoemaker; in 1820 removed to Emmitsburg. John was married two times & had 23 children. His first wife was Agnes Barnes & second was Mary Hobbs, d/o John, b. 1830 in Emmitsburg District. *FR2:965-6*

WALTER, JOHN, b. Germany 1825, to America at age 16. Was orphaned when young & was a res. of Frederick Co., MD "since his youth." He m. Elizabeth Pampel in 1848 [1847], she d/o his first employer, Mr. F. Pampel. Eight of their 10 children reached maturity: Sarah C. m. John O. Smith, lumber merchant of Hagerstown; Jacob W. of Hanover, PA; Alice V. m. Jacob F. Snyder, retired farmer of Germantown, MD; Charles G., dec'd.; Lewis C., locksmith of Frederick Co., MD; Florence M. m. William F. Snyder, res. Frederick City; Edward H., optician in Hanover, PA; Bertie E. m. (1) Prof. Mitchell E. Daniels of Vergennes, VT & (2) James F. Eldridge of Washington, DC. *FR2:981-2; 6TH:298-9*

WALTERS, BENJAMIN, from England to Eastern Shore of MD with 2 of his brothers. Settled on Kent Island. *6TH:776-77*

WALTON, DANIEL, 1 of 4 brothers, Quaker, left England in 1675 & settled near Philadelphia, PA. Desc. Samuel Walton to Harford Co., MD where he m. Elizabeth Hopkins Moore, d/o Benjamin P. They had 10 children, the eldest son being William Ellis Walton, who went west. In 1873 to NY & the next year m. Ellen Janney, d/o Henry & Hannah R. Janney. In 1876 moved to NE; 1893 moved back to MD. *TR4:180*

WALTZ, RINEHART, to America from Antwerp, Germany & settled in Liberty District, Frederick Co., MD, where he d. c. 1835. He is bur.

at Union Chapel; Luthern. His children were Isaac, Lewis, Solomon, Jesse, Mary & Jemima. *FR2:1273-4*

WALZI, JOHN, burgomaster of Stein, Austria, emigrated with his family to America & settled in Baltimore, MD 1852. His son Richard Edmund b. 14 Oct. 1843 in Stein, later settled in Harford Co. Photographer. He later removed to Baltimore. Richard m. in June 1874 Henrietta E. Scheib, 3d d/o Rev. Henry of Baltimore. *MDC:391*

WALZI, JOHN HENRY, b. 23 June 1833 in Stein, on the Danube, Lower Austria. To America to evade the German draft in 1853 & landed in NY. Two years later he removed to Hoboken, NJ & later to Baltimore, MD, in 1854 associated with him Beeckman Cooke in the daguerreotype business. He became a leader of photography in Baltimore and developed land in VA. He m. 1857 Augusta Eisenbrandt, d/o Christian H., musical manufacturer of Baltimore & native of Gottingen, Germany, to America 1812. *MDC:684-85*

WARBURTON, THOMAS, b. England & direct desc. of Bishop Warburton of Gloucestershire, England; to America in young manhood & settled in Cecil Co., farmer & Methodist preacher. He d. 1857, aged 84. He m. a d/o John & Elizabeth McCauley, of an old Scotch family that settled in Cecil Co. in an early day. *H/C:369-70*

WARD, JAMES, b. Ireland, to America at age 12, having left with parents & 3 sisters. He landed in New Brunswick, proceeded to PA & learned blacksmith trade. He resided in Frederick Co., MD & d. Nov. 1876, aged 71. Member United Brethren Church. His wife was Catherine Metzger, d. in 1882, aged 81. *6TH:498-500*

WARD, JOHN, b. London, England 1 Aug. 1747 (O.S.), m. Mary Ann Eustatia Forbes, b. London 1 Jan. 1752. To America 1770 & settled in Prince George's Co., & to Montgomery Co. 1776. John's ancestors had been from Yorkshire, England & his branch of the family removed to London at the beginning of the 18th century. *MDC:373*

WARFIELD, RICHARD, (1676-1755) from Berkshire, England in 1662 to Anne Arundel Co., MD; member of assembly for the county 1716-1723 & 1727-1731. He m. Ellen [Eleanor] Browne, d/o Capt. John of London who came from England in 1673. John Browne, with his brother Capt. Peregrine Brown, ran 2 transports from London to Annapolis.

Richard Warfield's will, probated in 1703, names his eldest son John. In 1696 John Warfield m. Ruth Gaither, eldest d/o John of South River, who had come into MD from VA in 1662. *GME:213; TR4:355, 810-16*

WARING, SAMPSON (CAPT.), of "The Cliffs," Calvert Co., MD, was in the province as early as 1641, atty. In his will, dated 18 Jan. 1663, he named wife Sarah & son Basil as his only child, then a minor. Basil was b. in Calvert Co. c. 1650. By his 2d m. to Sarah, d/o Richard Marsham & wife Ann, he had 2 children. Basil d. 1688. Richard Marsham emigrated to the province before 1650. He had no sons & refers to dau. Sarah in his will (probated 1713) as Sarah Haddock, formerly wife of Basil Waring. He also names grandson Leonard Brooke, s/o Baker Brooke. *TR4:321*

WARNER, JOSEPH, from England with the followers of William Penn & settled in Bucks Co., PA, where he m. Ruth Hayhurst, b. there. He moved to MD & settled in Harford Co. Son Andrew Ellicott Warner, b. Harford Co. 27 Nov. 1786. *MDC:184*

WARNER, WILLIAM (CAPT.), b. Draycot in the parish of Blockley, Worcestershire, England. Captain of the bodyguard of Oliver Cromwell, left England 1658. First to New England, then to PA; descendant Charles A. Warner, s/o C. Anderson Warner (b. 1832) & Margaret d/o Morris & Margaret (Ott) Hansell, to Burkettsville, MD to farm of his mother-in-law. Charles A. m. Carrie M., d/o Luther & Rebecca (Sheffer) Horine. *FR2:719*

WARNOCK, PHILIP, of Scotch desc., to MD from Northern Ireland 1774. His dau. Sarah m. 3 Dec. 1807, Silas Hollingsworth, b. 14 June 1766, of Harford Co., MD. Philip's Charity m. 1806, Benjamin Silver. *H/C:519-20; MDC:281*

WARRENFELTZ, JACOB, b. Germany 1751, to America with parents who settled in MD. He d. 1815, Frederick Co., MD. He m. Hannah Hartman & had: Jacob; John; Philip; Peter (1793-1864); Catharine, m. Conrad Green; Susan, m. William Patton; Hannah, m. Daniel Gernand; Mary, m. Christian Weller; Christina, m. Daniel Leatherman; Magdelena, m. John Firor & Elizabeth, m. Paul Marker. *FR2:727*

WATERS, EDWARD (LT.), of Yorkshire, England, to VA on the ship *Patience* in 1608 at the age of 40 & had previously been in the Bermudas. His wife was Grace O'Neil, who had also come out to Bermuda from the British Isles. Edward's immediate descs. settled in Somerset Co., MD. Their children, William & Margaret, b. in Elizabeth Co., VA & Lt. Edward d. 1630 at Great Hormead, Hertfordshire, England. His son William was b. c. 1619 and was left in the care of his uncle John Waters of Middleham, Yorkshire & lived to age 70, taking an active part in VA affairs serving as justice of Northampton in 1659. He m. several times & had sons William, Edward, Richard, John, Obedience & Thomas. Son Edward inherited lands in Somerset Co., MD at Annimessex, and Richard & John inherited half each of "Low Neck" at Annimessex. Son John settled on his Somerset Co. lands & his son William m. Rose Anne Harmanson in 1739. She was d/o Col. George & Elizabeth (Yardley) Harmanson of Northampton Co., VA.

In 1635 John Waters, supposed to be Edward's nephew, arrived in VA. A John Waters who appears on MD Rent Rolls in 1676 was the owner of Waters Adventure & supposed to be the progenitor of the family on the Western Shore. *TR4:305-6, 704-7*

WATKINS, THOMAS, of Wales, to MD. His dau. Sarah m. Edward Andre, b. near Seafrod, DE. Family to Dorchester Co., MD when son James Eidgway Andre was aged 10. *MDC:80*

WATSON, JAMES, b. Londonderry, Ireland, to America at age 50, settled Adams Co., PA; m. Mary Bond, widow of William Hineman. Son Dr. Robert (dentist) b. 11 March 1820, Adams Co., m. Hannah, d/o David & Mary (Bonebrake) Mentzer of Franklin Co., PA. Son John M. removed to Sabillasville, MD, m. Alice, d/o the late David and Maria (Hess) Crawford. *FR2:718*

WAXTER, WILLIAM P., b. Germany 1838, to US 1844, s. 1913. Ice manufacturer of Baltimore, MD. He m. Elizabeth Margene. *TR3:286*

WEBB, CHRISTOPER, to America in 1645 & Abner a desc., fought in Continental Army during the Rev. His son William Prescott Webb m. Anna Eliza Moore, was b. in Baltimore, MD & had son Armstead Moore Webb, b. Baltimore 29 Aug. 1862. *TR4:167*

WEBB, CHRISTOPHER, from Barking, County Essex, England in 1626, with 2 sons & 2 daughters. One son, Christopher Jr., settled in Braintree (now Quincy) MA. Nov. 18, 1654 Christopher Jr. m. Hannah Scott, dau. of Benjamin. Christopher Jr. d. 30 May 1694. Desc. Oscar

Everett Webb was a lifelong res. of Baltimore, b. there 2 June 1858, s/o Albert Lee & Catherine Ann (Deford) Webb. *TR4:760*

WEBB, ELIZABETH, from Gloucester, England, missionary, left her husband & children to travel with Mary Rogers to America in 1697. She returned to America & settled in Birmingham, Chester Co., PA, near Brandywyne in 1699. *H/C:119*

WEBB, RICHARD, from Gloucester, England in 1732, settled in PA. Accompanied by James Webb, b. England 1708, member of the PA assembly 1747-75 & other patriotic service. Desc. Elizabeth Ark Webb m. James H. Rowland of Port Deposit, MD. *TR4:395*

WEBER, CHARLES, b. at Obersuhl, Hesse Cassel, Germany, 18 Sept. 1821, s/o J. Weber, a minister of the German Reformed Church. His mother was of a French Huguenot family that setteled in Bremen. Charles was 4 years of age when his father died. He sailed from Bremen to Baltimore, MD in 1842 & m. Augusta, d/o Rev. J. C. Bachmann, minister of the German Reformed Church in Germany. *MDC:217*

WEBER, HENRY, b. province of Hesse-Cassel, Germany in 1835, s/o John & Elizabeth. Henry served in the British army in the Crimean war (1854-55) & for the next 10 years was stationed at points around the world. In 1865 to America & with his brother John, embarked in farming & market gardening near Mt. Savage, MD. After 5 years to Cumberland with John. He m. 1866 Catherine Schutz in Mt. Savage. *6TH:218-19*

WEBSTER, ---, From England with William Penn, brothers John (settled Roanoke, VA), Samuel, Michael & Isaac. [MDC:474 names the immigrating brothers as Richard (settled in MD), Michael (settled in New England), Isaac & John.] Isaac settled in Harford Co., MD on Bush River. 14 Nov. 1747 granted 265 acres by Lord Baltimore in what is now Churchville precinct, Harford Co. His wife was Margaret Lee. They had John b. 1670, & Henry W. Webster who m. Harriet J. Dallaran. Their dau., Sophia Horne Webster, m. Theodore Cook, Jr., M.D. of Baltimore. *H/C:173, 215; TR3:774-5; MDC:474*

WEBSTER, SAMUEL, held a commission from the English Crown as Inspector of Tobacco at Joppa, MD. His son Richard was a Methodist minister. Richard's son Henry resided near Churchville, Harford Co. & m. Martha Hanson, d/o Benjamin of Kent Co., MD. *MDC:530-31*

WEBSTER, SUSAN S., b. Montreal Canada, m. James Doeg Todd, b. NY. Son William Edward Todd, M.D., of Hagerstown, MD since 1910, b. Willow Creek, WI 26 April 1861. She d. 1912; James d. 1914. William m. 24 Nov. 1890, in Altamont, KS, Maude Augusta Roller, d/o Addison B. & Elizabeth (Bean) Roller, both b. Staunton, VA. *TR3:464-5*

WEEMS, DAVID, brought from Scotland to America by his uncle, Dr. Lock. He m. Margaret Harrison, of noble English descent & had 5 sons. Grandson Capt. George Weems, b. Marshall Seat, Anne Arundel Co., MD 23 May 1784. *MDC:607-08*

WEINBERG, ABRAHAM, b. Vienna, s/o Abraham & Margaret. He immigrated to the US in 1840, dealer in livestock. His wife was Regina Blum, d/o Joseph & Selma, who res. for a time in Budapest, Hungary, & also became res. of Vienna, Austria. Abraham d. in Baltimore, MD April 1922; Regina d. 24 Oct. 1911, aged 75. Their son, Daniel A. Weinberg, b. in Baltimore April 1871. *TR3:668-9*

WEINBERG, BENEDICT, b. Westphalia, Germany, emigrated to US prior to Civil War. His son, Abraham, b. Charleston, SC, m. Lizzie Iseman and their son, Dr. Myer A. Weinberg, physician of Baltimore, b. at Darlington, SC, March 1879. Myer grad. with M.D. from Univ. of MD in 1904 & m. 14 June 1910 in Baltimore, Regina Gichner, d/o Jacob. *TR3:361*

WEINBERG, LAZARUS, & wife Bertha Goldstein, to America & settled in NY in 1861; a short time later relocated to Baltimore, MD. Lazarus was a cantor & a Hebrew teacher. He d. 1916, aged 92. His wife d. 9 Feb. 1913, aged 80; both d. in Baltimore. They had 7 children & son Abraham I. was 2 years old when the family moved to Baltimore in 1865. In 1897 he m. Carrie Katz, d/o the late Kaufman Katz. *TR3:908-11*

WEINBERG, SAMUEL, German-Hebrew descent, emigrated & landed at Baltimore, MD in 1850, when he was age 16. He settled in Frederick, MD in 1860. In 1863 he m. Amelia Lowenstein, eldest sister of ex-Alderman David Lowenstein of Frederick, then a res. of Baltimore. Their living children: Henry, clothier of Hagerstown, MD; David of Frederick;

253

Isaac in Lexington, VA; Clara, m. E. E. Wachter, res. Hagerstown, MD; Leo & Jeannette, lives with her father in Frederick. *FR2:1463-4; TR3:42*

WEINER, MORRIS (M.D.), b. in Berlin, Prussia, 15 Jan. 1812, s/o Jasper, a banker, & --- Morris, b. near Glasgow, Scotland. Graduated Univ. of Berlin in 1836, to US 1842 & in 1849 settled in Baltimore, MD. *MDC:268*

WEITZMAN, LOUIS, & wife Lena --, b. Russia, to the US & settled in NY City. Louis, a minister, is now retired. Their dau., Frances Edith Weitzman, b. NY City, studied at the Woman's Medical College at Baltimore, grad. 1903. She first practiced at Norfolk, VA, but shortly removed to East Radford, VA. She then removed to Baltimore, MD until 1907, when she moved to Philadelphia, PA & from there to Annapolis, MD, where she remains. First woman doctor in the Annapolis area. *TR3:796*

WEST, ---, American ancestor of this family from England & settled in Prince George Co., MD. Desc. Joseph West, one of the early settlers of Petersville district, Frederick Co., MD & had son, Levin West, farmer of the same district. His children: Thomas H.; Patrick McGill (1825-1904); Erasmus; Sarah; Mary; Susan & Elizabeth. *FR2:872*

WEST, STEPHEN, s/o Sir John of "Houghton" (Buckinghamshire, England), m. Martha Hall in 1720. He was the immigrant & settled in Anne Arundel Co., MD c. 1720. His son, Stephen Jr., m. Hannah Williams, d/o Capt. Williams of Wales & his wife Christiana Black of Scotland. The immgrant's dau., Martha West, m. John Lawrence. *AAH:434; GME:394*

WESTCOTT, STUKELY, b. 1592, to America in 1636 in company with Roger Williams & settled at Salem, MA, where he d. 1677. Christopher Westcott, 6th in desc. from Stukely, was b. in NY 12 Jan. 1773 & res. Foster, RI in 1794. He m. Martha Gerauld 27 Nov. 1805. Their son Sardius D. Westcott m. Harriet Lord Walling, both b. NY. Their son, Dr. James Walling Westcott, b. Perrysburg, OH, 28 Dec. 1861, is pharmacist of Baltimore, MD who m. Minnie Shield Kendall there in 1890. *TR4:624-30*

WHEELER, JOHN (GEN.), immigrated to MD 1658. His son, Francis Wheeler m. Mildred Green, d/o Thomas, who came to MD in the *Ark and the Dove*, March 25, 1634. Thomas Green was appointed gov. *TR4:345*

WHITAKER, JOSEPH, s/o James, a large cloth manufacturer of Leeds, England, to US & m. Sarah Updegrove. Their youngest & only surviving son, George Price Whitaker, b. 31 Dec. 1803 in Berks Co., PA & later was ironmaster, Principio Furnace, Cecil Co., MD. *MDC:661-62*

WHITE, GUY, transported to Colony of MD 1648; m. Sarah Wright. Their son, Guy II, was of Prince George's Co., MD & m. Elizabeth Griffith, d/o Samuel, b. Wales, to MD before 1651 & settled on the Patuxent River in Calvert Co. Samuel Griffith m. in Wales Elizabeth Price whose will was filed in Calvert Co. 17 Dec. 1718. *TR4:516-18*

WHITE, JOHN, of Hulcote, England, who d. in 1501. John was s/o Thomas & Elizabeth (Fisher) White, of Bedfordshire, England, and was b. Aug. 1624. To America 1644-1650. John the immigrant d. in Somerset Co., MD Oct 3 1685. He m. Sarah Stevens in 1652 d/o Col. William Stevens; settled Pocomoke, Somerset Co., MD. *GME:26.*

WHITE, JOHN, rec'd. a warrant to 200 acres of land from Lord Baltimore. His son Israel had a son Milton who was b. 1802 in Cecil Co., MD, d. at age of 90 in 1892. Milton's wife was Martha Caldwell of Farmington, MD. *H/C:550-1*

WHITE, JOHN CAMPBELL, Irish patriot, settled Baltimore 1801. First president of the Ancient Order of Hibernians. Desc. changed spelling to WHYTE. *TR3:67*

WHITE, WALTER WALTON, & wife Grace Elizabeth Ewens, both b. England, Walter in Oxford & Grace in London. Walter s/o John W. & Anne (Walton) White; he d. 1904 aged 61, physician. Grace d. 1901, aged 48. *TR3:315*

WHITEFORD, MICHAEL & WILLIAM, to America from Ireland c. 1720 & located on PA-MD border. *H/C:286*

WHITMORE, ---, from Germany to America & settled in Carroll Co., MD. His son, Jacob Whitmore, b. Carroll Co., farmer, m. Susan Kuntz. They res. at Graceham, Frederick Co., MD, where he d. aged 80. Susan

d. 2 years later, being over 70 years old. Members of the Reformed Church. *FR2:1619-20*

WHITNEY, HENRY, settled in Watertown, MA 1715. Desc. Henry Whitney m. Lucy Sprague, res. Berkshire Co., MA. Their son Henry J. m. Jennie MacArthur, b. Glasgow, Scotland, d/o John & Jean (Gilespie) MacArthur of Paisley, Scotland. Son Peter Whitney, b. 8 Dec. 1863, in North Adams, MA, removed 1890 to NY City, where he was in the banking business until 1910, when he removed to Baltimore, MD. He m. in North Adams, MA 15 Dec. 1888, Carrie M. Smith, d/o Homer & Marie (Foss) Smith, res. of Berkshire. *TR4:393*

WHITNEY, JOHN, of old English family, in April 1634, with his family, on ship *Elizabeth & Ann*, landed in MA & settled at Watertown. He was a freeman there 1636 & appointed constable in 1641. His son John was b. in 1621 in London, England, d. Watertown, 1692. John m. Ruth Reynolds in 1642 & had Nathaniel Whitney, b. 1646. Nathaniel m. Sarah Hagar & d. at Weston, MA 1732. Their son, William Whitney, b. 6 May 1683, d. 24 Jan. 1720 at Weston. William m. 17 May 1706 Martha Pierce & had son Samuel, b. 1719 & m. Abigail Fletcher 1741. Samuel d. at Westminster, MA 1782 & his son, Silas Whitney, b. 20 Oct. 1752, served as capt. in the Continental army. In 1774 Silas m. Sarah Withington & he d. at Ashburnham, MA 1798. He was the father of Silas Whitney, b. 1 Oct. 1799, served as capt. in the War of 1812, m. Hannah Cushing 1801 & d. in MA 4 Sept. 1846. Silas & Hannah's son, Joseph Cushing Whitney, b. at Ashburnham 23 Jan. 1818, came to Baltimore, MD at age 12 to reside with an uncle, Joseph Cushing. Joseph's brother, Milton Whitney, served as state's attorney at Baltimore. Joseph C. m. Florence E. Weston. *TR4:146-7*

WHITWORTH, RICHARD, b. on an ocean steamer while his family en route to America from Manchester, England. He was raised in Baltimore, MD & later removed to Zanesville, OH, where he d. in 1858. He m. Isabella Willoughby, b. Baltimore. Richard's father, also Richard, b. Manchester, England & to US & engaged in the manufacture of woolens in Baltimore. Children of Richard & Isabella reside in DC suburbs of MD. *6TH:840-41*

WHYTE, JOHN CAMPBELL (DR.), Irish patriot, settled in Baltimore, MD in early 19th century. His son Joseph m. Isabella Pinkney, d/o Hon.

William & their son, William Pinkney Whyte, was Governor of MD, elected in 1871. *AAH:288; MDC:652-3*

WIEDEFELD, FRANCIS, b. Germany Feb. 1812, to US at age 15, d. aged 92 in 1904, tanner, resided in Baltimore, MD; m. Mary O'Reilly, d/o Thomas & Mary (McDermott), residents of Chambersburg, PA. Son Henry Charles Wiedefeld b. Baltimore 21 June 1845, funeral director. *TR3:240*

WIEGARD, BERNARD G., b. in Germany, to US in boyhood, res. Annapolis, MD. He m. Amelia J. Roebeck & had 11 children. Son Bernard J. b. 13 Oct. 1889, in Annapolis, served in 1st MD Regulars in 1915 as member of a machine gun company on the TX border. In active service in France in 1918; m. 16 July 1917, Annie Laurie Pippin, d/o Thomas K. *TR3:462*

WIENER, MICHAEL, b. town of Allzuheim, Bavaria 5 Feb. 1804, s/o George. He was worker in brewery from age of 14. He m. Margaret Goetz, b. Germany 15 May 1802. In June 1834 with their son Andrew from Breman to Baltimore. Short time in Frederick, MD; settled on a farm near the present location of the town of Harmony. Later removed to Middletown, MD where for 10 years he was employed in tannery of George Schlosser; to Burkittsville, where he bought tanyard of Ezra Slifer in 1846. Michael d. 11 March 1891 & is bur. in the cemetery of the Catholic Church at Petersville; Margaret d. 11 June 1872 & is bur. beside him. Their children: Andrew, d. in Frederick 1890, tanner; Andrew, m. Miss Cutshall; Mary Ann, widow of David Arnold of Burkittsville; Catherine, m. Dr. Thomas E. Hardy & she d. in Burkittsville; Henry M., b. Middletown 2 Sept. 1849, m. at St. Martin's Church in Baltimore, 6 May 1868, Ann Margaret Miller of Howard County, MD. *FR2:1122*

WIESENTHAL, CHARLES FREDERICK, Rev. Patriot, b. Prussia 1726; to Baltimore age 29, d. 1 June 1789; Surgeon-General of MD Line (1777). Lutheran. *TR4:34-5*

WIEST, WILLIAM, from Germany to US c. 1799, settled in PA. His son, Jacob Wiest, merchant, m. Sara Katherine Blingsinger. Their son, Charles McClellan Wiest, removed to Kabletown, WV & later to Rippon, WV. Charles' wife, Valley Virginia Foreman, was a d/o Peter & Mary Foreman of Darkesville, Berkeley. The son of Charles & Valley was

257

Paul Foreman Wiest, b. Kabletown, Jefferson Co., WV 7 Oct. 1895. He is physician of Baltimore, MD. Dr. Wiest's great-great grandfather on the maternal line was James Mahaffey, of Scotch-Irish desc., who left Ireland to come to America in 1753. He settled in Cumberland Co., PA; cabinet maker. Presbyterian. *TR3:906-7*

WILDEY,THOMAS, b. London, England, 15 Jan. 1782. In 1817 to US, settled in Baltimore City, MD. He was the founder of Odd Fellowship in the US. He d. 19 Oct. 1861, aged 80, & is buried in Greenmount Cemetery, Baltimore. *MDC:610-11*

WILEY, ---, b. Ireland, to America & had a son Matthew, b. Chester Co., PA, wealthy farmer. Matthew's son, another Matthew, m. Charlotte A. Norris. Their son, George N. Wiley was b. Harford Co., MD 21 Sept. 1837 & m. at the age of 38 to Zanna I. Wiley, also b. MD. *H/C:505-6*

WILEY, DAVID, b. Ireland, to America & located in Chester Co., PA, farmer. His son, Matthew Wiley, b. Chester Co., miller & farmer. Matthew was a veteran of the American Rev., a Presbyterian. He d. aged 88 & bur. Bethel Churchyard, Harford Co. He m. Rebecca Nelson, b. Harford Co., MD. *H/C:546-7*

WILHIDE, FREDERICK, b. Germany, to America with 2 brothers & settled in VA. He later removed to Frederick Co., MD, among the first of the settlers of that county. He had among his children a son, Frederick. Frederick owned a farm near Graceham, MD, adj. the Moravian Church. He later removed to Henry Co., IN, where he died. Frederick m. Catherine Peitzel & had: Benajmin; Henry, farmer of Mechanicstown District, now dec'd.; James of IN; Wilson, d. young; John, d. in early manhood; Maria [Mollie], m. John Booler of Graceham; & Savilla, m. --- Gernard, of Graceham. *FR2:729, 1458-9*

WILKENS, WILLIAM, b. 13 Oct. 1817 in Osterlinde, near Lesse, Dukedom of Brunswick, Germany, s/o Christian & Amelia (Deepe), members of the Lutheran Church. Family to Hildersheim in 1825 & William to America c. 1836. He landed in NY & removed at once to Philadelphia. In 1839 to New Orleans & later to Texas; 1841 back to Philadelphia, where he m. & eventually located in Baltimore, MD & founded the firm of William Wilkens & Co. *MDC:620-21*

WILKES, JAMES Jr., a Scotchman, later hardware merchant of Baltimore, MD. His dau., Mary A. Wilkes, m. Hon. James B. Preston. Mary d. 1874. Her son, Walter W. Preston, b. on home farm on Deer Creek, Harford Co., 14 Jan. 1863. *H/C:390-1*

WILKINS, THOMAS, with two brothers, to America from Fawsley, near Daventry, Northamptonshire, England, c. 1720 & settled upon the north side of Chester River in 1724, where he established a store & shipyard. Here he m. Mary, d/o William Comegys. Thomas drowned at age 92. *MDC:459*

WILKINSON, THOMAS, from Newcastle, England with his family, settled in Baltimore, MD; wife was Mary Ann Scott. Son Thomas, b. Newcastle, England 1809, d. Cumberland, MD 1877; m. Susan R. Oldham, b. Baltimore. *TR3:178-9*

WILKINSON, THOMAS, b. Ireland, to PA & settled New London Cross Roads, Chester Co., tanner & farmer. His son Thomas Jr. b. Chester Co. & removed to Harford Co., MD, farmer & miller. Resided near Deer Creek, d. 1602, aged 65. *H/C:162*

WILKS, JAMES, to America from Scotland & settled in Baltimore. Became large Baltimore City landowner. He had James Jr. who m. Mary, d/o Michael Kimmel, Jr. Their dau. Mary Amelia Wilks m. James Bond Preston Jr., b. Harford Co., MD 27 June 1827, s/o James Sr. & Eliza Johnson. Michael Kimmel Sr. came to America during the French-English war & was a brother officer of Gen. Washington in the army of Gen. Braddock. *TR4:96*

WILLIAMS, JOHN, b. Wales, settled in Harford [Co., MD] towards the middle of the last century. Desc. William Williams, contractor at Havre de Grace, where he d. 1848. His son, Dr. Lewis J. Williams, b. Harford Co. 1819, served in the US navy, d. at Baltimore 1888. *H/C:542-3*

WILLIAMS, RALPH, of Bristol, England, resided in 1672 in Towne Neck, Anne Arundel Co., MD. *AAH:43*

WILLIAMS, THOMAS, from Wales to America & founded the Williams family in Cecil Co., MD. His son Jesse had a son Thomas b. on farm in Cecil Co. in 1818 & m. Catherine Thompson, b. Cecil Co., d/o John Thompson. *H/C:428-9*

WILLIAMSON, ANGUS McINTOSH, b. 1814, Inverness, Scotland, to America 1832, res. for awhile in Philadelphia, PA, settled in Baltimore, MD, d. Philadelphia. He m. 1797 Elizabeth Reeves, of English lineage, her grandfather, John Bishop, a pioneer resident of Baltimore. *TR3:120*

WILLIAMSON, JOSEPH ALLEINE, to America from Scotland soon after the close of the Rev. War to visit a Philadelphian with whom he had become friends while a student of law at Edinburgh University. Studied to become Presbyterian minister & removed to VA where he m. Sarah North Newton of Essex Co. Their son, Joseph Alleine Williamson, b. Clarke Co., VA, removed to Orange Co., VA after his marriage, where he d. of typhoid fever in the prime of life. Joseph (2) m. Mary Mann Page, d/o Capt. Robert Page, officer of the Rev. Army & member of Congress. J. Alleine Williamson (3), s/o Joseph & Mary, b. Clarke Co., VA 1845, d. Frederick City, Frederick Co., MD 1896. He served in the Confederate Army in the Civil War, First Co. of Richmond Howitzers, Ewells' Division of Gen. Longstreet's Corps, Army of No. VA. After the war he settled in Westmoreland Co., VA, but in 1869 removed to Frederick, MD where he founded drug business now conducted by his sons, Thomas McGill & J. Alleine Williamson. *FR2:1550-51*

WILLIS, ---, three brothers from England to America. One settled on Eastern Shore of MD, one to TX & one settled in Berryville, VA. Levan C. Willis was a desc. of the first brother & was b. 15 Feb. 1792. Levan m. 1814 Eliza Orndorf & res. for a time in OH or IN, but later settled near Herring Run, Baltimore Co., MD & still later to Frederick Co., MD & settled on estate called Walnut Grove, near New Market. They renamed the place Williston. *FR2:1024-5*

WILMER, SIMON, from England to America in 1660 & settled in Kent, in Province of MD on "White House Farm," near Chestertown. Desc. Simon Wilmer m. Dorcas Hynson & had son William who m. Rose Blackiston in April 1790. *MDC:484-85; TR4:487-9*

WILSON, ---, b. Ireland & in 1770 located on a farm near Bel Air, MD. Son Humphrey Wilson m. Sarah H. Durham, b. Harford Co., d/o Abel, a veteran of War of 1812. *H/C:178*

WILSON, ARCHIBALD, b. Scotland, to America & settled in Harford Co., MD. His son James b. on home farm & d. there in 1870. James served in the War of 1812 & m. Letitia J. Wilson of Harford Co. *H/C:246*

WILSON, JACOB, JOHN & SAMUEL. Four brothers from England to America, the 4th's name is unknown. Sons of Christopher Wilson of England. Jacob's son, Samuel D., removed from DE to Cecil Co., MD in 1842, where he d. aged 62; m. Mary Pearson, also b. DE, & had John P. Wilson, b. Newcastle Co., DE 1836. *H/C:580-1*

WILSON, JAMES, from England to Province of MD & settled in Shrewsbury Parish, Kent Co. c. 1700; d. 1732. His wife was Catharine ---. *MDC:159*

WILSON, JOHN, b. England, to America & located in York Co., PA; subsequently removed to Stafford, Harford Co., MD. He was s/o Christopher Wilson, celebrated Quaker preacher of Yorkshire, England, near the Scottish border. John m. Miss --- Webster, 11 July 1764. They had 10 children, one was Christopher Wilson, b. 12 Dec. 1766. *H/C:352-3*

WILSON, N. J., b. Ireland 1836, to US at age 11. Wandered through the South and later settled Baltimore; 1851 to Frederick Co., MD. Catholic. Left widow & 8 children. One son, George I. Wilson, b. Frederick 1866, merchant. *FR2:725*

WILSON, WILLIAM, b. Limerick, Ireland 1750, s/o James, a native of Scotland who first removed to London & later to Ireland. William to America at age 20 & in 1773 m. Jane Stonsbury of Baltimore Co., MD. *MDC:511-12*

WINDER, JOHN, from Cumberland, England settled at Princess Anne, Somerset Co., MD; had son John who m. Jane Dashiel & they had son William Winder who m. Esther Gillis. William & Esther's 8th child was Levin Winder, 16th Governor of MD. *AAH:256*

WINDHAM, WILLIAM, from England to America at time of the Rev. War & farmer of MD. *6TH:797-98*

WINDSOR, ---, b. England & settled in Montgomery Co., MD. His son Henry b. & reared in Montgomery Co., farmer. Member of the Methodist Episcopal Church & m. Mary Simmons. Their son, James S., b. near

Clarksburg, 20 July 1839. James m. Oct. 1865, Sarah R., d/o John W. Darby. *6TH:671-72*

WINEBRENNER, JOHANN CHRISTIAN, from the Palatinate, a Rhenish province of Germany, landed Philadelphia 1753 and settled Mercersberg, Franklin Co., PA; later to Hagerstown, Washington Co., MD. His son Philip b. at Mercersburg, Franklin Co., PA before the Rev. War. Philip settled at Walkersville, Frederick Co., MD where he bought a farm that has been passed to several generations of descs. Philip had a son Christian who m. Phoebe Cramer. *FR2:708; 6TH:225; TR3:971-2*

WINTER, HENRY, and wife Elizabeth Burns, both b. Germany. He was a musician & settled in Hagerstown, MD. Elizabeth had come to America with her sister, Mrs. Burk, when aged 14. *6TH:858-59*

WINTERNITZ, CHARLES, b. 2 March 1815 at Deschnu, Bohemia, son of William, Rabbi of Patzau, Bohemia & Deschnu. Charles m. Wilhelmia Block, d/o Hiram of Dob, Bohemia & emigrated to Baltimore with wife & 5 children in 1844. Ironworker. *MDC:192*

WINTOUR FAMILY,, from England to MD with the first settlers of the province. Desc. Jane Winter m. Rev. Henry Lyon Davis, Episcopal clergyman, pres. of St. John's College in Annapolis & rector of St. Anne's. *TR4:872-4*

WIRT, ---, b. Scotland, m. ---, b. Germany; son William b. Bladensburg, MD 8 Nov. 1772. Both parents died before William's 8th birthday. *TR4:18*

WITHEROW, JOHN, from Ireland & m. Margaret Barber, settled near Philadelphia, PA c. 1760. Later settled on a farm about 5 miles from Emmitsburg, MD, where he died. Their children: John, David, Samuel, and daus. [not named here] who m. James Harper, Henry Williams, Andrew Marshall & a dau. who did not marry. *FR2:805*

WITHERS, JOHN, of family of Lancaster Co., England, to Choptank Parish, County Stafford, VA, where his will was drawn 1698. He m. Frances (Townshend) Dade. Their dau. Sarah conveyed land to Augustine Washington in 1727. Desc. James Withers, who d. in Fauquier Co., VA in 1791, had dau. Cynthia b. 1770 who m. Moses Duncan, b. Fauquier Co. in 1766, of Scottish desc. Moses removed his family to

Boyle Co., KY & had son John Duncan b. Roanoke, VA, d. in Oldham Co. in 1851. John's son, William Wesley Duncan, b. Oldham Co., KY 15 Jan. 1823 & d. there 13 July 1891. He m. Amanda Harrington, b. 10 Sept. 1833 in Shelby Co., KY & d. 9 Aug. 1894 in Oldham Co. Their son, John Thomas Duncan, b. on family farm near Crestwood in Oldham Co., 3 April 1851, now retired in living in Ft. Myers, FL. He m. Ida M. Smith, b. 8 Jan. 1854, d/o Joseph O. Smith, farmer of Jefferson Co. KY. Their two surviving children (1923): William Joseph b. 25 March 1876 & Alexander Edward b. 27 May 1878. Alexander Edward Duncan is financial leader of Baltimore, MD, where he has res. since 1907. *TR4:597-600*

WITTER, WILLIAM, settled in a part of Swampscott--now Lynn, MA in early 17th century; Baptist. Family established in Nova Scotia by Samuel Witter, b. 28 May 1723 in Norwich, CT, who removed to Horton, Kings Co., Nova Scotia in 1760. Desc. Rachel Louise Witter m. William John Wallace & their son Rev. Oates Charles Symonds Wallace pastor of Eutaw Place Baptist Church of Baltimore (1921). He served in Lawrence MA, Toronto Canada, Lowell MA & Montreal Canada. Rev. Wallace's wife is Helen Moore, d/o Rev. John Wright & Louisa (Fish) Moore of New Brunswick; they m. 2 March 1919. *TR4:478-80*

WOLF, CASPER, to US from Germany at close of Civil War; m. Annie E. ---, settled in Randallstown, Baltimore Co., MD. Dau. Annie Elizabeth m. Henry Buppert of Hebbville, Baltimore County. *TR3:238-9*

WOLF, MARCUS, b. 21 Dec. 1779, in village of Apinrod, County of Hochenburg, Duchy of Nassau, Germany, s/o Lewis & Lehna. He left Germany for America 31 Aug. 1818, landed in Baltimore, MD & joined an uncle in Owings Mills. He later removed to Baltimore & m. there 29 April 1824, Sarah Legare. He d. in Baltimore 21 Aug. 1875. *MDC:243-4*

WOLFE, ---, b. England, emigrated to PA c. 1720. Served in the American army in the Rev. War. After the war he returned to PA & married, leaving 7 sons. Three of his sons removed to MD. One son, Jacob Wolfe, b. near York Co., PA, located in the Middletown Valley of Frederick Co., MD, c. 1 mile from the village of Wolfsville & served in the War of 1812. He & his wife [not named here] had 6 children, the eldest son was Jacob. *FR2:1408-9*

WOLMAN, SOLOMON, b. Germany 1863, left an orphan when young, s/o Shepschel & Ella (Rosker) Wolman. 1877 to US, landed in Baltimore, to relatives in Gunpowder, MD, later to Baltimore, and still later merchant of Woodbine, MD. Associated with Chizuk Amuno congregation. He m. Esther Ida Schroeder, b. NY City 1869, d/o Aaron & Cecelia (Rosen) Schroeder, both b. Germany, to America in Civil War period & settled in NY. *TR3:307*

WOOD, HENRY, England to America at an early date with brother John, [second source says he arrived with two brothers, one settling in Baltimore & the other on the Eastern Shore of MD] settled New Market District, Frederick Co., MD. Elder brother Caleb remained in England. Henry m. Sarah Maclefresh & had 2 sons, John & Basil. Basil d. unmarried & John was a preacher of the Methodist Protestant Church & d. at his estate, "Rosedale," in 1839. John's wife was Ruth Burgess. *FR2:716, 1008*

WOOD, JAMES, b. Yorkshire, England 2 June 1809, m. Mary Caldwell, d/o Joseph of Yorkshire & had: Robert, Joseph, Richard, James, Ambrose & Sarah. He moved to the US with his family in 1842, settling first in Wilmington, DE. In 1844 James to Lycoming Co., PA with his oldest son Robert & engaged in lumber work. He was originally an Episcopalian, but later joined the Methodist Episcopal Church. Son Robert was b. 3 Dec. 1832, near Holmfirth, Yorkshire, England & was 10 years when he moved to the US with his family. He m. Hester Dorothy Straub, d/o Charles & Elizabeth Baker Straub of Whitepine, PA & they had 13 children. Hester Dorothy d. in Whitepine, 27 Feb. 1890, aged 52. Their son, George Leidy Wood, b. Whitepine 19 May 1873, formed a partnership with his brother Joseph in the lumber business. He later formed a partnership with William T. England. In 1896 he joined his brother, Robert E. Wood, in wholesale hardwood lumber business in southwest WV, in Welch, McDowell Co. In 1903 the R. E. Wood Lumber Co. was organized, with headquarters in Baltimore, MD & George L. was made vice president & general manager. He m. in Whitepine, PA 18 June 1902, Genevieve Anita McCullough, b. 11 Jan. 1878, of Scotch, Irish & English stock. Her mother, Emma Jane Lane, b. Woodstock, NY, d/o Alfred Henry & Catherine (Travis) Lane. Her father, Edward O'Neal McCullough, b. Marbletown, New York. His parents were William Henry McCulollough from Ulster, Ireland & Mary Wilson, b. near Edinburgh, Scotland. *TR3:936-46*

WOOD, JOSEPH, of England, one of the 1st settlers of MD under the charter granted to Lord Baltimore. *FR2:1327-8*

WOOD, JOSEPH, from England, settled at Hauvers Districk, Frederick Co., MD c. 1755. Patriot of the Rev. *FRI:11*

WOODALL, WILLIAM EASLEY, b. Liverpool, England 18 July 1837, s/o John, a native of Yorkshire, and Ester Easley, d/o Robert of Highfield House, near Stokesley, Yorkshire. William's brothers Henry E. & James also emigrated and settled in Baltimore, MD. William to America at age 15 & served as apprentice at Washington, DC shipyard of Capt. William Easley, a cousin of his mother. His father to the US in 1855 & settled near Bladensburg with his wife & 2 youngest children. John Woodall d. at Baltimore 19 May 1859; his wife d. 2 Jan. 1876. William Easley m. 13 Nov. 1860, Mary Eugenia, d/o Benjamin A. Hooper, of South Baltimore. Presbyterian. *MDC:350-51*

WOODWARD, ---, William of London, England sent 3 sons to MD: Henry, William & Abraham. Henry located on the Patuxent in Anne Arundel Co., m. Mary Garrett, sister of Amos of Annapolis. William, s/o William of London, m. & left 3 children. Abraham m. (1) Elizabeth Firlor, (2) Mrs. Priscilla Orrick, widow of James. Abraham's grandson, also Abraham, was killed in the Revolutionary War. *AAH:123*

WOODWARD, WILLIAM, of London, England, s/o William, to America & settled at Annapolis, MD. *MDC:418*

WOODYEAR, EDWARD, b. England; with his family to US from St. Kitts & settled in Baltimore, MD. His wife was Mary Fowler, d/o David of NC, who he met in England while she was attending school. Their son, Thomas Woodyear, m. 1817, Elizabeth Yellott, d/o John & Hannah, b. Yorkshire, England. Elizabeth d. 3 March 1876, age 84. *MDC:233-4*

WOOLFORD, ROGER, American progenitor of English lineage, to America in 1662 & settled in Dorchester Co., MD. Descs. fought in the Rev. War & Rev. Stevens Woolford m. Cassandra Waples, b. Dorchester Co., he a Baptist minister. Their son Thomas T. C. Woolford, b. 1829 in Dorchester Co., was orphaned at age 9 & was reared in the home of Mrs. Cassandra Skinner, an older sister who lived in Baltimore. He was a sea captain & d. 1900, aged 72. *TR4:302*

WORTHINGTON, JOHN (CAPT.), b. 12 Jan. 1650, s/o Rev. John Worthington, master of Jesus Collage at Cambridge, England who d. 1671. To America by 1675; 1686 bought "Greenberry Forest" from Col. Nicholas Greenberry. Capt. John appointed assoc. justice of Anne Arundel Co., MD in 1692. He m. Sarah Howard, d/o Matthew & Sarah (Dorsey) Howard, his neighbors. Their son John Jr., b. 13 Jan. 1689. Capt. John, the immigrant, made his will in 1699, d. in Annapolis in 1701 & he was bur. on the farm of the late R. Tilghman Brice, opposite the Naval Academy at Annapolis. Children named in his will: John, Thomas, William & Sarah. *TR4:630-1; AAH:145-7; FR2:728*

WRIGHT, ---, b. Wales, commissioned officer in the Rev. War. His son John Wright, b. Bucks Co., PA, d. aged 112 years. John's son, Joseph, b. Chester Co., PA, m. Martha McDowell Ford of Chester Co., & had 8 children. Joseph d. 1885, aged 77. Their son Robert F. Wright b. Penn Twp., Chester Co., PA 1833, served in Co. I, 175th PA Inf. in Civil War. In 1891 removed to Cecil Co., MD. *H/C:443-4*

WRIGHT, EDWARD, from England to Somerset Co., MD in 1660 & settled near Barren Creek Springs. *TR4:686-8*

WRIGHT, JOHN, b. England, was linen merchant of Belfast, Ireland. He & sister Susannah emigrated to PA & settled near Wrightsville, giving his name to the settlement. John m. & left several children. One son, Jesse, after the death of his first wife, removed to New Market, Frederick Co., MD, tanner. Here he m. the widow David (nee Hinkle) & had son Jesse. *FR2:938-9*

WRIGHT, NATHANIEL, from England in 1673 to Queen Anne Co., MD. His son Solomon Wright m. Anna ---, & had son Solomon who m. Mary Tidmarsh DeCourey. Their son, Robert Wright, was 3 times elected Governor of MD & b. at "Blakeford" in Queen Anne Co. Judge Solomon Wright (1717-1792), desc. of the immigrant Nathaniel Wright, was burgess in MD, chairman of committee of observation of Queen Annes Co. in 1775-76. *AAH:253; TR4:130*

ELLOTT, JEREMIAH, settled in Baltimore, MD & brought his brother John [see Edward Woodyear entry] & family to Baltimore in 1795. Jeremiah left no issue. John, farmer, settled in Harford Co., MD & later res. Dulaney's

Valley & later farm in Baltimore Co., "Auburn," where he died aged 75. *MDC:233-4*

YOUNG, CONRAD, b. Germany, to America & settled in Middletown Valley, Frederick Co., MD about the time of the French & Indian War. Henry, s/o Conrad the emigrant, b. Middletown Valley, farmer & m. Matilda Castle, b. Frederick Co. They had a large family. *FR2:1120-1*

YOUNG, CONRAD, to America from Germany c. 1770, with wife. All their children b. in America. They settled in Locust Valley & he erected a sawmill & farmed. Had two sons, Daniel & John. *FR2:931-2*

YOUNG, DEVAULT, b. Germany, he & friend Jacob Rhodes to America, landed at Baltimore, settled Ellicott City, MD and founded flour mill. Devault m. after coming to America, resided in VA and later to Western MD. He m. in America & had: Elizabeth, b. 13 May 1796, dec'd.; Barnet, b. 25 May 1798; & Jacob. *FR2:707*

YOUNG, GEORGE, b. England. His dau., Eleanor, m. Thomas Hillery & had son Henry Hillery who m. Cassandra Magruder. Henry & Cassandra had a son, Walter Hilery, (1752-1821) who m. Elizabeth Magruder. Family res. Prince George's Co., MD. *TR4:825-7*

YOUNG, HUGH, of Scotch-Irish extraction, resided Londonderry, Ireland. Implicated in the rebellion of 1798, fled Ireland & settled in Baltimore, where he died. His son, McClintock Young, b. 1801, d. 1863. Chief clerk of the US treasury, appointed by Andrew Jackson. McClintock m. (1) Susan Bird Newman, d/o Col. Francis Newman & (2) Josephine Causten of Washington, DC. *FR2:744*

YOUNG, JOHN A., b. Germany, to US in early manhood & settled in Reisterstown, Baltimore Co., MD. Later removed to Baltimore & d. in city of Washington DC. Member of the German Reformed Church, as was his wife, Rebecca Abrahams, of PA. *6TH:860-61*

YOUNG, PETER, b. Germany. He was a teacher of languages in America & d. in Frederick Co., MD at an advanced age. His son Jacob m. Anna Renner of PA. Member of the Reformed Church until his marriage & then belonged to the Dunkard. Their son, Jacob A., b. in Frederick Co., MD 22 April 1839, the youngest child & only son. *6TH:539-30*

YOUNG, RICHARD, Englishman, his will recorded in 1665 names him as of "The Cliffs." [Calvert Co.] Desc. James Young, printer & publisher, active in politics of early Baltimore City. He m. (1) Eleanor Parks & (2) Elizabeth Stretch. *TR3:823-4*

YOURTEE, PETER, to America from Alsace in 1731 & with his wife settled in what is now known as Sample's Manor, in the West of Washington Co., MD. Name was originally spelled Jourdeau. They had 5 children: Abraham (b. 1732), Jacob, Elizabeth, Mary & Barbara. Son Abraham m. Mary Magdalene Brown & settled on farm near Brownsville, MD. Abraham had son Aaron who had son John Tilghman (b. 2 July 1841), who had son Leon Ryno Yourtee, b. 31 May 1879. Leon is atty., res. Hagerstown. *FR2:1244; TR4:602-6*

ELL, ---, originally of Zell Town, Holland. Descendant Peter Zell was a veteran of the Confederate Army. His son Oliver Carroll Zell, reared in Baltimore, MD and his son, Arthur Stanley Zell, b. Baltimore 29 Feb. 1880. Protestant Episcopal. *TR3:337*

ZELLER, E. EDWARD, b. Hesse-Cassel, Germany 1850, eldest s/o John Frederick. John Frederick brought his family to America in 1853 & settled in Frederick City, MD. *6TH:387*

ZELLER, JOHN FREDERICK, of Hesse-Cassel, Germany. In 1853 with family to America & settled in Frederick City, MD. Son C. Edward b. Hesse-Cassel m. Miss --- Saddler, who d. 1885. Other children: John A.; Charles C., drowned age 18; Emma Virginia m. A. H. Rogers of Baltimore & Bertina, a half sister, m. F. W. Hoot of Locust Point. *6TH:387-88*

ZIMMERMAN, ---, 3 brothers b. Germany, emigrated to US. [Sources vary, one says there were only 2 brothers. See below versions.] One located in NY, another in PA. Progenitor of the Frederick Co., MD Zimmermans is George, the 3d brother. He had 11 children: John, Andrew, Benjamin, George, Henry, Michael, John Nicholas, a dau. who m. a Mr. Brunner, a dau. who m. a Mr. Simm, a dau. who m. a Mr. Byerly & a dau. who m. a Mr. Burkhart. George's son, John Nicholas Zimmerman, was the owner of the first paper mills in Frederick Co. His son, also John Nicholas, b. 1809 & d. 1875; was owner of farm in the

Tuscarora District & m. Elizabeth Albaugh, b. 5 Oct. 1812, d. 28 Aug. 1866.

The brother who settled in PA had at least one son, Henry Zimmerman, left PA for Frederick Co., MD as a young man. He settled on part of the old Carroll tract at Carroll's Manor; among one of the earliest settlers. Henry m. Charlott Thomas & had: Peter; Elizabeth, m. Edward Zimmerman, retired farmer of Carroll's Manor; Daniel, retired farmer of Jefferson District, Frederick Co.; Gideon M.; Rev. William; Ephraim & Josiah. All children now dec'd. Members Reformed Church. *FR2:882, 997-8, 1567-8*

ZIMMERMAN, HENRY, with 3 brothers to America from England & settled in Frederick Co., MD. His son Ephraim I. Zimmerman was b. in Frederick Co., where he d. 9 March 1894, aged 64. He m. Maria E., d/o Peter Thomas, of Frederick Co. *FR2:1198-9*

ZIMMERMAN, JOHN & MICHAEL, 2 of 3 brothers who emigrated from Germany to America. John res. on Carroll's Manor, Frederick Co., MD. He m. a Miss Holtz & they had a son John, b. Feb. 1792. John (2) was a farmer, m. Catharine Lashorn & had a son Edward D., b. in Frederick Co., 3 March 1822.

Michael Zimmerman the emigrant located in Frederick Co., MD, on land known as "Addition to Carrollton." He m. Eva Cronise & had 3 children: Michael & Henry (twins) & Sara.

The third Zimmerman brother, George, settled in Frederick Co., MD. His children: John, Andrew, Benjamin, George, Henry, Michael, John Nicholas; a dau. who m. a Mr. Brunner; a dau. who m. a Mr. Simm; a dau. who m. a Mr. Byerly & a dau. who m. a Mr. Burkhart. Son John Nicholas owned the first paper mills in Frederick Co., located on Tuscarora Creek, near Yellow Springs. *FR2:979-80, 1002-3, 1401-2; 1409-10*

INDEX

A

ABBOTT, John H. 1
ABEGG, Johanna E. 245
  William L. 245
ABELL, A. S. 1
  Caleb 1
  Preserved 1
  Robert 1
ABERCROMBIE, David 1
  Harry Netherclift 1
  John 1
  Ronald Taylor 1
ABRAHAMS, Galliston 1
  Joseph 1
  Rebecca 267
  William 1
  Woodward 1
ABRAKE, --- (Miss) 127
ABRAMS, Levy 1, 2
  Michael A. 2
ABRAMSON, Jennie 2
  Solomon 2
ACTON, Nathaniel 2
  Samuel Graham 2
ADAMS, Benjamin 2
  Benjamin T. 171
  George 2
  Henry 2, 157
  Jane 171
  John 2, 69
  John F. 2
  Laura E. 171
  Lydia 69
  Margaret 39
  Peter 2
  Thomas 39
  William 101
ADDISON, Elizabeth 3
  George Mitchell 3
  Isabella 3

ADDISON, James 3
  John 3
  Mary 242
  Mary Elizabeth 66
  Montgomery 3
  Nancy 3
  Robert 3
ADELSBERGER, --- 59
ADLER, --- 3
  Charles 3, 78
  Nytta 3
  Philip 3
  Simon 3
ADNEY, Alice 59
  Moses 59
AHALT, --- 3
  Henry 13
  Jacob 3
  John 3
  Joshua 3
  Matthias 3
  Samuel 3
ALBACH, Johan Wilhelm 3
ALBANY, Elizabeth 9
ALBAUGH, Elizabeth 269
  Guy 48
  Johan Gearhardt 3
  Johan Peter 3
  Johan Wilhelm 3
  Lydia 110
  Margaret E. 192
  Martha 176
  Zachariah 3
ALBERT, Jacob 3
  Lawrence 3
  William Julian 3
ALD 29
ALD, Sarah Harrison 29
ALES, Sarah 146
ALEXANDER, Amos 70
  Jane 47
  Martha 104

ALEXANDER, William D. 114
ALIBACH, Johan Wilhelm 3
ALLAN, Mary Kerr 4
  William 4
ALLEN, Asaph 4
  Benjamin 4
  Catherine 69
  Charles 4
  E. M. 165
  Edward 4
  Elizabeth 4
  George Hanford 4, 145
  John R. 4
  Jonathan 4
  Joseph 4
  Louis St. Clair 4, 145
  Mary 117
  Patrick 4
  Richard N. 165
  Simeon 4
  Solomon 69
  Thomas 4
  Thomas C. 4
  Zebulon 4
  Zilpah 23
ALLISON, Esther 29
  Mary 65
  Patrick 29
  Susan 70
  William 65, 66
ALLSTON, Joseph Blyth 4
  Joseph Waties 4
ALSIP, Josephus 186
ALTER, Abraham 142
  Annette D. 142
ALTVATER, Mary 2
AMBLER, Sarah 34
AMBROSE, Elizabeth 41
AMELUNG, John Frederick 5, 73
AMES, Josephine 99
  Levin 99
AMMIDON, Daniel C. 5
  John Perry 5
  Julia 5
  Roger 5
AMOS, Hannah 183

AMOS, Henry 229
  William 5
AMTHOR, Andrew 5
  Johann Michael Robert 5
ANDERSON, John 5
ANDERSON, Alice 242
  Allen 193
  Georgia 233
  Georgiana 193
  James 5
  John 193
  Mary 37, 112
  Mary Ellen 201
  Patrick 5
  Robert 201
  William 5
ANDRE, Edward 251
  James Eidgway 251
ANDREW, John W. 161
  William H. 161
ANDREWS, Debby 117
  Edith Branch 77
  Emma Delia 62
  John 117
  John D. 62
ANGUS, Annette 141
  Felix 5, 141
ANNAN, Andrew 6
  Robert 6
  Robert Landsale 6
  Samuel 6
  William 6
ANNE, Queen 99
AP LLEWELLYN, Daird (Prince) 143
APPEL, --- (Miss) 241
  John 109
APPLE, Susan M. 97
APPLEBY, --- 6
  Fanny 6
  Harriet 6
  Martha 6
  Mary Jane 6
  Nicholas 6
  Rufus 6
  Sarah 6

APPLEBY, Susan 49
  Walter 6
APPLEMAN, Alpheus R. 204
  Catherine 6
  Jacob 6
  John 6, 204
  Philip 6
  Sarah 6
  Susan 6
ARBUCKLE, --- 6
  Daniel 6
  Daniel T. 6
  Paul T. 6
ARCHER, Amelia 242
  John 6
  Robert 6
  Rolan Dutton 242
ARMS, Hannah 4
ARMSTRONG, Anna 7
  Elizabeth 7
  James 7
  Jane 7
  John 7
  Robert 7
  Samuel 7
  William 7
ARNDT, Amalia 209
ARNOLD, Abraham B. 7
  David 7, 257
  John H. 7
  Lydia 7, 8
  Margaret 114
  Peter 7
ARTER, Catharine 135
  Henry 7
ARVINGER, James R. 216
ASH, Daniel Heinrich 7
ASHE, Daniel Heinrich 7
  Rachel 7
ASHFORDBY, William 7
ATKINSON, Adelia Conant 239
  Alexander 7
  Joseph Townsend 239
  Lydia 113
  Mary 7, 38
  Ruth C. 8

ATKINSON, Stephen 7
  Thompson 7
  William M. 8
ATLEE, --- 40
AUCHER, Anthony 8
  Edward 8
  Elizabeth 8
  Joan 8
AULABAUGH, Johan Wilhelm 3
AULD, Bertie B. 208
  Harry 208
AUMEN, Barnabas 8
  Francis John 8
  Margaret 8
  Mary M. 8
  William Sylvester 8
AUSHERMAN, --- 8
  David 8
  John 7, 8
AYER, Mollie 82
AYLER, Sarah 219
AYRES, Henrietta Dawson 8
  John 8
  Richard Johnson 8
  Thomas 9
  Thomas J. 9

B

BABEL, Caroline M. 78
BABINGTON, Joseph 212
  Manada 212
BACHMANN, Augusta 252
  J. C. 252
BACKUS, Sarah 49
  William 49
BACON, Thomas Scott 89
BADAGLIACCA, Francis L. 9
  Vincent J. 9
BADER, Dominick 9
  Margaret 9
BAER, Elizabeth 9
  Lena 171
  Philip 9
BAETJER, Annie 68

274

BARTGIS, --- 11
Franklin 11
Mathias 11
Titus 11
BARTHELOW, Elisha 162
Jemima 162
BARTHOLOW, William 78
BARTLETT, Esther 11
James 11
John 11
Mary 11
Thomas 11
BARTON, David Walker 12
Frank 134
George C. 134
Randolph 12
Thomas 12
BASKIN, Andrew 12
Eldridge 12
Thomas Edmund 12
William 12
William Peebles 12
BATCHELLOR, Stephen 121
Theodate 121
BATSON, Margaret Josephine 97
BATT, Christopher 238
Jane 238
BAUER, Catherine 12, 105
John 12
John G. 109
BAUGH, Helen C. 238
BAUGHER, Lydia 208
BAUMGARDNER, Barbara A. 12
Catharine 12
Charles 13
Henry 12
John 12
John F. O. 12
Lizzie 13
Margaret 12
Rachel 176
Thomas 12
BAYLEY, Elizabeth 42
Henry 42
BAYNE, Colmore 13
Sarah Ann 8

BAYNE, Walter 13
William 13
BEACHAM, James 29
BEACHLEY, --- 13
Barbara 13
Catharine 13
Conrad 13
Daniel 13
Henry 13
Jacob 13
John 13
Mollie 13
Peter 13
BEALE, Rachel 179
BEALL, Fillmore (Mrs.) 8, 146, 205
Ninian 13, 179
Rachel 179
BEAN, Elizabeth 253
BEANE, Walter 13
BEARD, Barbara 215
George 14
Hugh 14
James 14
John 13, 14
John D. 13
Richard 200
BEATTY, Affordby Philip 240
Arthur 14
J. E. 239
John 14
Sarah 158
Thomas 14
William 14
BEATY, Jeannette 214
Jennette 215
BEAUMONT, Thomas 27
BEAVER, John K. 106
Martha J. 106
BEAVERS, Julia Ann 135
BECHTEL, Catherine 128
Lewis 128
Sarah 128
BECK, Elias 41
BECKWITH, George 108
Mollie G. 16

BEDINGER, Adam 14
Daniel 14
George M. 14
Henrietta 14
Henry 14
BEEDLE, Jane 86
BEIERFELD, Abraham 14
BEIRD, George 14
BEITLER, Samuel 14
BELANGE, Rebecca 52
BELL, --- 15
Adam 14
Alexander 15
Alton Cashell 15
Charles 16
Edward 15
Hugh 15
Isabella A. 24
Robert 15
Silas Adam 14
William 15
BELLESON, Annie 15
Corella 15
George W. 15
Henrietta 15
Mary 15
Richard 15
William 15
BELLICAN, Elizabeth 234
BELT, --- 15
Anna Maria 15
Humphry 15
James Harrick 15
John 15
Middleton 15
William Dyer 15
BENCHOFF, John 71
BENDANN, Daniel 101
Grace 101
BENEDICT, Phoebe 147
BENGSTON, Andreas 15
BENJAMIN, George 16
Henrietta 243
Joseph 16
Levi 16, 80, 243
Rachel 243

BENJAMIN, Solomon 16
BENNETT, Edward 16
Eli 163
Harriet 202
Ida Frances 51
Richard 16, 143, 171
William W. 51
BENSON, Elizabeth 16
Stephen 16
BENT, Magdaline E. 243
BENTON, Horace 157
Mary J. 157
BENTZ, Catharine 118
Jacob 118
BERESFORD, Isabel 68
BERGAN, Martha 163
BERGER, Edmund 112
John 201
BERLIN, E. H. 198
Hennie 211
Mary Josephine 198
BERNHEIMER, Sarah 205
BERNSTEIN, Esther 117
BERRY, Benjamin 16
Elizabeth 16
James 16
William 16
BESER, Louis 16
Nicholas 16
Sophia 16
BESLER, Charles S. M. 17
Christian H. 17
Johanna S. E. W. 17
BEST, --- 17
David 17
Edith 178
Simon 110
William H. 178
BESTER, William John 17
BETTLER, Jessie 14
John H. 14
Samuel J. 14
Sarah E. 14
Sophia 14
BETTS, Mary E. 98
William M. 98

BEVAN, Elizabeth 188
Julia A. 5
BEVARD, Charles 17
George 17
James 17
BIBB, --- 199
BICETINE, Mary 47
BIDDLE, John 17
Mary 17
Thomas William 20
BIELFELD, Herman 17
J. J. 17
BIGELOW, --- (Miss) 45
BILES, Rebecca 124
BILLINGHAM, Grace 39
BILLINGS, Louisa 207
BILLINGSLEY, Anne 214
BINN, John 10
BINNER, Adam 191
Susan 191
BINNEY, Elizabeth 245
BIRD, Andrew 108
Susan 108
BIRELY, --- 18
Charlotte 18
John William 18
Margaret 18
Mary Elizabeth 18
Rebecca 18
William 18
BIRNIE, Clotworthy 18
Rogers 18
BISER, --- 18
--- (Miss) 99
A. 99
Catherine 18
Charles C. 18
Charles Calvin 18
Daniel 18, 129
Daniel S. 99
Elizabeth 18
Frederick 18
Henry 18
Jacob 18
John 18
Peter 18

BISER, Polly 18
Sarah 129
Sophia 18
BISHOP, John 260
BITTINGER, Henry 18
William 204
BITTLE, --- 18
George 18
Jonathan 18
Thomas F. 18
BLACK, Andrew L. 19
Christiana 254
George 19
James 19, 70
John A. 19
Mary 203
BLACKISTON, Rose 260
BLACKSTONE, Henry 94
BLACKWELL, Annie 104
BLADEN, Thomas 19
William 19
BLAIR, George Smith 208
William 208
BLAKE, --- 57
Charles 19
Charles D. 19
Dorothy 19
Ellen 219
George A. 19
Henry C. 19
Joseph 19
Mary 198
Richard 10, 19, 20
Thomas 19, 20
BLAKISTONE, Nehemiah 83
BLAMEY, Mary 100
BLAND, John Randolph 20
Peter 20
Richard 20
Richard Edward 20
Theodrick 20
BLICKENSTAFF, Jacob 20
John 20
Yost 20
BLINGSINGER, Sara Katherine
257

BOWLY, Samuel 23
BOWMAN, Henry 23
BOYD, James Alexander 23
John 15
Margaret 15
BOYER, Catherine 23
Elizabeth 23
Gabriel 23
John Henry 23
Michael 23
Michol Magdalene 29
Peter 107
Polly 23
Sarah 23
BOYLE, Anna A. 85
Charles B. 134
Edward 24
Francis Edward 24
Francis W. 85
Margaret 134
Margarita 78
Patrick 24
Thomas 78
BOYLSTON, Martha 1
BOZMAN, Margaret 45
BRACE, William 24
BRACKEN, Fannie 44
BRACKENRIDGE, Mary 67
W. D. 24
BRADDOCK, --- 30, 203
--- (Gen.) 12, 226, 259
BRADEN, Jeannette Theresa 193
Mary E. 193
Noble S. 193
BRADENBAUGH, Mary 202
BRADFORD, William 24
BRADLEY, Ann 209
Henry 209
Mary Elizabeth 104
BRADY, --- 40
George F. 24
Henry H. 24
James 24
Mary Elizabeth 83
Samuel 24
William 24

BRAFMAN, Caroline 78
BRAND, Joseph 24
William 24
William Francis 24
BRANDEN, John 185
Katharine 185
BRANDENBURG, Henry 18
Jacob 25
Jesse 25
John 25
Lemuel 25
Mahala 25
Mary 32
Mary Polly 25
Mathias 25
Priscella 25
William 25
BRASHEARS, Benjamin 25
Mary 25
BRAUN, John R. 25
BREADY, George 25
BREATHED, Catherine 121
BREESE, Aseneth 25
John 25
Oscar F. 25
BREMOND, Francoise 126
BRENAN, J. F. 25
BRENGLE, George 63
William H. 108
BRENNAN, Catharie 238
BRENT, Margaret 25, 26
Mary 25
Richard 25
BRERETON, --- 237
BRETHED, Priscilla William 27
BRETTINGHAM, Margaret A. 99
BREUNINGER, Henry 26
J. Henry 26
Jacob F. 26
BREVITT, --- 26
John 26
BREWER, Angeline 170
John 26, 182
Rachel 182
BREWINGTON, Marion V. 79
BREWSTER, Elizabeth 159

BRIARLY, Sarah 103
BRICE, Ann 26
  John 26
  R. Tilghman 266
  Rachel 26
BRIDGES, Robert 26
  Robert Ferguson 26
BRILL, Christian 191
BRILLHART, --- 27
  Isaac 27
  Jacob 27
  Joseph 27
BRINEY, Jennie M. 67
  Mark D. 67
BRISCOE, --- 27
  George 27
  John 27
  John Hanson 143
  Philip 27
BROADWATER, Charles 27
BROME, --- 27
  Henry 27
  John 27
  Margaret 27
  Thomas 27
BROMWELL, Mary A. 103
BRONSON, Anna 210
BROOK, Jane 43
BROOKE, --- 27
  Baker 28, 219, 250
  Dorothy 219, 233
  Elizabeth 224
  Frances 240
  James 124
  Jane 219
  John 27
  Leonard 219, 250
  Michael 240
  Priscilla 28, 81
  Robert 28, 219
  Roger 28, 233
  Thomas 27, 28, 35, 81, 101
BROOKS, Annie E. 134
  Chaucey 82
  Jacob 28
  Nathan Covington 28

BROOKS, William E. 134
BROUGHTON, Mary 154
BROWN, --- 28
  Alexander 29
  Anna 89
  Anna M. 124
  Caroline 212
  Edward 127
  Elizabeth 8, 247
  Emeline 29, 34
  Frances 205
  George 29
  George John 29
  George Stewart 29
  George W. 29, 190
  Harry 8
  Henry 29
  Hugh 29, 34
  Ida C. 190
  James H. 29
  Jesse 29
  John 184
  John Smith 29
  Joseph L. 28
  Joshua 6
  Kirk 73
  Martha 62
  Mary 8, 15, 102
  Mary A. 30
  Mary Magdalene 268
  Matthew 89
  Peregrine 249
  Robert 30, 62
  Samuel 30
  William 28, 29, 30, 102
  William T. 28, 29
BROWNE, Abell 30
  Eleanor 249
  Ellen 249
  Hugh 30
  John 249
  Nicholas Manly 30
  Samuel 30
BROWNING, Joshua 30
  Meshack 30
  Ralph 30

BROWNING, Sarah 30
William 30
BRUCE, --- 213
Andrew 31
Elizabeth 210
Elizabeth T. 209
Norman 209
BRUENING, Meta 196
BRUNCH, Maria 6
BRUNDAGE, Mary 61
William 61
BRUNE, Frederick W. 31
BRUNNER, --- 31, 196, 268, 269
Ann Barbara 84
Anna Katherine 195
Elias 31
Henry 31
Jacob 31
John 31
Joseph 31, 195
Marai Elizabeth 195
Maria Elizabeth 191
Peter 206
BRY, Philip 189
BRYANT, Martha 110
BRYDEN, Cornelia 77
BRYLEY, Keziah 92
BRYNE, Philip 189
BUCCLEUGH, Dukes Of 184
BUCHANAN, Sarah Elizabeth
238
BUCHER, Howard 140
BUCKEY, George Peter 31
Henry 31
Susan 31
BUCKNALL, --- 119
BUDEKER, Carl A. 31
William 31
BUHRMAN, Henry 31
John 31
BULL, --- 31
Edmund 31
Jacob 31
John 31
William 31
BUNTIN, Elizabeth 82

BUNTING, James 32
Mary Alice Llewellyn 233
William 32
BUPPERT, Henry 32, 263
John 32
William Irwin 32
BURALL, --- 32
Adam 32
William 32
BURELY, Elizabeth 218
BURGER, Annie Margaret 32
Annie Rosetta 32
Charles Edward 32
Henry C. 32
William Alexander 32
William H. 32
BURGESS, Elizabeth 173
Ruth 264
William 60, 173, 200
BURK, --- (Mrs.) 262
BURKET, Peter 76
BURKHART, --- 268, 269
Charles H. 32, 171
George 32
Margaret 32
Peter 32
BURNESTON, Virginia 184
BURNHAM, John 94
BURNS, Elizabeth 262
Francis 32
Samuel 32
BURRIDGE, John 32
BURT, Alfred Patterson 33
BURTT, Thomas W. 33
BURWELL, Elizabeth 172
BUSH, Catherine 68
BUSSARD, Daniel 33
Hannah 129
John 77
John Wesley 33
Peter 33
Samuel 33
Sophia 33, 77
Susan 33, 77, 204
Ulstey 33
BUSSEY, Helen M. 103

BUTLER, --- (Miss) 99
    Absalom 33
    Mary 33
    Thomas 33
BUTT, Elizabeth 36
    Hazel 36
BUXTON, --- 33
    Basil 33
    Brook 33
    James 33
    John 33
    Lizzie 33
    Samuel 33
    Susan 33
    Susan P. 132
    Upton 33
BYE, Ann 65
BYERLY, --- 268, 269
    Jacob 101
BYERS, Gabriel 23
    Joseph 55
BYUS, Joseph 63
    William 63

C

CABELL, Elizabeth Caskie 33
    Nicholas 33
    William 33
CADDEN, Charles William 33
    R. 33
CADWALLADER, --- 33
    Robert 33
CADZOW, Elizabeth 182
CAILE, John 162
    Margaret 162
CAIRNES, George 34
    George A. 34
    William 34
CALDWELL, Joseph 264
    Lucy 67
    Martha 255
    Mary 264
CALLAGHAN, Daniel 34
    Patrick 34

CALLAGHAN, Timothy 34
CALVERT, --- 63
    Ann 219
    Anne 28
    Cecil 13
    Charles 208
    Cornelius 233
    Elizabeth 233
    George 226
    John 233
    Leonard 26, 27, 28, 59, 112,
        216, 219
    Lord 83
    Rose 209
CAMERON, Amor 29, 34
    James 48
    Mary 161
    Rachel 48
    Robert 29, 34, 161
CAMPBELL, --- 183
    Charles 34
    Christiana 158
    James 158
    Margaret E. 47
    William 47
CANBY, Letitia 85
CAPLAN, Lena 166
CAPLIN, Cecilia 214
CAPNER, Hugh 194
    Sarah Matilda 194
CAREY, Ellen 247
CARLIN, John 35
    John T. 35
CARLISLE, --- 6
CARLTON, Elsie 82
CARMICHAEL, Dugold 133
    William 133
CARPENTER, --- 233
    Abigail 35
    Elizabeth 119
    James Walter 233
    John 35
    Joseph 35
    Keziah 66
    Laura Maryland 233
    Samuel 35

CHEW, Samuel 38
　Sarah 38
　William F. 201
CHIDESTER, Eleanor 215
CHILD, Cephas 38
　Grace 38, 132
　Henry 38
　John 38
　Samuel 38
CHISELIN, Cesar 38
CHISOLM, Alexander 242
　J. Julian 242
　James J. 242
CHRIST, Elia Ann 171
CHRISTIE, George M. 38, 144
　James 38
　John 38, 144
CHRISTINA, Queen 97
CHRISTOPHER, Mary Rebecca
　210
CHURCHMAN, George 39
　John 39
CIOTTI, Andrew 39
　Joseph 39
　Marie 39
CLAGETT, --- (Miss) 16
　Edward 39
　Eleanor 71
　Mary 39
　Richard 39, 71
　Samuel 39
　Thomas 39
　Thomas J. 71
　Thomas John 39
CLAIBORNE, Edmund 39
　F. G. 39
　Thomas 39
　Thomas D. 39
　William 39
CLARK, Acsah Wilhelmina 123
　Alice 229
　Ann 31
　Anna 60
　David 40
　Eveline 10
　George 229

CLARK, Ichabod Eddy 169, 216
　James 40
　Jane 217
　John 40
　Martha 244
　Matthew 40
　Rachel 90
　Sarah Wilcox 169, 216
CLARKE, Elizabeth 42
　Lucy 9
　Reuben 9
CLATONIA, Mary 53
CLAUTICE, George 59
　Peter 59
　William Francis 59
CLAYTON, John 40
　Powell 40
　Richard 40
　Susan Smith 40
　Thomas 40
　Wesley 40
　William 40
CLEMENTS, Elizabeth 42
　Robert 141
CLEMSON, --- 40
　James 40
　John 40
　Margaret 40
CLESSON, Hannah 4
　Joseph 4
CLINCK, G. F. 61
CLINE, Alexander 41
　Caspar 69
　Casper 41, 69
　George 41
　George T. 69
　Mary 69
　Philip 41
　Thomas 41
CLUGSTON, Robert 71
CO, Susan 246
COALE, --- 38
　Elizabeth 41
　Hannah 41
　Hester 41
　Isaac 41

CRANWELL, James Harford 46
John 46
CRAPSTER, --- 46
Hannah 46
CRAWFORD, Alice 251
David 251
John 47
William 211
CREAGER, Susan 31
CREAMER, Henry 47
Valentine 47
CRESAP, Fannie 217
Michael 217
Thomas 47
CRESWELL, Charles E. 46
John 7
John A. J. 7
William 46
CRISSMAN, Abram 76
Daniel 76
CRIST, Daniel 47
David 47
George W. 47
Jacob Adam 47
John George 47
Philip 47
CROMBIE, Sarah E. 5
CROMWELL, --- 221
Edith 86
Henry 47
John Hammond 47
Oliver 47, 86, 250
CRONISE, Eva 269
CROSS, Andrew 48
Ellen 130
Jane 130
John 48, 130
CROSSBASKET, Laird Of 183
CROTHERS, Alpheus 48
James 48
John 48
John Lawrence 48
Richard H. 48
William 48
CROUSE, Frank E. 171
John T. 161

CROW, John 48
John Taylor 48
CROWE, Amelia 209
Michael 209
CROXALL, Charles Moale 48
Richard 48
CRUM, Alice 48
Casper 48
Catharine 48
Charles 48
Frank 48
George C. 48
Harry 48
Mollie 48
CRUMBINE, --- 133
CRUSE, Mary 49
Thomas 49
CUDDY, John P. 105
Rebecca A. 105
Ruth C. 105
CULLER, --- 49
Catherine 191
Elizabeth 49
Henry 49
Jacob 49
John 49
Michael 49
Susan 49
CULMAN, Caroline 140
CULVER, Edward 49
Jonathan 49
Samuel 49
Solomon 49
William Edward 49
CUMMINGS, --- 50
Andrew J. 50
James 50
James W. 50
CUMMINS, Jessie Stuart 107
CUNNINGHAM, Elizabeth 50
James Bell 50
John 50
Winifred 157
CUPPETT, Jacob 50
John 50
Thomas H. 50

DIAMOND, John 55
John B. 55
William C. 55
DICK, Elisha Cullen 182
Julia 182
DICKEY, Charles E. 204
Mazie 144
DIEHL, Albert 107
John 55
Julius F. 55
Lizzie 107
Matilda 74
DIELMAN, Adelaide Young 126
Henry 126
DIETZ, Elizabeth C. 219
George W. 219
DIFFENBALL, Catherine 55
John 55
DIFFENDALL, Samuel M. 71
DILL, John 146
Susan 146
DILLER, Casper 55
John 55
Martin 55
DILWORTH, Anne Brooke 90
Emma 150
Emma M. 150
Peter 150
DINSMORE, --- 136
DINTERMAN, George 55
DISTLER, John Cyrus 55, 56
DITTMAN, Amelia 42
DOBREE, Elizabeth Charlotte 50
DODSON, Daniel 56
John 56
Mary 56
Robert 56
Susannah 56
Thomas 56
DOERNER, Emma 195
DOHME, Charles 56
Charles Emil 56
Gustavus Christian 56
Louis 56
DOLLMAN, John 56
John G. 56

DONNELLY, James W. 56
DONOHUE, Charles 56
John 56
Rose 93
Terence Aloysius 42, 57
DONOVAN, Richard 57
DONSIFE, Catharine Mary 57
DORRITEE, Susan Arringdale
150
DORSEY, --- 163
Anne 57
Basil 58
Bridget 57
Cordelia 58
Daniel 57
Deborah 39, 71, 198
Edward 57
Elizabeth 198
John 39, 57, 71, 198, 205
Joshua 57, 197
Mary Hammond 47
Patrick 57
Philemon 100
Richard Brooke 57
Sarah 52, 118, 266
Vernon John 57
Vernon M. 57
William Hammond 57
DORTON, Frederick Theodore 58
Henry Frederick 58
DOSCHER, Laura 56
DOTTERER, --- 58
Frederick 58
John 58
Mary Catharine 58
DOTY, John 84
DOUB, Elizabeth 100
Elizaeth 99
Jacob 100
DOUGLAS, Henry 58
Robert 58
DOUGLASS, Mary Elizabeth 174
DOVE, Catherine 167
DOWNEY, --- 58
John 58
William 58

DOYLE, James 58
  Maria J. 58
DOYNE, Mary 53
  Robert 58
DRONENBURG, --- 59
  Jacob 59
DRAKE, Francis 58
  Mary 58
DREBERT, Mary Ann 95
DREHR, Annie M. 32
DRILL, Mary 138
DRIVER, Auguste 84
  Catherine 104
  F. 216
  John 104
  Pemla 216
DRUMMOND, John 103
DRURY, Charles 59
  Samuel 59
  William 59
DRYDEN, Joshua 200
  Sewell 200
DRYSDALE, Alexander 89
  Ellen 89
DU BOIS, Elizabeth 27
DU BOSE, Elizabeth 27
DU FIEF, Mary 59
  Nicholas G. 59
DUCKWORTH, Maria L. 213
DUDDERAR, Conrade 59
  George Philip 59
  William 59
DUDLEY, --- (Miss) 142
  Lord 142
DUDREAR, Ella V. 127
DUGAN, --- 38
  Frank 154
  Louis 114
  Sarah 114
DUKE, Abraham 190
  Gussie 190
  James 59
  Richard 59
  Thomas 59
DUKENSHEETS, --- (Miss) 59
DULANY, --- 59

DULANY, Daniel 60
  Edward 103
  William 59
DUNCAN, Alexander Edward 263
  Frances 11
  John 263
  John Thomas 263
  Margaret 158
  Moses 262
  William Joseph 263
  William Wesley 263
DUNKHURST, Dorcas 105
DUNLOP, James 183
  Jane 183
DUNN, --- (Miss) 120
  Andrew 60
  Charles B. 60
  George G. 60
  James F. 60
  Kate 166
  Katherine Wright 60
DUNNIGAN, --- 60
  John 60
DUNSTER, Henry 60
  Jane 60
DURHAM, --- 60
  Abel 60, 260
  David 60
  Samuel 60
  Sarah H. 260
  William A. 60
DURTOW, Elizabeth 24
DUSHANE, Anna Maria 122
  Nathan T. 122
DUTROW, Columbia 247
  Rebecca E. 247
  Samuel 247
DUVAL, Mary Alice 106
DUVALL, Benjamin 61
  Lewis 198
  Mareen 60, 61, 95
  Marsh M. 61
  Mary 95
  Susanna 60
  William T. 61
DUYCKINCK, Horace H. 61

EICHELBERGER, Martin 64
Mary Magdalene 64
Philip Frederick 64
EISENBRADT, Christian H. 64
Sophia W. 64
EISENBRANDT, Augusta 249
Christian H. 249
ELBERT, Elizabeth Anne 212
Hugh 212
William 212
ELDER, Aloysius 65
Anna 65
Arnold 65
Benjamin 64
Charles 64
Edward 64
Elizaeth 65
George 64
Guy 64
Ignatius 65
James 64
Joseph 64
Judith 64
Mary 64
Polly 64
Priscilla 64
Richard 64
Sarah 54
Thomas 64, 65
William 64, 65
ELDRIDGE, James F. 248
ELLET, Joan 132
Peter 132
ELLICOTT, Andrew 65
John 65
Joseph 65
ELLINGER, Jacob 65
Rosalie 65
Samuel 65
ELLIOTT, Elizabeth 103
Sarah 137
ELLIS, Anne 49
Charles 65
Charles M. 65, 119
Eleanor 34
Francis Asbury 65, 119

ELLIS, Rowland 65
ELMER, Edward 65
Horace 66
Jonathan 65
Lewis 66
Nathaniel 65
Samuel 65
William Stewart 66
ELTONHEAD, Jane 74
Richard 74
William 74
ELY, Charles Wright 66
Elias S. 66
Richard 66
EMMERICH, --- 66
Ellen Cora 66
George Washington 66
EMMETT, Robert 95, 140
William 140
EMMITT, Lydia 231
William 231
EMMONS, Ann S. 66
Arthur 66
Asa 66
Asaph 66
Burton 66
Carolus 66
Charles Cadwell 67
Charles DeMoss 67
Charles Trescott 66, 67
Elizabeth 66
Franklin 66
Hannah 66
Isaac T. 66
John 66
John S. 66
Katherine 66
Laura 66
Lewis 66
Lydia 66
Mariah 66
Mary 66
Mira 66
Nancy 66
Salmon 66
Samuel 66

FULTON, Charles C. 5
  Charles Carroll 79
  George 79
  Margaret 79
  William 79
FUNK, Catherine 104

G

G'FREY, Mary 241
GADDESS, --- 80
  Alexander 80
GAIL, Elise 238
  George William 238
GAILLAIRD, William 82
GAINER, Ann 182
GAITHE, Pauline Riggs 179
GAITHER, Amelia 77
  John 80, 250
  Ruth 250
GALL, Anna E. 67
  Barbara 96
  Charles M. 80
  Edward 80
  Elizabeth 67
  Eva 80
  Henry 80
  John 80
  William 67, 80
GALLAGHER, Alice 10
GALLATIN, Albert 180
  James 180
GALVIN, Thomas K. 131
  William 80
GANS, Henrietta 80
  William 80
GANTT, Edward 80, 81
  Elizabeth 39
  Roger 80
  Thomas 28, 80, 81
GARDY, --- 237
GARNER, Mary 202
GARNKIRKE, Laird Of 183
GARR, Helen A. 235
GARRETT, --- 60

GARRETT, Amos 81, 265
  James 81
  John 81
  John Work 81
  Mary 265
  Michael 81
  Robert 81
  Sarah 81
GARROTT, --- 81
GARTLAND, Catherine 160
GARY, --- 81
  James 81
  James Sullivan 81
  John 81
GASSAWAY, John 82
  Nicholas 82
GATCH, Eleanor M. 209
GATES, Eliza 125
  L. 125
GAULT, Andrew 82
  Cyrus 82
  Jane 82
  Matthew 82
  Patrick 82
  Samuel 82
GAVER, Daniel 82
  George 82
  Henry 82
  John 82
  John T. 82
GAY, Margaret 31
GAYLORD, Aaron 82
  Lorena 82
GAYSON, Jane 64
GEAR, George 234
GEARHARDT, --- 3
GEDDES, James 83
  James W. 83
GEESEY, John A. 178
  Susannah Rebecca 220
GEHAUF, Catherine 206
GEISBERT, Elizabeth Ann 247
GEMMILL, S. Alice 163
GEORGE, A. Frederick 83
  Anthony 83
  Jame E. 83

298

GEORGE, William E. 83
GEORGE III, King 182
GERARD, Elizabeth 83
  Richard 83
  Thomas 83
GERAULD, Martha 254
GERNAND, Daniel 250
GERNARD, --- 258
  Andrew 221
GERSTELL, Arnold 217
  Josephine 217
GESEY, Catherine 83
  Elias 83
  Martha 83
  Sarah 83
  Theodore 83
GETTEMULLER, Henry J. 83
  Herman H. 83
GETTY, John 83
  Robert 83
GETZENDANNER, Adam 84
  Christian 84
  Daniel 108
  Grace Ann 55
  Jacob 84
  John 84
  Jonathan 84
  P. D. 55
  Sarah Ann 55
GIBSON, Elizabeth 50
  Henriette Octavia 190
  Lewis 50
GICHNER, Jacob 253
  Regina 253
GIDDINGS, --- 99
  Elizabeth 63
  George W. 63
GIESKE, Gustave 84
  Walter M. 84
GIFFORD, James 84
  Joseph 84
GILBERT, --- 84, 228
  Adam 55
  Ann 203
  Elizabeth 84
  Ellen 55

GILBERT, George Henry 84
  Henry 84
  Humphrey 8
  John 84
  Lizzie 84
  Margaret 84
  Micah 84
  Michael 84
  Robert J. 84
GILDER, --- 146
GILES, E. Walter 85
  Edward Walter 95
  Emma 95
  Walter 84
GILESPIE, Jean 256
GILL, --- 85
  Ann 171
  Anne 233
  Benjamin 233
  Elizabeth 85
  George M. 85
  John 85
  Nicholas 85
  Stephen 85
GILLIS, Alexander F. 85
  Alexander James 85
  Esther 261
  Roderick 85
GILLY, Ann 28
GILMOR, Robert 85
GILPIN, Bernard 85
  Elizabeth 85
  Hannah 85
  John 85
  Joseph 85
  Mary 85
  Rachel 85, 182
  Samuel 85
GINGELL, George 86
  James Madison 86
  Joseph 86
GIST, Christopher 86
  Richard 86
GITTINGS, Thomas 86
GLADHILL, Catherine 78
GLASS, Christian 201

GLASS, Sarah Ann 201
GLAZE, David 228
 Elizabeth 228
GLEN, Alexander Lindsey 86
 Jacob Alexander 86
GLENDOWER, Owen 200
GLENKA, Viola 136
GLENN, John 182
GLIDDEN, Charles 86
 Edward Hughes 86
 Joseph 86
 William Pierce Harrington 86
GLOSS, C. H. 77
GLUCK, Aaron Manns 86
 Henry 86
GNAGY, Christian 86
 Elizabeth 86
 Emanuel 86
GODMAN, Thomas 199
GOETZ, Margaret 257
GOLDBACH, Otto 87
GOLDBERG, Hannah 206
GOLDHAWK, Mary 46
GOLDSBOROUGH, Anne E. 180
 Charles W. 14
 Felix Vincent 110
 Henry Paul 110
 Howles 180
 Judith 87
 Nicholas 87
 Rebecca 180
 Robert 87
 Robert Henry 87
 William 180
GOLDSMITH, Mathilda 176
GOLDSTEIN, Bertha 253
GOLDSTROM, Bernhardt 87
 Helen 87
 Isidor 87
 Marion 87
 Stella 87
GOODCHILD, Mary 11
GOODLEY, Mary P. 40
GORDON, Archibald 88
 Charles 88
 David 88

GORDON, Peter 88
GORMAN, John 88
GORSUCH, Ann 237
 Charles 88, 146
 Edward 88
 John 88, 146, 237
GORTEN, William 231
GORTER, Gosse Onno 88
 James P. 88
GOUFF, Mary C. 186
GOUGH, Elizabeth 88
 Hannah E. 88
 Harry 88
 Harry D. 88
 James 88
 Stephen 88
 Thomas Washington 88
 William 88
 William Joseph 248
GOULD, Alexander 89
 John 89
GOURLEY, Margaret 9
GRABILL, Abraham 89
 John 89
GRACE, Luther 121
 Miriam Rebecca 121
GRACIE, Jessie 192
GRAEBE, Sophie 56
GRAFF, --- 89
 Charles B. 89
 Elizabeth E. 89
 John P. 89
 Sophia T. 89
 William 89
GRAFTON, Basil 89
 Martin 89
 Nathan 89
GRAHAM, --- 53
 Edith 80
 Ellen 151
 John 151
 Mary 80, 193
 Robert 193
 Thomas 53
GRANDIN, Eleanor 194
 John 194

GRANT, Daniel 89
Isabella 89
James 89
John 89
Rachel 89
Robert 89
Ulysses S. 112
William 89
GREASLEY, Jacob 89
Philip H. 89
GREEN, --- 133
Abigail 113
Conrad 250
George 90
James E. 90
Mildred 255
Perry 15
Thomas 255
GREENBERRY, Anne 90
Charles 90
Katherine 90
Nicholas 90, 266
Ruth 90
GREENBURY, Elizabeth 87
Mary 96
GREENE, Thomas 90
GREENFIELD, Anne 81
Caleb 90
Nathan 90
Sarah Marie 90
Thomas 81, 90
GREENWOOD, Dorothy 90
GREGORY, Andrew 215
Henry 215
Judah 215
Mary Eleanor 215
GRIER, Elizabeth Helen 155
James 91
James A. 91
John 91
GRIFFISS, Blanche 91
Edward 91
Thomas J. 91
Warren 91
GRIFFITH, Elizabeth 142, 255
Henry 198

GRIFFITH, Mary E. 121
Ruth 198
Samuel 255
Sophia 61
Thomas 91
GRIGG, Harriet 19
William 19
GRIMES, --- 91
Lucy 172
Philip 172
Rachel 115
Samuel 91
GRINDALL, --- 91
John 91
GRINDER, --- 91
Michael 91
Samuel 91, 92
GRISBERT, Jennie 164
GRONS, Anna Mary 113
GROSS, --- 92
August 92
Henry 92
Jacob 92
Jonathan 92
Urias 186
GROSSE, Elizabeth 221
Roger 221
GROSSINGER, Louisa Anne 134
GROSSNICKLE, --- 92
Christianna 92
Daniel 92
Elizabeth 92, 100
Hannah 92
Jacob 92
John 92
Lydia 92
Mary 92
Peter 92
Rebecca 92
Susan 92
GROVE, Elias 128
John Henry 128
Mary Catherine 212
GROVES, Rebecca A. 106
GRUMBINE, Daniel M. 92
Jacob 92

GRUMBINE, Margaret 92
GUILFORD, Mae K. 222
　William F. 222
GUILFOYLE, Henry W. 92
　Mary E. 92
　William 92
GUNNING, Helen 93
　James 93
GUNTER, Frederick 93
　Sophia 93
GUNTHER, --- 93
　Frank Henry 93
　George 93
　George John 93
　John F. 93, 112
　Ludolph Wilhelm 93
　Rose Elizabeth 112
GURLEY, Mary 151
GURWITZ, Anna 164
GUTMAN, Ella 93
　Joel 93
　Moses 93
GUY, Nancy 185
　Richard 185
　Robert 185
GUYTHER, --- 41
GWYNN, Andrew Jackson 94
　David 94
　Elizabeth 94
　Hugh 94
　Humphrey 94
　John 94
　John Hillery 94
　Katherine 94
　Sarah 94

H

HAAS, Caroline Elizabeth 181
　John F. 181
HACHTEL, Barbara 75
　George L. 75
HACK, Elizabeth Smith 13
　Peter 13
HACKETT, --- (Maj.) 11

HACKETT, Henrietta J. Bedford
　11
HADDOCK, Sarah 250
HAENSLER, George 63
HAFER, --- (Miss) 196
　Abraham 196
　Annie 196
　Kate 196
　William 196
HAGAN, John 94
　John Ernest 94
HAGAR, Sarah 256
HAGENBROUZER, Louise 166
HAGUE, Pleasant 124
HAHN, Abraham 163
　Adolph 94
　Adolphus 94
　Annie C. 94
　Charles 94
　Clara A. 94
　Henry A. 94
　Jacob 145
　William A. 94
HAIG, Agnes 181
　Sarah 4
HAILER, Barbara 180
　Christian F. 180
HAINES, --- 94
　--- (Mrs.) 196
　Catharine 226
　John 95
　Joseph 95
　Margaret 95
　Mary 40
　Rebecca T. 74
　Richard 95
　Samuel 94
　Thomas 94
HALE, Mary 53
HALL, Elihew 95
　Elisha 95
　Haney 25
　Henry 95
　Joseph 95
　Martha 254
　Richard 95

302

HARGETT, Peter 98
HARLAN, David 99
  Etta 102
  George 99
  Jeremiah 99
  Michael 99
  Reuben S. 102
HARLAND, Hannah 24
HARLEY, A. G. 99
  Eliza 99
  Elizabeth 99
  Jane 99
  Joshua 99
  Mahlon 99
  Sophia 99
  Thomas 99
  Thomas H. 99
  William 99
HARMAN, Blanche Ferguson 62
  Walter 62
HARMANSON, George 251
  Rose Anne 251
HARN, John H. (Mrs.) 84
HARP, --- 100
  Catharine 139
  Daniel 99
  George 99, 100
  John 99, 100
  John Michael 99, 100
  Michael 99
HARPER, --- (Miss) 66
  Ann 229
  James 262
HARRINGTON, Amanda 263
  Prudence 69
HARRIS, --- 132
  Henry 189
  James H. 100
  Margaret 122
  Martha 148
  Mary A. 189
  Mary Elizabeth 100
  Nathan 100
  Thomas 100
  William 100, 122
HARRISON, --- (Miss) 235

HARRISON, Charles W. 128
  Margaret 253
  Mary 160
  Mary J. 34
  Sarah 41, 234
HARRY, Amelia Knode 18
HARSHMAN, --- 100
  Christian 100
  Daniel 92
  Elias 100
  John 92, 100
  Polly (Mary) 7
HART, Almira 184
  Joseph 88
  Margaret 231
  Rebecca 114
  Sarah 88
HARTING, Francese 220
HARTMAN, --- 215
HARTOGENSIS, --- 101
  Benjamin Henry 101
  Henry S. 101
HARTSHORNE, Rebecca 165
  William 165
HARTSON, Mary 99
HARVEY, Elizabeth 224
  Margaret 144
HARWARD, C. W. 136
  Ella V. 136
HARWOOD, Mary 101
  Richard 101
  Thomas 101
HASENMEYER, Caroline 208
HASGOOD, Elizabeth 77
HATCH, Hughby 231
HATHAWAY, Apphia 168
HATTON, --- (Miss) 90
  Eleanor 28, 101
  Elinor 35
  Margaret 101
  Mary 43
  Richard 28
HAUER, Barbara 101
  Catharine 101
  Daniel 101
  Elizabeth 101

HENDERSON, Eliza 92
George 106
John 106
Robert 106
Sarah 60
HENKEL, Harry A. 107
Henry A. 107
HENNECKE, Rosina 161
HENRIETTA MARIA, Queen 143
HENRIQUES, Joseph 107
Moses 107
HENRY, Elise Garr 235
Francis A. 235
John 198
HENSON, Elizabeth 158
Thomas 158
HEPBRON, Thomas 107
HEPPS, Anna R. 105, 106
HERBERT, Arthur William 107
Henry 107
James 99
Margaret Rebecca 99
Mary J. 37
HERING, Granville T. 133
Jennie Carroll 133
HERMANN, Charles M. 107
Gotlieb 107
HERON, Susannah 240
HERRICK, Lydia S. 179
HERRING, George 107
HERRMANN, Elizabeth 131
HERSBERGER, Bernard 52
Henry 52
Susan 52
HERSHBERGER, --- 107
Bernard 107
Catherine 107
Clarissa 108
David 108
Dorothy 130
Elizabeth 107
Henry 107
Hiram 108
John 108
John B. 107
Joseph C. 108

HERSHBERGER, Mary 107
Missouri 108
Susan 108
Thomas 108
HERVEY, Frances 108
Jane 108
Nicholas 108
HERWIG, Elizabeth 153
HESS, Charles 108
Maria 251
Samuel 108
HESSEN, Jacob D. 163
HETRICK, Adam 108
John 108
Nicholas 108
HETT, Henry 108
John 108
Margaret J. 108
HETZEL, Caroline Frederick 109
Christian F. 108
Christina Matilda 109
John Joshua 109
Philip Joshua 108, 109
HETZELL, George 109
John 109
HEUISLER, Joseph Anthony 109
HEWELL, --- 109
James Lewis 109
HEYN, Louise 46
Martin 46
HIBBARD, Hannah 49
Robert 49
HICKLEY, Elizabeth Cecilia 238
HICKMAN, Ella 109
George H. C. 109
John 109
John P. 109
Millard 109
William 109
HICKS, Lucy 9
HIESTER, Daniel 109, 110
John 109, 110
Joseph 109, 110
HIGGINBOTHAM, Ann 110
HIGGINS, Frank 11
John 11

HIGGINS, William 211
HILBERT, Samantha J. 149
HILD, Georgius 110
 Margaret Ann 110
HILDEBRAND, --- 110
 Amanda 110
 John 110
 Joshua 110
 Laura A. 110
 Lewis A. 110
 Louisa 110
 Lydia 110
 Sopohia 110
 William 110
HILDT, John 110
 Maggie E. 93
HILL, Charles E. 111
 Clement 110
 George 110
 Margaret Ann 221
 Mary 8
 Ralph 111
 Richard 8
 Thomas 110
 Thomas Gardner 110
HILLEARY, Ann Perry 111
 Elizabeth 111
 Ellen McGill 111
 John 111
 John Henry 111
 John William 111
 Sarah 148
 Thomas 111, 148
 Tilghman 111
HILLERY, Henry 267
 Thomas 267
 Walter 267
HILLIS, Frank Norman 111
 John David 111
HILTON, Benjamin 6
 Clement 111
 Robert S. 111
 Susan 111
 Thomas 111
HILTZ, John 111, 229
 Philip 111, 229

HIMES, Nancy J. 220
HINCHMAN, Elizabeth B. 164
 Harriet 164
 John G. 164
HINDMAN, Martha 91
HINEMAN, William 251
HINES, Ann Maria 29
 Matthew 111, 112
 Sarah 112
HINKLE, --- 266
HINMAN, Samuel 49
 Sarah 49
HITCHINS, Adam E. 112
 Owen Eaton 112
HOAG, Elizabeth 181
 Henry 181
HOAR, Katherine 157
HOBBS, John 248
 Mary 248
HODGES, Joseph 42
 Josephine 42
 Mary 152
 Thomas 112
HOEN, Augustus 112
 Berthold 112
 Dora 112
 Guida 112
 Martin 112
HOFFMAN, --- 112
 Alexander 112
 Daniel 112
 Elizabeth 11, 104
 Elizabeth M. 225
 Emily C. 142
 Joseph L. 225
 Mary 58, 225
HOFFMANN, Alexander 93
HOFMANN, Julius Kayser 112
 Peter 112
HOHF, Elizabeth 244
HOHING, Conrad 113
 George 113
HOHMAN, Therese 63
HOKE, Jacob 113
 Peter 113
 Sarah B. 107

314

KLIPP, Charles 134
  Elizabeth 134
  Henry 134
  John 134
  Paul 134, 135
KLOGOUR, William 131
KNABE, William 134
KNAPP, Deborah 192
  Frederick 134
KNIGHT, Daniel 127
KNIUGHT, T. J. 127
KNOTT, --- (Miss) 35
KNOX, Sallie 82
KOCH, Daniel 42
  Louise 42
KOEBER, Lena 134
KOEHN, Minnie 184
KOENIG, William 134
KOHN, Max 87
KOLIOPULOS, Demetrois S. 134
  Sophia 134
  Stratis 134
KOOGLE, Susan 165
KOONS, Abraham 135
  Frederick 15
  George 135
  George T. 205
  Henry 134, 135
  John 135
KOONTZ, Edward 63
  John 135
KOOPMAN, Jette 183
KORN, Charles 135
  Elizabeth Anna 135
KORRELL, Charles 135
  Elizabeth 135
  Frank 135
  John 135
  John A. 135
  Mary 135
KRAFT, Frederick 135
KRAMER, Susanna 14
KRANTZ, Frederick J. 135
  John D. 135
  William H. 135
KRAUSE, Charles 207

KREH, Charles 136
  Christiana 136
  John 136
  John F. 136
  Lewis T. 136
  Mary 136
  Peter 136
  William H. 136
KREITLER, Catherine 12
KROUSE, Elizabeth 197
  John H. 197
KROUT, Dora 26
KUCH, Polly 196
KUHL, Charlotte J. 149
KUHLMAN, Henry 136
  John Frederick 136
KUHN, Ann 2
  Henry 2
KUNDERS, Margaret 242
KUNKLE, Pauline 178
KUNKOWSKI, Andrew 136
  Catherine 136
  Frank 136
  Joseph 136
  Mitchell 136
KUNTZ, Susan 255
KURTZ, Edward 136
  Elizabeth 184
  Evaline 225
  John Nicolas 136
KYLE, Adam 136
  George 136
  Samuel A. S. 136

LA BARRE, --- 137
  Angeline 137
  George Royal 137
LACKLAND, Hester 124
LAFAYETTE, --- (Gen.) 137
LAMAR, John 137
  Peter 137
  Thomas 137
  William 99

MC CRONE, Margaret 24
MC CUBBIN, Atlanta T. 197
  Oliver 197
MC CULLOUGH, Edward O'Neal
      264
  Esther 193
  Genevieve Anita 264
  Margaret 197
  Martha 133
  William Henry 264
MC CURDY, Alexander C. 156
  Charles 156
  George 156
  Ira J. 156
  James 156
  James Crawford 156
  John 156
MC DERMOTT, Julia 189
  Mary 257
MC DEVIT, Jane 2
MC DEVITT, Edward 156
MC DONAL, William 156
MC DONALD, John 157
  Thomas 157
MC DONOUGH, Joh 157
  John 157
  Stephen J. 157
MC DOWELL, Alexander 157
  David 157
  Henry C. 157
  James 157
MC ELFRESH, Arianna 239
  David 157
  John H. 157
MC GAGA, --- 157
  David 157
  Duenna 157
  John 157
  Joseph 157
  Leanna 157
  Mary 157
  Thomas 157
  William 157
MC GANN, Bernard 157
  John H. 157
  Kate 157

MC GANN, Mary 157
  Nora 157
MC GAW, Jane 97
  Robert 158
MC GEE, Annie 8
  Annie Agnes 8
  Thomas 8
MC GILL, Eleanor West 158
  James 158
  Thomas J. 158
MC GINNIS, Hannah Marie 207
  Henry M. 207
MC GOUGH, Bridget 81
MC HENRY, --- 158
  --- (President) 158
  James 158
MC ILVAIN, Donald 158
  Elizabeth Grant 7, 14, 15, 123
  William 158
MC INTIRE, William 220
MC IVER, Eliza 129
MC KANNA, James 158
MC KELVEY, Ellen 5
MC KENZIE, --- (Miss) 88, 187
MC KEW, Susanna 90
MC KIM, David Telfair 158
  John 158, 159
  Thomas 159
MC KINNEY, David Ferguson
      159
  James Harris 159
  M. M. 159
  Matthew 159
MC KINSEY, --- 159
  Folger 159
  James 159
MC KINSTRY, Evan 175
  Mary Ann 175
MC KUSTER, John 57
  Sarah J. 57
MC LAIN, Daniel 159
  James 159
  John 159
  Samuel 159
MC LANAHAN, Isabella 29
MC LAUGHLIN, George 159

MC LAUGHLIN, Margaret 215
MC LEAN, Alice 72
Eugene L. 159
William J. 72
MC MANUS, Helena 110
MC MILLAN, Catherine 154
MC MURRAY, Caroline Selmann
118
MC NABB, James 160
Thomas 159
MC NAMEE, Francis 160
Merritt S. 160
MC NEAL, Archibald 160
Hector 160
MC NEIL, Margaret 155
MC PHERSON, --- (Miss) 73
Jane 124
Janet 160
John 160
Robert 160
MC SHERRY, --- 205
Edward 160
James 160
Patrick 160
MC VEY, John 161
Mary 193
Nancy 161
MC WILLIAMS, John 40, 161
Kate 40
MEAD, Marion Elizabeth 145
William 145
MEAKIN, Emma Louisa 161
Samuel 161
MEARNS, Abel 161
Andrew 161
MEDFORD, Anna Maria 161
Macall 161
MEDTARD, Barbara 174
MEDTART, Susan 174
MEERES, John 235
MEHRLING, Anna Mary 161
August 161
George W. 161
Henry 161
John Lewis 161
Lewis William 161

MEHRLING, Margaret Elizabeth
161
Phillipina 161
MEID, Conrad 161
MEIER, August H. F. 161
Gustav 161
Hency C. A. 161
Herman 161
Mary 161
William 161
MEIERS, Erustina 126
MEISER, John 219
MELTHORN, Adelaide S. 168
MELVILLE, James 162
John 162
John Graham 162
MELZER, Sarah 166
MENDSEN, --- 176
Sophia 176
MENGER, Amelia 77
Volantine 77
MENTZER, Catherine 163
David 251
Hannah 251
MERCER, Gracen 128
John 162
John Francis 162
Robert 162
MERCIER, --- 162
Archibald 163
Betsey 162
Cordelia 163
Cornelius 163
Fanny 162
John 163
John William 162
Keturah 163
Millie 163
Nancy 162
Rachel 163
Richard 163
Robert 163
Tivis 163
William 163
William F. 162
MEREDITH, Harry Lionel 163

323

N

NAYLOR, Mary 171
  Priscilla 132
NEAL, Anne Elizabeth 9
NEALE, Anthony 171
  Dorothy 28, 171, 233
  Henreitta Marie 19
  Henrietta 171
  Henrietta Maria 143
  Henrietta Marie 171
  James 28, 143, 171, 233
  Maria 171
  Raphael 171
NEEDLE, Sidney 171
  Simon 171
NEFF, Ann March 174
  Cordelia 159
  Mary Harnish 159
  Victoria 195
  William 159
NEIDENTHOHL, Henry Andrew
    174
  Jacob 174
  Norman Leslie 174
NEIDHART, Augustus 171
  Joseph William 171
  Lena 171
  Louisa 171
  Mary E. 171
  Rudolph 171
NEIGHBORS, Elizabeth 171
  Elizabeth R. 32
  John T. 171
  Martha 171
  Nathan O. 171
  Sarah 171
  William 171
NEIKIRK, --- (Miss) 117
NEIMANN, Edward 84
NEISTADT, Charles 172
  Maurice 172
NELSON, Elizabeth 191
  Francis 172
  Hugh 172
  John 174
  Keating S. 172
  Rebecca 258

NELSON, Sallie Page 172
  Scotch Tom 172
  Thomas 172
  William 172
NEUBERGER, Caroline 121
  Eli Baer 121
NEWBOLD, Adriana 172
  Jane 172
  Murphy 172
  Sarah 172
  Thomas 172
NEWCOMER, Catherine 172
  Henry 172
  John 172
  Samuel 172
  Wolfgang 172
NEWELL, Harriet 226
  John 172
  M. A. 172
NEWMAN, Francis 267
  Jacob 173
  Jacob M. 173
  John 52
  John Nicholas 173
  Susan Bird 267
  Susanna 52
NEWTON, Ann Mildred 48
  Sarah North 158, 260
NICHOL, --- (Gov.) 217
NICHOLS, Jacob 173
  John 173
  Susanna 20
  Susannah 10, 20
  William 10, 20
NICHOLSON, --- 173
  Francis 95
  Joseph 173
  William 173
NICODEMUS, --- 173, 174
  Conrad 174
  Henry 173, 174
  John L. 174
  Valentine 174
NIXDORFF, Henry 174, 208
  John George 174
  Mary 208

O

OBENDERFER, Mary 177
Sabean 177
OBRECHT, Christian 209
ODENBAUGH, Mary 120
OFFUTT, Sarah 100
OGG, Catherine 199
George 199
OGLE, Benjamin 177
Samuel 11, 177
OLAND, --- 177
Alice E. 177
Carlton E. 177
Charles F. 177
David P. 177
Frances 177
Frederick 177
Jacob L. 177
Lucretia 177
Virginia 178
OLDHAM, Susan R. 259
OLER, --- 178
George 178
Jacob 178
John 178
Peter 178
OLINGER, Anna 47
OLIVER, John Rathbone 178
Mary 70
Robert Shaw 178
Thomas 178
William 241
OPITZ, Mary 133
ORBEL, Joanna 67
Margaret 67
Samuel 67
ORDEMAN, Charles O. 178
Daniel T. 178
Emma C. 178
Frederick A. 178
Georgiana 178
Herman 178
John H. 178
Mary C. 178
ORGAN, Nancy 79
ORNDORF, Eliza 260
James 23

ORR, Anna B. 47
Robert 47
ORRICK, James 265
Priscilla 265
ORRISON, Charles 110
OSCHMAN, Fredericke 5
OTT, Margaret 250
OTTE, Augusta 178
Charlotte 178
Lewis 178
Louise 178
Minnie 178
Robert Adolph 178
Theodore 178
William 178
OTTERBEIN, Philip G. 179
OTTO, Christian J. 179
Jacob J. 179
OULD, Henry 179
Henry Longitude Seal 179
Jane 179
Robert 179
OVERHULTZ, Elizabeth 196
OWAINS, Richard 179
OWEN, Jane 200
John 179
Nancy 236
Robert 236
OWENS, Ann 154
John E. 179
Owen Griffith 179
Richard 179
OWINGS, Edward 69
Isaac 179
Joshua 179
Miranda 69
Rebecca 179
Richard 179
Samuel 179

P

PABST, Caroline 243
PACKARD, --- 179
Amos 179

PACKARD, Morrill Nathaniel 179
Samuel 179
PAGE, John 172
Lucy 172
Mary Mann 260
Robert 260
PAGELS, Christopher 180
Edward 180
George H. 180
PAGON, --- 180
William Watters 60
PAINTER, Hannah 239
PALMER, Elizabeth Jane 128
Ella 39
George 128
PAMPEL, Elizabeth 248
F. 248
PAPE, --- (Dr.) 189
Bertha 189
PAPIN, Joseph Marie 180
Pierre 180
PARKER, George W. 109
Jane 148
Laura Susan 111
Lewis B. 111
Mary 109
PARKS, Eleanor 268
PARR, Anna Maria 161
Catherine 62
PARROT, Elizabeth 148
Gabriel 148
Susannah 148
PARROTT, Augustin 180
John H. 180
PARSON, Hannah 152
PARSONS, Amanda 237
Isabel 188
Jehu 237
Mary 188
Thomas 188
PASCAULT, --- 180, 181
Jean Charles Marie Louis 180
Josephine Marie Henrietta 180
Louis Charles 180
Sarah Rebecca 180
PATERSON, Alexander H. 181

PATERSON, Eleanor 235
Henry 181
PATRICK, Anna 56
PATTERSON, Albert M. 181
Elizabeth 91
Esther 48
George 181
George Frederick 181
George M. 181
Mary Eliza 122
Mary Virginia 182
Sarah 39
William 122, 181, 182
PATTISON, --- 181
PATTON, William 250
PAUL, --- 181
Alexander 181
PAYNE, Henry 184
John 181
Mary 155, 181
Rachel 184
PEALE, Charles 182
Charles Willson 182
Charles Wilson 192
Margaret Jane 192
PEARCE, George 182
Gideon 182
James Alfred 182
Mary E. 217
Thomas 182
William 182
PEARRES, Charles B. 182
George A. 182
James 182
William 182
William T. 182
PEARSON, Mary 261
PEAT, John 182
William 182
PEEBLES, Sarah B. 12
PEIRCE, Elizabeth Cloud 179
George 182
Isaac 182
Joshua 182
PEITZEL, Catherine 258
PELCZAR, Frank 183

RAMSEY, William 7, 192
RANDALL, John 192
  Thomas 192
RANDOLPH, Alfred Magill 192
  Andrew Jackson 192
  Edward Fitz 192
  Mary 172
  Mary Isham 150
  Robert Lee 192
  Thomas 192
  William 192
RANKIN, Alexander 192
  Mary 230
RANNEY, Grace 55
  Israel 55
RANSOM, Charles E. 233
  Charles Edmund 193
  Cornelia Talcott 232, 233
  Samuel 193
RAPHEL, Eugene F. 193
  Stephen Joseph 193
RASIN, William 193
RASMUSSEN, Naren 222
RATCLIFFE, Richard 190
RATHBONE, Marion 178
RATOR, Elizabeth 108
RAUGHTER, Henry 145
RAUTH, Catherine 231
RAWLINGS, Greenberry 193
  John 193
  Robert 193
  Z. Taylor 193
RAY, Alfred 209
  Preston Blair 209
RAYMOR, Mary 82
REA, Davis 193
REABURG, Andrew 193
  Dora 193
  George William 193
READ, Martha J. 217
  Mary Lamar 63
  Nelson Clark 63
READE, Mildred 94
READING, Elizabeth 193
  Elsie 193
  John 193, 194

READING, Joseph 194
  William 194
READY, Ann 34
REAMER, Meyer 194
REBURG, --- (Miss) 49
REDMAN, Hattie 156
REDUE, Isaac 194
  John H. 194
REECE, Catherine 151
REED, Eliza 85
  Elizabeth 25
  Hettie 24
  John 194
  Joseph 194
  Thomas 194
  William 194
  William Bradford 194
REEDER, Charles 194
  Charles M. 194
  J. Dawson 194
REESE, --- (Miss) 79
  Gordon L. 194
  Harry S. 194
  John 194
  Rebecca 246
REEVES, Elizabeth 260
REGISTER, Henrietta 5
REICHERT, Katharine 121
REICHSTEIN, John 109
REID, Jennie Gibson 103
  Margaret 172
REIDER, Rebecca 210
REIFSNIDER, David 145
  Margaret 145
REIHENSTEIN, Rosa 172
REIK, Henry 195
  Henry A. 195
REILY, Patrick 184
REINEWALD, Charles 195
  Joseph Lewis 195
REINHARD, John Andrew 195
  M. E. 3
REMBOLD, Charles 195
  Henry 195
REMSBERG, Anna Margaret 195
  Anna Maria 195

RIDGELY, Ann 205, 221
  Charles 39, 87, 198
  Henry 26, 60, 198
  Martha 198, 236
  Robert 198
  Sarah 26
  William 198
RIGGS, Amon 198
  Christopher M. 137
  John 198
  Ralph 198
RILEY, Bridget Ann 154
RINE, Elizabeth 25
RINEHART, --- 198
  Andrew 198
  David 198
  Frederick 198
  George 198
  Jonathan 23
  Philip 198
  Sarah 23
  William 198
RINER, Mary 138
RINGGOLD, James 199
  John 199
  Thomas 199
RIPPARD, George 172
  James 173
  Susanna 172
RISCHEL, Elizabeth B. 68
RISTEAU, Ann 125
  Edward 125
  John 199
RITCHIE, Albert 33
RITTENHOUSE, --- 12
  David 12
RITZ, Christiana 134
ROACH, James 187
  John 199
  Mary Matilda 199
  Sara May 187
ROBAN, --- (Miss) 234
ROBBINS, --- 199
  Edwards 173
  Elizabeth 173
  George 199

ROBBINS, Henry Russell 199
  Isaac 199
  John 199
  Jonathan M. 199
  Obedience 199
  Orlando Douglas 199
  Thomas 173, 199
ROBERTS, Alfred 199
  Anne Maria 200
  Cadwallader 34
  Catherine 200
  Clara 199
  E. S. 140
  Hugh 200
  John 200
  John Joseph 129, 200
  Joseph J. 129
  Mary 132
  Rachel 245
  Rebecca 34
  Richard 4
  Robert 34, 200
  Temperance 200
  William M. 200
ROBERTSON, John 58
  Mary 58
  Sara 51
ROBINS, Edward 200
  Elizabeth 200
  Rachel 200
ROBINSON, --- 83
  Ann 154
  Christopher 200
  Emma 229
  Harry M. 201
  John 200
  Joseph 200
  Mary 224
  Maximillian 200
  Rose Elizabeth 93
  Samuel 83
  Sarah 151
  Sarah Peters 50
  W. 219
  Wilbert 93
  William 200

336

S

SHRINER, Jacob 59
  Johan Martin 214
  Johan Michael 214
  Margaret 59
  Michael 214
  Pieter 214
SHROYER, Susannah 135
SHULENBERGER, Adam 215
  Anthony 215
  Benjamin 214, 215
  Elizabeth 215
  John 214, 215
  Robert 215
  Samuel 215
  William C. B. 214
SHULTZ, Charles 162
SIEDLING, Frederick 215
  George C. 215
  George F. C. 215
  Julia H. F. 215
SIEGEL, Franz 140
SIEGWART, Andrew 215
  Charles 215
SIGGERS, George W. 215
  Harriet Elizabeth 215
SILBERMAN, Freda 210
  Tenchum 210
SILLS, Edward Pracey 215
  John William 169, 216
  Joseph 215
SILVER, --- 216
  Benjamin 216, 250
  Gershom 216
  John 216
  Mellicent 216
SILVERWOOD, William 216
SIMCOE, George 216
  John S. 216
  William 216
SIMM, --- 268, 269
SIMMONS, Abram 216
  Mary 261
SIMMS, Elizabeth 69
  John Edwin 215
  Robert Alexander 215
SIMON, William 216

SIMPSON, Ann 112
  John 112
SIMS, Joseph 163
SINCHELL, Henry 216
SINCLAIR, Duncan 217
  Malcolm 217
  Peter 217
SINGLEY, --- 151
  Ellen S. 151
SINN, Fannie 12
SISK, Joseph 217
  William 217
SKANE, --- 217
  Thomas H. 217
  Thomas J. 217
SKILES, --- 40
SKILLMAN, George R. 217
  Thomas 217
  Wilbur F. 217
SKIPWITH, George 41
SKUTCH, David 217
  Max 217
SLADE, Elizabeth 42
  Ezekiel 181
  Rachel 181
SLAGLE, Peter 23
SLAKE, Sarah 201
SLICER, John B. 217
  John T. 217
  Thomas 217
SLIFER, --- (Miss) 3
  Ezra 257
SLINGLUFF, Jesse 244
SLOAN, Alexander 217
  David 218
  Duncan 218
  James 218
  John 218
  Margaret 218
  Matthew 218
SLOCUM, Giles 168
  Joanna 168
SLOWEY, Ann 58
SMALLWOOD, --- 219
SMELTZER, Ann 147
SMITH, --- 218

SMITH, --- (Miss) 44
Alexander 218
Anna Margaretta 98
Buell J. 218
C. P. 220
Carrie M. 256
Catherine B. 191
Charles 218
Christian 218, 219
Conrad 218
David 220
Dorothy 220
Edward 220
Edward A. 218
Eleanor 220
Elizabeth 134, 218
Ellen 24
Frederick 218
Garrison 136
George 98
George L. Winfield 219
Henry 218, 219
Henry Lee 44, 150, 235
Homer 256
Ida M. 263
Isaac 218, 220
James P. 219
Jennie L. 220
Johanna Rebecca 221
John 23, 138, 219, 221
John C. 220
John L. 186
John O. 248
John Thomas 44
Jonathan 220
Joseph 213, 220
Joseph O. 263
Julianna 90
Katherine 125
Lena 220
Lizzie 220
Louisa 136
Lula 220
Malinda 220
Margaret 220
Martin 220

SMITH, Mary Ann 219
Matthew 235
Milton E. 218
Nancy 220
Nathan 41
Noah J. 220
Perry Green 220
R. H. 220
Rebecca 60
Richard 220
Robert 219
Robert V. 220
Samuel 157, 219, 221
Sarah 160
Saville 220
Solomon 220
Susanna 198
Thomas 220
Thomas Henry 221
Thomas L. 221
Walter 60
Washington Augustus 218
William 219, 220
William Frances 221
SMITHURST, Tabitha 1
SMYSER, Elizabeth 64
SMYTHE, Thomas 220
SNADER, Elizabeth 244
Jacob 244
SNELL, Rachel J. 17
SNOOK, --- 221
Daniel 221
Daniel J. 221
Jacob 221
John A. 221
Julia 221
Lewis A. 221
Lydia A. 192
Margaret M. 221
Simon 221
Susan M. 221
SNOUFFER, --- 221
Benjamin 221
George 221
SNOWDEN, Richard 221
Thomas 221

STANG, Frederick 196
STANLEY, Charles Harvey 224
   Dacy 224
   Harvey 224
   James Green 224
   John 224
   John Wright 224
STANSBURY, Hannah 156
STANTON, --- 61
   Mary 60, 61
STAPLETON, John 225
   John J. 225
STARK, Margaret 51
STAUB, Peter 61
   Rebecca 61
STAUFFER, Alvin Packer 225
   Daniel 83
   Hester 132
   Isaac Weaver 225
   Matthics 225
   Peter 225
STAUP, John 225
   John W. 225
STEEDMAN, Annie Frances 225
STEEL, --- (Mrs.) 203
   Mary 71
STEGMAN, --- 225
   Anna S. 225
   John Henry 225
STEHL, Elberta 225
   John 225
   Rudolf 69
STEIN, Eleanor 104
STEINACKER, Bertha Webb 4
   Joseph Toomey 4
STEINER, --- 195
   Catharine 54
   Jacob 101
   John 54
   John Conrad 225
STEINHART, Rebecca 202
STEINMETZ, Barbara 87
STEMPLE, Catherine 128
STEPHEN, Mary 175
STEPHENS, John 226
STEPHENSON, William 226

STERN, Clara 147
   Malchen 3
STERRETT, Eliza 152
   John 152
STEUART, Angeline 124
   William 124
STEVENS, Sarah 255
   William 255
STEVENSON, Henry 226
   James M. 226
   John 226
   John M. 226
STEWART, Flavila 111
   John 226
   Luther 66
   Nancy 23
   Susan 66
STIEFEL, --- 226
   Julius 226
STIEFF, Charles Maximilia 226
STIER, --- 226
   Henry J. D'Aertzlaer 226
   Rosalie Eugenia 226
STIGERS, Baltus 121
STIMMEL, --- (Miss) 83
STIMPSON, --- 90
   Thomas 90
STIRLING, James 226
STITH, Griffin 125
   Susan 125
STIVERS, Delia J. 144
   Joseph 144
STOCKBRIDGE, --- (Dr.) 226
   Henry 226
   Jason 226
STOCKETT, --- 226
   Francis 226
   Henry 226
   Lewis 226
   Thomas 226
STOCKSDALE, --- 226
   Edward 226
   John 226
   Mary 226
   Nellie 226
   Noah 226

STOCKSDALE, Ruhana 58
Solomon 226
STODDERT, Benjamin 226
James 226
Thomas 226
STONE, Daniel 228
Daniel Edward 226
Gregory 226
James Harvey 226
Mary 58
Thomas 226
William 58, 226
William F. 199, 226
William Huff 228
STONEBREAKER, John W. 12
STONEBURNER, Christianna 28
STONER, Rebecca 76
STONSBURY, Jane 261
STORR, --- 228
Henry C. 228
John 228
STOTTLEMEYER, --- 228
David 228
Elias 138
Margaret 228
STOUFFER, Benjamin F. 109
Elizabeth 81
Henry 81
STOVER, --- 101
Sarah 10
STOVIN, Mary 153
STRANGE, Robert E. 185
Robert Ellis 228
William French 228
STRAUB, Charles 264
Elizabeth Baker 264
Hester Dorothy 264
STRAUS, Levi 228
Solomon 65, 228
STRAUSS, Albert C. 117
STRAWSBURG, --- 228
Cassie 228
Jacob 228
Josiah 228
William 228
STRAYER, Elizabeth 27

STREET, David 229
John 229
Thomas 229
STREETT, Abraham 229
Charlotte 229
Elizabeth 229
James 229
Mary 229
Shadrach 229
St. Clair 229
William 229
STRETCH, Elizabeth 268
STROMEYER, Francis William 229
William Francis 229
STRONG, Joseph W. 181
STROUD, --- (Miss) 78
STUART, David T. 229
Samuel Ellicott Davis 229
William 229
William (Miss) 229
STUCKEY, Sallie 12
STUDD, Christina 229
STULL, Edward 177
Leander 190
STUMP, Esther 99
Henry 99
Hester N. 114
SUDSBURY, Joseph M. 230
Peter 230
SUEOR, Mary Catherine 222
SULCER, David C. 240
SULEY, Nancy 66
SULIVANE, James 230
SUMAN, Elizabeth 218
SUMMERS, --- 230
Annie E. 190
David W. 230
George W. 230
Henry W. 230
Jacob 230
Jacob V. 230
John T. 230
Joshua 230
Samuel M. 230
SURATT, Annie E. 238

347

THOMAS, Evan 234
  Gabriel 235
  George 234
  Henry 234
  Hugh 234
  James 234, 235
  John 234, 235
  John Henry 140
  Maria E. 269
  Maria Susan 115
  Mary 234
  Mary Ann 186
  Mary Jane 91
  Peter 269
  Philip 41, 234
  Rebecca B. 43
  Robert 235
  Samuel 234
  Sarah 234, 235
  Susanna 235
  Teretia 234, 235
  Thomas 234, 235
  Tristram 234
  Valentine 235
  William 137, 234, 235
THOMPSON, --- 235
  Adam 235
  Andrew 148
  Catherine 259
  Elda Katherine 149
  Elizabeth 148
  George 235
  Henry 235
  Jacob George 149
  James 236
  James William 50
  John 259
  John Jacob 236
  John W. 236
  Joseph 236
  Mary 148
  Mary Rosalie 50
  Robert 236
  Sallie 98
  Susan 102
  Thomas 236

THOMPSON, Walter Harrison
    235
  William 236
THORNE, Francis 233
  Mary A. 233
THRALKELD, Henry 116
THRASHER, Benjamin 236
  Thomas 236
THURSTON, Elizabeth 41
TIDINGS, Elizabeth 15
TIERNAN, Luke 236
  Paul 236
TILDEN, Charles 237
  John 237
  Marmaduke 237
  Rebecca 122
TILGHMAN, James 61
  Mary 61
  Oswald 237
  Rebecca 237
  Richard 237
TILYARD, Josephine V. 218
TIVIS, --- (Miss) 163
TOADVIN, Edwin Stanley 237
  Nicholas 237
  Purnell 237
TODD, --- (Miss) 186
  Elizabeth Frances 237
  James Doeg 253
  Robert 237
  Thomas 237
  William Edward 253
TOMLINSON, Benjamin 237
TOMS, Catherine 100
  Jacob 237, 238
  Lydia 164
  Samuel 164
  W. 164
  William 100
TONRY, William 238
  William P. 238
TOPHAM, Robert 233
  William 238
TOPPAN, Abraham 233, 238
  Anne 238
  Peter 238

TORMEY, Leonard Jamison 238
Patrick 238
TOUILLON, Bouchard 44
Pauline 44
TOULSON, Andrew 239
John 239
Nathan 239
Patrick 239
TOWDIN, Nicholas 237
TOWER, Lydia 245
TOWNSEND, John 239
John Shotwell 239
Joseph 239
Levin 243
Mary 11
Priscilla A. 243
Richard Hallet 239
Robert 11
TOWNSHEND, Frances 262
Samuel 239
William 239
William Belt 239
TOWNSLEY, Mercy Bardwell 4
Mercy Cooley 4
TOWSON, --- (Capt.) 80
TRACY, Isabel 180
TRAIL, Charles Bayard 239
Charles E. 239
TRAINOR, Alice 125
Bernard 125
TRAPNELL, Joseph 239, 240
Sarah 240
TRAVERS, Abednego 240
Catherine 240
Henry 240
Jane L. 218
John 240
Meshach 240
Samuel K. 218
Shadrach 240
Susan Margaret 146
William 240
William Hicks 240
TRAVIS, Catherine 264
Samuel Hicks 240
TREADWAY, Mary A. 167

TREADWELL, Elizabeth 164
TREAT, Johanna 232
Richard 232
TREGO, Mary E. 159
William 159
TRESCOTT, Mehitable 66
TRIGGS, Margaret 182
TRIPPE, Henry 240
Mary Emerson 87
TRITAPOE, Ada Va. 240
Alvira E. 240
Earl E. 240
Edward H. 240
Gertrude A. 240
Harry G. 240
John 240
Michael 240
Samuel 240
TROTT, Christina 113
TROTTER, James 240
John Reynolds 240, 241
Peter 241
William 241
TRUEHART, Sarah 78
TRUMBULL, Susan 170
William 170
TRUNDLE, David 241
John 241
TRUOG, George 241
TUERKE, George 241
Otto 241
TUNSTALL, Alexander 241
Baynham 45
Robert Taylor 241
TURNBULL, Annie 19
John 19
Lawrence 143
TURNER, --- 242
--- (Miss) 25
Benjamin 242
Daniel 242
Edward 35
John 242
John Duffield 242
John Street 242
John W. 242

WALLACE, Margaret 19
Mary 17
Oates Charles Simon 247
Oates Charles Symonds 263
Rachel 48
Randall 17
Robert 247
Thomas 48
William 247
William John 247, 263
WALLING, Harriet Lord 254
WALLIS, Albert 247
Albert A. 247
Albert E. 247
Samuel 247
WALSH, Catherine 247
John 247
John Carroll 247
May Ellen 247
Michael 247
Rabuck 247
Thomas 247
William 177, 248
WALTER, --- 248
Alice V. 248
Bertie E. 248
Charles G. 248
Edward H. 248
Florence M. 248
Jacob W. 248
John 248
Lewis C. 248
Mary Ann 76
Sarah C. 248
WALTERS, Benjamin 248
WALTON, Anne 255
Daniel 248
Jane 144
Samuel 248
William Ellis 248
WALTZ, Isaac 249
Jemima 249
Jesse 249
Lewis 249
Mary 249
Rinehart 248

WALTZ, Solomon 249
WALZI, John 249
John Henry 249
Richard Edmund 249
WARBURTON, Thomas 249
WARD, --- 40
James 249
Jemima 40
John 245, 249
Julia 64
Julia A. 204
Maria 50
Martha Kelto 97
WARDROP, --- 235
WARE, Ann 79
WAREHAM, Mary J. 232
WARFIELD, Elizabeth 125
John 77, 250
Mary 77
Perrigrene 205
Richard 249, 250
WARING, Basil 250
Sampson 250
Sarah 250
WARNER, Andrew Ellicott 250
C. Anderson 250
Charles A. 250
James 212
Johanna 212
Joseph 250
William 250
WARNOCK, Charity 250
Philip 250
Sarah 250
WARRENFELTZ, Catharine 250
Christina 250
Christine 139
Elizabeth 250
Hannah 250
Jacob 250
John 250
Joshua A. 61
Magdelena 250
Mary 250
Peter 250
Philip 250

WIDEGAN, Christopher 234
WIEDEFELD, Francis 257
Henry Charles 257
WIEGARD, Bernard G. 257
Bernard J. 257
WIENER, Andrew 257
Catherine 257
George 257
Henry M. 257
Mary Ann 257
Michael 257
WIESENTHAL, Charles Frederick
257
WIEST, Charles McClellan 257
Jacob 257
Paul Foreman 258
William 257
WILCOX, John 10
Sarah 10
WILDE, Augusta 168
John 168
Mary 168
WILDEY, Thomas 258
WILES, --- (Miss) 107
James 107
WILEY, --- 258
David 258
George N. 258
James D. 26
Matthew 258
Zanna I. 258
WILHIDE, Benjamin 258
Elizabeth 163
Frederick 258
Henry 258
James 258
John 258
Maria 258
Savilla 258
Wilson 258
WILKENS, Christian 258
William 258
WILKINS, Thomas 259
WILKINSON, Rebecca 54, 81
Thomas 259
William 54, 81

WILKS, --- 32
James 32, 259
Mary Amelia 259
WILLARD, George 49
WILLIAMS, --- 90
--- (Capt.) 254
Cornelia 111
Elizabeth 200
Hannah 29, 254
Henrietta 20
Henry 262
Jacob 220
Jesse 259
John 259
Lewis J. 259
Mary E. 94
Ralph 259
Roger 243, 254
Thomas 259
William 259
WILLIAMSON, Angus McIntosh
260
Ann 11
J. Alleine 158
Joseph Alleine 158, 260
Thomas McGill 260
WILLIER, Margaret 71
WILLIS, --- 260
Josiah Engle 34
Levan C. 260
WILLOUGHBY, Alice 212
Isabella 256
Thomas 212
WILLS, Catherine 241
WILMER, Ann 237
Lambert 237
Rebecca 237
Simon 237, 260
William 260
WILMOT, John 84
Margaret 84
WILSON, --- 260
Archibald 260
Catharine 261
Christopher 261
Franklin 49

355

YOUNG, Peter 267
  Richard 268
YOURTEE, Aaron 268
  Abraham 268
  Barbara 268
  Elizabeth 268
  George W. 151
  Jacob 268
  John Tilghman 268
  Leon Ryno 268
  Mary 268
  Peter 268

Z

ZACHARIAS, Elizabeth 62
ZAFFARANO, Josephine 9
ZAJDEL, Katharine 183
ZEALER, Catharine 101
ZELL, Arthur Stanley 268
  Oliver Carroll 268
  Peter 268
ZELLER, Bertina 268
  Charles C. 268
  E. Edward 268
  Emma Virginia 268

ZELLER, John A. 268
  John Frederick 268
ZIMMER, Michael 180
  Rosina 180
ZIMMERMAN, --- 268
  Andrew 268, 269
  Ann Mariah 220
  Benjamin 268, 269
  Daniel 269
  Edward 269
  Edward D. 269
  Elizabeth 269
  Ephraim 269
  Ephraim I. 269
  George 220, 268, 269
  Gideon M. 269
  Henry 268, 269
  John 268, 269
  John Nicholas 268, 269
  Josiah 269
  Michael 171, 268, 269
  Peter 269
  Sara 269
  William 269
ZINLAND, Mary Elizabeth 36
ZWINGLEY, Otho 138